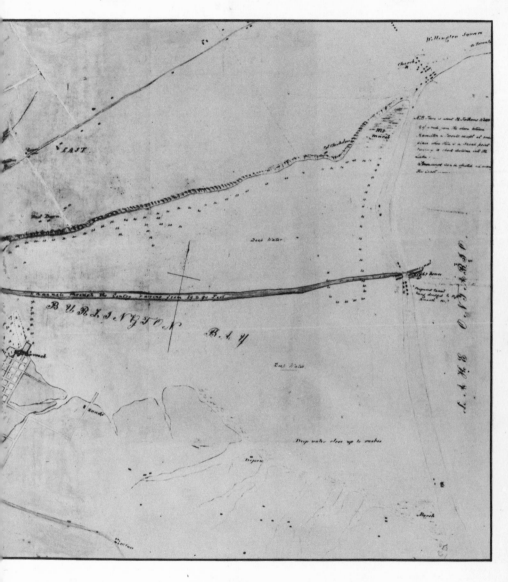

1846: BURLINGTON BAY, HAMILTON, SHOWING ROADS AND
DESJARDINS CANAL ROUTE AND HOMES OF EARLY SETTLERS.

A Mountain and a City

The Story of Hamilton

Marjorie Freeman Campbell

McClelland and Stewart Limited
Toronto/Montreal

The Canadian Publishers

McClelland and Stewart Limited
25 Hollinger Road, Toronto 16

1st printing October, 1966
2nd printing December, 1966

Printed and bound in Canada
by
The Hunter Rose Company

TO THE PEOPLE OF THE CITY

Contents

page

Preface   The Right Hon. Lester B. Pearson   ix
Foreword   Victor K. Copps   xi
1   Mountain, Stream, and Lake   1
2   The Loyalists, Depew, and Land   6
3   Richard Beasley   12
4   Land Surveys and Settlers   17
5   Brock and War   32
6   Hamilton and its Founder   45
7   Police Town, 1833   56
8   Adolescence   69
9   Allan Napier MacNab   79
10   The City, 1847   91
11   Market Place, Lights, and the Whistling Iron Horse   101
12   Sewerage, Waterworks, and a Glass Palace   116
13   Common Schools vs. Ryerson and Central School   124
14   Bankruptcy and a New Economy   134
15   Confederation, Fire Fighters, and Police   147
16   Churches, Horse Cars, and Access Roads   159
17   All Around the Town   170
18   Hospitals and the Medical Profession   180
19   Further Hospitals and a Bevy of Murders   191
20   War and Industry   200
21   Radial Age   209
22   Works Department, Health, and Schools   223
23   The Second World War   235
24   Labour, Lawrence, and a Look-back   244
25   The Jacksonian Era   255
26   Victor Kennedy Copps   270
27   Today   288
    Acknowledgements   296
    Notes   299
    Bibliography   319
    Index   329

Illustrations follow pages 96 and 192

Preface

The Right Honourable Lester Bowles Pearson
Prime Minister of Canada

My first reaction to arrival in Hamilton was annoyance at having to leave Peterborough where my father had spent three years as Minister of George Street Methodist Church and where we had had a very happy time.

But we soon were equally happy in Hamilton, at the Wesley Church Parsonage, a big red brick building on Catharine Street North—Number 137, I think—much too large to be looked after alone by an overworked Minister's wife with three active boys.

The district wasn't exactly "a desirable residential suburb," but it was pleasant, the neighbours were friendly, and there was room to play without worrying about traffic. I gather there have been many changes since then in that part of Hamilton.

My vivid memories of those years—1910-14—centre around home, football, or any other kind of game for the season in the back yard, often with my father; church, Sunday morning service, Junior League (I used to spend the time looking at a pretty girl whose name I still remember); and Sunday School. Father preached well and briefly, but the choir sang even better.

Then there was school—the old Central Collegiate. Mr. Thompson, I think, was Principal but the teachers I remember best were Mike McGarvin, an inspired and wonderful man; Ben Logan, who made Latin tolerable; and Ben Simpson, whom we admired perhaps more as a football half-back than as a mathematics master.

Those were the great days of the pre-war "Tigers." I can still remember the name of nearly every member of the team that lost to Varsity in the Canadian finals of 1911. I tried to become a "Tiger" in the 110-lb. City League and later in the Collegiate Team. But my favourite games were basketball in the winter and baseball in the summer, when I played on a "Y" team in the Intermediate City League.

I seem to be writing only about myself, not Hamilton. It was becoming a big city—as we thought. I remember that in Centennial Year, the boast was that the population had reached almost one hundred thousand.

ix

But the country was very close to the city, and a picnic up the mountain and beyond was an adventure into the wilds. To get to Burlington Beach for a swim was an exploit, and to get to Grimsby to pick fruit was a trek.

I recall that, when I took on an early morning paper-route for the old *Toronto World*, departure time was 6.30 a.m. from an office near the old T. H. & B. station, and I seemed to have covered a large part of the city before I got home for breakfast. But perhaps it only seemed that way!

Looming large in my memory of those days was the Kinrade murder case (we read the newspapers avidly each day for the latest reports) ; the new factories springing up around the Bay; the Centennial celebrations; the men's store on King Street, where I purchased my first "long" suit; the market behind the City Hall where I used to go with mother on Saturday morning; the 1911 election, when Sir George Foster spoke at the "Y"; my own first attempt at election when I ran for President of the H.C.I. student society (why can't I remember its name? Our magazine was called *Vox Lycée*) and was defeated by "Red" MacLennan.

Those were wonderful days and Hamilton was a good place in which to live.

When we left in June 1914 for Chatham, Ontario, I felt just like I did on leaving Peterborough. On that earlier occasion, I took my Entrance examination certificate with me. On this occasion, I took my Senior Matriculation. For that I owe much to the teachers of old Hamilton Collegiate Institute, as I do for the lasting friendships I made there.

May Hamilton continue to flourish!

Foreword

Victor K. Copps
Mayor of Hamilton

A Mountain and a City is more than just a book about the history and development of a municipality. It is a Centennial project for Hamilton.

During the past several years, Canadian cities and towns have come forward with a great variety of projects to be undertaken at the local level as their part in the observance of Canada's Centennial of Confederation. These cover a wide range of plans for libraries, parks, arenas, community centres, and restorations of municipal buildings, among other things.

Hamilton's major and official Centennial project is the restoration of Dundurn Castle, the unique 72-room mansion at the western entrance to the City. Built from 1835 to 1847 as his residence by Sir Allan Napier MacNab (1798-1862), one of the most prominent public men of his time, the mansion is being restored to the 1850 period. Completion of this restoration will give the City a wonderful link with his historic past.

A Mountain and a City as an unofficial, but most important Centennial project, does even more than that. It recounts the history of our City between the mountain and the bay from its establishment before MacNab's time, up to its development as the centre of one of Canada's most prosperous and fastest-growing metropolitan areas.

It is appropriate that the author of this story of Hamilton should be Marjorie Freeman Campbell, an enthusiastic historian of local activities, whose interest and pride in her community are evident in every page of this work. It has been her labour of love.

We welcome its publication as a record of the spirit of Hamilton in the past and the expectancy with which "a Mountain and a City" look to the future.

1

Mountain, Stream, and Lake

FOR hundreds of millions of years the Mountain has stood guard above the priceless land corridor below, the chameleon bay and the blue wash of lake beyond.

In the beginning, the corridor rippled with the wind in sedge grasses, crawled with rattlesnake and terrapin, and gabbled with waterfowl feeding on the wild rice and millet that fringed the deeply indented inlets and escarpment streams.

In spring the ear-piercing chorus of green frogs pulsed to the stars like a mating paean, while in winter the frozen marsh and ice-locked bay echoed under the hungry howl of the wolf pack that homed in the willow thicket where later a market place would blossom.

Far below, a Precambrian platform of igneous basalt, born of fire, supported mountain, corridor and lake.

In the beginning only the Precambrian existed, spun out from the earth's bubbling core and cooled through centuries to solid lava. Over this most ancient of global rocks, four hundred million years ago the seas descended. Where city and mountain stand, millenium after millenium the ocean held its sway.

In the transparent depths life was created, multiplied in numbers and in forms, perished, and sinking to the bottom was preserved in the accumulating layers of sand and marl—detritus from the exposed old-lands of the crystalline Precambrian Canadian Shield and the westward-draining mountains of the future New York State.

Layer by layer, sandstone, shale, and limestone . . . limestone, sandstone, shale . . . dolomite and chert . . . the strata were laid down. As the rugged Shield eroded, its deposits under the sea grew in proportion.

Tens of millions of years later, after the land had risen from the ocean and the waters had run away in rivers, carving escarpment and plain, after the glittering Pleistocene glaciers, one to two miles high, had ground inexorably across the land, back and forth, four full times, scooping out the Great Lakes and remodelling the surface of the land; after the final glacial Lake Iroquois had subsided from the base of the escarpment and become Lake Ontario—millions of years after this, men quarried the limestone for city homes, and dug out shale and sandstone to lay streets.

Broken grey macadamizing stone from the top of the quarry to the blue stratum below, delivered and spread on the streets, $3.75 a cord. The blue stratum in Hamilton Mountain, or stone not less hard or tough than the blue, $7.50 a cord from private, $5 a cord from city quarries.

Few cities have been more affected by topography than Hamilton, restricted as it is to a narrow plain, one and one-half to three miles wide, between the escarpment on the south and the bay and adjoining marsh to the north.

When the first white settlers landed below the escarpment at the head of Lake Ontario, they found the site largely swamp, watered by spring-clear streams that flowed from the foot of the Mountain and by deep inlets that stretched long fingers inland from the bay. Interspersing inlets and streams were rolling grass-green meadows, low clay hills dark with scrub pine, and forests of virgin oak, maple, ash, hemlock, and spruce, with nut trees—walnut, beech, chestnut, butternut, and hickory—offering abundant harvest.

Behind loomed the Mountain, clad from head to foot in dense foliage. Below, dancing in the sunlight against its green north shore, glinted the blue bay once known as the finest natural harbour on the Great Lakes, and so beautiful that the Indians had named it Macassa (or Marcassah) Bay, meaning "beautiful waters." The harbour still has beauty in outward form although the people of the city have made it today what has been described as "the largest septic tank in the world," so that no one dare bathe in its waters or eat its fish.

So limpid had those waters been before the white man came that pebbles on the clean sandy bottom ten and fifteen feet down were clearly visible, and the schools of minnows darting in and out of the long glancing shafts of underwater sunlight.

Mirrored in the still water, huge willows and elms had fringed the shoreline, crowning the cliffs at the western end, and in the east trailing willow plumes in the marshes that spread where industry now stands.

At dawn and sunset thousands of gabbling waterfowl had fed in the opalescent bay, herds of deer had come to drink from it, long-legged herons had fished the shallows, and kingfishers, like blue jets, flashing with raucous cries from willow to willow, had dive-bombed the depths.

Offsetting these attractions was the saw-toothed Indian swordgrass edging the inlets, which bound the soil in a vise and slashed to ribbons all clothing but buckskin; swarms of mosquitoes and other flying pests; giant ant-hills; rattlesnakes by the hundreds, big as a man's leg, black and venomous; and bears and wolves with a lust for sheep and hogs which made the keeping of the smaller domestic animals a frustrating battle.

Discovering these obstacles, early newcomers to the area mostly struggled up the mountainside and retreated inland to higher, drier, and more easily cultivable soil. Those who remained to hack out a holding where

Hamilton now stands were a sturdy breed who were influenced by attraction to the locale which deepened into attachment, and by an appreciation of the value of its economic position at the junction of the two great corridors of migration thrusting into the continent of North America from the eastern seaboard—the St. Lawrence waterway and the Hudson-Mohawk River system, one of the overland escape routes to Canada of the United Empire Loyalists during and after the American Revolutionary War of 1775-83.

Situated at the western end of the Niagara Peninsula, most important gateway region on the Canadian-American border, and highly accessible by water, the natural transportation system of the pioneer, the Head of the Lake, as it came to be known, was largely settled by loyalists, many of whose descendants still people the city. As the province opened and roads developed, the east-west traffic between the Niagara border and southern Ontario centred upon the lakehead community, while northern traffic added its quota to the city's trade.

All growing cities possess problems in common. But it is the problems unique to itself which a community faces by reason of its topography, situation, environment, people or background history which provide its individuality.

In addition to the disadvantages resulting from a surplus of ground water, and the constraint on settlement imposed by escarpment, bay, and marsh, development at the lakehead was affected by further geographical features. In early days the lack of streams capable of generating water-power proved a severe economic handicap. While Ancaster and Dundas, served by rapid, tumultuous streams, became bustling mill-towns, Hamilton remained a slowly developing mercantile hamlet, released to industrial growth only upon the invention of steam power. Furthermore, while access to the area—otherwise water-locked to the north—is afforded by two unusual natural land bridges, today's Burlington Heights and Burlington Beach, these causeways have always been a potent source of trouble and a bottleneck to traffic.

A sand and gravel bar, varying in height from ninety to one hundred and sixteen feet, Burlington Heights separates Hamilton Harbour[1] from the sedgy waters of the Dundas Marsh, or Coote's Paradise,[2] which fills the lower reaches of the wide, lovely valley carved by the once torrential Dundas River. The Heights provides the city today with its main western entrance; carries Highway 403 and two railway lines; furnishes the site for Hamilton's famous Rock Garden; and supplies Hamiltonians also with a public park and the city's oldest and most historical public burying ground, Hamilton Cemetery.

Nearly three and one-half miles in length and one-quarter mile wide, the high level bar is a beach deposit built by glacial Lake Iroquois across the mouth of the Dundas Valley through the backwash action of wind and lake currents, just as the low level bar of Burlington Beach was built by later Lake Ontario across the mouth of Hamilton Harbour.

3

To understand the formation of Burlington Heights one must appreciate that Lake Iroquois, during its lifetime, varied in depth by as much as one hundred feet, so that its beaches may be found at widely varying levels. East of the city, Highway 8 runs for much of its course on Iroquois beach. Yet within the city the Iroquois beach extending west from Wentworth Street along Charlton Hill to James, lies forty feet above Highway 8. Today, hundreds of thousands of years after it was laid down, the old Iroquois beach is Hamilton's perennial headache, slipping and sliding like new shingle and carrying the current roadway with it.

Two factors were responsible for the lake's variance in depth: the damming up of the St. Lawrence outlet by ice; and the recoil of the earth following release from the mountainous glaciers. As the St. Lawrence ice-lobe gradually shrank and lake waters found successively lower outlets, the Iroquois level dropped, until at the end of the glacial era, the lake was invaded by the salt sea flooding up the Hudson and St. Lawrence valleys. Until little over a century ago, salmon and other salt water fish abounded in Burlington Bay.

With the removal of the tremendous weight of the glacial ice, however, the basin to the east began to rise, tilting the land towards the northwest, shallowing the water at the eastern end of the lake and deepening it at the western.

For centuries the high bar grew—from its junction with the escarpment at the later head of James Street, curving slightly northwestward across the site of the future city, past the present Queen Street and Dundurn Castle, out York. Just beyond the gravel pit that would become a noted rock garden, almost 18,000 feet from its beginning, the peninsula halted a stone's throw from the north shore, with only a narrow ship channel of open water between—the old natural Dundas Marsh outlet.

On the stratified sand and gravel of the Heights the history of the lake and lakehead is recorded: the depth of the lake in the height of the sandbar; a tropical climate in the bones, teeth, and tusks of mammoth and wapiti discovered at various levels from thirty-three to eighty feet above Lake Ontario;[3] invasion by the sea in deposits of marine crustacean fossils.

Behind the bar, over tens of thousands of years, the site of the city developed—a wide high-level coastal plain built by Lake Iroquois, with delta deposits contributed by the tumultuous escarpment streams of the day, one of the most extensive still being known as The Delta; and a wide low-level plain north of this, the handiwork of later and shallower Lake Ontario, its low shoreline invaluable as sites for industry, with stream mouths forming harbours, and deltas for quays.

Storied and picturesque as the high bar is and important as is its role in the history of the city, it is matched in all respects by the low bar to the east which cuts off Hamilton Harbour from Lake Ontario. Created by the latter in much the same manner as the high bar, the low bar is an eight-foot-high sandstrip four miles in length, varying from three hundred

4

to one thousand feet in width. Originally the bar was broken by a narrow natural outlet between bay and lake, slightly less than half a mile north of the later man-made Burlington Canal—a shallow sand-choked passage deep enough at all times for the Indian's canoe or the flat bottomed batteaux of the early traders, but only with spring and fall high water affording sufficient draft for sloop or schooner.

As it grew, the bar developed different characteristics on east and west shores: on the wave-swept lakeside, a clean and sterile sweep of sandy, pebbly beach; on the protected bay front, an indistinct shoreline rich in accumulated silt and humus—virgin soil for the wind-and-water-borne seeds which soon grassed the strip with green, peppered it with wild flowers and running vines, and shaded its reedy west shore with huge willow trees and oaks.

This was the habitat of the city-to-be. Hundreds of thousands of years before the first tree was felled at the lakehead to build the first pioneer's log cabin, the good and ill fortunes of distant generations were written in rock, soil and water. Take for instance, the Mountain, Hamilton's individual stretch of the 350-foot cuesta formation which rises in New York State near Rochester, skirts Lake Ontario to the vicinity of Hamilton, then swinging north through the Blue Mountains and the Bruce Peninsula, dips under water, to reappear in Manitoulin Island and again in the Michigan Peninsula where it fades out.

"If future historians," wrote Stan McNeill in *The Hamilton Spectator*, "ever try to assess the role of the Mountain in the development of Hamilton, it is almost certain it will be measured in terms of dollars and cents. But how can you put a price tag on the pride, despair, affection, hatred, fear, or concern that Hamiltonians have felt at various times for this craggy, overgrown pile of rocks?

"How could historians comprehend that a whole city could be united in the pursuit of a common hobby—and that hobby a 300-foot mountain?"[4]

2

The Loyalists, Depew, and Land

UNTIL the year 1781 the area to the west of the Niagara River—the Niagara Peninsula—was virgin wilderness broken only by the hunting trails of the Mississauga Indians. At the head of Lake Ontario and throughout the surrounding countryside no white settlement existed. The land belonged to the Mississaugas, and the Indian, with good reason, was jealous of white encroachment.

As early as 1725 a fur trade route to the far west had been obtained by the white man on the east (American) bank of the Niagara River, and Fort Niagara established.

Since the chief interest of the French and later the British in Canada lay not in colonizing but in the rich fur trade, both countries were satisfied to preserve their Niagara portage rights on the eastern side by respecting Indian sovereignty west of the river.

Until the American Revolutionary War of 1775-83, this condition prevailed. At this time, however, the flood of Loyalists escaping to British Canada from the seceding American colonies, and the thousands of loyal Indians dispossessed of their lands by war, forced a change in British policy. On May 9th, 1781, His Britannic Majesty George III completed negotiations for purchase of a four-mile-wide strip of Mississauga territory extending the length of the Niagara River on the west side.

So desperate however was starving, overcrowded Fort Niagara for land and the food to be raised upon it[1] that settlement apparently preceded conclusion of the tedious purchase negotiations. Helping to establish the date of arrival of Hamilton's first settlers is an item in the diary of Francis Goring, chief clerk at Fort Niagara, dated August 4th, 1780: "Secord commenced farming over the river," and the editor's comment: "With little doubt the first attempt at agriculture by the British in the Province of Ontario."[2] Supporting this conclusion is Peter Secord's later petition for crown land in the upper province. "The First Settler," he records, "on Land in this Country."

Once opened, Loyalists crowded the four-mile strip faster than the

6

surveyors could lay it out. On foot, on horseback and by homemade boat portaged laboriously from stream to stream, by oxcart and by conestoga— the covered wagon of the Pennsylvania German, similar to but smaller than the western prairie schooner—through the dense unfriendly wilderness, strife-worn, hungry, and frequently destitute men, women and children followed the trails north.

Reaching the Niagara River, refugees crossed the stream on rudely constructed rafts, or dismantling their wagons and caulking the seams with clay, paddled their household goods across while they swam their farm animals alongside. In such numbers they entered at Niagara and future Black Rock, that in 1784 a further purchase of land from the Mississaugas was required.

Listed in the first census taken across the river in 1782 were two future Hamilton pioneers and their families: John Depue (later Depew) Sr., his wife Mary and six children, and his son-in-law, George Stuart, his wife (née Mary Depue) and their two infant sons.

The so-called New Purchase consisted of a tract extending westward from the first along Lake Ontario to Burlington and from there at an angle north 45° west twelve miles, thence to the sources of the River La Tranche (Thames). On Burlington Beach the line of the New Purchase ran through the old natural outlet between Lake Ontario and Burlington Bay and, later extended by four miles, forms the present county line between Wentworth and Halton counties, crossing North Shore Boulevard East near Indian Point.

No sooner were negotiations for the New Purchase concluded at Niagara on May 22[3] than settlers began to push into the wilderness. At Niagara the choice frontier lots facing on road or waterway were hard to obtain. Being most accessible they were earliest claimed, and were largely awarded to officers and men of standing while "back township" sites in the dense bush fell to the private soldier and lesser colonial.

Beyond the reach of settlement, however, lay land which the settler might occupy under squatter's rights, with the expectation that his formal application for his chosen site would be recognized with a location ticket, a later land certificate and an eventual crown patent.[4]

It was to discover such a site that George Stuart and his young brother-in-law, Charles Depue (later Captain Charles Depew, Sr.), set out from Niagara. Paddling along the north shore of Lake Ontario the two portaged their canoe across the southern Carrying Place on Burlington Beach, where a natural channel curving into the beach strip cut the portage by two-thirds, and entering Lake Geneva coasted slowly along its reedy shoreline until they found a satisfactory homesite.

Within a deep entrance, later Stipe's Inlet, they landed, and as the land was not yet surveyed, laid claim to it by driving in a flattened stake bearing Depew's name. Then paddling westward up the bay, past the Big Bog and two sizable inlets, they staked George Stuart's claim, later the Grant farm, lying east and west of Sherman Avenue. A year later, in

1786,[5] John Depew and his grown family moved to the lakehead. George Stuart and Charles Depew remained at Niagara a further year, possibly because of a new infant born to each family.

On the 935 acres granted John Depew and his family by crown patent[6] stands much of Hamilton's present industry: The Steel Company of Canada Limited; Hamilton By-Products Coke Ovens; the Hamilton municipal incinerator, shortly to be closed and the site incorporated into The Steel Company; Procter and Gamble Company of Canada Limited; Canadian Industries Limited; and among still other plants, Dominion Foundries and Steel Limited, on Depew Street.

The willows and reeds of the Depew ancestral acres have vanished with the deer at the waterhole and with the wild berries that gave its name to Huckleberry Point, a onetime favorite picnic and duck hunting ground for Hamiltonians. In their place stretch hundreds of acres of reclaimed land, filled inlets, slag heaps and rusting stock piles, and the stark grey walls of the mighty mills and factories that have made Hamilton. The clouds of passenger pigeons that darkened the sky for days in migration have been replaced by the mills' grey banners by day, their pillar of flame by night. The wolves have gone and the rattlesnakes, but so have the salmon and whitefish, the water fowl and the fresh transparent air and waters of the bay.

Gone are the Depew orchards with their pink and white spring fragrance, their autumn tang of fallen fruit rotting on the brown earth; the green and gold chequer of fields; the grateful coolness and the bird songs of the wood lot; the dry heat and the whirring grasshoppers of the sun-drenched cow pasture. All this has disappeared beneath city streets and city homes, leaving no trace except here and there a gnarled apple or pear tree clinging indomitably to life.

Yet the waterfront today has its own terrifying beauty of turret and towering blast furnace, of straddling crane, of flame and the roar and hiss of molten slag quenched in the long-suffering bay; the beauty of unloading bridges, like wingless planes, servicing berthed ships; the regimented beauty even of a parking lot, typifying the dignity of steady labour and the basic security of the regular wage cheque.

Today in the midst of the eight hundred acres of Hamilton Works, mother plant of The Steel Company of Canada, where the sunken graves of the Stipes-Depew family cemetery greened in the sun,[7] coke ovens distil coal into fuel to run the plant's blast furnaces. Similarly to the west, in 1930, the site of the Stewart (Stuart)-Depew cemetery was incorporated into the holdings of the International Harvester Company of Canada, located on the northern end of George Stewart's crown grant in Lots 8 and 9.

Inasmuch as Captain Charles Depew, Sr. and his wife, Magdalene Showers (also Shervers and Scheurs) had fifteen children, and their son, Captain Charles Depew, Jr., and his wife, Elizabeth Horning, had nine, the range of intermarried pioneer connections, many of whose names

8

appeared on stones in the pioneer cemeteries—Gage, Grubb, Neff, Water-
bury, Bernitt, Osborne and Bates—is not surprising. Today descendants of
these marriages and intermarriages make a considerable contribution to
the city's population.[8]

While the Depews and Stuarts were toiling doggedly from sunrise to
sunset to fell enough trees and break the soil amongst the standing stumps
for their first planting with the corn, potatoes and wheat they had raised
as seed at Niagara, a neighbour was establishing himself to the west.

On a slight rise on solid ground beyond a long finger of Lake Geneva
(on the south side of later Barton Street, near Leeming) Robert Land
built first a dugout then a crude slant-roofed, skin-windowed shack.
Alone and morose he fought the pioneer's lonely battle with the wilderness. The story of Robert Land typifies Loyalist history. Born in New
York State about 1736, Robert Land first lived in Connecticut, then as
an employee of the Delaware Land Company, he settled in the Delaware
valley where about 1757 he married Phoebe Scott, a tall dark girl three
years his senior and a fitting complement to Land who was short, stout
and fair.

A loyal adherent of the British crown, young Land was obviously a
brave and fearless man attracted to warfare, danger, and intrigue.
Scarcely was he married when he enlisted for service in the Seven Years
War, which won New France (Canada) for Great Britain.

Following the end of the war Land located in a rambling community,
today Cochecton, on the bank of the Delaware River. Here he built a
cabin for his growing family, found employment as a wood turner, and
served as District Magistrate.

The outbreak of the American Revolution, however, saw him by
1776-77 again in service, this time as an undercover agent of the British,
running despatches through the wilderness between British headquarters
in New York City and western headquarters at Fort Niagara. As local
suspicion of his activities grew, his position in the community deteriorated
from one of trust and respect to that of a suspected and hated spy and
enemy. Possibly his wife and family of seven children, ranging from
nineteen years to an infant, suffered more than their father.

During his absence Land's home was twice burned and his family
attacked, on the second occasion house and household belongings being
totally destroyed. When her eldest son, John, was thrown into jail where
he was held until the end of the war, and seventeen-year-old Abel, a chip
off the paternal block, enlisted with the British, Phoebe with her remaining children made her way to New York City, mecca of loyalist refugees.
British garrison records there show her application for rations.

While his family was undergoing these trials, Robert Land was meeting with his own troubles. In March, 1779, he was captured by a band of
"patriots" in the Delaware valley, carried to Minisink, New Jersey, for
trial,[9] and sentenced to be hanged. For an unknown reason the sentence
was recalled and on September 30th he was released from jail on bail

9

posted largely by a neighbour, Nathaniel Skinner, whose daughter would later marry Robert's son, John. Forfeiting bail, Land returned immediately to service.

A year later he was again in trouble, from which he would again escape although it would cost a friend his life.[10] While guiding Robert Land and a party of four recruits through the sheer ranges of the Alleghenies, Ralph Morden, a Quaker of Mount Bethel, Pennsylvania, was ambushed, captured, tried, condemned to death, and hanged,[11] although his trial disclosed that he had carried no weapon and made no attempt to escape, following the tenets of non-violence of his faith.

Although wounded, Robert Land escaped with his companions and made his way to New York where Phoebe nursed him back to health. On July 10th, 1780, he applied for crown aid for himself and family, addressing his petition to Sir Henry Clinton, K.B., General Commander-in-Chief of His Majesty's Forces, and detailing the above events.[12] On January 21, 1781, he and his wife attended the baptism of seven-year-old Ephraim in storied Trinity Church in downtown New York.[13] Some time subsequent to this the short stout greying loyalist in the wilderness garb of fringed buckskin jacket, buckskin trousers and leggings and fur cap left on his final trip to Fort Niagara, records from this period forward showing him in this western theatre.

On August 18th, 1782, Brigadier General H. Watson Powell, commander at Fort Niagara, reports Land as having arrived at the fort and anxious to return to New York.[14] The war was ending, however, and apparently Land determined to remain in the western area. In 1783 the British evacuated New York. Among the ten thousand loyalists they transported to the Maritimes was Robert Land's family.

A year later we find Land listed among those who had subscribed their names "to Settle and Cultivate the Crown Lands Opposite to Niagara," with a rations allowance to December 24th, 1784.[15] Across the river he was allotted a tract of two hundred acres at Niagara Falls,[16] later to become the farm of William Lundy and site of the bloody battle of Lundy's Lane in the War of 1812. A record preserved in the family relates: "He lived alone and brooded on the past. The sound of the nearby Falls . . . their nearness and the sight of them filled his soul with gloom. To escape he fled the vicinity and settled at the lakehead." This record estimates his sojourn at Niagara at three years.

This would seem to be correct, for in 1786 his name appears between those of Charles De Pugh and George Stewart on the rations list at Niagara.[17] Like the others his name is missing from the 1787 list. John Depew therefore apparently preceded all three to the lakehead, making him Hamilton's first settler.

In the Maritimes, meanwhile, Land's family had not prospered. In 1789, at the instigation of seventeen-year-old Robert, Jr., they determined to migrate to Canada, returning to New York and travelling overland to Niagara. En route they are said to have visited John who had been released from jail and allowed to resume the Cochecton farm and who was now married to Lillian Skinner.

Refusing John's appeal to remain, the group pushed on to Niagara where they spent a year, with the men hunting and trapping and working for neighbouring settlers. Then from an itinerant trader they learned that a white man named Land was living alone at the Head of the Lake and to satisfy their mother, who still believed she would find her husband alive, Robert and Ephraim accompanied her to the lakehead.

According to family legend, at the end of a day's labour Robert was seated outside his rude home enjoying his evening pipe when his wife and sons entered the clearing. The joy and relief of the faithful mother and wife after her long years of trial may well be imagined.

With the arrival of Abel and William, Rebecca and young Phoebe in 1791, the Land settlement progressed steadily. With the three hundred and twelve acres patented to Robert, Sr.,[18] stretching from the waterfront to the mountain top immediately west of Wentworth Street, with grants to the sons and daughters, and with purchases, the Land family came to own a solid block of over a thousand acres, extending from today's Wellington Street to Sherman Avenue and from the bay to the Mountain.

On this square mile and more of initial wilderness were dotted the Land homes—the first log cabins in rude clearings, and the later more substantial frame, brick or stone residences. Flanking the patriarchal cabin of Robert, Sr. was a weeping willow planted to commemorate the family reunion. Through the years of the cabin's replacement, first by a frame cottage, later by a two-storey red brick residence, square-towered and commodious, the willow flourished as a familiar neighbourhood landmark. A landmark also for decades were the two pointed stone pillars inscribed "Landholme," which flanked the entrance to the grounds and which, following purchase of "Landholme" about 1914 by the late Stanley Mills, well known Hamilton merchant and loyalist descendant, were transferred to the driveway of the home at 341 James Street South, now occupied by H. H. Leather, Esq., M.B.E.[19]

On April 13th, 1915, the site of the original log cabin was commemorated by a stone tablet placed by the Wentworth Historical Society in the W. A. Freeman Coal Company office building. Missing after removal of this building, the memorial reappeared publicly in November, 1953, when it was installed by the Robert Land Home and School Association in the entrance hall of the Robert Land School, which stands on former Land property.

In the light of more recent knowledge the tablet must be accepted with reservations: "Here Robert Land the first settler built his cabin, A.D. 1779."

3

Richard Beasley

WHILE the two focal points of clearing and cultivation, Depew-Stuart and Land, were expanding in the east end of the future community, a similar development was occurring well to the westward on a site adjoining the high bar—one of the choicest locations on Lake Geneva.

On a gentle, tree-shaded park-like slope above the western curve of the bay Richard Beasley, fur trader and merchant, built a fairly commodious log cabin. At the water's edge below, he erected the first wharf on Lake Geneva and a trading post which would become a popular rendezvous for the numerous wandering Mississaugas and the white settlers of the lakehead area.

At the time of his location on this site, young Richard already had several years of trading experience behind him. Born in Albany, New York, Beasley was descended from English and loyal Dutch stock, his grandparents having been John Beasley and Lydia van Benthuysen, widow, of Albany. This marriage had two offspring: a son, Henry, who in turn married Maria Noble; and a daughter, Johanna, who married Richard Cartwright. Of these latter unions, among other children, Richard Beasley was born in 1761, Richard Cartwright, Jr., in 1758.

This lineage is important, for Richard Cartwright, Jr., became one of the foremost trading merchants and leading political figures of Upper Canada, and his interest in and influence upon his first cousin, three years his junior, proved a considerable factor in shaping the latter's life.

Growing up in Albany together, the two cousins apparently left home in the same year. In a later petition for crown land Beasley states: "Your Petitioner came into the Province[1] in the year 1777—and served two years as Acting Commissary." Richard Cartwright's land petition gives the same date of entry, 1777, a date obviously applying to Fort Niagara and not the area across the river.

Following his two years as Acting Commissary, young Beasley entered the fur trade in company with one Peter Smyth, or Smith. In view of the long controversy as to whether Richard Beasley or Robert Land first arrived at the lakehead—John Depew prior to these findings not having been considered a claimant as founder—the following petition from Beasley on behalf of himself and Smith, dated Kingston, 24th August, 1788,[2] is significant:

". . . Your memorialists did in the Year '83 erect a House at Toranto River and Another at Pomitiscutiank on the North side of Lake Ontario for the purpose of carrying on the Indian trade, since which time they have been constant Residents at these Places and have made considerable improvements. . . ." They requested that they be allowed to retain the houses with an adjoining allotment of lands. On June 19th, 1789, the Land Board confirmed the houses and two hundred acres each to the petitioners. Edwin C. Guillet, well known Canadian historian, is authority for locating Smith at the post near Port Hope, and Beasley therefore at Toronto.

Until establishment of this trading house it would seem that Richard made his fixed headquarters with his cousin Cartwright, since in a listing of families resident at Niagara, December 1st, 1783, Richard Beasley, aged twenty-two, appears as a member of the household of Richard Cartwright, twenty-five.[3]

These records would seem to indicate that until the year 1788 Beasley's place of residence was established by his own claims. Says T. Roy Woodhouse, Dundas historian, "In Augustus Jones' survey map of 1791 Robert Land's name appears on the lots later patented to him. The lots which Beasley came to own—Lot 18, Con. 1, and Lot 19, Cons. 1 and 2, Barton Township—appear on this survey map in Captain Robert Lottridge's name."

J. H. Smith, public school inspector of Wentworth County for almost half a century, 1871-1917, and an authority on county history, places Richard Beasley's arrival at the lakehead as "about 1785," when, he states, Beasley laid claim to the land where Dundurn Park was later situated, and also preempted the adjoining property known as Beasley's Hollow.

Richard Beasley's claim to the land was the not unusual one of that day of squatter's rights. While Captain Lottridge had a certificate issued by the Land Board of Nassau in 1792, and presumably a location ticket, since the lots were already inscribed to him on Augustus Jones' survey of 1791, Richard Beasley had possession. For years the lots were in dispute, the matter finally in 1796—the year crown patents were granted—being submitted to the committee of the Legislative Council at York (Toronto), land boards having been abolished by Lieutenant-Governor John Graves Simcoe in 1794.

With the death of Captain Lottridge, the matter was amicably settled with his heirs, who were willing to accept land in another location. On June 15th, 1798, the legislative council allowed Richard Beasley's claim to Lots 18, 19 and 21, Con. 1, and Lot 19, Con. 2, Barton Township. A month later, on July 10th, Beasley petitioned for the broken fronts of these lots and received them, in addition being granted: "leave to build a wharf and storehouse in the most convenient place, on the beach, with an acre of waste lands of the crown thereunto adjoining," a somewhat belated permission, as both wharf and storehouse had been in operation for at least a decade.

By the 1790's the fur trader's establishment at the head of Lake Ontario was widely known. On February 10th, 1792, Captain Patrick Campbell of Scotland, while travelling from Niagara to the Grand River Indian reservation with a festive party, records arriving by sleigh at "the house of a Mr. Beasley, who keeps a shop at the head of Lake Geneva."

By 1791 Richard Beasley had become a miller as well as a fur trader and merchant. With James Wilson he built a saw and grist mill in Ancaster Township. Later these well-known Ancaster mills were purchased by St. Jean Baptiste Rousseau at the turn of the century.

The mill was a definite milestone in Beasley's upward progress. By 1791 the province was settling, its social development already patterned to the design of Colonel John Graves Simcoe, first Lieutenant-Governor of Upper Canada, 1792-96. Simcoe's plan included establishment of a colonial upper class of gentry composed of half-pay officers of good family; the leading mill owners, merchants, and traders who were also the provincial bankers and financiers; and its landed proprietors.

From the ranks of this aristocracy would come magistrates, justices of the peace, and members of the legislative council; distinguished citizens to fill substantial offices and serve on important public and private boards and committees; and the holders of honorary appointments in the upper echelon of provincial militia units.

In the inner ranks of these "Gentlemen of Upper Canada" moved Richard Cartwright, Jr., merchant, mill owner and shipper, partner in the forwarding business of the powerful and wealthy Robert Hamilton of Queenston whose son, George, would in 1816 become founder of the city of Hamilton. Together Robert Hamilton and Richard Cartwright helped shape the destiny of Upper Canada. Both served as early magistrates, sat on the land board, and were appointed to the legislative council of the first parliament, opened in Newark on September 17th, 1792.

The extent of Cartwright's influence on Beasley cannot be estimated. Certainly as Cartwright's kin, Richard received Robert Hamilton's support. As Beasley's trade merchandise was provided by the firm of Hamilton and Cartwright—and later by Cartwright who moved to Kingston and founded his own company—the two cousins were in constant business connection. Although only three years the elder, Cartwright acted as self-appointed adviser and mentor to Beasley, increasingly so as the latter's affairs bogged down in debt.

Whatever the motive power, step by step Beasley assumed more responsibilities. In March, 1793, Lieutenant-Governor Simcoe visited the Ancaster mills while on a tour of the province and, snowbound by a blizzard, put up at Beasley's. The following month, addressing Governor-

General Lord Dorchester on the provisioning of troops in Canada, Simcoe wrote: "I had also desired Mr. Beasley who has a mill at the head of the lake (now Burlington Bay) to reserve a quantity of flour, as it may be possible I shall establish a Post in this neighborhood."[4]

The renaming of Lake Geneva as Burlington Bay by Simcoe in a proclamation of June 16, 1792, was in keeping with his propensity for changing prevailing Canadian names to English. On the northeast coast of England, Burlington or Bridlington Bay with its seaport resembled Lake Geneva. To the west of Burlington Bay in Yorkshire, moreover, loomed a promontory, Flamborough Head, similar to the bold mesa-like outlier where the Niagara escarpment, west of Waterdown, swings at right angles to run northward. This gray dolomite bluff, white as Dover's chalk cliffs in bright sunlight, became a second Flamborough Head.

In similar fashion Simcoe changed the names of the four districts into which the upper province had been divided in 1788. Lunenburg, Mecklenburg, Nassau—in which the Head of the Lake was situated—and Hesse became respectively the Eastern, Midland, Home, and Western districts.

To govern each district a body of magistrates—the District Court of General Quarter Sessions of the Peace—was appointed by the Lieutenant-Governor In Council. Over the years Quarter Sessions Courts, which operated until 1841, came to have wide powers, including many assumed after this date by municipal councils. In 1795 Beasley was appointed a justice of the peace, a post belonging traditionally to the gentry, being nominated for this honour by the Hon. Robert Hamilton.

At this period in Upper Canada the position of justice of the peace was no sinecure. If its duties sometimes proved onerous, however, this was balanced by the prestige the position afforded. The title of Esquire accompanied the judicial role and the squire was a man of importance to whom hats were doffed.[5]

In the issuing of liquor and marriage licenses the J.P. came closest to the settlers' hearts. In pioneer life liquor was the universal panacea; and in a day when only the Church of England had lawful right to marry, bury or baptize, the power vested in the J.P. to marry—provided the participants could prove they lived at least eighteen miles from an Anglican clergyman—was the only escape from the Anglican ceremony. This was so unpopular with other sects that many couples lived together out of wedlock or suffered irregular marriages performed by a "dissenting minister" (not belonging to the Church of England), although such a marriage left children illegitimate.

Upper Canada was opening up. In 1792 Simcoe divided the province into nineteen counties to elect representatives to the provincial legislative assembly, and established sixteen electoral ridings. The following year an act to establish an Upper Canada militia system was passed. To speed the distribution of land, townships were surveyed and concession roads and side lines run.

In the district of Nassau the Head of the Lake lay in Township 8, later renamed Barton Township by Simcoe; Township 7, today partly annexed to the city, he named Saltfleet; and the township in the rear of No. 7, Binbrook. On the north shore of Lake Geneva the former Township of Geneva became East Flamborough.

These townships were surveyed by Augustus Jones, appointed in June, 1791, as deputy provincial land surveyor of the district of Nassau, following more than two years' service as assistant to Philip Frey, provincial surveyor.

In 1788 the first line surveyed in the future city of Hamilton was run between Lots 14 and 15 (west side of James Street) from the second concession (King Street) "North Eighteen degrees East down to Burlington Bay, blazing both line trees and side marks and laying off a road allowance of one chain between the lots. Registered, Nassau, 25th October, 1791,"[6] the survey of Barton has inscribed on each lot the name of the owner at the time of survey.

Above and below the mountain new settlers were locating: the Hornings, Rymals, Ryckmans, Burkholders, Mills, Hesses, Fergusons and Hughsons, and the Springers—Daniel and Richard and their widowed mother, Margaret Springer, whose husband, David, a circuit rider minister of New York State, had been a casualty of the American Revolutionary War. Stripped of extensive inherited possessions, Margaret Springer had travelled on foot through the wilderness with five of her nine children to settle at the foot of the mountain.

Riding one day through the willow swamp which still borders the southwest sedge of Coote's Paradise—today part of the 1,900 acres of the Royal Botanical Gardens—Beasley came upon a frightened white girl who greeted him with joyful tears. While busy outside their cabin Henrietta had been seized and carried off by Indians.

As Beasley carried her home on his horse he learned that she had not been harmed. Following Indian custom, she was to be given for adoption to an Indian mother who had lost her child. Outwardly acquiescent, the captive had waited and watched for the opportunity to escape. When it came she had slipped away only to become hopelessly lost. Had it not been for Richard—she shuddered and clung to him tightly—she might even then have been recaptured.

Richard Beasley was surprised at his own relief at the rescue of this young descendant of good Amsterdam stock. So relieved that his return of Henrietta to her mother was merely temporary. In 1791 for greater safety he made her Mrs. Beasley and removed her to his own comfortable hearthstone. The marriage resulted in Richard achieving at least one first in the new community. Henrietta made him the father of the first white child born at the Head of the Lake—Henry, who arrived in 1793.

4

Land Surveys and Settlers

IN 1794 Lieutenant-Governor Simcoe had the King's Head Inn built at the southern end of Burlington Beach, at the Carrying Place. A large two-storey frame house with auxiliary buildings, the inn contained eight rooms, as well as two low rear wings joined by a colonnade. Facing northwest towards today's La Salle Park, it stood about two hundred feet from the bay shore, near a curving arm of Big Creek which materially shortened the portage between lake and bay.

In addition to accommodating travellers, the inn served as a depot for military stores and provisions and provided accommodation for troops on their way between Newark (renamed from Niagara) and York or Detroit.

The inn stood strategically at the junction of three Indian trails: the Mississauga which followed the shore of Lake Ontario from Newark to York (and which vanished east of Van Wagner's Beach in storms, especially Hurricane Hazel, in the 1950's); Brant's trail, which crossed Burlington Beach from the northern end possibly using the Mississauga trail, swung west along the southern shore of Burlington Bay past Beasley's trading house, then climbed Burlington Heights to strike inland and up the escarpment to Ancaster; and a third trail that turned off from the Mississauga at the southern end of the Beach, traversed the site of the city, mounted the escarpment near later John Street, and headed south to the Grand River and Lake Erie.

Running west along the line of Cannon Street the trail would have turned south to today's King Street—itself a major Indian trail—before reaching the present Wellington Street where an inlet extended from the bay to south of Main Street.

Here in the days of the Indian, and the 1790's and early 1800's of white settlement, lay the crossroads of the plain below the escarpment. Here the Indian trail—later Highway 8 and King Street—running from the Niagara River at Queenston to the Head of the Lake and westward through Dundas, with a branch-off up the mountain to Ancaster, was joined by the trail from the Humber River and "muddy York" which snaked through the forest along the course of today's Highway 2. Crossing

Burlington Heights, the trail followed the present course of York Street past Beasley's homestead, and angling cornerwise into the future heart of the community, passed James Street a few rods north of King, to intercept King Street to the east, just short of the inlet.

Here, eighty feet west of Wellington and the same distance north of King, in a silver-leaved poplar grove, stood the first public house of the area—Smith's tavern, in operation prior to January 31st, 1796, when it housed the first full meeting of The Barton Lodge, Free and Accepted Masons.[1] Here, too, in 1824, on the southeast corner, site of today's First United Church, previously First Methodist, on land secured two years earlier from Colonel Robert Land, Jr., the earliest church in the city was erected and dedicated by the Methodist Episcopalians. And here, also, east of the church site, the first log cabin schoolhouse in Hamilton was taught by William Applegarth, whose scholars came from the "First Families" of the east end, and whose scanty salary was supplemented by his "boarding round" after the fashion of the day.

In 1796 Smith's tavern, Beasley's store, and the widely scattered cabins of the settlers comprised the community at the lakehead. "The country generally was in a very unsettled state," wrote Thomas Hamill, whose family moved here from Grimsby in 1797. "Hamilton was not in existence; Toronto was composed of but a few shanties; and London was still a wilderness. Indians in large numbers roved up and down the country at will, camping where they pleased, and wolves were numberless."

Said John Ryckman, born in Barton Township, later a justice of the peace in St. Catharines: "The city in 1803 was all forest. The shores of the bay were difficult to reach or see because they were hidden by a thick, almost impenetrable mass of trees and undergrowth . . . Bears ate pigs, so settlers warred on bears. Wolves gobbled sheep and geese, so they hunted and trapped wolves. They also held organized raids on rattlesnakes on the mountainside. There was plenty of game. Many a time have I seen a deer jump the fence into my back yard, and there were millions of pigeons which we clubbed as they flew low. I saw 112 killed with one charge of shot."

With hardy hands each pioneer made his crude clearing in the forest, squaring the felled logs to build his one-room shack, plastering chinks with clay, and using basswood bark for roofing. Barns were made of logs thatched with straw. Both houses and barns had earthen floors. "Straw or dried grass was used for beds," said John Ryckman, "and frequently during the night harmless milk snakes used to crawl into bed beside you to get warm."

Heart of the home was the stone fireplace which must be large enough to roll in a back log to hold the fire. Heat against the bitter cold, light and cheer the crackling blaze of the hearth provided. In addition it could roast the haunch of venison or the wild turkey turning on the spit; boil the suspended soup kettle, and bake the cornbread in the covered iron pot nested in the coals.

One of the bitterest of pioneer memories, as frequently recorded, relates to mornings when the last carefully banked coal on the hearth was found to have succumbed during the night; in the icy chill within the room, water stood frozen solid in the bucket; the flint would not spark; and before the fire could be lighted and water boiled, the first riser must wade through unbroken snowdrifts half a mile, a mile or more to the nearest neighbour to "borrow fire."

From the beginning excess water plagued the plain: perpetual streams, flowing from the mountainside, northeasterly across the plain; seasonal torrents and floods; springs at the foot of the escarpment creating a marsh (still commemorated in Spring Street); inlets that took the names of the settlers upon whose lands they encroached.

From east to west: Ghent's Inlet, Jones', Secord's and Ogg's, Gage's, Stipe's, Lottridge's and Harvey's, Sherman's or Coal Oil Inlet of evil-smelling fame, Land's and Ferguson's, and reaching south to Main Street, a perpetual aggravation to city fathers, a deep marshy ravine between future Caroline and Hess Streets.

On King Street, between Wellington and John, a swamp later crossed by a low bridge lurked for the unwary. On James Street North a greater bog in spring and fall severed communication between the town and "the lake," as the bayfront was then termed.

Yet to its settlers the attractions of the site overcame its disadvantages. In his *Topographical Description of Upper Canada,* Sir Francis Gore speaks of the area as "perhaps as beautiful and romantic as any in the interior of America. . ."

Mrs. Simcoe shared his opinion, as her diary indicates. In June, 1796, the Lieutenant-Governor and his wife interrupted a voyage from Newark to York to stop at the King's Head Inn and were detained by an east blow. "This place is so delightful," she writes, "I do not regret it." Riding on the sandstrip, "We passed an Indian encampment," she comments. "Their huts and dogs among the fine oak trees formed a picturesque appearance." She admired the red clay cliffs of the north shore. Only the sandflies were not appreciated.

"At eight o'clock," she writes, "we set out in a boat to go to Beasley's, at the head of Burlington Bay . . . The river (Big Creek) and bay were full of canoes; the Indians were fishing; we bought some fine salmon of them. When we had near crossed the bay, Beasley's house became a very pretty object. We landed at it and walked up the hill, from whence is a beautiful view of the lake, with wooded points breaking the line of shore and Flamborough in the background. The hill is quite like a park, with large oak trees dispersed, but no underwood.

"Further west of this terrace we saw Coote's Paradise . . . It abounds with wild fowl and tortoises; from hence it appears more like a river or lake than a marsh, and Mordaunt's (Morden's)[2] place in the distance takes a fine shape. I was so pleased with this place that the Governor stay'd and dined at Beasley's."

19

That evening, "A violent east wind and terrific surf—a prodigious sea," she notes. "I stood for some time under an umbrella to admire its grandeur."

The Indians whom Mrs. Simcoe mentions were not the first inhabitants of the lakehead area. Of the earliest aborigines and their successors little is known. In 1615 when Etienne Brulé reputedly paid the first white man's visit to Lake Ontario and the lakehead, the Attiwandarons, or Neutral nation, had long occupied the territory.

Before the autumn-tinted mid-September day in 1669 when Robert René Cavelier de La Salle and his priestly companions, Francis Dollier de Casson and René de Brabant de Galinée, first saw bay and mountain, the Neutrals had been eliminated by the Iroquois. Skimming the sandbarred lake outlet and skirting the northern shore of the bay, La Salle and his party landed near today's La Salle park. Briefly they lingered, then with their company of "more than fifty savages and savagesses" the white men disappeared westward on the arduous overland portage to the Indian encampment of Tinawatawa in the great swamp.

By the time George III negotiated the New Purchase at one-tenth of a penny per acre, the migratory Mississaugas of the Ojibwa nation from the north had infiltrated the land.

To understand the distribution of this land to white settlers, one must know something of surveying methods then in practice. Like Saltfleet, Barton was laid out in eight concessions running east and west, with a broken front bordering the water. Between concessions one chain (sixty-six feet) was allowed for concession roads which lay five-eighths of a mile apart.

Starting point in the survey was a base line, the later Burlington Street, at that period so deeply and widely slashed with inlets that the survey line was run in winter across the frozen marsh. North of Burlington Street extended the broken front; southward to Barton, Concession 1; Barton to Main, Concession 2; Main to Concession Street (later named Aberdeen Avenue below the escarpment), Concession 3; Concession to Fennell Avenue, Concession 4; and southward: to Mohawk Road, Concession 5; to Limeridge Road, 6; to Stone Church Road, 7; and to Highway 53, Concession 8.

Dividing these concessions into pairs of lots were side roads running north and south, commencing on the east with the township line between Saltfleet and Barton, the present Strathearne Avenue, and ending on the west with a line one lot allowance west of and parallel to today's Paradise Road. One-half mile apart, the side roads divided the concessions into ten blocks of two lots each—with the western lot making twenty-one lots in Barton Township. With a frontage of twenty chains and a depth of fifty, each lot, excepting the irregular broken fronts, contained a hundred acres. In both Barton and Saltfleet lots number from the east westward.

Today, with city expansion far beyond these earlier township limits, the old side roads, like the concession roads, have become main city arteries: Strathearne Avenue, Kenilworth, Ottawa, Gage, Sherman, Wentworth, Wellington, James, Queen, Dundurn and Longwood Road.

"These side roads," said William C. Cust, chief draughtsman in the city works department of city engineer Waldo A. Wheten, B.Sc., "are remarkably straight, with only the odd error, but the east-west concession roads such as Main Street and Barton have a deflection at every intersection with the side roads. This is especially noticeable on Main Street at night. Run your eye along the line of street lights and you will see them jog at Ottawa Street, at Gage Avenue and Sherman, at Wentworth, at Wellington, and particularly at Queen."

The reason for these bends lay in the sixty-six foot surveyor's chain of the day, composed of one hundred jointed links. As this chain was dragged over rocks, across stony streams, and through the tangle of fallen trees and undergrowth, the joints wore thin and the chain lengthened, resulting in inaccuracies.

In surveying Barton and Saltfleet Townships Augustus Jones used the front-and-rear system, marking the base line and throwing a line around the township, then running the side roads and marking the lot corners on them. Starting from the base line, Burlington Street, and a point one concession west of present Strathearne Avenue, he ran up the east side of Kenilworth to the southern boundary, the present Highway 53; west along 53 one concession (two lots) to Ottawa, and north on the east side of Ottawa to Burlington; west on Burlington to Gage, south on Gage to Highway 53, west to Sherman, down Sherman, and so on.

"The lot corners marked at this time," said Bill Cust, "were the lines of the future concession roads. When the surveyors later came to lay out the concessions, however, from marker to marker, the inaccurate chain had resulted in a variance in lines run from the north and from the south. The deflections are the measure of that variance."

When one considers the primitive equipment of the day; the lack of roads and the fact that supplies and equipment had largely to be back-packed over bush trails; that lines must be run through impenetrable wilderness in bush heat aggravated by snakes, flies, mosquitoes and ague, and conversely by sub-zero cold, blizzards, ice and snow, it is little wonder that so many early surveyors took to the bottle, the popular pioneer tranquillizer.

Yet today the city of Hamilton stands as a monument to the diligence and painstaking care, the skill, ability and powers of endurance of solemn, dignified Augustus Jones, underpaid and sometimes not paid at all, overworked, frequently berated and seldom officially praised. Born in 1763 in Duchess County, New York, Mr. Jones was of Welsh extraction. Following completion of his training as a land surveyor and service as an officer in a Hessian regiment in the American Revolutionary War, he came to Canada in 1784 with recommendations to Lord Dorchester which led to his immediate employment in Upper Canada.

Coming into everyday contact with the Indians in his taming of the

21

wilderness, Augustus Jones learned their language and employed them in his work. His liking of the Indian character and disposition led him (according to the autobiography of his second son, the Reverend Peter Jones, Indian missionary), to marry Tuhbenakanguay, daughter of a Mississauga chief, by whom he had five sons and five daughters.

Peter Spohn Van Wagner, son of pioneer Henry Van Wagner, however, states that Augustus Jones had two Indian wives. "By his first squaw, Wap-pa-noos, he had two sons, John and Peter, who both in time filled Methodist pulpits. By his second squaw, Sally, for the first had been divorced, he had several children."[3]

This would tend to explain the Reverend Peter Jones' statement that the two elder sons, left to their mother's management in their father's absence, for over fourteen years lived and wandered with the nomadic Mississaugas. Later Augustus Jones settled his family on a crown grant north of Stoney Creek. Possibly his desire to live in a fixed abode as a white man led to the divorce from his first wife who preferred the ways of her people.

"My father," said Peter Spohn, "knew him and lodged at his house. He always spoke very respectfully of him and his second squaw, who was a chief's daughter, and though retaining Indian costume presided at the table with a taste equal to a refined lady's."

Until after the War of 1812 the Indian was still much a part of the Canadian scene. "In my father's time," wrote Peter Spohn, "there were as many or more Indians as whites. The Indians were quite peaceable and quiet living, hunters rather than warriors. As a boy I played more with Indian children in the woods than with playmates of my own race. My parents never doubted my safety.

"For several years," he concludes, "the Mississaugas pitched their tents in my Father's bush in warm weather," and here in their camp he recalls, "having frequently met his (Augustus Jones') first squaw, as a little boy would meet an old woman."

On the 1791 survey by Mr. Jones are recorded the names of Hamilton's pioneer landholders by location ticket. While many of the grants had changed hands even before patents in 1796 established final ownership, a surprising number of pioneer names are still to be found among descendants in the city today. Prior to 1791 and the passage of the Canada, or Constitutional, Act giving settlers in the upper province the right to hold land by British rather than French feudal tenure, the transfer of land was not legally permissible.[4] Legal or not, land did change hands, however, by sale, exchange, gift and inheritance.

Where a property had been transferred several times, the resulting documents of ownership made the awarding of patents an involved and difficult problem. Such papers included pencilled notations on the back of playing cards, on birch bark, and even on scraps of cloth.

Yet beneath Simcoe's guiding hand the province was taking shape. On February 14th, 1798, the lakehead gained one of its most colorful citizens of all time—Thayendanegea, or Chief Joseph Brant, of the Six Nations Iroquois. For his services to the British crown during the American Revolution, Brant was granted for himself and his family 3,450 acres of land at the northern end of Burlington Beach—as much as he could walk around "from sunrise to sunset." Known originally as Brant's Block, this choice and beautiful location, bounded in part by Burlington Bay and the western curve of Lake Ontario, later became the site of Wellington Square, forerunner of today's thriving town of Burlington.

In the northeastern corner of the bay, sheltered from the storms of Lake Ontario, Brant located his home just north of the old lake outlet. On a grassy tree-shaded meadow he built a dignified two-storey Georgian house. Erected in the wilderness at a time when the log cabin was the prevailing form of neighbourhood architecture, the home provides a measure of the man.

An account of the interior speaks of a spacious hall and a parlour well furnished and carpeted, with a pier and chimney glasses, mahogany tables and fashionable chairs. On the wall hung a guitar and a bookcase in which, among other volumes, was a Church of England Prayer Book which Brant had helped translate into the Mohawk tongue.

Breakfast, brought in on a tray by an Indian woman servant wearing a man's hat, consisted of "tea, coffee, hot rolls, butter in ice coolers, eggs, smoked beef, ham and broiled chickens; all served in neat style."

Whether Brant patterned his home on Johnson Hall in the Mohawk valley of New York State or on dwellings he may have admired in Great Britain is not known. Either is possible. Joseph Brant had frequently visited the home of Sir William Johnson, British Superintendent of Indian Affairs in North America, where his sister, the beautiful and famous Molly (Mary) Brant presided as chatelaine and mother of eight of Sir William's children. On the other hand Brant was conversant with English architecture for he had visited the mother country in 1776 and 1785. He had been received by George III and accepted widely in court circles.

Tall, erect and majestic, Thayendanegea possessed the air and mien of one born to command. When presented to King George III, it is said he refused to kiss the royal hand, but in declining observed gallantly that he would gladly kiss the hand of the queen. In England Brant wore European dress except for formal attire when he was provided with splendid native costumes. His portrait was painted by Romney in Indian dress.

On his second visit to England the Mohawk was attended by two Negro slaves, chosen from a number captured in the American Revolutionary War and later retained in his service. In *The Life of Joseph Brant*, William L. Stone explains that Brant stated the slaves were happy and willing to live with him, liked Indian habits and customs, and had no desire to return to white masters. Substantiating the story of slaves was the much later unearthing of a considerable number of skeletons buried separately in the Brant house grounds, which proved to be the remains of Negroes.

In common with his race Chief Brant was noted for his hospitality, and the low shoreline and quiet reed-fringed waters before his dwelling were frequently crowded with the canoes of his tribesmen. His door stood open to all, poorest and most distinguished. On May Day, 1800, one thousand Indians are said to have gathered at a housewarming to do him honour.

With the arrival of Joseph Brant a new era began at the lakehead. At the southeastern end of the beach strip on a crown grant of twelve hundred acres lived Augustus Jones. Jones and Brant were old friends, Mr. Jones having surveyed the crown grant of Indian lands along the Grand River and having received for his services some forty-eight hundred acres from the grateful Six Nations.

Both surveyor and chief were equally friendly with Richard Beasley. By horseback along the hardpacked sand of the lakeshore, by Brant's trail, or by water the three were close neighbours. They were compatible. In a hospitable era all were recognized for their liberality; all had capabilities beyond the ordinary; and all had a common interest. The life of Augustus Jones was bound to the land; Brant, at this period, was acting as official agent of the Six Nations in a scheme to sell part of the Grand River grant and invest the proceeds in government annuities to provide financial security for his people; and Beasley, with James Wilson and Jean Baptiste Rousseau as silent partners, had acquired for speculation a block of 94,012 acres located some distance upstream from Brant's Ford (Brantford).

For a decade these three shared honours and friendship as the leading citizens of the lakehead. In 1796 Richard Beasley was elected to the Legislative Assembly for Durham, York and the first riding of Lincoln, a post he held until 1800. For the following four years he represented the newly divided electoral district of West York, the first riding of Lincoln, and the new County of Haldimand, in the final year of this term serving as Speaker.

In addition to these duties, Squire Beasley was also clearing, fencing, farming and setting out in orchards his Burlington Heights property; was actively engaged in fur trading and operating his store; still owned his mill; served as lieutenant-colonel of the 2nd York Regiment of militia; was fathering a growing family; and was involved with extensive land transactions.

It was in this last field that Richard Beasley created the difficulties that dogged him throughout his lifetime. Aside from the profit he undoubtedly anticipated in his large scale transactions in Indian lands, only an itch for land itself could explain his acquisition of property throughout Hamilton and in various parts of Upper Canada which he received, says Mabel Dunham,[5] "from the Crown through the influence of friends in the Legislature." On the Heights alone, through further crown grants and by purchase, Squire Beasley consolidated his various holdings into an integrated property exceeding 1,100 acres in extent. It was his misfortune that land was a commodity from which it was difficult to extract money.

While these events transpired, the lakehead too was developing. From all states to the south sturdy, stout-hearted men and women, many unused to wilderness life, were pushing into the plain below or locating on the heights above the escarpment.

From Montgomery County, Pennsylvania, Abraham and Isaac, sons of Holland-born Ludwig Horning, arrived in 1787 to settle on the mountain; while their brother, Peter, his family and two sisters, arriving the following year after shipwreck and loss of much of their belongings in a Lake Ontario gale, established their cabin south of the Depew and Stewart farms. On land extending today from Main Street to the Mountain and from Sherman Avenue east to Gage, the Horning log cabin stood on the site of the later Springer homestead, which in 1890 was converted into the initial unit of today's flourishing St. Peter's Infirmary.

From Pennsylvania too came William Rymal whose descendants, ardent liberals, would include Jacob, representative of Wentworth County in the Legislative Assembly. A reformer and close friend of William Lyon Mackenzie, Jacob provided the fiery red-wigged Scot with shelter and a fresh mount during the fugitive's flight from York along the Niagara Peninsula and across the River.

On the thousand-acre Rymal farm—a hundred acres of which Jacob purchased for a yoke of oxen and a shotgun—William built the inevitable first log cabin, and Jacob the subsequent homestead. A one-and-a-half storey frame, eighty-four feet long by thirty-four wide, with a Dutch oven on the ground floor and another in the basement, and three huge stone fireplaces, "big enough to drive a team through," the home was unusually commodious even in a day of large homes for large families. Mute testimony to the giant pines of Upper Canada were the floor boards, fifteen to twenty inches wide, and the pine plate upon which the rafters rested. A single timber, eight by ten inches, it ran the full length of the house.

Cornelius and Samuel Ryckman, who founded Ryckman's Corners; William Terryberry, proprietor of the famous two-storey frame coach stop, the Terryberry Inn; Beckett, Markle, Kirkendall, Green, Munn, Secord, Neff, Taylor, Young, Almas and McBride: all of these, industrious and thrifty, helped convert the mountain top from wilderness to prosperous and ordered farms.

Immediately west of James Street in 1789 settled Michael Hess of Northampton County, Pennsylvania. With his wife, Charity, and their ten children, Michael settled on Hess Creek which ran through the later Ontario Hospital farm and the Gourlay-Colquhoun farm, to drop over the Mountain at Chedoke Falls into the Chedoke ravine. One wonders if the ten Hess children and their children and the Gourlay and Colquhoun offspring suffered from living near this treacherous beauty spot and hikers' paradise from whose tempting rockbound walls children—and occasional adults—have required frequent rescue for the past century and more.

Far to the east along the mountain brow a pioneer from the deep south settled upon still another escarpment stream, Big Creek, and used its falls to establish one of the earliest grist and saw mills in Barton Township.

In 1792 William Davis, of Welsh descent, with his wife, the beautiful Hannah Phillips of Virginia, their seven children, a number of slaves who refused to leave the family, and twenty "hoss beasts" laden with belongings, migrated from North Carolina. With them came Thomas Ghent who had recently married Elizabeth, eldest daughter of the household. Hannah, an outstanding horsewoman, is said to have ridden the five hundred wilderness miles seated on a hunting saddle trimmed with blue velvet and ornamented with a pair of brass powder horns.

When they reached the mouth of the Genesee River, Simcoe, a friend of the family, despatched a gunboat to carry the party to Niagara. Wilderness and danger Hannah could brave, but Canada's climate proved too harsh for both mistress and the family's faithful retainers. None survived long in this northern land. When Hannah died in 1794 William Davis and his family moved to the lakehead. On a grant of five hundred acres in Saltfleet—with an additional three hundred acres to Thomas Ghent—located above and below the mountain, they built Albion Mills. Today Mount Albion and the Glendale Golf and Country Club in part occupy their land.

Although erected before 1800, Harmony Hall which William Davis built in the tradition of the southern plantation house is still occupied and well preserved. For years the Albion Mills operated, the hard burr stones of the grist mill grinding the coarse, dark, precious pioneer flour and the buckwheat daily used in pancakes.

West of Albion another family settled—so numerous in its second and third generations that it became a community in itself, complete with cemetery, school and church. Near the corner of today's Sherman Avenue and Mohawk Road, Jacob Burkholder built his cabin on land selected in 1793 by his eldest son, Christian, then aged twenty-one, who walked from Pennsylvania to the head of the lake and back to inspect and report on the land promised settlers by John Graves Simcoe.

"Until Jacob Burkholder settled there," said Miss Mabel Burkholder, Hamilton writer, whose weekly feature, "Out of the Storied Past", appeared regularly in *The Hamilton Spectator* from 1946 to 1962, "the eastern portion of the mountain lay in its centuries-old sleep. Jacob chose it as it was less heavily timbered than land near the lake and therefore more easily cleared. The mountain offered two alternatives: a fine view from the brow or location on an open road, the Mohawk trail from Niagara to Ancaster, then merely a slash through the woods. Jacob elected the road, a mile from the brow."

Of Pennsylvania German stock, Miss Burkholder is great-granddaughter of Jacob Burkholder, Swiss Mennonite, and Sophia de Roche, daughter of a Huguenot family of southern France, whose romance aboard the sailing vessel, *Myrtilla*, in 1765, led to their marriage in America. They settled near Harrisburg. Being Mennonites the family refused to engage in the American Revolutionary War. In 1794, however, they joined the exodus of "later loyalists" and with their six children abandoned their well established homes and trekked into the wilderness. On the mountain Jacob and his sons received 800 acres.

"Life wasn't easy for the pioneer," says Mabel Burkholder. "Shortly after their arrival in October, Joseph, the youngest child, was killed in a fall from the roof of their log hut. Early that same winter the last child, Peter, was born. Great-grandmother Sophia was French and dainty and loved the fine fabrics she had known in France. In the wilderness everyone dressed in homespun and if Mennonite, dyed the homespun drab. Sophia had a little box of silk and satin patches of all colours. To the backwoods women it was like a box of jewels; they came for miles to look at the patches and touch them.

"Sophia's greatest pride were her small feet. She had one pair of stylish shoes she had brought with her and these, treasured and used only on special occasions, lasted for years."

If settlement was progressing on the mountain it was also moving apace on the plain below where land holdings in the early 1800's were stabilizing themselves as they would remain for some decades.

South of Main Street to the Mountain in tremendous farms, James Mills, father of the Hon. Samuel S. Mills and founder of the well-known Hamilton mercantile family, owned land west of Queen Street; William Wedge, between Queen and James; John Springer, east of James to the line of Mary Street; Richard Springer from Mary to Wellington; and Ephraim Land from Wellington to Wentworth. On the north side of Main Street Peter Hess owned west of Bay Street; Samuel Kirkendall, from Bay to James; Nathaniel Hughson, from James to Mary; Archibald Ferguson, from Mary to Wellington; Robert Land, Sr., from Wellington to Emerald; and Abel Land from Emerald to Wentworth. Only the farms of William Wedge and John Springer would shortly change owners.

As for soil: ". . . between the Mountain and Lake," wrote Patrick Campbell in his *Travels in North America*, "is in general a deep clay soil with black and fat mould of some inches on top. The land on the mountain is of much lighter soil intermixed with sand . . . but produces heartier wheat than the lands below though not in such quantities. . . . The top of the Mountain would make good pasture for cattle in its present state, particularly for sheep, could they be preserved from the wolves . . . The lands on the Mountain appear to be the fittest I have yet seen for the poor man to begin upon, as it requires scarce any clearing, there being no more wood upon it than sufficient for rails, inclosures and necessary purposes of farming so that if he chooses he may plow down the land the moment he acquires possession of it. Clearing land of heavy timber is both expensive and tedious but if one has sufficient patience to go through with it, he may be assured of being amply repaid in the end."

As clearings increased in number and size the community grew with them. Stores appeared: on the southeast corner of King and John Streets,

William Sheldon's small frame general store; on the south side of King at the future Gore, John Aikman's wagon shop; and later nearby a tin shop operated by Edward Jackson. On the northwest corner of King and John, Barnum's tavern added its pioneer comfort to Smith's at King and Wellington. Homespun clothing began to replace buckskin as Jacob Burkholder set up as a skilled weaver, his first customer Abraham Horning. Later James Mills would commence tailoring.

On James Street North, crossing the great bog, a corduroy road was laid, with hundreds of small trees placed side by side and the spaces between filled with mud and stones. Where Wellington Street would run, Land's Lane (also, Lovers' Lane) wound its rutted grassy track through thick bush to Land's wharf, second on Burlington Bay to Beasley's. Here Abel Land supplemented farming with a modest carrying business, employing the flat-bottomed batteaux of the day capable of clearing the old shallow outlet, his cargoes at first chiefly salt, whiskey and potash, with later grain and flour.

On Samuel Kirkendall's farm, where the City Hall of 1888 would stand, Mr. Kirkendall's apple orchard came into bearing, with McIntosh Reds, Spitzenbergs, Red Astrakhans and Early Harvests ripening in the sun. On the future Court House Square a cornfield rustled in the summer breeze and in the adjoining potato patch a small boy picked slugs into a wooden bucket while a block to the west, at the corner of Main and James, his father, John Springer, shot the downtown area's first pigeons raiding his ripening wheat.

Only in the west end on the heights was life proving difficult. For some time, as the "Cartwright Letter Book" discloses, Richard Beasley's trading business had been running in the red, for reasons which Cousin Richard Cartwright did not hesitate to point out. In contrast with today's accepted economy of credit buying and government subsidies, his letter offers an interesting comparison with the past and its simple code of supply and demand.

"Let me intreat you," Cartwright warned, "to be cautious in giving Credits, for when once begun there is no knowing where to end. A man may have property to pay but of such a nature as not to be convertible into Remittances, on the Punctuality of which the Credit and Profit of a Man of Business principally depends. Accidents may happen to prevent the best intended People from fulfilling their Engagements. The Weather and the Seasons are not under our Controul; yet on these depend the fruitful or scanty Harvest, and if the Farmer loses his crop what Resources has he for the Payment of his Debt? Consider too that the Price of Produce is on the Eve of being very much reduced with you, and that Wheat next year will perhaps be not more than 3/S Halifax Currency."

When Richard Beasley's mounting debit balance with his cousin (£1,740) indicated disregard of the above advice, Cartwright's letter salutations testified to the exhaustion of his patience and of Beasley's credit. From the customary friendly, "Dear Cousin" or "Dear Richard," they chilled to a cold, "Dear Sir," then to a forbiddingly formal, "Mr. Beasley, Sir."

Yet, gainsaying his preaching, Cousin Cartwright saw that the *Lady Dorchester*, the *Kingston Packet*, and the *Governor Simcoe* continued to carry Beasley's orders—13 Bbl. of Rum, 16 Bbls. Salt, a Smithy Bellows, Glass, Nails, Earthenware, a Chest of Tea, Cloth, Sheeting. There seems little doubt of Cartwright's family feeling for this first cousin whose birthplace of Albany was his own.

On February 27th, 1797, Beasley sold his half of the Ancaster Mills to Robert Wires for eight hundred pounds, under double indemnity pledging the land to which he had not yet received patent.[6] In the issue of June 21st, 1800, of the *Canada Constellation*, published at Niagara, he advertised the land at the Head of the Lake to which he had received a patent less than a year earlier:[7]

> *FOR SALE*: To be sold, a valuable and pleasant situation at Burlington Bay (head of little lake), containing 976 acres of land, 150 of which are under good improvement. There are on the premises a comfortable dwelling place and stables; also a wharf 100 feet long and 52 wide; a store house, 30 x 20, and an excellent saw for a saw mill, with a quantity of valuable pine, walnut and other timber. It is an excellent stand for business, being the head of the water communication with the western part of the province, and the main road from the Grand River and the River La Tranche leads from this place. Persons wanting to purchase may know terms by applying to the printers of this paper in Niagara or to R. Beasley, Esq., on the premises.

The funds Beasley hoped to raise from the unhappy sale of his homesite were desperately needed to cover overdue payments on the Indian lands purchased on February 5th, 1798. Although James Wilson, Beasley's former partner in milling at Ancaster, and Jean Baptiste Rousseau, who later replaced Beasley in that partnership, were both included in the purchase, the block was known from the beginning as the Beasley tract and was so-named in the legal documents pertaining to it.

"Beasley," says Mabel Dunham in *Grand River*, "conducted all business pertaining to it. He had it surveyed and subdivided into farm lots and he was solely responsible for the payments on the mortgage, principal and interest, a substantial amount, since only £600 had been paid on the £8,887 purchase price of the property."

Under these circumstances one may estimate Beasley's delight when Mennonite emigrants from Pennsylvania, having sent emissaries ahead to inspect the Beasley tract according to their custom, expressed willingness to buy, to pay cash for their purchase, and to bring in other cash-paying settlers of their faith. Beasley sold them land and gave them deeds. He omitted to mention that he was only one of three owners of the tract and that the land was heavily mortgaged.[8]

Until 1802 all went well. The "plain people" struggled through the deadly bog of Beverly swamp, reached their new land and built the first homes in the vast interior south of Georgian Bay. Others followed until it seemed as if the whole tract would be settled and Richard Beasley's monetary difficulties at an end. Then the bubble burst. Bachelor Sam Bricker, a late arrival, walked to York one day on business and heard talk there of the plight of the settlers on the Beasley tract whose deeds were not worth the paper they were printed on. Redheaded, short-tempered Sam Bricker investigated. Then instead of returning home he walked to the head of the lake and confronted Beasley.

Squire Beasley admitted the truth of Sam Bricker's accusations. Furthermore he offered to make amends. If the Mennonites would buy sixty thousand acres for ten thousand pounds he would pay off the mortgage with the purchase money and give them a clear title to the land.[9]

To the Mennonites who had already invested all their capital in purchasing their farms, this was a cruel jest. But not to Sam Bricker. How he and Joseph Sherk journeyed to Pennsylvania to raise the money and how Sam in a final desperate bid succeeded after Joseph had departed in despair, is an Horatio Alger success story, too long for this book but available and well told by Mabel Dunham in *Grand River*.[10]

When Sam and a strong escort arrived with a wagon specially built to carry the canvas bags into which the Mennonite women in Pennsylvania had sewn the required precious silver dollars, they found the settlers packed to leave. Joyfully all restored their belongings to their homes. The silver hoard was conveyed to York, and after a reputable lawyer had searched the title and drawn up an airtight deed, it was paid for sixty thousand acres of land. On this tract within Waterloo County the original settlers and compatriots founded the thriving cities of Preston, Kitchener and Waterloo.

To Chief Brant the result of his stewardship of Indian lands was a disaster which clouded his last days. Sale of the lands had been entrusted solely to him, and while Brant was exonerated by his own people of any motive of self-seeking or personal profit, the outcome of his unbridled generosity was litigation for the Six Nations, loss of their land, and little of the capital they had been promised. To his difficulties at this time was also added trouble with his worthless son, Isaac, a dangerous maniac when intoxicated. In a drunken scuffle in Beasley's store one evening, the old chief in attempting to disarm his son who is said to have attacked him with a knife, inflicted a head wound with his own dagger. In itself the injury was superficial, but Isaac refused treatment and death ensued from infection.

Although Brant reported the case the police considered action unnecessary. Overcome with grief and remorse, however, the old chief resigned his commission as captain in the army and forfeited his pay. On November 24th, 1807, he died at his home at Brant's Square, his last whisper, "Have pity on the poor Indian!" a plea for his race.

Brant's remains were laid to rest in St. Luke's cemetery, Burlington, at an impressive service attended by Six Nations' chiefs, government officials and mourners of both races and all classes. For twenty-four hours the bell in His Majesty's chapel of the Mohawks on the Grand River tolled the passing of one of the Six Nations' greatest leaders. His death marked the end of an era at the lakehead.

For forty-three years Brant's remains rested at Wellington Square. Then in November, 1850, they were disinterred and carried—with those of his son, John, who died in 1832—on the shoulders of Mohawk braves across Burlington Beach and through the forest to a final resting place beside the Mohawk chapel. Again, as at his death, the tolling of the chapel bell accompanied the passage of the funeral cortege.

At its termination the memorial service was conducted by the Rev. Peter Jones, son of Brant's good friend, Augustus Jones, and of his first wife, Wap-pa-noos.

5

Brock and War

In 1812 the smouldering animosity of America towards Great Britain burst into open flame for a second time.

From his knowledge of the temper of the victorious American colonies, gained as a British officer during the American Revolutionary War, John Graves Simcoe had foreseen further hostilities. He had also foreseen Canada as the battleground and during his term of office, 1792-96, had tried to prepare the upper province against assault and invasion.

In turn General Isaac Brock had also appreciated the inevitability of war. So outstanding had been Brock's reports of Canada's needs, its resources and their cultivation, its settlement and defence, that the customary term of five years of military service in the colony in his case had been doubled. At the outbreak of war Brock had spent ten years in Canada and was then president of the government of Upper Canada and Major General commanding His Majesty's forces in the province.

Involved as she was on land and sea in the global Napoleonic War, Great Britain was anxious at all costs to avoid conflict with the United States. Yet with the obtuseness which had earlier helped provoke the War of Independence, she moved steadily towards a new outbreak with her former colony.

Main causes of dispute centred in the British and French blockading of European ports, with seizure and search of neutral vessels, including American, resulting in United States' claims of violation of its sovereignty on the high seas; in impressment of United States sailors by the Royal Navy; in United States reprisals for the above courses of action; and in their belief that Britain had helped foster, within the United States, Indian uprisings against the white man's westward expansion.

Add to these causes of friction American desire to annex the rich, continentally and territorially important provinces of Canada; to increase United States prestige and decrease British by their conquest; and to come again to grips with the mother country, and one has in general the inducements which led President Madison—ignoring the French blockade —to declare war formally against Great Britain.

Again, as in the American Revolutionary War, Canada found herself engaged in an internecine combat which divided families within themselves, set friend against friend, and separated business associates into opposing lines of battle.

In the War of 1812, the field commander of the American forces at Niagara, later Commander-in-Chief of the United States army and General, Winfield Scott, was the nephew of Phoebe Scott, wife of Robert Land, Sr. Fighting against their cousin in the battle were five of Phoebe's sons and nephews. Similarly Private Isaac Corman of Stoney Creek was first cousin of Kentucky William Henry Harrison, Commander of the American northwestern army.

As for business associates, it is of interest to note that while war was formally declared in Washington on June 18th, 1812, official notice did not reach Governor-General Sir George Prevost in Quebec until July 7th, and London, England, until July 30th. Unofficially however, Sir George received the information from Montreal on June 25th through officials of two leading fur trading companies.

At Niagara the news arrived similarly. On June 26th a weary messenger from Albany, New York, crossed on the ferry from Lewiston to Queenston carrying a letter from John Jacob Astor to Canadian associates in the fur trade. When it developed that Mr. Astor's warning arrived a day ahead of official notification of war to Fort Niagara, incensed Yankees clamoured for an investigation which resulted in the jailing of the unfortunate messenger,[1] a commercial cartman named Vosburgh, whose only offence had been his professional speed.

The War of 1812 is confusing in that its operations by land and water were fought on long and disconnected fronts and in many different theatres of action. Its engagements were spasmodic, both sides lacking the momentum of a forceful and coordinated plan of campaign, British failure in this respect resulting from the premature death at the battle of Queenston Heights on October 13th, 1812, of General Brock.

In the Hamilton area the interest of the opposing forces throughout the war centred on Burlington Heights, a strong and defensible position which commanded the interior of the province. The strategic heights served as British headquarters for Major-General John Vincent after his forces were driven from the Niagara frontier. They became an overcrowded "City of Refuge" for troops, civilians and Indians fleeing after the occupation and burning of York and following the disastrous defeat of Major-General Henry Procter at Moraviantown on the River Thames, both in 1813.

All active engagements at the lakehead—the neighbouring land battle of Stoney Creek and two of the three minor naval skirmishes at Burlington Beach—were spearheaded at the Heights.

Indirectly, however, in the enlistment of their men for service with the militia and in the requisitioning of food and other commodities to meet the army's demands, war came closest to the settlers.

Under Brock's amended short-term pre-war Militia Act, formation was authorized from each regiment in the province of two flank companies of volunteers, to be trained six days each month until reported efficient. Limited to a captain, non-commissioned officers and forty rank and file, the chief object of the flank companies, according to Brock, was to establish a stock of loyal, brave and respectable young men capable of assisting the government in emergency in forming a force of militia engrafted upon them.

The flank companies were Brock's counterpoise to the strong pro-American element in the upper province derived from settlers drawn north of the border, not by loyalty to Great Britain, but by the lure of free land offered to promote settlement of the wilderness. Even in the Legislative Assembly pro-American sentiment was sufficiently powerful to prevent passage of needed loyalty and alien laws.

"We can take Canada without soldiers!" proclaimed William Eustis, United States Secretary of War. "We have only to send officers into the Provinces and the people, already disaffected towards their own government, will rally to our standard."

Brock largely agreed. "The great influence which the fear and number of settlers from the United States possess over the decisions of the Lower House," he wrote from York on February 25th, 1812, to Sir George Prevost at Quebec, "is truly alarming." Again, on July 29th, 1812: "My situation is most critical, not from anything the enemy can do, but from the disposition of the people . . . a full belief possesses them all that this Province must inevitably succumb."[2]

As far as American settlers in Canada were concerned they were right. United States settlers would gladly have become the fourteenth state, shucking off distasteful colonial dependence in favor of liberty, and substituting for Canadian conservatism and acceptance of traditional dogmas, American democracy and its freer and more radical culture.

That the province did not fall may be directly credited to Brock himself and to the United Empire Loyalists[3] and their descendants who still cherished a vivid memory of the wrongs they had suffered at the hands of American patriots, with resultant hatred of Americans and American ways.

At the Head of the Lake, largely settled by Loyalists, enlistment in the flank companies was so enthusiastic that the 2nd Flank Company of 5th Lincoln Militia under Captain James Durand and Lieutenant William Davis, instead of the prescribed forty, enrolled eighty-three privates, providing transfers to other companies for equalization. In this company and the sixty enlistees of Captain Samuel Hatt's Flank Company of Volunteers of the 5th Lincoln and 2nd York Militia under Lieutenant Robert Land, Jr., are found many family names of Loyalists who fought in the earlier American War of Independence: Depew, Reynolds, Gage, Kribs, Van Every, Forsyth, Ryckman, Campbell, Shafer, Clement, Bates, Showers, Lucas and Green.

In addition, the rolls carried family names of others who would be closely associated with the future history of the growing community above and below the escarpment: Hughson, Ferguson, Sipes, Storms, Wedge, Burkholder, Jones, Loudon, Bastido, and Young. By the time war was declared, the training of these flank companies had progressed so favourably that Captain Hatt's Company was included in some of the earliest action of the war. Beginning with the United States invasion of the western (Detroit) peninsula by General William Hull on July 11th, 1812, the war ended in the west with the final withdrawal of United States forces across the Niagara River at Fort Erie on August 15th, 1814.

Throughout this period the development and improvement of civilian property came to a standstill. Because of the staggering drain of the Napoleonic War a British government "no expenditure" policy for Upper Canada had effectually tied Brock's hands. At the outbreak of the War of 1812 the King's stores contained no blankets, haversacks, tents, kettles or other camp equipage, clothing or shoes. The militia were required to clothe themselves and to provide, each man, his own musket or rifle, cartridge box, knapsack, blanket and canteen. Many did not have these articles.

"The militia," said Brock, "assembled in a wretched state in regard to clothing; many were without shoes, an article which can scarcely be provided in the country."

In this emergency most soldiers lacked the resourcefulness—and literacy—of Sergeant Angus McAfee who when he found blankets would not be issued wasted no time in writing his wife, Thamar, daughter of Nathaniel Hughson (after whom Hughson Street is named). In a letter from Niagara, dated July 2nd, 1812, Sergeant McAfee not only asks for a blanket for himself but two also for his brothers, Samuel and David, and suggests that Phoebe, wife of his brother-in-law, George Hughson, send her husband a coverlet.

Having displayed his capability, it is little wonder that the big bluff good-natured sergeant was appointed quartermaster, a post he held throughout the war, combining it with active service in almost every major battle.

In a war such as that of 1812 where an army to the greatest possible extent lived off the land, the office of quartermaster was no sinecure. A quartermaster's duties demanded that he scour the countryside, requisitioning supplies from kin and neighbours as well as settlers at large. Cattle and other domestic animals were required for food, and horses to mount the cavalry and move the army. Each family was permitted to retain one milch cow and every farmer one working team.

In addition, quartermasters were urged to obtain bread, flour, and other domestic commodities for use of the troops. Again displaying his resourcefulness, Sergeant McAfee, during the occupation of Burlington Heights by the British forces, operated Smith's old tavern at the corner of King and Wellington Streets "both as a tavern and the bakery for His Majesty's troops."[4]

Throughout hostilities this then became the familiar daily visage of life at the lakehead: this and the difficulty of operating a farm with its menfolk in service; the nursing of sick and wounded, the deaths, and the constant anxiety concerning husbands, fathers and sons fighting frequently barefoot and in rags, poorly fed and indifferently sheltered, throughout the rigours of a Canadian winter.

The first contact with the regular army came to the lakehead early. Following a special session of the legislature, during which Brock had surprised a necessary supply bill through the hostile Assembly, then moving swiftly and decisively had prorogued that body and proclaimed martial law in the province, the tall, fair-haired, ruddy-faced soldier-statesman had sailed with a small force from York to Burlington Bay. Major-General Brock was on his way to evict Hull from the western peninsula. Prior to setting out from the lakehead, however, he and his officers dined with Captain James Durand in his commodious stone mansion—the only stone house at that date at the head of the lake.

Writing of the event in his *Reminiscences*, Charles Durand relates: "General Sir Isaac Brock, Lieutenant John Beverley Robinson, afterwards Chief Justice in Upper Canada, Colonel Macdonald, who was killed at Queenston Heights afterwards . . . with a company of soldiers, in August, 1812, took dinner at my father's house, passing on quickly through the woods."

Situated immediately below the Mountain at the head of Mountain Road, today's John Street, Durand's home enjoyed an outstanding view of land and lake. As Captain George Hamilton, its later owner and the founder of Hamilton, was one of Brock's officers at Detroit, it seems reasonable to assume that he saw or heard of the property as a result of this visit.[5]

At the Head of the Lake General Brock added Captain Hatt's Volunteers to his small force. To reach Long Point on Lake Erie, where he embarked, Brock took the Governor's Road, built by Simcoe between Dundas and London.

Nine months later the lakehead received its initiation by fire. On April 27, York had been burned by that portly, jolly old sea dog, Commodore Isaac Chauncey. On May 10, preparatory to attacking Fort George at the mouth of the Niagara River, Chauncey despatched two armed schooners, the *Governor Tompkins* and *Conquest*, to Burlington Beach to destroy the King's Head Inn and its stores. Throughout Upper Canada the inn's oval sign was known to travellers—on one side the bewigged head of the king surmounted by a crown, with the legend, "George III—King of Great Britain," and on the reverse, "King's Head Inn, 1794." Among its proprietors it had numbered Augustus Jones, William Lottridge and William Bates.

Commandeered by Major Samuel Hatt, the inn was garrisoned by a force of sixty-three officers and men of the local militia. Under the onslaught of an invading force of two hundred, supported by the shot of the United States ships, the defenders were forced to fall back to await reinforcements from the Heights. Before these arrived, however, the inn and its stores and the boats maintained for the transport of troops were destroyed.

If Major Hatt and his men were intimidated by the enemy, Mrs. Bates was not. According to local history, Mrs. Bates, daughter-in-law of William, who had been absent during the bombardment, returned to find her home in flames and her household goods destroyed or carried off. Undaunted by ships and invaders, Mrs. Bates grimly located a boat that had escaped enemy fire and, rowing out to the ships, demanded of the commander the return of any goods aboard and payment for property destroyed. As it was well known that Commodore Chauncey frowned on civilian looting—he having returned, with apologies, rare books and church plate carried off from York—the captain surrendered certain articles and meekly, so the story goes, paid the amount demanded. He then had her and her belongings rowed ashore.

A month later to the day, Fort George was in United States hands and the Stars and Stripes flew the length of the Niagara River. To escape annihilation or capture by a force several times larger than his thousand regulars and four hundred militia, Major-General John Vincent retreated from Fort George to Burlington Heights, where he took up position.

Today in Dundurn, Harvey Park and Hamilton cemetery, the lines of Vincent's defences against the invaders may still be traced. Within the cemetery near the main gate remains of embankments, gently rounded by time and in places invaded by the tombs of leading citizens, create a hazard for the motorist on narrow, winding cemetery roads. Here across the heights, Vincent's first line of trenches and earthworks extended. Over the years, with construction of the York Street highway and evolution of Harvey Park, the left flank vanished, only a cannon and an historical marker today indicating its onetime location.

Advance bulwark of Vincent's main defensive system was the redoubt which now juts, as perilously as a rocky headland, into the heavy traffic at the intersection of York and Dundurn Streets. Here a battery of one or two guns was mounted to delay or repulse the enemy depending upon the strength of his attack.

Protecting this advance post and two lines of entrenchments to the north, an *abatis* of felled trees with cruelly sharpened trunks and limbs faced outward amid a welter of dead leaves. Behind these defences lay Vincent's camp with its crude barracks, its stores, magazines and further batteries, and its hospital and cemetery where twenty years later, in the cholera epidemic of 1833, victims of the plague would be rudely tended and graved in mass burials beside the casualties of this War of 1812.

Stemming also from this later period is the masonry reinforcing the battlement at York and Dundurn, the picturesque stone Battery Lodge and graceful stone archway. Erected by Allan Napier MacNab in the 1830's, the Lodge was the gatehouse of Dundurn Castle and housed the lodgekeeper, while the archway was the original entrance to the grounds.

During the War of 1812 Richard Beasley's home was commandeered as army headquarters, but the tale that the Lodge served at the same time as a fort or quarters for soldiers is erroneous. In 1837, however, during the William Lyon Mackenzie Rebellion (in suppressing which MacNab played an active part), a protective guard was stationed at Battery Lodge.

By the end of May, 1813, General Vincent and his British regulars had gained the Heights, previously held by a small force under Lt.-Col. John Harvey, and had there been joined by all the regular forces formerly operating throughout the peninsula. In all, Vincent had eighteen hundred regular troops. In addition, although the militia had been dismissed after the fall of Fort George, 131 had reported for duty at Burlington Heights. The remainder had gone home to protect their families and dwellings.

In the early days of June the United States army under Generals John Chandler and William H. Winder moved slowly up the peninsula. As the Americans advanced, farm animals were driven into the woods and penned, valuables buried, and homes in many cases evacuated. Other householders refused to leave, feeling that their presence might help protect their possessions from enemy looting.

Before Mary (Chisholm) Land, wife of Ephraim, left her log cabin in the Land block, south of Main Street—site of the later residence of Seneca Jones, insurance executive, at 67 Ontario Avenue—she carried certain household treasures to the garden and with the help of her two young sons buried them. She then planted a flower to mark the spot. Since Ephraim was absent with the militia she also buried the jewels and warrant of the Barton Lodge which were in his charge. Half a century later, B. E. Charlton, Right Worshipful Master of the Lodge, was shown the exact spot by Stephen Land who had helped his mother.

"He said the flower, a large peony," reported Worshipful Brother Charlton, "occupied the centre of a circular bed. He helped dig up the flower, bury the box in the place it had occupied and then put the flower in its original position. The enemy," concluded Worshipful Brother Charlton, "was surprised during the ensuing night at Stoney Creek and thoroughly routed. The next day the members of Ephraim Land's family returned to their home and to their great joy found their treasures undisturbed."

At noon on June 5th the United States army reached Grimsby, crawled around the bend in the trail below the peak and headed west towards Stoney Creek. Beneath the overarching trees the force of thirty-five hundred appeared like an enormous undulating blue serpent, with the mounted dragoons and cavalry its reared head. Like flames struck from its burnished scales, the sun glinted on musket barrels and cannon.

Entering Stoney Creek, the Americans overran John Brady's log tavern, hungrily appropriating the day's bake of bread fresh from the oven, ate everything edible in sight and drained the town pump dry. Then wearily, with a clatter of hoofs, the rumble of artillery and wagons, and the measured beat of marching feet, the force advanced westward. West of Stoney Creek, beyond James Gage's house and his Uncle William's, at the small Wesleyan Methodist church standing in its yet unseasoned graveyard—one of the earliest churches in the province to which settlers came twenty and thirty miles to attend service—the United States advance guard encountered a British picket. Driving the picket westward, the Americans advanced past Red Hill House, the log tavern of William Davis, Jr., son of William of Albion Mills, to Big (now Red Hill) Creek. On the west bank the British halted.

Since dusk was then falling and the terrain unsuitable for encampment, the blue-clad ranks turned and fell back on Stoney Creek. There they pitched their tents and with Saltfleet fence rails fed their camp fires. Against the darkening forest the fires flickered like will o' the wisps. By the time the fragrance of wood smoke mingled with the fresh lake smell and the evergreen scent of cedar from the swamp to the north, the camp was set up—headquarters established in the James Gage farmhouse and its family locked in cellar and outbuilding; neighbourhood residents seized and imprisoned; cannon planted to sweep the road to the west; sentries posted; and an advance guard set in the Methodist church.

After they had eaten, the weary soldiers lay down upon their arms. The night was hot and still, with black clouds in the moonless sky and the dark tree-tops brightened fitfully with the sultry flicker of heat lightning.

In the meantime, nineteen-year-old William Green, better known as Billy the Scout, was living a day of rare drama. With his brother, Levi, he had watched for the Americans and parallelled their advance from Grimsby along the mountaintop. Reaching Stoney Creek, he learned that his sister Keziah's husband, Isaac Corman, had been taken prisoner by the enemy and carried to United States auxiliary headquarters beside the recently sacked King's Head Inn. Immediately Billy set off through the woods, bird calling at intervals. Shortly he heard Isaac's answering owl hoot and met him returning, alone and free.

Questioned concerning Vincent's forces and proving uncommunicative, Corman, a militiaman invalided home with wounds, had been treated with scant courtesy until it developed that he was from Kentucky and first cousin to General William Henry Harrison. On the strength of this Corman was released by his interrogator, a fellow Kentuckian, and even given the day's password—Will-Hen-Har, composed of the first syllables of the General's name—to enable him to pass through enemy lines and reach home, but on condition that he would not carry it to the British.

"I'll carry it to the British," offered Billy, "and you can still keep your word," a specious argument, but in keeping with the disregard for the rules of warfare observed on both sides in this conflict.

Scarcely had the two parted company when Corman was overtaken by three American soldiers detailed to escort him home. There they mounted guard over him, unaware that his secret was already on its way to British headquarters.

Vincent's swift decision to carry the attack to the enemy was influenced by several factors: advice by Colonel Harvey who had reconnoitred the United States camp and noted its weaknesses; a similar report from Lt. James Fitzgibbon of the 49th, who is supposed to have toured the camp disguised as a countryman peddling fruit; the weakness of Vincent's own defences on the Heights; his shortage of ammunition; and the fact that the Americans outnumbered him two to one. On the lake moreover a strong United States fleet was supporting the land force. If the Heights fell, Upper Canada clear to Kingston fell with it. And here suddenly was the American password, key to the enemy camp, and the best woodsman and scout in the countryside to guide the attacking force.

The startled officers and men were roused from sleep and swiftly preparations to march went forward. By 10.30 p.m. the last of the "704 forelocks" selected to rout more than five times their number ". . . disappeared," says E. B. Biggar,[6] "from the waning light of their camp fires down the lonely road eastward. Stealthily they took their way beneath the grand wall of trees that rose on either side of the road and in places arched together overhead, closing them in profound night and darkness. . . . On they stole down the west bank of Big Creek, then up the eastern like a train of ghosts."

"I shall never forget," wrote a member of the 49th, "the agony caused to the senses by the stealthiness with which we proceeded to the midnight slaughter . . . not a whisper was permitted; even our footsteps were not allowed to be heard." One by one outposts and sentries were removed.

In his account of the battle the member of the 49th describes all similar battles of all wars of that period: ". . . Following the dreadful flash and crash came a silence yet more impressive, broken by the clinking of ramrods. Now an ominous 'click! click-click!' rattles along the gloomy hill, succeeded by another echoing roar of musketry and shock of artillery; and again the trees, the tents, and everything about lives as in momentary day; and again the whizzing bullets are followed by moans and dying words. But now the flashes come from the flats also, and from simultaneous volleys the firing runs into an incessant roar, the hill and valley are continuous sheets of living flame and the sky is bright with glare."[7]

At daybreak, with Generals Chandler and Winder and 125 officers and men taken prisoner and some 55 killed and wounded,[8] the Americans retired to Forty Mile Creek. Later, about seven or eight o'clock, a strong detachment returned to the field and destroyed their abandoned provisions, spare arms and camp equipment. At noon, leaving American dead to be buried by the British, they departed finally to the jaunty and then popular tune, "In My Cottage by the Wood," struck up by their band. At this point settlers hidden in the woods, knowing the American

40

strong fear of Indians, set up a lusty war whooping, whereupon the band broke off and the force retreated at a greatly accelerated pace.

In the meantime Harvey, who had conducted the British action, withdrew his men to the Heights, fearful lest the enemy should discover the meagerness of his force, further weakened by the loss of 23 killed, 136 wounded and 55 taken prisoner,[9] and by the disappearance of Vincent who became lost in the woods and did not emerge until early afternoon of June 6th.

From far and near, residents of the countryside flocked to view the battlefield with its mounds of dead and dying men, of horses, guns, swords, tents and baggage. Working under a British flag of truce, some carried the wounded into neighbouring homes, James Gage's and William Gage's being filled. At William Davis' Red Hill House, the wounded drinking thirstily from tubs of water set upon the floor reddened it with their blood and stained the furnishings of the room, marking a new corner cupboard which Mrs. Davis, née Mary Long, granddaughter of the Widow Morden of Dundas, had had built by an itinerant cabinet maker.

By inheritance, the cupboard descended to the late Mrs. J. Bryce Mundie, former curator of Dundurn Museum, and great-great-granddaughter of Mary Long Davis. Handmade of walnut and put together with wooden pegs, the closed two-section cupboard stands over seven and one-half feet high.

Mrs. Mundie once said, "The stains are still there. In spite of sanding and revarnishing they always reappeared. My grandmother used to tell a story of the battle. The family were shut in the cellar. Looking up through the small window they could see the legs of the British soldiers, like darker shadows in the night, creeping up the road to the attack. To the family it seemed an endless parade of legs!"

More than two hundred pairs of legs failed to return. When neighbouring homes could not accommodate the British and American wounded, Dr. William Case converted his three-year-old frame residence on present King Street, near the Delta, into a hospital, the first in the community. Assisting him, his wife became Hamilton's first army nurse.

For the dead, other residents performed the last simple rites, burying some in a communal grave where they fell, the remainder in the Methodist chuchyard, their funeral bier an ox-drawn stoneboat. The church itself became a casualty of war, its walls pockmarked with shot and riddled with cannon balls. In 1820 its wounds were hidden by boarding. Fifty years later, when it was torn down, boys gathered pocketsful of shot and handfashioned nails that dropped from its time-shrunken lumber.

With the American retreat, the active stage of the war moved from the lakehead except for two brief visitations by water. On July 29th a seaborne force of several hundred men under Lt.-Col. Winfield Scott was landed by Chauncey on the beach sandstrip below "Brant's house," now Chief John Brant's, to attack the British camp on Burlington Heights.

Learning however that the British were well prepared for him, Scott destroyed a redoubt near the old outlet, reembarked his men and stood away for York which he and Chauncey again plundered.

Two months later the final lakehead engagement occurred. In late September, 1813, the British squadron under Sir James Lucas Yeo, met the United States fleet under Chauncey, off York. In the ensuing skirmish in which the Americans had the advantage in both armament and tonnage, Yeo's flagship, H.M.S. *Wolfe*, lost her maintop mast and mainyard, H.M.S. *Royal George* her foretop mast. Knowing that to remain meant capture or destruction, the British flotilla took to its heels, the *Wolfe* in the lead, the *Royal George* bringing up the rear. More manoeuvrable in rough weather than the United States ships, the British were favoured by the east storm blowing up.

When Flamborough Head appeared to starboard through the swirling mist the Americans were close astern. Yeo made a desperate decision. Ahead lay Burlington Bay with its shallow natural outlet. If his ships could win the sheltered bay they were safe. Yeo summoned the master and pilot of the *Wolfe*, Lieutenant James Richardson, who, although only twenty-three years of age, had served a five-year apprenticeship on the Great Lakes and was probably unexcelled in his knowledge of their navigation.

"Mr. Richardson," demanded Yeo, his chin as hard as the peak of an anchor, his eyes spitting black lightning, "can you take us through the Burlington outlet?"

The youthful master of the *Wolfe* studied the line of creaming whitecaps racing shoreward. Yeo scowled and waited. "He was a hard fighter," says an old account, "a hard driver, a hard loser. He went black in the face every time things went wrong, and in the season of 1813 he went black very often." Richardson knew his commander. He appreciated that the Burlington outlet was Yeo's only hope of saving the British fleet, and on the fleet depended British survival, for in this war in the upper province the waterways commanded the land. Clearly, incisively, Richardson's mind weighed the problem. If he said no, he was safe, for no man could question his decision. If he piled the British fleet on the sandstrip he would be ruined.

"Well, Mr. Richardson?" Yeo barked.

Richardson met the burning black gaze. "Aye, aye, sir," he said quietly.

A heavy sea was running, with huge white-capped rollers crashing on the beach. It was a dangerous surf, yet at the same time the waves with their lift and added depth made the entrance possible. Out in the lake the United States ships were turning about for Niagara. Chauncey was having his own troubles. He had no desire to founder on this enemy coast and his large fleet of schooners was cranky and unweatherly, the guns on their decks giving them a tendency to capsize. In the flying mist and spray no American eye saw the *Wolfe*, her after-sails gone, her shattered spars trailing overboard, drive straight before the wind into the

42

outlet. In she rode on a comber, hung for a sickening moment as the backwash caught her, then was carried forward by the next "white horse" into the deeper water beyond.

In her wake, under the command of the renowned Captain Sir W. H. Mulcaster, followed the *Royal George*, 510 tons to the *Wolfe's* 637. Astern the smaller ships steered for the gap in the wave-pounded sandstrip: the *Melville*, 279 tons; the *Earl Moira*, 262; the *Sir Sidney Smith*, 216; and the *Beresford*, 187 tons. On the crest of a comber one after the other rode into the bay, the *Melville* with water spouting from her scuppers and her crew furiously manning the pumps.

The Americans never learned the secret of the British disappearance. Arrived at Niagara, Chauncey that evening sent the schooner, *Lady of the Lake*, back to the lakehead to discover what had happened to the British ships which he had last seen so dangerously inshore. The *Lady* found no trace either of ships or wreckage.

It was a long day of drama. Drawn by the thunder of the guns to the brow of the Mountain the people of the countryside watched the running battle on the lake. Nor did the British escape end the affair.

"Mr. Richardson, how do we take the ships out?" Yeo had demanded.

"We must wait for another east storm, Captain," said the pilot. "An east blow always raises the water at the head of the lake."

"And when," roared Yeo sarcastically, "may we expect another east gale?"

"With the full of the moon, Captain. The lake's just finding its level now after the last storm. With the full moon we can look for another shift of east wind."

Meanwhile, safely screened by the towering oaks and poplars of the beach strip, the repair of the damaged ships went forward, members of the garrison on the Heights and countryside craftsmen lending a willing hand to the ships' carpenters. With spars cut from the tall pines along the shore—reserved to the crown for use of the Royal Navy—the topgallant masts and yards were mended, bloodstains were sanded from decks and scuppers, and the ships made seaworthy.

With the full moon the pilot's prediction came true. The wind rose, waves began to roll in and the water piled up along the beach and deepened in the bay. A dank fog rolled in off the lake, shrouding water and land in wet cotton wool.

"Now!" ordered Richardson. First the smaller vessels were towed through the channel and anchored. Then the guns and all movable equipment from the *Wolfe* and the *Royal George* that could be slung by yard tackle were loaded on to the little ships; the anchors of the two larger vessels were planted deep in the lake, and with hundreds of men helping to heave the capstans around, the big hulls were worked through the channel, their keels leaving a deep furrow in the sand.

In 1815 in the disbursements made by the Loyal and Patriotic Society, established in York under the Right Rev. John Strachan to relieve wartime distress and commemorate conspicuous bravery, the sum of £100 was allotted to Mr. James Richardson for "his uncommonly good conduct."

Said Frank L. Jones, military historian and authority on Richardson: "I think it safe to assume that the escape of the British Squadron after the action off York can be attributed to Richardson's knowledge of these waters and his superb seamanship. The balance of naval power on Lake Ontario was in his hands when he took the *Wolfe* and the rest of the squadron through the channel to find safety under the guns of Burlington Heights."

6

Hamilton and its Founder

LIKE all conflicts, the War of 1812 ushered in a postwar period of want and hardship and eventually of discontent. Freed from military service the militia returned to reclaim their neglected farms, lately sown and harvested on sporadic leaves. Now that they had time to cultivate their fields and stock, however, they no longer had the lucrative customer of war years, the army; and they no longer drew militia pay, erratic as its receipt had sometimes been. Furthermore, with the end of the war had come an end to the army bills, paper currency authorized by the government of Lower Canada, backed by the government of Great Britain, and redeemable at par—the first adequate circulating folding money Upper Canada had known.

Compared to other parts of the Niagara peninsula where homes had been burned and looted and whole communities put to the torch, the Head of the Lake had escaped lightly. Possibly Richard Beasley had greatest cause for complaint as his detail of war damages to the Board of Claims at Fort George discloses.

If compared with his "For Sale" advertisement of June 21st, 1800, the letter, dated Barton, 12th September, 1815, shows the extent of Beasley's property improvements, including a new home. On a present 950 acres, 160 cleared and under fence, he lists "a Brick house, Barn, Storehouse and Outhouses, an Orchard containing 200 bearing apple trees, a Garden with a number of choice fruit trees, and a Nursery of Young Apple trees."

On June 1st, 1813, these premises, on whose produce Beasley stated he depended for the support of himself, his wife, eight children and servants, "were taken forcible possession of by His Majesty's troops under command of General Vincent," he and his family having to seek other shelter. War losses included provisions on hand, crops maturing in the fields, and later crops which could not be sown.

Despondently he concludes, "Shortly after the Battle of Stoney Creek . . . the Army commenced fortifying on my premises, the Destruction that they and the Indians who were encamped on my Land made in my timber was Astonishing, my Farm Buildings are left in a most Desolate Situation, the depreciation and Waste of my Property at Burlington has been Great."[1]

At the opposite end of the peninsula a similar case of wartime loss would materially affect Hamilton history. In a letter written from Queenston on August 22, 1816, Captain George Hamilton, 2nd Troop, Niagara Light Dragoons, complains of the occupation by His Majesty's forces of his "very valuable" premises at Queenston, the destruction by fire of his home, "an Elegant Stone Building", and the "wanton Devastation" visited by the army on fences, outbuildings and property in general.

In common with Richard Beasley and the majority of other claimants, Captain George Hamilton would receive little satisfaction. Because of Canada's postwar impoverishment, lack of assistance from Great Britain, war-depleted by the long Napoleonic conflict, and government tardiness, veterans would become old men before their claims brought compensation. Not until sixty years after the war did Canada grant a pension to veterans of the War of 1812. On October 4th, 1875, at ten o'clock in the morning, local payment commenced in the city council chamber, Hamilton, granted by the city for the occasion, with Colonel McPherson of the headquarters staff, and Colonel Villiers and Major Alger, paymasters, officiating.[2]

Assembled about the tables in the chamber were forty-two old soldiers who recognized one another and recalled old times with all the glee of children. In age they ranged from the seventy-seven years of Christopher Abcowser to the ninety-seven years of Timothy Downs, with David Fonger on that day celebrating his ninety-fifth birthday. Some veterans came on crutches and some, too feeble to walk, were carried into the room. One, however, William Green, eighty-two, of Stoney Creek—Billy Green, the Scout—when his name was called advanced to the table "as spry as a kitten", says the press, received his certificate and pension money and "retreated with the martial tread of a soldier."

In turn each aged soldier received the munificent pension of twenty dollars, an amount dictated by government error. Believing that three hundred veterans of the War of 1812 survived, the government voted fifty thousand dollars for their reimbursement. Actually the veterans, a sturdy breed, numbered twenty-five hundred. "Were it not," commented *The Daily Spectator*, "that some recognition is better than none, the brave old men would be justified in refusing the pittance. It appears our sapient rulers blundered in this as in most other things."

Following the ceremony the veterans were entertained by Mayor George Roach and city council at a dinner at two p.m. in the Mansion House.

Lack of redress for war claims was only one of the causes of dissatisfaction in the period following the War of 1812. Additional causes were the almost complete demoralization of Canadian trade and commerce, and a government policy of discouraging entry of American immigrants into Canada. While this exclusion affected the population in general by preventing the inflow of needed hard money and by holding settlement at an unproductive standstill when reputable settlers such as the Mennonites were available, to large landholders such as Richard Beasley the policy spelled disaster.

Upon the outbreak of war and throughout hostilities the presence of pro-American Canadians in Upper Canada was a constant concern to military authorities and the political leaders who formed the executive council, the legislative assembly being itself pro-American. Of the twenty-five thousand American sympathizers in Upper and Lower Canada, many had migrated solely for the benefit of trade and of free or cheap land and were still American by conviction; others were pro-American from expediency, being determined to side with the apparent victor-to-be; and a small but troublesome minority displayed active hostility, deserting to the enemy and serving throughout the war as spies and raiders, employing their knowledge of the countryside to despoil and harass former friends and neighbours.

In July, 1813, a commission was appointed to administer properties abandoned by deserting Americans, Richard Beasley being appointed a commissioner. On March 24th, 1814, a further commission was established "to secure and detain persons suspected of treason," with Squire Beasley again a commissioner. Dozens of suspects were brought to trial and sentenced. Believing that even stronger measures must be taken to control the flagrantly disloyal, a special commission was appointed by the law officers of the Crown to try certain prisoners for the crime of high treason.

By a special act the court was held at Ancaster, then a more important town than Dundas or Hamilton. It was also adjacent to the military camp on Burlington Heights from which guards and supplies could be provided for prisoners and court. Ancaster was also sufficiently removed from the victorious American forces in the Thames River and Lake Erie area that the latter could not attempt a prisoner rescue.

Presided over by Chief Justice Thomas Scott, assisted by puisne Judges William Dummer Powell and William Campbell, and with John Beverly Robinson, aged twenty-three, Attorney General for Upper Canada, acting as prosecutor, the court made legal history, coming to be christened, "The Ancaster Bloody Assize."

On May 23rd, 1814, the trial opened, with the judges sitting in turn on the Bench. About the courtroom lingered the cloying odour of sickness and disinfectants, the commodious Union Hotel, scene of the trial, having been converted for the occasion from a hospital for wounded from the Thames area. Here the prisoners, guarded, in leg irons and heavily manacled, were transported from York in heavy wagons that lumbered and creaked over the narrow forest roads and up the escarpment to Ancaster.

During the ensuing trial four men were acquitted, fifteen found guilty.[3] On Tuesday, June 21st, 1814, Chief Justice Scott, donning the black cap, pronounced a sentence never before or since invoked in Canadian history: "The law demands, and the sentence is that you shall be drawn to the place of execution where you must be hanged by the neck but not until you are dead, for you must be cut down alive, and your bowels taken out and burned before your face (on your being still alive). Then your head must be severed from your body which must be divided into four parts, and your head and quarters to be at the King's disposal. And may God have mercy on your soul!"

Throughout the trial and during the month granted for appeal, petitions poured in from counties, communities, and from loyal Canadians of all ranks pleading for the lives of the doomed men. At the lakehead Richard Beasley and Samuel Hatt, justices of the peace for Barton and Ancaster, added their plea.

Nevertheless, one month later, on July 20th, 1814, sentence was carried out upon eight of the convicted, seven having been reprieved by the executive council, to be later sentenced by the Crown to confiscation of property and banishment from British territories for life. The execution on a single gallows took place on Burlington Heights outside the camp, on the west side of what was later Dundurn Street near its junction with York.[4] It was conducted by Sheriff Thomas Merritt of Niagara.

If the judges knew no mercy, it is believed that unofficially the hangman did, and that he tried to ensure that life was extinct before the victims were cut down and beheaded. As he must use a loose knot, however, the best the condemned could hope for was death by slow strangulation.

Today when the traffic light at York and Dundurn is red, if an imaginative motorist in the line of idling cars should turn his gaze beyond the buildings crowding the corner—at a time when light and shadows artfully combine—he might conjure against a westering sky a monstrous gibbet and eight dangling forms.

Although a wartime measure, the setting up of this court with its obligatory medieval and inhuman penalty may be taken as a measure of the fear evidenced by the ruling Family Compact respecting American influence in the province.

It is said that Richard Beasley never fully recovered from the shock of the punishment meted out on his doorstep. The war had cost Beasley dearly. Actual war service he had not suffered, having resigned his command at the outbreak of hostilities in favor of Major Titus Geer Simons, but his property and business had suffered severely. Other changes lay ahead. With the death of Joseph Brant in 1807 the lakehead triumvirate lost its first member. Next to leave was Augustus Jones.

In 1799 the latter had given up government work to devote himself to private surveying and to development of his extensive land holdings. Throughout the war Captain Jones served with the 5th Lincoln Regiment.

Following the war he moved to Brant County, to live, it is said, in considerable style with servants, a carriage and coachman. In this move he left behind his brother, Philip, and his sister, Mary (Jones) Gage,[5] mother of James Gage of Stoney Creek and sister-in-law of William Gage, whom he had helped locate at Stoney Creek.

Prior to this move he sold his property in Saltfleet, Henry Van Wagner securing Lots 24, 25 and 26, Concession 2, Saltfleet, south of Barton Street.

Henry was the second son of Dr. Henrih von Wagner, German surgeon of Albany, New York, who died in 1789 when his son was a year old, leaving him to be reared by his mother who shortly remarried. Following apprenticeship to a millwright, young Henry married Mrs. Edith Spohn, a widow, in 1811. Five years later he left Albany by rowboat for Canada to inspect the country, taking the Loyalist route up the Hudson and portaging his boat by oxteam from stream to stream—the only man, neighbours later joked, who had travelled the whole way to Canada backwards.

In 1818 Henry returned from Albany with his family. With the surveyor's land he purchased also the Jones' home in which he had earlier lodged. Until this house—"built somewhat after the style of those old Continental days, with profuse and elaborate carpenter and joiner work" —became available, Henry settled his family in a log house a mile away in the woods. Here in 1818 his son, Peter Spohn, was born.

A highly skilful millwright, Henry Van Wagner left his mark on the countryside, remodelling old-fashioned mills, surveying sites, planning, drafting and building new mills. John and Elijah Secord of Mount Albion, Robert Nelles of Grimsby, and the Honorable James Crooks of West Flamborough were only four of the many who engaged his services. His last work was a flouring mill built for Ebenezer C. Griffin of East Flamborough.

"After work one evening," said Henry's great-great-granddaughter, Miss Myra M. Hamilton, now of Toronto, "on his way to Mr. Griffin's home where he boarded, Henry paused a moment on the log bridge to watch the stream tumbling down the rugged face of the mill. 'It all depends on water coming down,' he thought.

"When the building was completed, the final pair of rafters placed on the frame, and the bottle, according to custom, thrown from the highest part, Henry christened it, 'The Waterdown Mill!' 'The Waterdown Mill!' everyone shouted, until the hillside echoed it back. And that," concluded Miss Hamilton, "is how the snug village of Waterdown gained its name!"

As his prosperity increased, Henry added to the comforts and conveniences of his home. One of the family's most cherished possessions was a wall mirror, twelve by twenty inches, a marvellous luxury which had cost as much as six or seven precious dollars, and which hung on the back wall of the livingroom, opposite the front door.

"It was a great attraction for the Indians," wrote Henry's son, Peter

Spohn. "Indian men are much vainer than women. They would come in the front door which always stood open in summer, and pose before the mirror, admiring their good looks, arranging their black locks, assuming and studying expressions of dignity or fierceness, all with intense satisfaction to themselves and great interest to the children of our family who maintained a discreet and polite silence. After the brave had satisfied himself concerning his appearance, he would draw himself to his full height and stalk out with much dignity.

"Usually," said Peter Spohn, "the Indian has a great sense of humour, loving jests, games, dancing and merrymaking."

Henry Van Wagner lived and died on the land south of Barton Street. It was Peter Spohn who through his marriage to the widowed Eliza Jane (Pettit) Carpenter, following her death acquired the lake front property which she had inherited from her first husband, the well known Van Wagner farm which gave its name to Van Wagner Beach. In 1962 some fifty-odd acres of this land, in Lots 25 and 26, Concession 1, Broken Front and sandy beach, was purchased by the city for Confederation Park.

If the lakehead lost Augustus Jones with the end of the War of 1812, it gained a new citizen, Captain George Hamilton, second son of the Hon. Robert Hamilton of Queenston and his first wife, Mrs. Catharine (Askin) Robertson, both then deceased.

Throughout the war young George Hamilton had been engaged in various actions. Following the taking of Detroit by General Brock he served with the 2nd Troop, Niagara Light Dragoons, during an American attack on Fort Erie, and on October 13th at the battle of Queenston Heights. In writing to an aunt, Mrs. Henderson, in Scotland, on July 4th, 1813, his brother, Alexander, stated:[6] "George and myself with Mr. Robertson are attached to Colonel de Hearn of the 104th Regiment, who commands the advanced Guards, from our knowledge of the country and roads about the place to assist him in his movements, etc. James is attached as a Lieutenant to the Incorporative Militia . . . one or other of us, sometimes two and three together, have been in almost every action."

On July 19th, 1814, George Hamilton fought in the battle of St. David's and six days later in the battle of Lundy's Lane. Not until final withdrawal of American forces from Fort Erie did Captain Hamilton have time to turn his thoughts to James Durand's property at the Head of the Lake. Immediate action was necessary, for war's end found Captain Hamilton, his wife (the former Maria Lavinia Jarvis, eldest daughter of William Jarvis, provincial secretary of Upper Canada under Governor Simcoe) whom he had married in 1811, and their infant son, Robert Jarvis, homeless.

The ending of hostilities also gave Captain James Durand, C.O., 2nd Flank Company, 5th Lincoln Militia, an opportunity to promote a promising business venture—the manufacture of salt in Belleville, Canadian production of salt having been revived when war halted cheap import from the United States.

50

Prior to moving, however, Durand had to dispose of his property at the lakehead, which consisted of several parcels of land including the hundred-acre crown grant farm of Loyalist Daniel Springer which Durand had purchased about 1806, but the deed to which had vanished. In the stone mansion he had built on this property—Lot 14, Concession 3, Barton[7]—Durand had entertained Brock and his officers.

To offset loss of the deed, on January 24th, 1815, John Springer and his wife, Sarah, acknowledging disappearance of the document and destruction of the office of enregistration in consequence of the war, reconveyed to James Durand the title to Lot 14, Concession 3, Barton, extending from James Street eastward to the continuation of the line of Mary, and from Main Street to the mountain top.

The following day, January 25th, 1815, James Durand and his wife, Keziah, for £1,750 sold to George Hamilton, gentleman, 257 acres of land at the lakehead, one parcel being Lot 14, Concession 3. The same day by separate deed the Durands also sold George Hamilton the 14 acres in Concession 2, purchased in 1809 from Nathaniel Hughson—the block of land between Main and King Streets, extending from James to the line of Mary—the most important piece of land below the Mountain, later nucleus of the city of Hamilton.

Having disposed of his property, James Durand left in January, 1815,[8] for Smith's Creek, near Belleville, embarking in three sleds with the five children of his first marriage and with his second wife, the former Keziah Morrison, and their three sons, born in the stone house at the head of John Street—Charles in 1811, Ferdinand in 1813, and Alonzo in 1814,[9] the two latter births having occurred after George Hamilton is popularly reported as having occupied the house.

In the meantime George Hamilton had brought his wife and son from their wartime residence with friends in York.[10]

In her family chronicle of George Hamilton's settling at the lakehead, "Biographical Sketch of a Noted Pioneer,"[11] Agnes Hannah Hamilton Lemon (Mrs. Charles), granddaughter of George Hamilton, may have originally misdated the event since she places it in 1813—an error resulting in the exuberant week-long celebration by the city in 1913 of the centennial of its founding by George Hamilton.

Scarcely was the latter established in his stone mansion, Bellevue, with its widow's walk, its double French doors and floor-length windows opening onto upper and lower verandas on the north and east sides, than the Upper Canada legislature dropped a plum in his lap.

In the early 1800's settlers at the head of Lake Ontario who had to attend a court, land board, or registry office on business had to travel either to York in the Home District or Niagara in the District of Niagara. Either required an arduous journey of several days.

In 1810, in a rash of petitions, the lakehead communities, Dundas, Ancaster and Brant's Block, appealed to parliament to form a new district from the two existing ones, with a county town convenient to the area. Extolling its own virtues, each municipality begged to be selected as county town. Chairmaned by Richard Hatt, who pledged $500, Dundas citizens offered for the town an additional $3,960 towards the cost of erecting a court house and gaol.

Not to be outdone, James Durand likewise petitioned, recommending "the south side of Burlington Bay, and nigh the head, on Lot 14 in the 2nd Concession of Barton Township, owned by James Durand and Nathaniel Hughson"—Mr. Hughson's property lying east of James Street to Mary and from King north to the bay, its owner having sold Durand the block from King to Main. Durand secured 264 petition signatures.

Meeting legislative approval, the bill to form a new district passed the lower house in 1812, but was shelved on the outbreak of war. With the end of the conflict however, parliament removed the bill from its pigeonhole, dusted it off and on March 22nd, 1816, passed an act "to erect and form a new District out of certain parts of the Home and Niagara Districts, to be called the District of Gore," (after Sir Francis Gore, Lieutenant-Governor), said district to "include two counties, Wentworth and Halton."[12]

The bill further established: "That a Gaol and Court-House for said District of Gore shall be erected and built in some fit and convenient place, on Lot 14, in the 3rd Concession of the Township of Barton, to be called the Town of Hamilton," thus initially naming the community and doubly defining it to George Hamilton.

Whether the latter had already had his property surveyed into town lots, and now incorporated into this survey a site for the gaol and county house; or whether his survey postdated the act, may never be established, as the Hamilton survey, still in use in the County Registry office, Main Street East, Hamilton, is undated.

What is known is that on December 30th, 1816, as a site for court house and gaol, Mr. Hamilton surrendered to His Majesty George III, two blocks of land in Concession 3, south of Main Street, containing two acres each, extending (by today's limits) from Hughson Street to Catharine and from Main Street to Jackson, "having one chain of an allowance for road between said blocks"—today's John Street.

As no surrender deed for the Haymarket, south of the Court House, is available, it has been assumed this might have been dedicated to the community without instrument of gift, by including it on the survey. Actually George Hamilton gave a deed to the market place in 1834.

In dedicating the Gore—the triangular wedge of land separating the north and south sides of King Street from James to Mary—a duly executed deed of conveyance was drawn up by George Hamilton and, with an exact transcript, was entrusted to the Hon. John Willson, M.P.P., at the ending of a Quarter Sessions Court, with the request that he carry it home and read it.

At home, Mr. Willson tossed the papers unread into a drawer where they lay for twenty-odd years, until some time after George Hamilton's death in 1836, and after a suit had been entered and won by Mr. Hamilton in 1833 to restrain the town from building a market house on the Gore.

Says Mr. Willson:

Some time since the case was tried respecting that plot of ground in King Street in the Assizes at Hamilton, Mr. Justice McLean presiding, as I believe, I went to a drawer of papers promiscuously mixed together, with a view to assort them, in the doing of which I find two sheets of paper . . . one of them a conveyance from George Hamilton, Esq. and duly executed conveying a certain Gore of land in King Street in the Town of Hamilton to the public use and benefit of the Town, or to the Police of the Town to and for the use and benefit of the Town for ever as an Area or Promenade and not to be applied to any other use or purpose. Such was the purport and tenour of the said instrument . . . the other sheet I find to be an exact copy or transcript of the original . . . I making this discovery was much surprised, and regretted it had not been made before the case was tried in Court. . . .

I believed these papers to be of very little consequence as the case had been disposed of, as I thought, at the Assizes, but as the original one of them, whether by endorsement or whether in the instrument I do not now remember, was to be deposited in the Clerk of the Peace's office and the other to be kept by Mr. Hamilton, I took some after opportunity when going to Hamilton to take the said papers with me, delivered them to the Clerk of the Peace, who I believe was Mr. Berry, and stated briefly to him the circumstances, and desired him to send the copy to the present Mr. Hamilton and file the other in his own office. I took no copy nor memorandum at the time, neither of dates nor details, supposing the documents would always be forthcoming.[13]

Strangely, in spite of diligent search made by city solicitors in the office of the clerk of the peace, as directed by city council,[14] no deed was ever forthcoming.

As to its shape, the Gore was laid out by George Hamilton on the understanding that Nathaniel Hughson would give an equal quantity of land on the north, "recovering the angles to form an oblong square." When Mr. Hughson laid out his farm in town lots, however, he "declined adhering to his agreement."[15]

With an established name, status and county seat, and land set aside for the new combined court house and gaol, market place, and promenade, Hamilton was ready to advance. The 14 acres in Concession 2, between James and the line of Mary, King and Main, George Hamilton divided into four blocks, as today, containing 32 lots, 16 on King Street, 16 on Main. Later an alley running east and west through each block provided rear access to the properties.

Yet the lots moved slowly. At twenty-five pounds each, only seven had been disposed of by 1820, six to family members and one at half-price to James Durand. This concession may have been in recognition of Durand's contribution in obtaining location of the county seat; in appreciation of Durand's natural chagrin in having sold the property; or merely as a generous gesture. The salt venture having proved a costly failure, Mr. Durand had returned to settle in Dundas.

Until 1816 the Head of the Lake was included in the Township of Barton, and records of community and township were combined. In 1816 the population of the whole township was only 668. In a census taken the previous year Barton, including Hamilton, showed 102 ratepayers; 72 homes built of logs squared on two sides, 25 frame houses, Richard Beasley's brick residence, and George Hamilton's stone mansion. In the township only "twelve additional fireplaces" were listed, meaning a second in a home. William Terryberry's abode, the Terryberry Inn, rated special mention as two-storied.[16]

Of the huge farms earlier cited, in 1815 William Rymal had 160 acres of cleared land; Jacob Rymal, 80; William Terryberry, 168; Samuel Ryckman, 26; Cornelius Ryckman, 45; Peter Horning, of 5,000 acres, only 80 cleared; Richard Beasley, assessed for 13,000, 350 cleared; and George Hamilton, with 1,416 acres, 141 cleared.

In Hamilton the only industry was a small chopping mill at Miller's spring, on present Bay Street, which chopped grain for an equally small distillery situated below the mountain, west of Mountain Road (John Street). Although the war had improved roads, there were still only two thoroughfares in Hamilton, King's Street leading from Niagara to Dundas and Ancaster, and Mountain Road up the mountain and southward to the Grand River. Not yet had pathmaster Peter Horning opened the line of Main Street to relieve King's Street of its congestion of swine, cows, horses, fowl, wagons and humans, mounted and on foot. Prior to its opening an old deed bears the notation: "Main Street, commonly called the south side of King Street."

For social life men gathered at the taverns: Samuel Price's Inn near Wellington Street, previously kept by Smith and McAfee, Barnum's on the northwest corner of King and John Streets, and Richard Beasley's store on Burlington Heights. Meetings of the Barton Lodge, A.F. and A.M., were well attended. If one may judge from the minutes of meetings, as recorded by George E. Mason, lodge secretary, members were not averse to "a little stimulant while discharging the arduous duties of the various offices," an average attendance of twenty requiring four gallons of rum as an evening's fitting stimulant, or an equivalent one barrel of spirits and one of wine. Surely, however, a special occasion inspired the entry: "Feb. 8, 1805. That Brother Showers furnish ten gallons of whiskey against the next lodge night."[1] Chartered in 1795 with Davenport Phelps as first Master, Lodge No. 10 of Barton Township had as lifetime members Richard Beasley and Col. John Aikman, at whose homes meetings were held, James Henry, Capt. Joseph Birney and John S. Dodds.

At the bees attended by the women of the household as well as its menfolk, hard liquor also circulated, but not so freely as at stag affairs, while at bees predominantly feminine—as spinning, preserving, dressmaking—tea, coffee, cider, raspberry vinegar or blackberry cordial accompanied refreshments. In addition to work accomplished, the bee provided a much needed social outlet for the lonely settler. "The afternoon tea," said W. S. Herrington, "serves today's purpose very well, but modern society has yet to discover the equal of the quilting bee as a clearinghouse for gossip."

Especially popular with the young was the corn husking bee, held in a dimly lit barn filled with the fragrance of new hay, where a red ear of corn earned a kiss; the springtime sugaring-off of sap, with accompanying romps in the woods; and pumpkin and apple paring bees where these commodities were peeled and strung for drying. All ended with a supper and dance. Nor must kissing games be omitted from the simple pleasures of early days. Sparking bees were the forerunner of the modern petting party, with candles extinguished and only the hearthfire to supplement the moonlight, social activities being timed to full moon; while "bundling" in bitter winter weather was an accepted institution, the young couple enjoying the comforts of bed and bedding, but chaperoned by a monitoring centre board.

For the more soberly inclined, as early as 1798 Methodist Episcopalians began to hold regular services in the community under leadership of Richard Springer, brother-in-law of Richard Beasley, who became the founder of Methodism in this part of Canada. Included in the founding class were Sarah Springer, wife of Richard; John and Hannah Aikman; John and Sarah Springer; Peter and Florence Ferguson; Heziah Lockwood; Charles and John Depew; Robert Jones; George Stewart, Sr. and Jr., and Ann Stewart; Caleb Forsyth; and Nathaniel Hughson.

These were the men and women who forged the future city above and below the Mountain; who had found the attractions of the site greater than its disadvantages; who had known and loved mountains at home and turned now to this elevation in a foreign land.

The Mountain was not like the mountains they had left—the high-peaked Alleghenies, the Adirondacks and the Catskills, with their long green flanks sliding down into the chasms of purple misted valleys. This was a mountain for a weary toiler at the end of day, for a tired mother and housewife worn with the endless tasks of pioneer-providing. A mountain for the fearful, strangers in a harsh new land. A wall of protection standing to the south, long, strong, stalwart, calm and permanent, a veil of green in spring, in summer, cool and dense, a Jacob's cloak of colour in the fall, and a silvery fantasy in winter.

"I will lift up mine eyes unto the hills," said the psalmist. Notably he did not say, "I will lift up mine eyes unto the mountains!"

7

Police Town, 1833

BY 1817 Hamilton's first combined court house and gaol stood completed, near the southeast corner of John and Tyburn (now Jackson) Streets, directly opposite the eastern entrance of its successor, the handsome stone court house erected ten years later on the west side of John Street.

Built on a slight elevation and facing west, the log and frame building was set back far enough from the road to allow space in front for pillory and stocks. Instead of a whipping post, this first gaol was equipped with three ring bolts sunk in the gaol wall, to which the unfortunate culprit under sentence was triced. For the first storey, logs were obtained by dismantling a blockhouse on Burlington Heights.

The building is described by Henry Lutz, son of Loyalist Conrad Lutz of Jersey and son-in-law of William Davis, Jr., of Red Hill House, who became one of the city's leading builders. "It was 30 by 30 feet," wrote Mr. Lutz, "with basement . . . first storey of square hewn logs, second storey of frame with seats all round the sides. It was heated by a fireplace with wood. Prisoners were secured by chains on one foot, long enough to reach from the woodpile to the fireplace and also to the bed." Apparently dissatisfied with the heating, one prisoner, it is said, warned the gaoler that if fires did not improve he would leave. Another, named Springstead, disdaining warnings, burrowed under the logs and departed, earning the nickname, "The Fox."

The gaol consisted of four rooms of equal size: two for prisoners in general, one for the numerous debtors of the day, and one for the gaoler, Rolston. This latter accommodated also his wife, their three sons and three boarders. Boarders and boys, however, slept outside the gaol yard in a building used during court sessions as a jury room.

Surrounding the gaol yard was a fourteen-foot palisade of sharp-pointed logs. In each cell a narrow slit opening onto this yard provided light and ventilation, while an eight-inch hole in the inside cell door permitted passage of food and water. Each cell was provided with a pail

56

emptied every 24 hours. On an average, seven debtors and other prisoners enjoyed the community's hospitality, the pound of bread and quart of water a day of prison fare. Bread was strictly weighed but water was more plentiful, ". . . some of the boys," one account conceding, "generally being on hand to fill their pannikens when handed through the door."

Above the gaol extended a frame court room, its outside entrance on John Street reached by a wide flight of steps. Here for the first time, in 1818, recorded court sessions were held in Hamilton. Commencing October 9th, 1816, a district court sat locally under Richard Hatt, but its location is not known. Clerk of the court was George Rolph. The following year court was "holden" in Ancaster. In 1819 the court sat in Hamilton; in this year Joseph Cole, convicted of petty larceny, received a gaol sentence, following which he was "at midday . . . to be publicly whipped with 40 lashes, lacking one, on the bare back, and then discharged." The sentence was administered before the court house in view of a large gathering of intent spectators, floggings, hangings and pillories being then the most popular form of public entertainment.

The judge who sentenced Cole was Judge Thomas Taylor, Colonel of the 3rd Gore, who had been seriously wounded at the battle of Stoney Creek. Judge Taylor, who died in 1837, should not be confused with the noted jurist, Sir Thomas Wardlaw Taylor, born in 1833, who resided in Hamilton for the final fifteen years of his life, his death occurring on March 2nd, 1917. Sir Thomas, who served as Chief Justice of Manitoba for twelve years, attracted international attention when he presided at the trial of Louis Riel which resulted in his hanging for treason on November 16th, 1885, near Regina.

In 1819 also, the first Court of General Quarter Sessions of the Peace for the Gore District was held in the log court house, with Magistrate James Crooks, chairman, and George Hamilton and Richard Beasley among the magistrates on the bench.

In 1827 the old court house, then close to replacement, saw the faithful court clerk, George Rolph, shed his familiar role for a more exciting one as plaintiff in a *cause célèbre* of the day. In his *Reminiscences* Charles Durand, himself an early Hamilton barrister, describes the case.[1]

There was much excitement about a wicked and wanton assault made upon George Rolph, of Dundas, by some disguised (so-called) gentleman in that year. At first they were not known . . . but Dr. James Hamilton and Titus G. Simons, of West Flamboro, and a Mr. Robertson were found out, tried, and Hamilton and Simons convicted and fined $80 each—Robertson got clear. Justice James B. Macaulay, of York, was the judge assigned to try this special case.

Dr. John Rolph, Robert Baldwin and Dr. William Warren Baldwin, his father, acted for George Rolph as counsel; Allan N. MacNab and a Mr. Chewett for the defendants. The cause of the outrage arose from

57

political envy and private hatred . . . Mr. George Rolph was elected a member of the Legislature in 1828, after the trial, showing what the public thought.

In Upper Canada the cleavage between the Tory Family Compact and the Reformers, or Radicals, as the government termed the opposition, was widening under the influence of two Scotsmen, fiery redheaded William Lyon Mackenzie and Robert Gourlay, who had entered the province two years earlier, a sincere and public minded man but a fanatic and quarrelsome to an unfortunate degree. In this trial of 1827 the lines of the future bitter struggle in Hamilton between Tory MacNab and Reformer Mackenzie were clearly drawn. On the one hand MacNab, his later physician, Dr. Hamilton, and Colonel Titus Geer Simons; on the other, Mackenzie, the Rolphs, the Baldwins, and James and Charles Durand. It speaks ill for Tory Hamilton that the 1827 trial would have almost an identical counterpart five years later when Family Compact member William Johnson Kerr, Esq.,[2] prominent member of parliament and justice of the peace would enlist three henchmen, following a heated political meeting, to set upon and murderously assault Mackenzie in the Court House Square.

Before this occurred, however, Hamilton's first court house would have been succeeded by its second, built by William Hardy with Peter Hunter Hamilton, half-brother of George, as chief contractor. Prior to passing from the local scene the old log building had its most dramatic role to play. In 1828 a resident of Beverly Township, John Vincent, was tried by Judge Hagerman for his wife's murder, found guilty, and condemned to die on the gallows. There being no official hangman, the offer of a local negro prisoner to officiate in return for his freedom was accepted, his complete inexperience apparently not considered important.

Instead of the customary gallows a platform containing the drop was erected against the John Street front of the building, a window removed from its frame offering access. Buying a brand new rope the hangman installed it. When the time of execution arrived he and his victim stepped through the window onto the platform, to become the focus of attention of a crowd so large that the cavalry had been called out to control it.

In his haste to adjust the noose about the prisoner's neck, the hangman failed to bind his legs. As the trap was sprung and the doomed man plummeted downward, the crowd surged forward to savour in full the supreme spectacle of death. Unfortunately death did not occur. The green rope stretched so that the toes of the strangling man occasionally touched the earth, his resultant leap giving him air.

Straddling the drop the terrified hangman attempted unsuccessfully to lift the rope to shorten it. Finally he re-entered the building, descended the stairs, and throwing his full weight upon the swinging figure, ended Vincent's life. An eye-witness account states that although the negro was very black skinned, at the end of his agonizing half-hour ordeal he had turned pale blue.

Following this case, the new court house was put into operation. In the first issue of *The Gore Gazette,* dated Ancaster, March 3rd, 1827,[3] an advertisement had called for stonecutters and masons to work on the new building, now completed. Replacing the old court house and gaol, demolished shortly after 1830, would be a substantial stone hotel operated by innkeeper John McGee. Subsequently this became the Court House Hotel which flourished for many years; until passage of the Ontario Temperance Act, its big hospitable taproom providing a welcome retreat and meeting place for barristers and their clients, jurymen, witnesses, court clerks, and even, on occasion, a judge or two.

McGee's hotel was one of a rash of hotels, inns, taverns and ordinaries that mushroomed in Hamilton in the 1820's and '30's, one record stating that at one time there were more hotels and taverns in the community than houses. In 1833, F. W. Fearman, later Hamilton commission merchant, estimated there were only three brick dwellings in Hamilton, this antedating the establishment of brick kilns and resultant rows of brick homes. Probably the most notable hostel was Plumer Burley's Hamilton Promenade, situated near the southeast corner of King and James, so-called because of its upstairs balcony overlooking the Gore where stylishly attired guests strolled in unfavourable weather. A stage coach stop, the Promenade was brightened by all the colour and stir, the prancing horses and bugling horns, the change of relays of arriving and departing coaches.

Eastward, on the site of the later Terminal station, stood the Grove Inn, named because of a fine stand of oak trees which lined King Street from John to Mary and which were eventually sacrificed by the pathmaster, Mr. Gray, as interfering with traffic. At Wellington and King flourished Mrs. Price's tavern, Mr. Price, deceased in 1822, having been the first burial in the Methodist graveyard across King Street. Overlooking the bay loomed Nathaniel Hughson's big two-and-a-half-storey brick hotel, later to become the city hospital, while on the Market Square, Andrew Miller's popular Steamboat Hotel was named to draw shipboard travellers. Gracing the corner where the Wanzer sewing machine factory later stood was Chatfield's Hotel, noted, according to Mr. Fearman, for the size of its bedbugs.

Different in type, the select, family Cambria boarding hotel of Mr. Cattermole, immigration agent, on John Street south of Main, catered to the better class of old country immigrants. Among mountain hostels the romantic Terryberry Inn, a main stage coach stop, was outstanding, serving for decades as a gay centre of social events.

In Upper Canada, inns served as a barometer of the community economy. A flourish of inns spelled prosperity; inns closing their doors warned of decline. By this yardstick then, Hamilton had freed her feet from the sword grass and swamp of pioneer days and had embarked on her next phase as a promising young community.

With growth came the pressing cry for education and the first fumbling efforts to satisfy that need. The first school in Wentworth County was built at Ancaster in 1796;[4] the first in the present Hamilton area at the east end of Burlington Beach, in Saltfleet, in 1816, a log cabin, eighteen by twenty feet in size.

Within the city the first school, presided over at one period by schoolmaster Vaux, stood just east of the site of the Methodist Church erected in 1824 and known variously as the Hamilton Church, the King Street Church, and the White Church. School fees varied from $2.50 to $3.25 per quarter for each student, with parents also providing cut stove wood and boarding the teacher "round." Primitive as the first schools of Upper Canada undoubtedly were, they possessed elements which would thrill the hearts of today's children. "The Indians were peaceable and honest," says an account of 1899. "They made baskets, brooms and moccasins and traded them with the whites. Boys going to school would give their dinners for several days for bows and arrows."

In 1819 the Legislature passed an act establishing a public school in Hamilton, but not until 1821 was the Gore District School opened under the act. Located at the southwest corner of Hughson and Tyburn Streets, the school developed a high reputation, drawing pupils from across the province. Its first schoolmaster, John Law, a native of Kirkcudbright, Scotland, was persuaded by Anglican John Strachan to leave a tutoring position with a nobleman's family and come to Upper Canada as a teacher. Mr. Law's residence was a small frame house which stood immediately east of what was later the Y.M.C.A. building.

Among the school's many pupils probably the most outstanding was Egerton Ryerson who helped found the educational system of Ontario, becoming in 1844 chief provincial superintendent of education.

About 1830 Stephen Randall (or Randal), described by Charles Durand as "a very odd but gifted young man from Quebec . . . a protégé of Bishop Mountain," opened a private school in the old court house. Here Charles Durand studied Latin, Greek, Euclid, and the lower branches of mathematics. Mr. Randall relinquished this enterprise in 1832 to become assistant to Headmaster John Law in the Gore District School, at a salary of fifty pounds per annum; in 1833 succeeding Mr. Law when the latter entered the legal profession prior to assuming George Rolph's position as court clerk. The same year the school moved to "the new building on Mountain Street fronting the Court House Square"—probably McGee's Inn.

As advertised, terms of tuition ran: "for day scholars, in the classics, £1; in the common branches, 16/S . . . for boarders, who must supply their own beds and bedding, 12/S 6d. per week, or £32 per annum. For an evening school, to be opened as soon as 12 applications were received, from 7-9 p.m., £1 per quarter, payable in advance."

On December 27th, 1833, an assistant, James Cahill, was authorized for Mr. Randall by the board of trustees: James and Matthew Crooks, Thomas Taylor, William M. Jarvis and John Law.

In all, the year 1833 marked a milestone for Hamilton. On January 8th an act was passed by the legislative council of Upper Canada and by the house of assembly ten days later: "To define the limits of the Town of Hamilton, in the District of Gore, and to establish a Police and Public Market therein."

In an old calf-bound minute book, the colour of faded chocolate, the clauses of the act have been inscribed in flowing longhand by the first clerk of the newly incorporated town. With its successors,[5] mostly thicker, heavier tomes of varying shades of brown, the first minute book lies safely locked in the vaults of Hamilton's new city hall. Worn though it is with attending on 130-odd years of municipal government, the old record has survived three city halls and reached a fourth.

By the 1833 Act of Incorporation the boundaries of the new town became Wellington Street on the east, Queen on the west, Burlington Bay on the north, and Concession Street (later, below the mountain, Aberdeen Avenue) on the south.

Within these boundaries the town was divided into four wards for elective purposes. Dividing lines between the wards were the street heretofore called Mountain Street or Ancaster Road, hereafter to be called John's Street, and the street leading from the Eastern part of the District in the direction towards Dundas, hereafter to be called King's Street; Wards 1 and 2 lying west of John's Street and respectively south and north of King's Street; Wards 3 and 4, east of John's Street and respectively north and south of King's Street.

From each ward one representative was elected annually. These four elected members then elected a fifth to constitute a five-man Board of Police. From their number the board elected a president. The act required that an eligible voter should be a British subject, male, resident in the ward in which he voted, and should possess certain property requirements, the latter being increased for the aspirant to the board of police. Elections were set for the first Monday in March, at a polling place in each ward appointed by the sheriff, with notice given at least six days in advance, and were to be presided over by the sheriff or a deputy.

Should the four elected members fail to elect a fifth, the act provided for the calling of a general election to this end. A clause governing grounds of complaint regarding the validity of an election would find ample use in future years, early elections being lively, frequently violent, and succeeded by an aftermath of charges and countercharges.[6]

Covering every aspect of early community life, the act authorized the corporation to pass ordinances and by-laws for the proper government of the town and appointment of town officers; the regulation of all types of licenses; and means of fire prevention and establishment and maintenance of a fire fighting department.

Certain functions and authority previously exercised by justices of the peace relating to control of streets and roads were now given to the board of police.

Finally and importantly, the corporation was authorized to establish a

61

market, at least one acre in extent, in a place determined by a majority of the justices of the peace for the District of Gore at any Court of General Quarter Sessions, not less than ten magistrates being present. To erect a market house upon this plot, to purchase one or more fire engines, as necessary, and to provide a fitting place to keep them, the board was empowered to borrow the sum of one thousand pounds.

Hamilton's application for incorporation as a town had been based on a recent marked increase in population. In 1826 the population of Barton Township had been 1,195. In 1833 an assessor's census of Hamilton alone showed a population of about 1,400. By September, 1834, this had increased to 2,101 and by May, 1835, had jumped to 2,600. These figures were published by Dr. Thomas Rolph, of Ancaster, in 1836, in reporting a trip through Upper Canada. "By now," concludes Dr. Rolph, "the population is probably 3,000."

Maps also indicate the rapid development of the town. In 1830 a Hamilton map by Lewis Burwell shows a hundred acres surveyed. Six years later one by Alexander Mackenzie shows eight hundred acres.

This increase in population and extension of boundaries was due largely to the building of the Burlington Bay canal. On March 19th, 1823, an act of parliament authorized construction of a navigable waterway to replace the shallow natural outlet which provided passage only for small schooners and the flat bottomed batteaux used widely at that time in the carrying trade. With larger vessels, cargo was unloaded on the Lake Ontario side of Burlington Beach and trans-shipped. The new canal was built in its present location, south of the natural inlet which was later filled in.

Although reports show a "drudge" was used in construction of the canal, the work was done mainly by hand with pick and shovel and required an army of labourers. From far and near workmen flocked in, many bringing their own wagons, teams and tools. Hamilton became their headquarters and to accommodate them, dwellings, storehouses, barns and wharves sprang up along the bay shore—unpretentious frame homes mostly, with a sprinkling of better class residences. In the resultant boom, land and water lots were at a premium, capital was attracted, and wharf building flourished.

Simultaneously receiving attention was the project of Pierre (Peter) Desjardin[7] to cut Coote's Paradise by a canal which would permit ships entering Burlington Bay to proceed by the natural navigation route— across the bay and north of the present Valley Inn—into the marsh and by canal to Dundas. On November 1st, 1820, Desjardin's petition for land and water rights was granted. Not until January 30th, 1826, however was the Desjardins Canal Company (capital, £10,000) incorporated to construct a canal three to four miles in length, including natural navigation within the marsh. Unfortunately Peter Desjardin did not see his dream realized. His death on September 7th, 1827, postponed the opening of the canal for another decade.

Simultaneously John Galt, founder of the Canada Land Company, after whose family Galt, Ontario, is named, determined to profit in the new mercantile era. Applying for land adjacent to the Burlington canal, Galt planned to establish a depot where immigrants and cargo might be unloaded and forwarded overland to Guelph and other hinterland points. His plan was confounded by the impossible roads of the day.

In the meantime the Burlington canal had gone its own way. In 1829 Hamilton's first steamer, the *John By,* a barge equipped with engines and paddles and drawing only two and one-half feet of water, is reported as running between Hamilton and Toronto, taking a day and night for the trip. In keeping with the times her first cargo was whiskey.

Accounts of the canal are conflicting but pieced together provide a fairly accurate overall story. "The Burlington canal," wrote George E. Mason,[8] "was commenced in 1823 and completed in 1826 by Captain John McKeen and James G. Strowbridge, both of whom are buried at the southeast corner of King and Wellington Streets.[9] The width of the canal was originally only 30 feet. Prior to the digging of this canal Ancaster . . . (had) in 1818 twenty prosperous stores; but many of her most enterprising business people, such as Edward Jackson, Richard and Samuel Hatt, &&, removed to Hamilton on the opening of the canal."

Contractors of the canal we find listed as Spohn & Mann; while Inspector J. H. Smith, county historian, gives the complete cost of the project as $94,000.

By an act, dated February 17th, 1827, the provincial legislature provided for a survey of works at the Burlington canal and *further aid to complete the same.* Autumn and spring gales and winter ice undoubtedly took heavy toll of the channel. In a report submitted in the autumn of 1828 to the canal commissioners—William Chisholm, William Applegarth and John Aikman—William Johnson Kerr, superintendent, gives a graphic picture of canal renovation of that day with the tools available.

I . . . put the Drudging Machine in repair, and commenced deepening the Canal about the 10th May . . . and by the 10th June I discontinued the Drudge, having a depth of water averaging twelve feet through.

I then began repairing the South Pier which was in a very Shattered State—I carried it out 800 feet upon the foundation laid by Mr. Hall (first superintendent) 200 feet of it had been washed away six feet below the surface of the water and the other 600 feet I took down principally to the water level—which I have tied with timber of one foot square fastened with two inch treenails 22 inches long.

The whole 800 feet are perfectly filled with heavy stones, 700 feet of this pier I have decked over with 2 and 3 inch plank, crossing the top ties at every four feet—well spiked with seven inch spikes—with heavy oak gunwales on both sides . . . secured with treenails and iron bolts, 22 and 18 inches long.

To protect the foundation of the pier 40 cords of larger boulders from the Islands below Kingston were deposited on the south side, thus giving the ground swell an easier ascent upon the pier. The north pier was similarly repaired and 100 feet that had been washed away renewed.

In concluding, the superintendent suggested the need of bridging the canal after navigation closed, for the convenience of travellers and because of the expense of the ferry, which cost five pounds per month in wages to the ferryman who attended "late and early as well as on Sunday." That the suggestion bore fruit seems proved by an item which appeared in the Gore Balance, Vol. 1, 45, October 1, 1830: "The Swing Bridge over the Burlington Bay Canal will be opened October 2, 1830."

In another part of his report Mr. Kerr refers to the "Stone Scowmen" employed on the canal. From this section of workers comes the gruesome story, "The Ghost of the Canal," told by Peter Spohn Van Wagner, half-brother of Mr. Spohn, canal contractor.

Between the Burlington canal and the northern mainland lies a stretch of dry barren sand, an almost treeless waste, part of which covers the original outlet to the bay. This no man's land is said to be haunted by the ghost of an unfortunate and neglected boatman injured by having his leg crushed as he helped unload a heavily laden stone boat when it was caught between the boat and the timber crib into which the stones were being thrown. The injured man was carried to an old house standing on a narrow strip of land beside the outlet, a former tavern, where he received scant attention or sympathy, he having been noted for his roughness.

Finally his unceasing cries and groans attracted a gentleman passing who sent to the village of Hamilton for a surgeon—the well known Dr. Case—who was forced to amputate the leg. This the doctor gave to a fellow scowman, named Wheeler, with instructions to bury it. After unbelievable suffering Jem Horner died, an enquiry was called and Dr. Case instructed Wheeler to disinter and produce the leg as evidence. Wheeler however had not buried the leg. He felt that if Jem Horner died, as seemed likely, he should have his leg placed in the coffin with him for fitting burial. To preserve the leg for this eventuality, he now admitted, he had placed the appendage in a keg of whiskey. He departed to bring this. Shortly Wheeler returned carrying the keg. His face was puzzled: his burden was unaccountably light. An examination quickly provided the explanation. The keg produced a highly colored, highly odorous leg but the preservative whiskey had vanished.

Finally the story came out. Three of Wheeler's boon companies had seen him disappear with the keg and upon search had found it hidden away. Unaware of what the keg contained in addition to the liquor, they had considered it an excellent joke to visit the hiding place several times, remove the bung and empty Wheeler's keg for him, gleefully anticipating his surprise and chagrin when he made the discovery. It was unnecessary for the court of enquiry to seek beyond the culprit who had confessed, for the guilt of the other two was plainly written on their blanched and horror-stricken faces.

Until the house was razed, years later, wayfarers who passed in the night frequently swore that they had heard echoing from the dark dilapidated abode the bloodcurdling moans and cries of the dying scowman.

According to W. F. Johnson, Beach historian, the Burlington canal opened in 1830, the first boat making the passage being the *Rebecca and Eliza,* under Captain Zealand. Since the *Western Mercury* of October 6th, 1831, states that "the Canal is to be finished this year," it seems obvious that use of the canal predated its formal completion. Confirming this is a *Gore Gazette* item of April 14th, 1827: "Mr. (John) Chisholm's three vessels, the *Mohawk, Brock* and *Rebecca* passed through the Burlington canal from the bay (where they had wintered) last week; each having some part of its cargo on board. The *Jane,* a topsail schooner belonging to Colonel (James) Crooks, is now loading opposite Burlington Heights with flour, etc., from Dundas and is expected to pass the canal without taking out any of her loading."

In contrast to the later lazy somnolence of the Beach as a summer resort, the sandstrip now hummed with activity—the taking on and discharging of cargo by ships laying alongside the wharves and freighthouses on the lakeside of the canal, the sawing of lumber and rattle of hammer and caulking mallet in the shipyard of Irish Philip Magee who launched the first ship built at the canal on May 11, 1831, a 50-ton schooner, the *Daniel O'Connell of Burlington Canal.*

To maintain the canal the government imposed tolls and appointed John Chisholm as collector of customs. Tolls were universally disliked, by ship owners and carriers and by Hamilton and district merchants and wholesalers. In their way canal tolls were as unpopular as the hated road tolls of the day, to avoid which citizens frequently travelled roundabout bone-shaking miles. Merchants cried ruin. Yet as early as October 6th, 1831, the *Western Mercury* was boasting, "Since the Burlington Canal started, Hamilton has increased from 3 to 18 stores. Its former trifling trade and its houses have doubled."

Much of the new settlement occurred on the waterfront, so that Hamilton became two communities separated by a swamp, the senior in the centre of town with a growing jealousy of the upstart "at the lake." Thus the city's colourful lively "North End" was born, the district that lies today north of the Canadian National railway tracks, west of Wellington Street, and bounded north and west by the waters of the bay. In the early nineteenth century the area at the foot of James Street and John was settled by a "rough tough reckless lot, hard working, hard playing, hard living, hard swearing, hard drinking," but they founded, said the late David M. Nelligan, "the liveliest, loveliest part of Hamilton, set apart by the neighbourliness and fierce pride of its people, home of cock-fights, good times and a legion of the city's most colourful characters."

As houses, stores and inns mushroomed, elation grew in the plain below the Mountain. The canal had made Hamilton a port on the important St. Lawrence waterway. As a port town she would have her chance. Lacking water power she had lagged far behind Dundas and Ancaster with their busy mills. This superiority on their part caused the two communities to be continually incensed by Hamilton's appointment as county town. After campaigning throughout the early 1820's, Dundas in 1825 called a meeting chaired by Titus Geer Simons and with William Lyon Mackenzie as secretary, to which residents of Halton County were invited, in an attempt to have the appointment revoked and the seat established in Halton. Not until the new county court house and gaol actually stood on Court House Square did the lobbying cease.

Now with the opening of the canal came promise of development as a mercantile centre. Let Dundas and Ancaster have their industries, Hamilton would make her place in trade. She would become an entrepôt for the area, would seek her future in wholesale houses and company headquarters. With good fortune and judicious cultivation in the right quarters, Hamilton might become the banking centre of Upper Canada.

All that the canal brought, however, was not good. In 1832 it brought the plague. At first it was merely a whisper, a bare line in the paper: "The Asiatic cholera has crossed Europe and is in England." And later: "The cholera has reached Ireland. It is an epidemic." When the news-paper said: "Even the Atlantic is no barrier to the cholera," barrister Robert Berrie, of Ancaster, clerk of the peace for Wentworth and Halton, called a public meeting to clean up the town.

On June 20th, 1832, householders met at the court house and resolved to remove the piles of garbage, ashes and rubbish that adorned streets, alleys and yards; to scrub dwellings and public buildings; and to clean out and disinfect cess pools, privies and all other germ breeding sources. If Hamilton had been inland she might have escaped. Being a port town she was doomed, for cholera bred in the stinking holds of immigrant ships and the ships arrived in relentless succession. "One hundred immigrants a week land in Hamilton," one paper estimated; while another reported, "Immigrants by schooner loads arrive all summer."

The first schooner met a hostile reception. Armed with pitchforks and clubs, terrified citizens refused to allow the vessel to dock or its anguished passengers to land. Even the sight of the pale listless children clinging to their mothers' skirts moved only one individual. Proclaiming that no Christian would leave human beings imprisoned in the polluted hold of the ship, George Hamilton persuaded his fellows to build rude shelters on the bay shore for the newcomers to occupy.

Many years later a Hamiltonian related how her grandmother, aged seven, newly arrived by ship in this foreign land, lay wide eyed in the night listening to the ominous chant of the town crier: "Bring out your dead! Bring out your dead!"

Since Hamilton had had no previous experience with the plague and was utterly lacking in health services as we know them, the community became a vast charnel house. Many well known citizens died, among them Chief John Brant. When Jailer Tidd, a giant Irishman of six and one-half feet, and his wife both fell victim, all prisoners were released from the new jail excepting one condemned to death, George Hamilton, Allan Napier MacNab and a Mr. Steven going surety for them. It is interesting that MacNab, imprisoned for debt at seventeen, went surety for the debtors.

Since the influx of hundreds of immigrants, many ill, many destitute, who were dumped upon port towns by a government which then washed its hands of them, constituted a major catastrophe for those towns, Hamilton's motto: "Bread! Quicklime! And transportation out of town!" is understandable.

In the beginning an abandoned time-raddled barracks on Burlington Heights, dating from the War of 1812, was used as a hospital, there being no other in town, and the dead were interred in quicklimed pits in the adjacent military cemetery. In jolting carts dead and dying were transported over the Heights' narrow sandy track to the hospital and left to the care of its sole attendant, an old soldier named Hyslop.

Hyslop claimed he feared neither cholera nor the footpad desperadoes of that era. His defence against the plague was a quart of raw whisky tippled daily; against footpads a flour barrel by his cot caging two pet rattlesnakes, large enough to rear and flicker a wicked tongue above the open barrel top but unable to escape.

In its horror the death scene of the victims of the black plague suggests a Hitchcock nightmare. As background the rough isthmus covered with hazel bushes and crawling with timber rattlesnakes; the creaking dead carts, ill-kept road and mouldering, empty windowed barracks. Overhead, black clouds that would not loose the prayed-for rain to drown the heat lightning flickering above Coote's Paradise or still the thin wind keening eerily above the unhallowed burying pits.

Outside the hospital a pile of voiceless corpses begging burial; within, the groans, the prayers and curses, the agony of the still-living; the flies, the stench. And over all, a requiem for dead and dying, the maunderings of the drunken old man feeding and conversing with his jewel-eyed companions.

Hitchcock, 1966? Believably. Unbelievably, yet truly, Hamilton in 1832.

Hyslop's lack of fear did not save him from the cholera. When it struck it proved as swift and deadly as his rattlers. Within three hours of his first seizure he was dead. Following his death the barracks on the Heights was closed by the board of health of the District of Gore, the epidemic occurring prior to incorporation of the community as a town, and an emigrant hospital was erected within the community on land rented by the government from leading citizen George S. Tiffany.

As the plague waned with cold weather, the other ever-threatening scourge of early communities, fire, swept the town. With wooden houses heated by wood stoves and fireplaces, hazardous chimneys and inadequate water supply, it is little wonder that the majority of Ontario cities have a major conflagration in their background.

On Friday, November 16th, a raw blustering day, fire broke out between eleven and twelve o'clock in the morning in MacNab's new tavern in the heart of town. In less than an hour the flames, fanned by a strong wind, had spread to five other buildings, wiping out the stores of Messrs. Ferguson and Company and Mr. MacNab, the dwelling and shop of Mr. Scobie, the post office, and the offices of the Desjardins Canal Company and the *Western Mercury*. Within three hours of its first discovery the buildings were completely razed. While the loss was serious, buildings then were not commensurate with those of today, the post-office being a single room up a narrow flight of stairs above the *Western Mercury* office on James Street North, where the postmaster not only performed all postal duties but acted also as janitor.[10]

At the first business meeting of the newly elected board of police of the town of Hamilton, held on March 16th, 1833, one pressing item of business was fire protection for the growing community.

8

Adolescence

On March 4th, 1833, Hamilton's first election ran an amicable and uneventful course. In three wards only one candidate stood for the police board. In Ward One Colin C. Ferrie polled seven votes and was declared elected.[1] In Wards Two and Four Ebenezer Stinson and Peter Hunter Hamilton, half-brother of George, won seats with three votes apiece. Only in Ward Three, north of King's Street and east of John's, did a contest occur, Joseph Rolston winning with twenty-two votes against Samuel Mills' eleven. Of the young town's forty-six voters therefore, thirty-three lived in Ward Three.

One week later the four members met at the Court House to elect a fifth member of the board, unanimously choosing Judge Thomas Taylor and then further electing him president. For its first item of business the board resolved to take the opinion of householders concerning the best location for the town market place.

Of the two sites available, one on King's Street, not otherwise specified, the other, George Hamilton's plot on John's Street[2] at Haymarket, the former received ninety-seven votes, the latter forty-eight. Never popular, Hamilton's gift site was always regarded as too far removed from the centre of town, especially considering the condition of early streets and its difficult uphill location, south of the later Toronto, Hamilton and Buffalo railway tracks.

In his presentation to the magistrates at the following court session, Judge Taylor reported the above figures, implemented by a board majority. Nevertheless the magistrates pronounced in favour of the Hamilton plot, the later Haymarket.

Having appointed Stephan Randal (or Randall) clerk to the board and assessor; David Beasley, son of Richard, collector and treasurer; John J. Ryckman, high bailiff and inspector of highways and chimneys; and John Kennedy, market clerk and inspector of weights and measures, the board turned to drawing up the by-laws and regulations of administration. From establishing the weight and cost of bread, rules governing

69

slaughter houses, fines for speeding, for obstructing streets, and for domestic animals running at large, by-laws ranged to determining the width of sidewalks and prescribing licences. Possibly the two most vital issues the by-laws grappled with were property assessment for taxation purposes, and fire prevention.

With the recent fire as a grim warning, by-laws ordered that every dwelling should have a ladder permanently in place extending above the eaves, with a chimney ladder where needed; one or more three-gallon leather buckets bearing the owner's name; and regular chimney inspection and cleaning, with a heavy fine for a chimney fire if the chimney had not been cleaned within the set time. In addition compulsory citizen assistance was required at fires if demanded by bailiff, magistrate or a member of the police board.

With by-laws established, the board turned to another phase of fire prevention, and a pressing need of the growing town—an adequate water supply. By September, five wells, each of eighty cubic feet capacity, had been dug in public places and pumps installed. In addition the first sidewalks in the community were laid on King Street and John, nine feet and eight feet wide respectively.

Hamilton was progressing. At Port Hamilton four steamboats touched regularly: the *John By, Queenston, William IV* and *St. George,* the last described as a beautiful schooner-rigged vessel propelled by a ninety horsepower engine, accommodating upwards of sixty cabin passengers. Exports were steadily climbing. In one week seventeen thousand bushels of wheat at one dollar per bushel were shipped from only one of the town's four wharves. Hamilton had three newspapers: The *Canadian Wesleyan,* The *Western Mercury* and The *Hamilton Free Press,* as well as the semi-monthly literary journal, The *Garland.*

Moreover, augmenting steamboat service coach lines now offered Hamiltonians regular connections with Canadian and United States centres and intermediate points. From Hamilton coach travel took twelve hours to York, four hours to Brantford, and six days to Sandwich. Fare between Hamilton and York was thirteen shillings and ninepence, and passengers were allowed thirty-six pounds of baggage, with excess at the rate of one seat for two hundred pounds.

In 1833, Hamilton's growing importance as a mercantile community led Henry Fowle, of Dundas, to inaugurate a local stage coach service. Operating twice a day between Bamberger's tavern, Dundas, and Burley's Promenade, the stage also made connection with the York boats.

As in 1832, however, there was an obverse to the bright face of growth and progress. In 1833 the ships again brought cholera, although the visitation this year was less deadly since the town had learned some of the measures necessary to combat the disease. Besides cleaning up the town, disinfecting buildings, and controlling slaughter houses, the board frowned on public meetings and forbade exhibitions of animals and circuses, theatres and shows without board permission. By this latter stricture they possibly saved Hamilton the fate of Galt, Ontario, where in 1834 an epidemic of cholera carried by a travelling circus wiped out one-third of the village population.

In 1833 Hamiltonians were assessed their first municipal tax, the rate being established by the board at two pence halfpenny on the pound.

In 1834 John Law, schoolmaster, became president of the board of police, John J. Ryckman was replaced as bailiff by Thomas Gillesby, and William Frank assumed the new office of poundkeeper.

On May 5th, 1834, George Hamilton launched the town on its most important enterprise to date. For the market place, say the minutes, he "made his deed to the Police and tendered the same which was accepted by Mr. Law as President . . . on the part of the Town"—a document apparently later misplaced as no record of it exists today.

In consequence on July 1st, Messrs. Law and Stinson were deputed to procure, from Toronto or elsewhere, a loan of one thousand pounds as authorized by the act of incorporation so that the town might erect a market house[3] and purchase and house a fire engine.

With money in hand the work proceeded speedily. On August, following the resignation of Joseph Davis, clerk and assessor, Charles Durand received the appointment. In his *Reminiscences* Durand states that as clerk he oversaw the erection of the small frame market building constructed by James Scott and Robert Biggar to a plan for which Samuel Shenton was paid five pounds. On October 20th the board met to dispose by auction of the eight market stalls, at monthly prices ranging from nineteen to six shillings.

To protect the interests of these stall holders, stringent regulations governing the sale of foodstuffs in the community were established and strictly enforced, including produce offered in licensed groceries and shops, and from wagons on the market place or peddling door to door. Forestallers and regraters—persons buying goods to resell at a profit— were promised full punishment. In other words, from the inception of the market the lines were drawn between licensed stall holder on the one hand and shop and pedlar on the other, echoes of resultant battles punctuating early police records.

Simultaneously with the building of the market house, erection of a second public building in town was progressing—a hospital made possible by a government grant of fifty pounds. In 1832 the Gore District board of health, composed of Judge Taylor, Peter Hunter Hamilton, Colin C. Ferrie, Myles O'Reilly and Robert Berrie, had closed the hospital on the Heights following Hyslop's death. After disinfecting and whitewashing, the barracks was then used as a shelter for newly arrived immigrants.

Apparently the cholera hospital ordered erected in town at that time was impermanent, for a hospital was now built by A. S. Searls under direction of the board of health at a cost of £13.13.0.

Although purchase of a fire engine was investigated by the 1834 board, not until July 16th, 1835, under President Andrew McIlroy, was the apparatus purchased from Wm. Platt & Company (not otherwise identified). Total cost, with fifty feet of hose, pipe and hose boxes, freight and duties, £190.17.6 ($763.50), with £64 paid on delivery and the remainder in two debentures maturing in one and two years.

In early years the city's universal payment of all but minimum accounts by issuing debentures, accepted by the creditor who then faced the sometimes bleak prospect of collecting his money, resulted from scarcity of municipal funds and the fact that taxes were not payable until fall. In 1835 town revenue, including taxes, totalled £430 ($1720.), to cover all community expenditures.

So desperately hard up was a board on occasion that members contributed their own funds to carry on municipal business. In 1838, under President Miles O'Reilly, the board subscribed £200 on a ninety day note drawn by the president and endorsed by board members,[4] John Bradley, Ward Four, abstaining. Falling due on November 15th, the note was renewed from that date for £113.

Unfortunately, in 1839 (William J. Gilbert, President), neither Judge O'Reilly nor Alexander Carpenter was elected and ironically, in 1840 and '41, only the abstainer, John Bradley, was returned to office. Furthermore, over the years Bradley's tenders on lumber for town works were repeatedly accepted. In 1842 his four-year run was ended by James Gage but neither Mr. Gage nor his successors had Bradley's hold on the ward, a series of one-year terms ensuing.

After the renewal of the board's note the matter drops from the minutes until 1846. On May 4th of that year we find board members repeating history and under President Daniel MacNab, wholesale hardware merchant, raising £500 on "their individual responsibility," to defray wages of labourers engaged in essential work, the amount to be repaid from taxes collected in July.

Three months later, on August 8th, the board resolved to undertake no more contracts until "the £150 note granted by the members of the late Board and now in suit be paid out of the revenue of the present year."

With accrued interest the £113 note of the board of 1838 would now total £150, and as Hamilton was about to assume new status as a city, even the most long suffering creditor would doubtless feel the time had come for liquidation of the civic debt.

As usual in municipal affairs, purchase of the town's first fire engine set up a chain reaction of events. On November 16th, 1835, the board authorized James Scott and Robert Biggar to erect a fire engine house at a cost of £300, to specifications drawn by William Hardy. For two plans of the engine house Mr. S. Wood received £2.10.0.

On January 13th, 1836, the first engine company in Hamilton was authorized by the board, and the names of members reported. Over the next three months the board approved payment for chains to the Hook and Ladder Company; for "necessaries" to the Fire Engine Company;

C. Kimble's account for painting hooks and ladders and varnishing wagon; and an expenditure for forty caps and forty belts at a price of £1, furnished by William Bullock, captain of the Hamilton Fire Company.

Since this was the hazardous winter fire season, even more stringent regulations were added to existing ones. Shavings might not be burned within a hundred yards of a dwelling; fire could not be carried from house to house except in a closed pan or covered scuttle; and chimneys must be swept and stove pipes cleaned once a month. To enforce this, Hamilton's first official chimney sweep, John Garah, was appointed, to receive 7½d. for sweeping a chimney, 1s. for cleaning stovepipes, and sole right to sweep.

In the meantime, since its arrival, the fire engine had been housed in rented quarters. On July 25th, 1836, John Stinson, of the firm of T. E. & J. Stinson, King Street East general merchants, deeded the board gratuitously the plot of ground, thirty feet wide by forty deep, situated on the north side of King William Street between John and Hughson.[5] The land was given—"to have and to hold . . . forever"—with one provision: that a fire engine house be erected upon it to house one or more fire engines and that the property be retained in perpetuity for this purpose, or one in conjunction with the same. Otherwise the land should lawfully revert to John Stinson or his descendants, upon a fair payment being made for the fire house.[6]

On September 19th, 1836, the first debenture issued to Wm. Platt & Company as an instalment on the fire engine, with sixteen months interest amounting to £67.10.3, was presented to the board. Finances being customarily straitened, the board issued a note on the Gore Bank, Hamilton, payable at sixty days, to be met with the first monies paid the treasurer.

Fire protection was costing the town dear. On the credit side were fines for chimney fires and infractions but in the winter of 1837 these were exhausted by citizen awards for outstanding service at fires; a premium of £1.5.0 for each fire, applied for and granted the fire department; and additions to engine and hose. Finally the fire department asked for and was granted all fines for chimney fires. On March 27th, 1837, James English was engaged at £15 per annum to service the fire engine.

His salary compared favourably with those of other civic officials. In 1836 William Hale, high bailiff and town inspector, received £20 annually plus the emoluments of his office which included, for service of a subpoena or summons, one-third the penalty imposed; for an arrest or for issuing a licence, 2s.6d. Services outside his regular duties brought additional sums.

The following year Mr. Hale's fortunes fell abruptly. In addition to a bailiff at Port Hamilton, appointed in 1835, assistants were appointed in Wards One, Three and Four. All received ten pounds a year and emoluments. Although Mr. Hale remained high bailiff and was given a residence, he resigned on May 1st.

Early town fathers believed strongly in incentive. In 1835, in addition to a yearly salary of £10 as town clerk, Charles Durand was paid for issuing summons or subpoena, half the fine imposed, and for each licence issued, 1s. 3d. As assessor he received four per cent of all assessments, and as tax collector, five per cent of all taxes received. Under this system the number of assessment protests crowding the minute books is understandable.

Following election, the board of 1836 determined that Mr. Durand should serve without salary, receiving only the perquisites of his office. They also appointed an assessor at three per cent assessments; a collector at four per cent collections; and a treasurer at two per cent of all monies passing through his hands. When Charles Durand resigned, George C. Street became clerk and treasurer, serving until 1839.

If the town fathers dispensed little actual cash to civic employees, they were equally frugal with firms, individuals providing services, and the general public. For all but minimum amounts, debentures were issued. When a debenture fell due, if funds were lacking as they usually were, the debenture was renewed, but with the creditor's current taxes endorsed as payment on the note.

Board minutes bristle with items: Thomas Wilson appeared to state that a vagrant, one Flanagan, had died that morning. Mr. Wilson had by desire of the board supplied blankets and provided an attendant. An order to Mr. Wilson for £3.2.6., the amount of his taxes. . . . Order written on John Young & Company for 2 lbs. of nails for the John Street Market, to be deducted from their taxes.

In the 1820's and '30's money was an almost unknown commodity, barter being largely the means of exchange. Doctors, lawyers and ministers were most frequently paid in produce and firewood. Newspapers advertised their rates in currency but if not forthcoming were pleased to exchange newsprint for commodities. Even Masonic dues were taken out in trade, and most shops accepted certain types of produce. Francis Leonard, King Street East, Dry Goods, Hardware, Groceries, Books and Variety, listed his wants in the *Hamilton Free Press* as 5,000 bushels Oats; 2,000 Deers' Horns; 2,000 lbs. Bees-wax; 10,000 lbs. good Firkin Butter; Furs; and House and Field Ashes; with cash offered for good merchantable wheat delivered at Hatt and Chisholm's storehouse, Abel Land's, George Chisholm's, or Hatt & Chisholm's, Dundas.

Obversely, for a very young country, the scope and variety of merchandise offered by the better class of tradesmen was astonishing. In December, 1823, Robert C. Campbell, King Street East, advertised his fall supply of groceries in the *Western Mercury*. Contained in chests, boxes, hogsheads, pipes, puncheons, kegs, bags and bottles, these included: teas of all kinds; loaf sugar, Muscovado sugar, New Orleans sugar and East India sugar; Cognac brandy, Jamaica spirits, Holland and Schiedan gin, old Port in wood and bottles, Madeira, brown and pale sherries and Scotch whiskey; Carolina rice; Havana coffee; 20,000 Spanish and other cigars, 20 kegs plug tobacco and 50 jars Maccoboy snuff; raisins; 50 boxes glasses, 100 boxes mould and dip candles, and 90 boxes American soap; molasses; shrub; peppermint; chocolate and cocoa; figs, prunes, Zante currants; filberts, walnuts, soft shelled almonds; pepper, mace, allspice, nutmegs, whole and ground ginger, orange and lemon peels; cinnamon, cloves, carraway seeds; mixed pickles, gherkins; French anchovies, anchovy paste; Brandy fruits; olives; orange and ginger marmalade; cordials; macaroni, vermicelli; English and American cheese; and just received direct from New York, a few barrels of fresh oysters.

Below the Mountain the town on the plain was like a half-grown child, not yet adolescent but out of first childhood. Agnes Hannah Hamilton Lemon, daughter of George Hamilton's eldest son and heir, Robert Jarvis, writing of Hamilton in the 1840's, said:

At our feet the green fields stretched out one after another down the gentle slopes till they reached the clustering houses of the little town below. Then came the fields again in all their varied tints of green, with blossoming orchards between, and beyond all sparkled in the sunshine the blue waters of the bay, making a picture of surpassing beauty never to be forgotten while memory holds her place.

In the 1840's Land's virgin bush still extended east of Wellington almost to King Street, and Archibald Ferguson's property—Lot 13, Concessions 1 and 2, a crown grant to his father, Peter, in 1802—stretched west of Wellington to Mary and from Main Street to the bay in unbroken farm land, excepting for a strip fronting on the north side of King Street from Wellington to Mary, purchased by Richard Beasley. In March, 1837, a dozen freeholders of the town petitioned the board "to have the 1st and 2nd concession roads of Barton (Barton Street and Main) through Lot 13 opened at once," and the board so instructed the seemingly reluctant Mr. Ferguson.

Peter Hunter Hamilton's fields, west of James Street, laid out now in lots (but still farm land) bore some of the finest nut trees in town, his sweet chestnut trees a lure each autumn to the town's youths armed with sticks and bags. Mr. Hamilton's log house, half frame and clapboarded, stood at the head of today's Charles Street at the end of a long shady lane entered from Main Street. East of the house a great orchard spread to James Street. To this house in 1824 Peter brought his bride, Harriet Durand, daughter of James and sister of Charles. Six years later he replaced the frame house with a spacious brick residence which eventually, with additions, became the well known Holmstead of William Hendrie, Sr.

Between Mr. Hamilton's acres and the Hess land to the west, the Bowery—the earlier name bestowed by a homesick loyalist from Manhattan on Bay Street South—was a path winding through pasture fields to the foot of the mountain, "where the family cows," said F. W. Fearman, provision dealer, "roamed at will during the day, to be driven home with tinkling bells for milking when the sun was going down."

In the eastern part of town there were few houses south of Main Street except Richard Springer's log homestead standing in a grove of trees near the corner of Hunter and Spring Streets, where Corktown's Irish shanties and cottages would mushroom with the building of the Port Dover railway. In this homestead in 1801 Richard Springer held the first Methodist service in the community. Of greater interest to local youths however, were the extensive orchards surrounding the house. Not only did they produce delicious fruit for pilfering, but in cider time lads armed with sufficiently long straws could steal their fill of tangy cider.

In the 1840's Hamilton streets were mud holes under rain or snow, and deep in dust in drought. On windy days suffocating clouds of dust would whirl down King Street, York and Main, temporarily disrupting business. These, however, were growing pains common to all communities of that era.

Standing on the Mountain one could mark the sidewalks beginning to edge the streets, and the streets themselves pushing into the green fields, sometimes only a block long to service a single dwelling, sometimes two or three blocks, but never at one time much longer. Where the corduroyed swamp had stretched on James Street North, side streets now right-angled east and west and buildings had appeared: Anglican Christ's Church begun in 1835 and completed four years later under the Rev. John Gamble Geddes, a handsome wooden edifice with a classical portico and tall tower and spire; and counterpoised across James Street, Judge Thomas Taylor's landscaped residence and gardens.

Along King Street brick buildings were replacing wooden structures. Manufacturing plants began to appear—initially often set up in the manufacturer's home or in a building on his property. Mr. Harris, gunsmith, produced a small output of excellent guns; an unnamed craftsman manufactured augers which gained a reputation; the Hamilton Tin factory, manufacturers of all types of tin and sheet iron ware, was reorganized under Edward Jackson, Charles Gilbert and Moses C. Nickerson, moved into larger quarters and expanded its operations; next door Alexander Carpenter set up a new shop to manufacture cook and box stoves, Franklin stoves, brass and tinware, stove pipes, wagon boxes and hollow ware; while on King Street Joseph J. Carpenter began business, making carriages, wagons and sleighs.

Lists of manufactured articles appearing at this time give an insight into the life and habits of the day: James Finney opened an extensive chair factory, producing both common and fancy chairs; W. J. Gilbert, cordial manufacturer, offered all manner of cordials of a superior quality, being made on the London principle; while H. Clark advertised his intention of manufacturing and stocking sideboards, sofas, secretaries; dressing, column and plain bureaus; pillar and claw dining tables, breakfast and card tables, common dining, side and tea tables; ladies' work, writing,

76

wash-hand and candle stands; and high post, field, French, fancy and common bedsteads.

In 1835 Calvin McQuesten, M.D., came to Hamilton to join his cousin, John Fisher, in manufacturing the first threshing machine in Ontario, invented by Mr. Fisher. For two decades their foundry stood on the northwest corner of James and Merrick Streets, to be replaced in 1857 by the famous Royal Hotel.

Already a recurring motif was evolving in the community below the Mountain, new figures appearing to replace familiar ones that vanished. No matter how strong, how wise, how indispensable an individual seemed, when he went, another or others took his place. Like sand filling a desert excavation, the vacancy closed silently and almost unnoticed. Each according to his merit and desire gave to the city and what he gave became part of the city and could never be withdrawn.

Where Calvin McQuesten came, Titus Geer Simons went, as did Judge Taylor and William Davis, Sr., of Albion Mills. Robert Land, Sr., had long been dead. In 1834 James Durand was killed, strangely in the same manner as his first wife, by being thrown from his carriage, in Beasley's Hollow. On February 20th, 1836, the town lost its founder, George Hamilton, at forty-nine years of age. His wife had predeceased him. In his latter years Mr. Hamilton had taken an active part in politics, representing Wentworth in the provincial legislature from 1821 to 1830, and for several years officiating as treasurer of Wentworth and Halton Counties.

Always interested in education and a close friend of John Law, whose home site was his gift, George Hamilton[7] had scarcely time before his death to become acquainted with the latest headmaster of the Gore District public school, Dr. John Rae,[8] graduate in medicine and scientist and economist of repute, or with his assistant, William Tassie.

With the help of Scottish William Tassie, an able pedagogue and firm disciplinarian, Dr. Rae revolutionized the curriculum, introduced scientific studies, and established a province-wide reputation for the school, attended in 1838 by thirty-five boys. In 1839 when local municipal grants were introduced, the name was changed to the Gore District Grammar School. Text books used included the *English Reader, Mavor's* spelling book, *Murray's* and *Lennie's* grammars, *Daboll's* and *Walkingame's* arithmetics, *Olney's* and *Parley's* geographies, and *Goldsmith's* history.

In his diary the Rev. George A. Bull, son of George Perkins Boothesby Bull, printer and editor of *The Hamilton Gazette*, tells of attending the school in 1841-42. His books he obtained from the shop of John Leslie, Dundas.[9] He writes:

Dr. Rae's Grammar School was then on James Street North. A narrow lane led from James Street to the school, standing about halfway to Hughson Street. The building had been a stable and its former use was betrayed by the hayseed and dust from the old loft. The floor

77

and posts added to the roughness, inconvenience and discomfort of the place. Outside accommodation and playground—nothing! William Irwin was a classmate and William Lister and William Bickle, my seniors.

In 1848 Dr. Rae resigned from the Gore Grammar School to open a private school in the neighbourhood of the later Queen Victoria School, his place as headmaster being taken by George Elmslie, with Mr. Tassie as assistant.

9

Allan Napier MacNab

THE death of George Hamilton brought his eldest son, Robert Jarvis, home from Texas.[1] In the presence of the family, friends and leading members of province and town, the city's founder was laid in the family burial plot, a shaded, stone walled nook on the mountainside above Ferguson Avenue (immediately west of the Ferguson Avenue steps). Here too Judge Taylor was buried and James Durand was laid beside his first wife.

Since he died intestate, George's eldest son, Robert Jarvis, inherited the Hamilton estate. In 1836 the latter divided the property, sharing it with the other members of the family, settled himself in the ancestral home and in the fall married Miss Catharine Robertson. In 1844, with five of his twelve children now on the scene, Robert replaced Bellevue the first with Bellevue the second.

Three stories high and built irregularly in Tuscan villa style, with a veranda across the front, the new Hamilton home of dressed stone facing was a handsome addition to the mountainside. In the rear stood a stone stable with stalls for six horses and upstairs quarters for a groom, and one of the daily neighborhood events was the opening of the great gates of Bellevue to permit departure and return of the family carriage drawn by a spirited matched pair, the gleaming metal on their harness jingling to the horses' lively prancing.

Three years after the new house was built Mrs. Hamilton died. In 1851 Robert Jarvis married Miss Mary Wright. Today the family still lives in streets named in honour of its members by George and Peter Hunter: George, Catherine, Augusta and Caroline still survive. James Street South was once Jarvis Street; Catherine South was Robert; Charlton Avenue, Hannah; Young Street was Catharina; and Forest Avenue originally Maria. At that period city streets bore different names east and west of James and north and south of King. Bay Street in fact had three: Bowery, south of King; Bay, north of King to Burlington; and Brock, east to its termination at MacNab, the latter named after young Allan Napier MacNab who in 1826 became Hamilton's first resident lawyer.

Within ten years MacNab had proved his acumen. By the time opening of the Burlington canal attracted professional men in various fields into the new port town, the former Toronto law graduate was solidly established. Not only did Allan MacNab have an extensive local practice, as his legal notices in publications of the day disclose, but he had developed a roaring land office business with the Pennsylvania Germans of the later Waterloo-Kitchener area who stopped in the county town to procure their land deeds before pushing into the wilderness. Frequently, say old accounts, the Gore was white with the canvas tops of conestogas, the eastern prairie schooner.

With the knowledge of realty gained while acting as land agent for the Hon. Henry Boulton while articled as a law student—a service which had included laying out the later abandoned village of Dundurn, between Toronto and Thornhill on Yonge Street—MacNab had acquired not only whole surveys of land in Hamilton but also some of the choicest lots in the business and residential areas.

As president or director, Mr. MacNab's name appeared on the board of every important company or institution in the community, including the Bank of Upper Canada, Gore Bank, Desjardin Canal, proposed Burlington Bay-York-Niagara Steamboat line, proposed London and Gore Railway Company, and proposed Hamilton and Port Dover Railway Company. An ardent soldier, MacNab served actively as Colonel of the Gore militia—the so-called Men of Gore. And since 1829 he had represented Wentworth County in the provincial legislature, a high Tory in the Family Compact government.

These various activities were largely bent towards one objective, a vision that from earliest colonial days held a dangerous fascination for the Scot—that of establishing in this new land an estate and mansion worthy of his ancestors and probably much more pretentious than the builder could ever have attained at home. With unerring judgment MacNab chose Richard Beasley's location on Burlington Heights as setting for his intended establishment.

That he was able to purchase it resulted from an unfortunate chain of circumstances in Beasley's affairs. The War of 1812 had drained the latter's resources; Family Compact policy following the war had slowed the sale of his extensive land holdings; settlement of the country had gradually eliminated the fur trade; and as a merchant he now had to compete with an influx of shrewd, knowledgable traders, many with capital and overseas connections.

On October 9th, 1819, for the sum of £4,963.17.2 Richard Beasley had granted Francis des Rivières, Esq., and Thomas Blackwood, Montreal merchants, a mortgage on thirty-six hundred acres of land comprised of three thousand acres on the Grand River and six hundred on Burlington Heights, date of expiry being April 10th, 1820.[2]

Ten years later, on September 4th, 1829, Mr. Beasley wrote Thomas Blackwood in response to demands for payment of the mortgage. He had advertised his lands widely without success, said Beasley,[3] and he had no other means of paying his debt.

Beasley's letter illustrates the widespread dissatisfaction with the Clergy Reserves—established by the Constitutional Act of 1791, which set aside permanently one-seventh of the lands of the province for support of the established Church of England—which lay like a dead hand on the province, obstructing its opening up with undeveloped tracts of land and forest.

> . . . the Government and Clergy at present monopolise the market not from their low price—but from the extensive credit they give. They sell from 10/S to 20/S per acre at ten years Credit by paying one Instalment in hand. I offer mine at 10/S the acre, one Instalment in hand. I can sell none on these terms. To sell for Cash is impossible at present.
>
> I have offered my lands to you and am still willing to let you have them . . . I have no other means of paying the Debt unless by sale of my fixed property. At the present time if the sale is forced it must be at a great sacrifice, it would not meet the Debt. I am sensible the Alien you have on my lands at a fair valuation will amount to more than the Debt . . . Probably you will consider and make me an offer.

On March 1st, 1831, Thomas Blackwood, co-partner with the late Francis des Rivières in the firm of Des Rivières, Blackwood and Company, Montreal, assigned all holdings of the firm to John Solomon Cartwright, Kingston. A year later, on February 20th, 1832, Mr. Cartwright accepted in discharge of Richard Beasley's indebtedness to the firm, then £2,463.18.7, the conveyance of two tracts of land, consisting of three thousand acres on the Grand River and five hundred and fifty acres in Barton Township District of Gore.[4]

Since 1815 Cousin Richard Cartwright, Beasley's early adviser, mentor and creditor, had been dead. His son, John Solomon, as Beasley discovered, was a very different individual and lacking in his father's family feeling. Although Richard Beasley had reduced his indebtedness by more than half — £2,500 — he was required to surrender the full amount of land, less fifty acres, originally pledged as security. On November 16th, 1832, Mr. Cartwright sold to Allan Napier MacNab for £2,500 the property on the Heights, thus achieving a clear profit of three thousand acres on the Grand.

The reduction from 600 to 550 acres in the Burlington Heights property—which does not seem to appear in the legal description of the lots— may have an unhappy significance. "Richard Beasley," emphatically says his tall, broad shouldered and handsome great-great-grandson, David R. Beasley of New York,[5] "always maintained that he never intended to include his dwelling house and farm—his fixed property—in the lands he agreed to surrender in payment of the mortgage. He was cheated out of them. That is a legend in the family."

Beasley's letter, above, to Blackwood drawing a line between his "lands" and his "fixed property" would seem to substantiate this.

One must leave to individual interpretation a letter from Allan N. MacNab to Cartwright, dated Hamilton, 13th August, 1832:[6] "Mr. Beasley is particularly anxious to get the release from you of lot No. 18 in 2nd Concession or third Range—I think you had better send it up to me—that I may hand it over to him when the arrangements with me are completed on his part—You had better have it down immediately and quiet the old gentleman's fears." Lot 18, Concession 2, holds Dundurn.

In an undated Memo re Dundurn Park, in City Hall records, appears the item: "Richard Beasley moved to the property on the north side of King Street of which Walnut is a part, in 1832. Signed T. Beasley, City Clerk (Taken from my deeds in my office)." At this time Mr. Beasley was seventy-one. His store, standing "west of Ferguson Avenue at Walnut," was built of hewn timbers subsequently covered with clapboard.

Strangely, for a man active for so long in Hamilton affairs, little description of Beasley or his wife exists. "All I have ever heard," confesses David Beasley, "is that great-great-grandmother Beasley, as one of the Springers, always had a hymn book in her hand, no matter what she was doing!" Of her husband, "Colonel Beasley," states one writer, "was a man of much personal charm and no mean ability."

Bishop John Strachan disagreed. "Colonel Beasley," he wrote,[7] " . . . behaved poorly during the war and is a disagreeable weak discontented Character. When General Brock was going to Detroit he took the Bucket and Chain from his well that the Volunteers of the York Militia marching with the General might not drink."

If there was the slightest truth in this, possibly Colonel Beasley did not want his well drunk dry, as occurred at Stoney Creek. Possibly there was no truth in it, for Bishop Strachan was an unfortunate man to cross and this Richard Beasley, M.P., had done. As Speaker of the House in 1804 Beasley gave the casting vote against bringing in a bill to provide public schools for the province—not today's schools for the offspring of the general public, then a crying need, but schools to provide education for the children of Simcoe's favoured class of gentry.

Schools were not the only innovation citizens were demanding. In the community below the Mountain, water works to replace wells, and sewers to drain swamp areas and to carry off seasonal and flash floods were being urged.

In Upper Canada discontent with government was waxing to open rebellion, with the first mayor of Toronto (renamed in 1834), radical William Lyon Mackenzie, and Hamilton's high Tory, Allan N. MacNab, implacable enemies at the heart of events. In 1837 at the town pump at the corner of John and Main Streets Sheriff Macdonald proclaimed the young Victoria Queen.

The only constant is change. Beyond the town pump on its new site stood the recently completed county Court House and gaol, the first court, according to the *Gore Balance,* sitting in the new building on July 14th, 1830. As if timed, completion of the new Court House provided a dramatic setting for the final act of a murder case whose earlier scenes had been staged in the old log and frame building across the street.

In 1827 or 1828 (accounts differ) the Young-Sheeler case opened in Potter's Hotel on the northwest corner of King and James Streets. A chill fall mist was rolling up James, shrouding the Gore and Potter's in white, but inside the inn all was warmth, light and good cheer except in one corner where Farmer Hess was angrily decrying the loss of prize turkeys stolen from his farm, west of James near Caroline Street. An interested listener was the village constable.

At this apt moment an attendant informed the innkeeper that a man was at the kitchen door offering turkeys for sale. While the proprietor bargained with him, Peter Hess from a vantage point determined the turkeys were his and the constable slipped around the hotel and cornered the salesman, a handyman from the Christian Young farm on the mountain. Questioned later that night Farmer Young and his two sons, James and John, implicated a neighbour, John Sheeler, as the thief, claiming he had also robbed their henroosts. Before action could be taken against Sheeler, Jesse Masters disappeared, so that he would not have to testify, it was generally believed.

Shortly after this, Sheeler, apparently tipsy, cornered the constable in Potter's Hotel to enquire the penalty for knowing a crime had been committed and remaining silent. Under the constable's questioning, Sheeler confessed he had been present when the Youngs, fearing Masters' testimoney would convict them of the theft, had seized the latter, carried him to the rear of the farm and there murdered him and burned his body in an ash pit.

Sheeler's lurid tale of waiting while the Youngs took Masters into the woods; of the sounds of a struggle succeeded by cries and groans; and of a statement by one son that he "had hard work of it but he had killed him," led to the arrest of two of the Youngs and their trial on a murder charge. The third, reportedly on his way to the United States to locate Masters, was apprehended, returned, and tried separately. With no corpse and only the evidence of Sheeler, of poor repute, to convict them, all three were acquitted. Bones were found in the pit but they were not human.

Although freed the three Youngs remained suspect. Finally, in despair, James and John with money raised by sale of their land and belongings, augmented by funds contributed by friends, set out to find Jesse Masters and bring him back. One went to New York, the other to Montreal, travelling from village to village and enquiring of stage and steamship lines. Neither succeeded and both finally turned homeward, their resources exhausted. At Buffalo, as he boarded the ferry, James Young came face to face with Masters. The latter, previously ignorant of the trial, returned willingly to Hamilton. "Jesse Masters," proclaimed the

Gore Balance of July 1, 1830, "whose resurrection was announced in our last *Balance*, has paid a personal visit in proof of his mortal existence . . . John Sheeler, who testified to the murder, is now in gaol."

Tried before Chief Justice Sir John Beverley Robinson in September, 1830, John Sheeler was found guilty of perjury and sentenced to eight months' imprisonment, with two appearances in the stocks, possibly the last such exposure in Hamilton.

Contemporary with the stone Court House were new and imposing Hamilton homes. From the western Mountain brow Colonel James Matthew Whyte's square-towered Italianate stucco villa, Barton Lodge, completed in 1836, looked down on town and countryside. With its casement windows lighting the low-ceilinged rooms, furnished with priceless family heirlooms brought from England and filled with unusual and fascinating *objets d'art*, silver, fine china, rare paintings and first edition volumes that had graced the most distinguished circles, Barton Lodge was unique.

Nearby stood twenty-four-roomed Chedoke built by Scotch stonemasons for W. Scott H. Burn, wheat producer, with thick stone walls and deeply embrasured windows shuttered inside, with hand hewn beams and lath to outlast the centuries, even if the masons failed to plumb the walls or truly square the corners. Chedoke was noted for its seven water cisterns, its private schoolroom that doubled as a chapel, its enormous bake oven occupying a whole wall, and the fireplaces in most of its two dozen rooms, including the very large drawing room and small withdrawing room.

Colonel Whyte, his brother John Lionel Whyte, who inherited the Lodge from him, and Mr. Burn would all play their part in the community's unfolding story. Both were close friends of Allan MacNab who also boasted a new mansion, ". . . unequalled in the province," said a contemporary, ". . . a most extensive building, beautifully designed and elegantly finished."

When Allan Napier MacNab was born at Newark, now Niagara-on-the-Lake, on February 19th, 1798, history suggests that his father was confined in the common gaol. Certainly Lieutenant Allan McNabb, chief aide-de-camp to Lieutenant-Governor Simcoe, was in jail a month or so later, for on April 6th, 1798, a notice appeared in the *Upper Canada Gazette* offering two hundred dollars reward for apprehension of an escaped debtor, one Allan McNabb, a reduced lieutenant of horse on the half-pay list of the late corps of Queen's Rangers, who had broken gaol on April 1st.

Son of the above Lieutenant McNabb (also McNab, MacNab and Macnab) and Anne, daughter of Captain William Napier, commissioner of the port of Quebec, Allan Napier MacNab was descended from a Scottish landed family whose modest estate, Dundurn, was situated on the borders of Loch Earn in Perthshire. His grandfather, Robert MacNab, a captain of the 42nd of the Black Watch, had served as royal forester of Scotland.

84

With the family motto: *Timor Omnis Abesto*—Without Fear—and the family coat of arms with its Gaelic war cry: *Gun Eagal*—No Surrender—Allan Napier inherited two family characteristics, military blood in his veins, and a propensity for spending money faster than he could acquire it.

When Simcoe moved the seat of government from Newark to York, McNabb was appointed gentleman usher of the black rod, slightly augmenting his inadequate half-pay. Young Allan Napier's formal education in the Home District Grammar School of John Strachan, now Bishop of Upper Canada, ended abruptly in 1813, at the age of fifteen, when American forces attacked and burned York. Father and son, the MacNabs both fought in the battle of York and later marched in the laborious retreat through spring snow, slush and mud to Kingston.

Following the end of the war in which he had gained a commission and the nickname, "Boy Hero," for gallant action, Ensign MacNab remained in the army until its reduction. Returning then to York he began again the lifelong battle with debt which had already acquainted him with the inside of a debtor's prison and the limiting of his freedom 'on the bounds'—the promenade about the gaol outlined by blue posts within which the debtor was allowed his freedom.

Already, in his teens, MacNab's most dominant characteristic was firmly established. Dr. Pangloss in Voltaire's *Candide* might well have spoken of MacNab when he said: "This youth was doubtless designed to move in the circles of fashion, for he's dipt in debt and makes a merit of telling it." In young MacNab's case a proper ambition to attain the fashionable sphere supported his predisposition. Through employment as carpenter, pedlar, sailor, actor and government copying clerk, the penniless ex-soldier finally reached the office of the Hon. D'Arcy Boulton, where he then became articled as a law student. To supplement his meagre income he engaged in real estate transactions as agent for the Hon. Henry Boulton, son of D'Arcy. This profoundly affected his life, undoubtedly leading to his later extensive land holdings and manipulations, and resulting also in his second marriage on September 30th, 1831, to Mary Stuart of Kingston, niece of Mrs. Henry Boulton.

MacNab's first marriage, on May 6th, 1821, to Elizabeth Brooke, daughter of Lt. Daniel Brooke, Toronto, ended with her death in 1825, leaving the young widower with a son and infant daughter. The following year MacNab was called to the bar and determining his course, established himself in practice in Hamilton.

Three years later the youthful lawyer's star of destiny, in which he firmly believed, shone upon him. In Hamilton on January 28th, 1829, an effigy of Lieutenant-Governor Sir John Colborne was paraded through the streets and was offered indignities. Called before the House in its investigation of the affair was Hamilton's lone lawyer. Ardent Tory though he was, MacNab refused to testify, rumour hinting that certain of his clients were involved. In its annoyance the Assembly committed him to gaol for "contumacy" and kept him there ten days, in spite of repeated motions for his release.

MacNab emerged the "martyr of Toryism," was persuaded to run for the county seat, and so inaugurated thirty years of undefeated success at the polls, representing the County of Wentworth, Hamilton, and finally the Western Division in the Legislative Council of United Canada. As complement to the promising career opening before him, MacNab needed a suitable setting. Following purchase of the Dundurn property, he commenced construction of Dundurn Castle, believed designed by architect Robert Wetherell, completing it to the point of occupation about 1835.

Built in Regency style, and certainly in the grand manner for Upper Canada, the imposing stucco-covered villa with its seventy-two rooms reached eventual completion in stages, as funds became available. Today three different periods of construction are visible to experienced eyes. Laid out in final form with terraces, gardens, lawns, lodges, stables, eight-sided cockpit, walled cemetery and handsome entrance gates, Dundurn is estimated to have cost $175,000.

For his initial funds MacNab could thank a fortuitous real estate boom in Toronto which enabled him to dispose of certain holdings at a handsome profit. In 1833, also, MacNab raised £3,000 on a mortgage on the Dundurn property taken by David C. Beasley, son of Richard, further proving, according to namesake David of New York, that funds were not lacking in the Beasley family and that its members, had they appreciated that anything but their father's too extensive land holdings were at stake, would have moved to save the family property. Possibly some hope of its recovery led to David Beasley's acquiring the mortgage.

Five years later Allan MacNab discharged the Beasley mortgage, the Bank of Upper Canada assuming a mortgage of £9,000 on Dundurn and other MacNab properties, so diverse and extensive that their listing without legal description fills half a folio page. Showing the extent of Mac-Nab's contribution to the town's development, the *Western Mercury* of 1831 mentions twelve stores and houses built by the young lawyer within the past two years and thirty-eight lots sold by him that season, to be built upon. In 1837 he possessed twenty town lots, four frame houses under two storeys and four of brick or stone of two storeys. His office stood on the northeast corner of King and James Streets, and on the waterfront, at MacNab and Brock, he owned a wharf, storehouse and a stone tavern "with full appurtenances."

In 1833 he advertised in the day's press one of his properties—of special interest as showing the final development of Beasley's estate:

Dwelling House To Let:[8] The handsome and commodious Brick Cottage on Burlington Heights, lately occupied by Colonel Beasley, will be let for two years . . . beautifully situated on the edge of Burlington Bay, commands an extensive view on all sides, and is very roomy being 50 feet long by 40 feet wide with two wings each 20 feet square, frame kitchen 18 x 30, with cellarage under the main body of the building. On the premises are a good icehouse, wash house, smokehouse, an excellent garden stocked with superior fruit trees and an extensive peach orchard said to be the best in this Province.

Today it is generally conceded that the turret-crowned brick and plaster building isolated on the bluff east of the Castle was a cockpit where Allan MacNab privately entertained his male guests. Now that the heavier land clearing was achieved, at least within settled communities, leaving more leisure time, sports were gaining in popularity. Cockfighting, horse racing, foxhunting, iceboating on the bay, fishing, balls, soirées and garden parties, theatricals, musicals, debates and travelling shows — all flourished in a society largely responsible for its own entertainment.

So famous was Land's wharf, at Emerald Street, for its pike and bass fishing that one ardent fisherman frequently walked from Eramosa, thirty miles away, and back with his catch. Hamiltonians today can scarcely appreciate to what extent the bay featured in the life of the earlier community. During navigation the arrival and departure of the lake steamers was a well attended event. "The passenger business, between the boats, hotels and stage lines," said Frederick W. Fearman, merchant on Mac-Nab Street near Market, "was lively. In early morning and at evening James Street and the wharves were crowded with coaches, buses, cabs and various baggage craft."

In winter the Indian method of fishing through holes in the ice was popular, and the boating and bathing of summer gave way to skating, curling, and sleighing. In 1836 the first iceboat was launched on the bay. Built by the combined efforts of William Johnston, Nathaniel and Angus McAfee, and William Rayner, the craft was a clumsy triangular structure of scantling, shod with skate runners. An old quilt served as sail.

Under a brisk southwesterly breeze the boat with the four aboard shot down the bay on its maiden run, gathering momentum until it approached the beach at express speed. As the front runner was immovable the craft could not be braked. Unavailingly its passengers dropped sail and applied their pike poles. With sledge hammer force the boat struck the beach, propelling its occupants thirty feet through the air into the scrub fringing the frozen shingle. Tattered and torn, their hands and faces cut and bruised, the four took refuge in John Dynes' nearby windmill until nightfall might hide them from their friends' gleeful jeers.

In the early community, practical jokers flourished, as F. Kidner demonstrates in the tale of Sheriff Macdonald's foxhunt. A gentleman sportsman, the good sheriff had imported a pack of hounds from the old country and was given to appearing in Hamilton's rather primitive streets in full huntsman's regalia. When he arranged a grand foxhunt to gather at the Court House Square, it proved an irresistible temptation to a fellow Hamiltonian, Dennis O'Brien.

On the day preceding the hunt, the hounds were brought down from their kennels at Isaac Scuse's tavern near the present high level bridge on Burlington Heights and were lodged at Buckland's slaughter house which stood on James Street South on land now occupied by St. John's Presbyterian Church. By nightfall all was ready for the great event. After nightfall, however, the irrepressible Mr. O'Brien took over. Beginning at the slaughter house he trailed a course of pungent asafoetida criss-cross throughout the town, ending at Faulknor's brickyard beyond Garth (Dundurn) Street.

In the morning the hunt assembled importantly on the square. A block away the hounds were released. Immediately they gave bay and to the astonishment and discomfiture of their handler and the hunt, streamed past the Court House in full cry on their way to parts unknown. Not until late afternoon was the exhausted pack finally coralled and returned to Buckland's.

Keeping pace with sports was culture. If taverns graced every corner, private schools ran them a close second. F. W. Fearman, a profuse writer of the day, estimates that Hamilton at one time could boast twenty-eight.

In a house on the corner of King and Walnut Streets, rented from Dr. Case, Miss Sewell conducted a select ladies' establishment for females, with a few lads from exemplary families admitted. . . . On King Street West, near the corner of Bay, the Burlington Seminary flourished . . . Mr. Sherbrooke, a specialist in a non-specializing age, opened a school on John Street to teach penmanship. . . . For 15s. quarterly for the common branches and 20s. for the higher, Miss Eliza Eastman instructed young ladies in Reading, Writing, Grammar, Composition, Rhetoric, Logic, Arithmetic, Geography, History, Astronomy, Natural Philosophy, &&. This was a stern curriculum . . . Tending to a more social development was the fare offered by Mrs. and Miss Blennerhassett who provided French, Reading, Writing, Arithmetic, and all sorts of Needlework, both useful and ornamental at $2.50 per quarter, and for $4 quarterly, Music, Drawing and Geography additional. Mrs. and Miss Blennerhassett had no desire to turn out blue-stockings. Arithmetic would enable the sweet girl graduate to keep household accounts while geography would prepare her for travel and conversation.

In December, 1837, external events interrupted the even tenor of the town's routine. Erupting into ill-advised action, William Lyon Mackenzie's radical followers gathered north of Toronto to march on the capital and oust the Family Compact government. Informed of this rebel activity, Allan MacNab called out the militia. Then mounting his horse, Sam Patch, he rode headlong to the waterfront, commandeered the steamship *Traveller*, and embarked with sixty "Men of Gore" for Toronto and the battlefront.

In Toronto Colonel MacNab was welcomed with open arms and made commander-in-chief of the government forces by his staunch admirer, Lieutenant-Governor Sir Francis Bond Head. During the absence of MacNab and his wife in Toronto, the MacNab children and their nurse were removed for safety to the postoffice in Hamilton, threats of their abduction as hostages having been circulated. A guard was also posted in the lodge.

Following the march up Gallows Hill and dispersal of the rebels at Montgomery's tavern, MacNab returned home. Posses under Colonel William Chisholm scoured the countryside around Burlington, Dundas and Hamilton, seeking Mackenzie who had escaped. Yet although a reward of £1,000 was offered for capture of the small, fiery, impetuous rebel, none betrayed him and many risked their necks to assist him in his flight to the Niagara frontier. On the Mountain the son of pioneer Joseph Rymal, Jacob Rymal, M.P.P. for Wentworth County, provided Mackenzie with shelter and a mount.

After a brief campaign in the London area to disperse rebel forces under Dr. Charles Duncombe, Colonel MacNab marched his militia to the Niagara River to oust Mackenzie from Navy Island where, with the assistance of American sympathizers, he had established himself and set up a provisional government for Upper Canada.

For most of the winter MacNab and his militia remained at Niagara. F. Kidner described their departure from the Gore. They left, he said,

... full of martial ardour and perhaps a sufficient quantity of the liquor so cheap in those days. Among the number were about two hundred stalwart Indians, painted and feathered, anxious to manifest their loyalty to the great white mother across the sea. George Lees . . . had the contract for supplying bread to the warriors while Charles Buckland furnished meat. The bond stipulated beef, but anything edible in the flesh line, from ancient mutton to salt pork, was accepted without demur by the exhilarated soldiery. These rations secured, they were promptly skewered on the bayonets of the force, presenting a most ludicrous appearance as it departed towards the east.[9]

Lifeline to Mackenzie on Navy Island was the American owned steamer *Caroline* which transported men and supplies and maintained communication between the island and the American shore. With his customary arrogance and hotheadedness, MacNab instructed Commander Andrew Drew, R.N., to destroy the ship. Failing to locate the *Caroline* on Navy island, Drew crossed the river to the American side, boarded the ship as she lay at her moorings, cut her loose, fired her and sent her ablaze downstream.

In the operation one American was killed, others injured. By the narrowest margin an international crisis between the United States and Great Britain was averted. Yet, with his star of destiny in the ascendant, instead of severe censure Allan MacNab was knighted by a grateful sovereign and received a sword of honour from the legislature of Upper Canada for his services in suppressing the rebellion.

Ostensibly Mackenzie's uprising failed. Two men were hanged, the leaders of the movement were banished to Van Dieman's Land or fled into exile, while hundreds of reformers rotted in filthy, unheated verminous jails throughout the bitter months of the long-remembered "white winter."

Yet ill advised and misdirected as the rebellion of 1837 was, it hastened establishment of responsible government and brought correction of long standing ills and abuses: the clergy reserves and tracts of wild land owned by landgrabbing absentee owners that delayed development of the country; lack of roads and public schools; corruption of local government; nepotism that controlled all public offices; paternalism instead of democracy; and a legislative assembly impotent if opposed to the all-powerful lieutenant-governor and his council.

In every hamlet in the land Mackenzie's rebellion and its fellow in the lower province made itself felt. In Hamliton it cost the town its new market place and market hall.

10

The City, 1847

IN THE early life of the community John Street housed the commercial district while James Street was the Lake Road (south to King) from the Steamboat wharf.

In 1835 the corporation purchased from Robert Jarvis Hamilton for £175 a road allowance between Lots 14 and 15 at their southern extremity, permitting the opening of James Street to the mountain brow and establishing direct communication with Caledonia, Ancaster and Brant's Ford.

The day subscribing property owners celebrated their conquest of the Mountain would be long remembered. With banners, a parade and general pandemonium, James Street merchants signalized Hamilton's new business and mercantile centre. To emphasize its future effect on rival John Street they hired a farmer to sow John Street with grass seed. Commencing at King Street the yeoman progressed southward, scattering seed with a lavish hand, and before the John Street merchants could rally, had reached the new court house. There however a barrage of rotten eggs ended his demonstration.

With the gradual improvement in roads leading to the city and the resultant greater influx of farmers with produce, dissatisfaction increased with the John Street market, never overly popular. In March, 1837, the current board of police determined to erect a second market in a more central location, easier of access and affording greater accommodation—including closer proximity to taverns—for both farmers and townsfolk. Two offers of free land followed: from Messrs. Stinson, donors of the fire engine property, of a site at King William and Hughson Streets, and from Andrew (Yankee) Miller, land speculator and innkeeper, of one on the corner of James Street and York, the present market site.

Within a month the latter had been accepted, a deed received and notices published calling for tenders and plans for a market building of brick or stone, measuring 50 feet by 90, with a hall above the market place and cellars beneath.[1] On June 21st, 1837, to erect a market house, the

91

board of police borrowed two hundred pounds from George B. Harvey, payable with interest in one year. The following June, of course, funds for repayment were not available. On the back of the small weathered parchment, taxes for several years are credited against the note, and interest payments recorded.

On Monday, June 3rd, 1839, market stalls were first sold on the James Street market, with all members of the board in attendance. Leases ran for a year and the upset (minimum) overall price was £150. Stalls Nos. 1 and 2 to William Duff at £30.5.0 and Nos. 15 and 16 to Charles Buckland at £31.10.0 were costliest.

Unfortunately by the time this auction occurred, through a peculiar chain of circumstances, neither market nor market house belonged to the corporation.

In accepting Andrew Miller's land as a market site[2] and proceeding to build a market house, the president and board of 1837 overstepped legal bounds. By the act of incorporation the town had been empowered to establish a market place and borrow funds to build a market house. As this had been accomplished, the corporation had no authority in law to purchase, take or hold lands for a second market without amending the act to provide for this development.

On December 3rd, 1838, the current board, apparently discovering the situation, inserted a notice in the *Upper Canada Gazette* declaring the corporation's intention to apply at the next session of parliament for leave to effect an additional loan, to authorise selection of a spot for a new Market House, and to amend the Act of Incorporation, an outstanding example of the municipal horse trailing the cart.

Had it not been for William Lyon Mackenzie's rebellion the matter would have doubtless progressed uneventfully to a satisfactory conclusion. Had Andrew Miller been a staunch conservative, nothing untoward would likely have happened. But Yankee Miller was a radical, in sympathy with Mackenzie, and as such was well known to Allan MacNab. With hundreds of others throughout Upper Canada, Miller was arrested and jailed and his lands seized for debt, a simple matter since all land dealers were in a chronic state of financial embarrassment.

Andrew Miller's debt, for which suit was entered by the Bank of Upper Canada of which MacNab was a director, amounted to £486.6.3½, a trifling sum considering his extensive holdings and hotel business. Included in Miller's seized lands and tenements was the Hamilton market site and market hall, his conveyance of the land to the town having been rendered inoperative and void by the inability of the police board to accept it under the act of incorporation.

Faced with the unhappy task of auctioning city property, the sheriff of Gore, William Munson Jarvis, brother-in-law of the late George Hamilton, postponed action by various pretexts for over a year. On March 2nd, 1839, however, after due advertisement, as required, Miller's lands were put up for auction at the court house. Sale of the municipal property brought the bank little return, site and market house going to Miles O'Reilly, president of the board of police, for an undoubtedly prearranged three pounds.

Although notices of applications to the legislature for an amended charter to authorize additional markets recur at various times in board minutes, not until September 6th, 1849, did eventual legislation result in Judge O'Reilly returning the city property to the corporation for a token five shillings.[3].

The James Street market was not the only Hamilton institution affected by the rebellion. In 1838 the three-year-old Gore Bank, founded by Allan MacNab over the bitter opposition of William Lyon Mackenzie, was forced to suspend payment in specie until the end of 1839. One of the leading authorities in the province on matters of finance, currency and banking, Mackenzie was opposed in general to chartering of banks with note-issuing privileges and limited liability of shareholders. He had been doubly opposed to such a charter being issued to MacNab and his friends.

During his campaign against the bill Mackenize published in his paper, the *Correspondent* and *Patriot*, a list of Allan MacNab's unsatisfied debts. And when the bill finally passed, "The Hamilton or Gore District Bank," he said bitterly, ". . . is a machine job got up by Allan Napier MacNab and a few of his cronies and will completely answer his purpose."[4] Later events would prove Mackenzie largely correct.

From the beginning the intimate relationship between the Bank of Upper Canada and the Gore Bank becomes apparent. Subscription books for the new bank were opened in Hamilton and provincially at offices of the Bank of Upper Canada. In Hamilton, having sold the Gore Bank all the discounted notes in its Hamilton office, including MacNab's, and seen its manager, Mr. Andrew Steven, installed as cashier of the new institution, the Bank of Upper Canada closed its Hamilton office on April 30th, 1836.

On Monday, May 2nd, the Gore Bank opened for business, with Colonel James Matthew Whyte, MacNab's close friend, as president, young Colin Campbell Ferrie, secretary, and MacNab, solicitor. On the board of directors was David Archibald MacNab, Allan's brother. Two years later John O. Hatt, MacNab's brother-in-law and legal partner, joined the directors. Already rumours were circulating that Allan MacNab's indebtedness to the bank and the bank's loans to other directors were causing concern to shareholders. By 1839 dissension between MacNab's supporters and the opposition, led by Messrs. Ferrie and Steven, made the press.

Discussing the question of Sir Allan's indebtedness to the Gore Bank, including debts absorbed from the Bank of Upper Canada, the *Toronto Examiner*, published by Francis Hincks, wrote on July 2nd, 1839: "We are inclined to doubt, however, the extent to which the Gore Bank is said to be involved, namely £25,000."[5]

"MacNab had countless ways of making money," said Dr. Freda Waldon, for twenty-three years chief librarian of the Hamilton Public library. She continued:

And he was so bland and charming that people found it difficult to refuse him. Take, for instance, the site he presented free of cost to the Gore Bank the year it opened.

As solicitor he knew the bank wished to move from its original location on the south side of King Street, between MacNab and Charles. MacNab owned a single lot on King William Street just east of James. To make it large enough he bought another lot and presented the whole to the directors of the Gore Bank as a gift, asking only that they bar his wife's dower. When they came to pay however they found the dower valued at eight hundred pounds, more than twice the price of the property on the open market. In addition the land was impossible as a bank site. Yet the directors accepted his offer, held the property a few years, then sold it at a loss.

Later, on the southwest corner of King and Hughson Streets, a dignified square stone building topped by a widow's walk and entered by a handsome arched doorway was erected, which housed the bank and provided living quarters above for the manager. An integral part of city life, the history of the Gore Bank is the history of the community throughout the pioneering years of canal, bridge, road and railway building. Over the next three decades, "As good as the Gore Bank," came to be an accepted province-wide comparison.

In its growth the community below the Mountain was approaching incorporation as a city. One by one it had expanded its municipal adjuncts, adding a town pound, a town bell, a corporation Seal, and a Mechanics' Institute; holding its first Agricultural fair on May 30th, 1835; and two years later receiving the first petition for a public burying ground.

Hung first in the belfry of the American Presbyterian Church,[6] a small wooden building on the east side of John Street, the bell was removed in 1838 to the engine house on King William Street. From this vantage point it announced the hours of six, morning and evening, twelve noon, and nine at night; summoned worshippers to services on Sunday; clanged alarm for fires; and tolled for deaths and funerals. As bell-ringer the bailiff, George Cheevers, received £15 a year additional to his salary.

In an era prior to labour laws, when a man's daily wage for a minimum ten-hour day ranged from fifty to seventy-five cents, the town bell featured in possibly the first clash in Hamilton between labour and management. In 1840 clerks in Hamilton stores petitioned to have the bell rung at seven o'clock, store closing time. With a police board composed largely of business men, including merchants, refusal of the request is understandable.

94

Five years and various petitions later, however, the clerks won their case, the board ordering the bell to be rung at seven, provided the clerks paid the bailiff an annual £2.10.0 for his services. For several years the regulation remained in force.

Forerunner of the modern public library, the Mechanics' Institute succeeded the circulating library operated by James Ruthven and Company, books and stationery, and the reading room established by A. Crosman, editor of the *Canadian Casket*, a literary publication, in J. G. Hathaway's hotel. To his stock of "Religious, Political and Literary newspapers from all parts of British America and the United States," Mr. Crosman added as a bonus the ample attractions of Mr. Hathaway's bar and table.

To this era belongs one further important development. In 1834 under Allan MacNab, Hamilton took one of the first steps in the province towards railway development—a development which would "make" the city but in the process would also bankrupt her—by obtaining a charter to build the London and Gore railway from Burlington Bay to London, with an extension to Windsor and Sarnia.

To kindle public interest the first railroad meeting in the city was held on the John Street market. *Pièce de résistance* was an ox roasted whole— ". . . or rather warmed up," says a record of the day, "for it proved almost completely raw and hunks were used by the boys to play ball, with catchers coming off worst."

The following year MacNab obtained a second act authorising shareholders to construct a railroad between Hamilton and Port Dover on Lake Erie, with Oswego the American terminus across the lake. MacNab himself became president.

Although the road was publicized widely in the United States by agent MacNab and a considerable block of stock subscribed, the project lapsed for many years. Although numerous lines were chartered in the 1830's and early 1840's the time had not yet come for railroad building in Canada for various reasons: the convenience, comfort, cheapness and romance of steamship travel; the rebellion of 1837 and its ensuing economic depression; and diversion of funds to the building of canals and the public roads whose improvement was vital to existing stage coach travel.

In his appreciation of the commercial importance to both province and city of rail facilities, Allan MacNab was before his time. Without his efforts and those of Jasper T. Gilkison, secretary of the Great Western railway company, successor to the London and Gore, and of Isaac Buchanan, a prominent pioneer Upper Canada wholesale merchant and federal member of parliament for Hamilton from 1857-1865, the Great Western undoubtedly would not have been built when it was and furthermore would have bypassed Hamilton for the escarpment top and Ancaster or Dundas.

The arrival of rail would find Hamilton a city. Although the Act of

Incorporation[7] was passed by the legislature in the summer of 1846, it did not take effect until the January 1847 election, the city-elect in the interim being governed by the board of police under President Daniel MacNab. Hamilton did not attain cityhood without pointed comment from neighbouring communities, with insinuations that her census of 6,832 had been attained by including names of citizens then domiciled in local graveyards and/or taking the city roster on the day a well publicized festivity had swelled town ranks with visitors.

As a city Hamilton widened its boundaries to Emerald Street on the east, Paradise Road on the west, Aberdeen on the south, and Burlington Bay and the marsh (Coote's Paradise) on the north. By the new City Charter of September 9th, 1846, city wards were increased to five and names substituted for numbers, the wards being now St. George's, St. Patrick's, St. Lawrence, St. Andrew's and St. Mary's. Each ward elected two councillors, these ten members at a later date elected an eleventh, and at a subsequent meeting the eleven from their number elected a mayor.

On January 15th Alexander Carpenter was chosen as the eleventh councillor,[8] and on the 16th Colin C. Ferrie was elected first mayor of the city of Hamilton. Besides routine procedures the new council took steps to obtain a loan to "liquidate the Debt of the late Corporation of the Town of Hamilton, and to devise a city Seal."

On March 15th city council held the first council meeting in the market hall, from this time forward known as City Hall. An unimpressive building, the hall's thirty feet of frontage facing on James Street contained two entrances, each gained by a short flight of steps. As an architectural gesture the hall was surmounted by a small square tower and dome, replaced in 1873 by a four-storey patterned brick tower, partly projecting beyond the old frontage. On the ground floor and in the basement a brisk trade was carried on in butter and eggs, poultry and meat. The upper storey was an open hall with the city clerk's office at the rear, and opposite, at the east end of the building, a stage for local and travelling talent.

The community centre of the future, the little hall afforded entertainment as diverse as boxing matches and balls, including the highly popular Bachelors' Ball, an annual return for hospitality offered by the town's eligible males; performing bears and panoramas, the latter the forerunner of modern cinema; vocalists and elocutionists; and painters with their accompanying exhibits. Impartially the hall hosted business and social meetings; accepted sessions of the Amateur Hamilton band; and welcomed church bazaar, Oriental juggler or the Young Men's Debating club.

Theatre was always popular, performed either by touring troupes or by the local Gentlemen Amateurs of the Theatre, undoubtedly originators of Little Theatre in the community. The Amateurs' success seems proved

Hoax picture of George Hamilton, founder of the city. (Public Archives of Canada.)

Market house and later city hall, built in 1839, with projecting five-storey clock tower of patterned brick added in 1873. (J. Ross Robertson Collection, Toronto Public Library.)

Fourth and present municipal building, opened by Governor-General Georges P. Vanier, November 21, 1960. (Tom Bochsler.)

Colin C. Ferrie, 1847, first mayor of the city of Hamilton. (Hamilton Spectator.)

Lloyd D. Jackson, mayor, 1950-1962. (Rose Photography, Hamilton.)

Victor Kennedy Copps, elected mayor 1963. (Cambridge Studio.)

Third city hall, erected 1888. (City Engineering Department.)

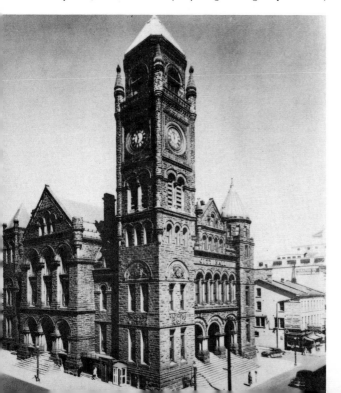

Royal Hotel, 1858-1935, with its 186 rooms the centre of Hamilton's social life in the 19th century. (V. Karklins, City Engineering Department.)

Original pumping station, opened 1860. (Hamilton Public Library.)

Interior of the old pumping station, still usable. (Hamilton Spectator.)

Gore Park, 1862. Fountain in rear stands before Wesleyan Ladies' College, site of today's Sheraton Connaught Hotel. (Public Archives of Canada.)

Soaring hyperbolic paraboloid pumping station in colourful orange, green and grey.
(City Engineering Department.)

Dundurn Castle from the rear. Residence of Sir Allan Napier MacNab in the 1850s. (Bochsler Studio Ltd.)

Fire equipment at the gutting of Nicholson's Block, February 15, 1875. (Public Archives of Canada.)

*Mrs. William Gourlay, nee Emily
Esther Elizabeth Whyte, daughter of
Isabella Hyde.* (Frank Wright.)

Colonel William Gourlay, aged 25.
(Frank Wright.)

Barton Lodge, mountain-top home of the Whyte-Gourlay families. (Frank Wright.)

Early Tiger football team. Left to right: W. Marriott, R. Isbister, G. Ballard, R. C. Ripley, D. McCarthy, H. Murray, S. S. Dumoulin, D. McKeand, A. Moore, D. Lyons, B. Simpson, D Tope, W. Burkholder, J. Craig. (A. M. Cunningham.)

At Oldtimers' Night of the Leander Boat Club, three 1912 Grey Cup champion Alerts greet Pinky Lewis. From left: Dutch Becker, Pinky, star lineman Norm Clark who was also on Tiger Grey Cup teams of 1913 and 1915, and outside wing Red Fisher. (Hamilton Spectator.)

by their donating fifteen pounds, net profit of a first night's performance, to council who established a fund for a town clock.

On certain evenings, determined by the president of the board of police, the hall's first concessionaire, Sam Webb, was licensed to sell ginger beer within its walls.

With advent of city status the upper hall was outfitted as a council chamber, complete with mayor's chair, council meetings having previously been held in the Engine House or—possibly more enjoyably—at John Bradley's or some other tavern. To outfit the chamber the old furnishings were moved from the Engine House.

Following establishment of the James Street market the John Street fell into disuse, eventually becoming restricted to Tuesday and Saturday sale of hay, augmented by one butcher stall. Its principal customers were livery stables and delivery companies. The motor age spelled the death warrant of the old Haymarket, the rows of wagons of fragrant hay dwindling with the disappearance of the horse from city streets. Briefly it served as the city wood market. Today the only evidence of the once active market with its stalls, drinking fountain and trough and busy hay scale lies in the name Haymarket Square.

By the 1840's Hamilton was well advanced as an entrepôt and distribution centre of growing importance, with commercial interests far outstripping industry. Although the Desjardins canal had been built to establish Dundas as a port, it had also contributed to Hamilton's advancement, especially when deepening of the Burlington canal provided entrance to shipping of too great tonnage for the Desjardins canal.

In 1845 Dundas boasted twenty mills and factories to Hamilton's nine. Yet Hamilton's exports for the year totalled 85,049 barrels of produce to 63,926 from Dundas, an excess of twenty-five per cent.[9] Hamilton's completion of the famous Plank Road to Port Dover had opened to her the settlements on the Grand River and Lake Erie which MacNab had planned to link still more closely with his proposed Hamilton-Port Dover rail line. From surrounding districts came much of Hamilton's exports.

Hamilton had also profited from the opening of the Welland canal in the 1820's and had supported through her parliamentary representative, Sir Allan, reconstruction and deepening of the waterway in 1845. Coinciding with the 1848 completion of the St. Lawrence canals this enabled shipping, up to 140 feet in length, or 26-foot beam, and 9-foot draught, to sail for the first time from Montreal to Chicago. In the following decade would come the railways. Together the two would ensure Hamilton's future as the leading community at the head of the lake.

Elated with the town's developing economy thirty-six prominent businessmen met on April 29th, 1845, at the Royal Exchange hotel and inaugurated a board of trade to foster the community's interests. First president was the Hon. Isaac Buchanan, with Daniel MacNab, vice-president, and Hugh Cossart Baker, secretary-treasurer.

97

Mr. Baker, then twenty-six years of age, was the first manager of the first branch of the Bank of Montreal in Hamilton, opened in November, 1843. In August, 1847, with other Hamilton businessmen he founded the Canada Life Assurance Company, the first Canadian company to write insurance, and became its first manager, actuary and president. Desiring to insure his life Mr. Baker applied to British companies and learned that to obtain a policy he would have to travel to New York for the necessary examination. After making the arduous thousand-mile round trip he determined to found a Canadian company for Canadians. The first policy issued by the new company, established in rented quarters in the Mechanics' Institute, James Street North—a site now occupied by the T. Eaton Company Limited—went to Hugh Cossart Baker.

In 1856 the young Canadian company moved to the handsome three-storey stone Canada Life building which it erected on James Street South, where the Pigott building now stands. Founding of the company added another head office to the city.

On the opposite, east side of James Street North, facing the market, another Hamilton institution was founded in 1846 when the first edition of a semiweekly *The Spectator* was peeled from the flatbed press in a small print shop above the drugstore of Dalley and Stevens. A family affair, *The Spectator* was owned and edited by young, zealous Robert Reid Smiley, with John Douglass as associate editor and Mr. Smiley's brothers, Hugh and John, assisting in publication.

The first issue of *The Spectator,* named in admiration of Joseph Addison, dealt with the defects and annoyances of the postal system in Canada with its high rates of postage and slow and awkward delivery; and with Sir Robert Peel's unpopular Free Trade measure. Abolition of the preferential Empire tariff was feared in Canada, and nowhere more than in Hamilton, where free trade threatened the town's budding mercantile development. Yet eventually Britain's Free Trade policy would have a worldwide effect and work to Canada's advantage by relaxing United States' trade barriers.

If there was a changing economic tempo at mid-century, there was also a changing political atmosphere. *The Spectator* itself was witness to that change. Hamilton was a Tory city, a city that favoured Allan Napier MacNab not William Lyon Mackenzie, the Family Compact not the reformers. A city as class conscious as any British rural shire, with its distinction of yeoman and squire. A city where birth and breeding were passports to position, and wealth while an asset, was less important than good connections. A city where learning was considered an upper class prerogative.

Yet in the very heart of this conservative stronghold a new element was rising, one favouring a broader conservatism than that of the high and hidebound tories, the policy of John A. Macdonald rather than that of John Strachan. To give voice and leadership to this new conservative cause Robert Smiley was invited by Hamilton businessmen to set up his journal in Hamilton in competition with the extremist Tory *Western Mercury* edited by James Johnson, and the Liberal *Hamilton Free Press,* publisher, William Smith.

While failing dismally, Mackenzie's rebellion had nevertheless achieved its end. It had focused attention of the home government on the colony and led to the despatch to Canada of John George Lambton, Earl of Durham, to enquire into the recent trouble. Durham's celebrated "Report on the Affairs of British North America," to the indignant disbelief of MacNab and other Family Compact leaders, advocated responsible government as a solution of the country's problems.

In Canada the report was published and debated at widespread "Durham meetings." In Hamilton for the first time MacNab found his militant conservatism opposed not only by staunch reformers such as Jacob and Joseph Rymal but by men of his own party, as William Chisholm, who had fought beside him in suppressing the rebellion but who now espoused a program of reform and moderation.

In 1840-1841 the Act of Union reunited the provinces of Lower and Upper Canada as Canada East and Canada West, in the first rudimentary step towards Confederation. When the first united legislative assembly formally resolved that the executive council should "possess the confidence of the elected representatives of the people," namely the legislative assembly, the Hon. Robert Baldwin achieved a significant advance in his long struggle for responsible government. In 1842 the outmoded rule by magistrates of the Quarter Sessions Courts ended with establishment of district councils in Canada West, the first measure of municipal government. In the District of Gore, Henry Beasley, eldest son of Richard, was appointed first registrar, holding office four years. In 1844 he also became treasurer of the town of Hamilton. His marriage to Sophia, daughter of Jacob Burkholder and Catherine Maria Hesse, united three pioneer lakehead families.

On February 16th, 1842, Richard Beasley died and was laid in Christ's Church burying ground, his stone proclaiming him: "The first settler at the head of the Lake." His wife survived him four years. Through succeeding generations their family would serve the community, two of his daughters as wives of Hamilton mayors, Catherine marrying Colin Campbell Ferrie, son of the Hon. Adam Ferrie, and Keziah wedding Nehemiah Ford, Hamilton's chief executive in 1852, while Thomas C. Beasley, son of Henry, would serve for fifty-three years as city clerk.

With Richard Beasley, another era of public figures passed from the civic stage. In 1843 Col. James M. Whyte died at the age of fifty-five and was buried on the north side of St. Andrew's Presbyterian Church, James Street South, a small frame edifice built in 1833 for the congregation of the Rev. Alexander Gale, and occupying the site of later St. Paul's. Colonel Whyte's death preceded by a year the disruption of the Presbyterian Kirk in Scotland, which had its repercussion of schism here, splitting St. Andrew's and resulting in founding of Knox Church, James Street North, by Mr. Gale.

On July 1st, 1844, the town lost one of its most faithful citizens, John Law, aged forty-six, schoolmaster and barrister, and noted also as father of "golden-haired Maggie, the prettiest girl in Hamilton."

In 1848 William Case, M.D., the Elder, born in 1776, was laid to rest in the Hamilton family plot on the mountainside, his grave being later marked by the Hamilton Medical Society as that of the first medical practitioner in the district. When construction of mountain roads led to removal of remains from the Hamilton burial plot to the Hamilton cemetery on Burlington Heights, the box tomb of Dr. Case was left in lonely solitude. In 1951 it was similarly removed.

Still another casualty, with its disbanding in 1843, was the 1st Battalion, Incorporated Militia, raised three hundred strong in the district late in 1838 following the rebellion and trained to an unusual degree of military efficiency for the times. First O.C. was Sir Allan MacNab, succeeded by Col. William Gourlay of the 12th Regiment, Gore District Militia, a veteran of the Napoleonic Wars, and MacNab's right hand man during the Mackenzie rebellion. Drilling with military precision before Burley's Promenade Hotel the 1st Battalion had afforded a lively spectacle with their shakos, scarlet coatees, pipe-clayed crossbelts and blue "trowsers".

Yet since there is always compensation, in the years ahead the city would have Dr. William Craigie, the tall spare Scottish physician known and loved by the whole countryside, founder in 1850 of the Hamilton Horticultural Society; Isaac Buchanan, ardent supporter of the Free Kirk, who laid the cornerstone of Knox Church in April, 1856, and whose public announcement that he would contribute two hundred and fifty dollars to every congregation in Upper Canada that within a stated time would build a church and name it Knox[10] led to acceptance of his offer at least in Dundas, Galt, Guelph, Acton and St. Catharines.

The future would bring the Right Rev. John Farrell, D.D., first bishop of the Roman Catholic diocese of Hamilton, founded on February 17th, 1865, with St. Mary's Church the Cathedral church of the diocese; the gentle Sisters of St. Joseph; the still active Hamilton Association for the Advancement of Literature, Science and Art, founded in 1857 under President Rev. William Ormiston, first minister of Central Presbyterian Church; and Rev. David Inglis, pastor of MacNab Street Presbyterian Church from 1855 to 1872.

11

Market Place, Lights, and the Whistling Iron Horse

IN 1850 Hamilton's population topped 10,000. With 1860 it had almost doubled. Of necessity such an increase brought its changes to the city. In 1849 a new act,[1] with revisions in 1850 and '51, extended city limits on the east to Wentworth Street; provided for an annual salary not exceeding £100 to the mayor at discretion of council; and increased the number of city council members by adding an alderman to the two councillors in each ward. From these aldermen, superior in standing to councillors and requiring greater property qualifications, the mayor was chosen.

Understandably two clauses of the new act elicited council's express disapproval: one restraining the issue by the city of notes, bills, or other security for an amount less than £25, thus eliminating a former important source of revenue, and the other requiring the corporation to pay, within the year of their falling due, all debts and liabilities. The act also required the annual publication of corporation accounts by the city auditors.

On January 9th, 1850, the first council under the new act was elected and sworn. Two weeks later council met and elected John Fisher mayor, then adjourning, accompanied His Worship to the chambers of Miles O'Reilly, socially conscious, handsome and popular judge of the county court, where the oath of office was administered.

In 1851 another innovation was introduced with the election of two aldermen, two councillors, an inspector of houses of public entertainment,[2] and a school trustee for each ward. This was accomplished on three consecutive days of voting, with the mayor, John R. Holden, elected two weeks later. In 1854 the disadvantages of this method of electing a chief executive became apparent when all ten aldermen on council were successively nominated and voted down, and Aldermen Charles A. Sadleir, lawyer, and Hutchinson Clark, architect and contractor, were refused a second time.

On the thirteenth ballot James Cummings—who ironically had been first nominee—received a tie vote and Councillor Joseph Faulkner, as member having highest assessment, was called upon to cast the deciding vote which he gave in Mr. Cummings' favour. Although Alderman Sadleir verbally protested Mayor Cummings' election, on the ground that Councillor Faulkner did not own and had not paid his taxes on the land assessed to him, the election was upheld by the exhausted council. On February 20th, however, the Court of Queen's Bench pronounced Alderman Cummings' election null and void, whereupon Alderman Charles Magill was elected by council and sworn in by Chief Magistrate G. H. Armstrong. Interestingly, the same court also declared invalid the election of Charles A. Sadleir, who was replaced. In 1859 election of a mayor was established at the polls.

Whatever the manner of election, each year the city's new council was confronted with the intensifying headache of the city debt. By 1849 and the new act of incorporation, city indebtedness had reached an overall of £18,962.14.4 in hand, plus the sum of the corporation's unsettled and later maturing accounts. Against this the city had on the credit side real estate estimated at £11,250; certain unpaid taxes of 1848; and amounts, frequently of long standing and difficult to collect, owed by absentee landowners.

It was the city's backlog of debt that constituted the chief stumbling block to financial solvency. Otherwise population was increasing, assessments were high enough to arouse protest, the tax rate had mounted from 2d. to 1/s in the £, and city revenue from market rentals, licenses and fees was satisfactory.

On December 31, 1849, the retiring finance committee reported the net debt of the city as £27,234.8.1, with £1,150 additional accounts unsettled, an amount notably in excess of its estimates.. The committee offered a helpful hint to its successor in office.

"Committee of 1850," suggested committee of 1849, "being entirely unrestricted in its powers of taxation,³ will be able to stay the increase of city debts, and may well deem it more prudent to make an effort to liquidate the present debt as it falls due." Accepting the suggestion the committee of 1850 established a tax rate of 1s.6d. in the £;⁴ a rate increased in 1854 to 3s; and in 1860 to 20 cents (not mills) on the dollar.

Not all of this rise in tax rate was due to council. Nor did it result from normal community growth and expansion. With the mounting tide of immigration from the British Isles came recurrent bouts of ship fever and cholera. Smallpox too made periodic visitations.

On June 7th, 1847, in expectation of government support, a board of health was established in Hamilton prior to the immigrant season and a health officer, Henry John Williams, appointed with authority to erect hospital buildings and engage nurses; to arrange for special constables to protect immigrants; and special scavengers to promote sanitary measures in the immigrant sheds and the town. At this time garbage and refuse heaps were ordered cleared from streets and back yards only twice a year, open cess pools were common, privies frequently drained into roadside ditches, and a by-law was later passed to fine individuals who dumped offal, decayed meat or dead carcases in the street.

In January of the new year an epidemic of smallpox led council to procure a house for patients afflicted with the disease; and resulted in the first public mass health program in city history, free clinic vaccination of the children of the poor. Operating in pairs, ten doctors[5] conducted after-noon clinics at city hall on Wednesdays and Saturdays for three weeks in February. Almost simultaneously with this, discovering that government funds were not forthcoming, council dispensed with the board of health, dismissed the health officer, and closed the hospital.

Confronted with a population crowding 10,000, however, and the century's seasonal epidemics of typhus, smallpox, diphtheria and scarlet fever, even a frugal city council had to surrender. Within two weeks, the city established another board of health, appointed Dr. John W. Hunter city physician and later re-engaged Mr. Williams as medical health officer.

The city physician received a salary of £30 per annum, finding his own medicines; the health officer a monthly £5, later, because of the unpleasant, arduous and even dangerous nature of his duties, raised to £7.10.0 and made five months retroactive, an unheard-of procedure. Again the health officer was empowered to obtain a building for a hospital. The small house on Catharine Street which he rented and which was visited and approved on October 2nd, 1848, by a committee of city council may be considered Hamilton's first permanent hospital, since the city's monthly financial statements show it was still in operation in July of the following year. It was superintended by a matron, Mrs. Woodside, who received a pound a week and board. Later, upon admittance of male patients—"the first three labouring under typhus, one in a filthy state and all requiring an immediate change of linen, to be purchased by the health officer"—Mr. Woodside was engaged as assistant at 15s a week.

Although they approved the Catharine Street hospital the committee found it already crowded with only four patients. They recommended rental or erection of a building which might combine facilities of hospital and workhouse, thus relieving council of the problem of caring for indigents whose number was increasing alarmingly with the growth of the city, and who had an embarrassing habit, on occasion, of dying in unconventional and public places. Although burial charges of the day would send a modern mortician into shock, they were paid grudgingly by the city, as council minutes show: "For making a coffin for a man that died under Mr. Chatfield's shed, 10/S . . . Coffin for Cornell and digging a grave, 12s. 6d. . . . Burial of Annie Boyle, a woman of the town, 15/S. Coffin, 10/S.; coffin and grave digging, 12s. 6d.; coffin, grave digging and burial, 15/S: $2.40, $3 and $3.60." Even at this figure there must have been a margin of profit for we have record of one taxpayer petitioning council to take coffins in payment of his taxes.

As a result of the committee's above recommendation it was determined to erect a hospital on two acres of city property, previously purchased from Robert J. Hamilton, lying just below the Mountain at the head of Cherry Street, the present Ferguson Avenue. That Robert Jarvis and his neighbours did not appreciate a city hospital and workhouse in their midst seems obvious from a petition against the proposed site carrying Mr. Hamilton's signature and three hundred others. Already community encroachment on Hamilton suzerainty had led to disputes with council over a road right-of-way to the mountain top at the head of James Street, and another easterly across Hamilton property from John Street, later Arkledun Avenue.

A comfortable two-storey white frame building shaded by oaks and willows, the hospital hugged the lower hillside beneath the Wellington Street quarry, immediately south of the present high level pumping station. Situated on two acres of forested land later fenced, the building faced north on Aurora Street which ran east from Cherry. Although a single building, the hospital served in a dual capacity as a hospital housing in-patients and "out-door pauper patients", and as a poorhouse. Rules of admission required a certificate signed by a clergyman or magistrate attesting to the applicant's destitution, or by the city physician stating the patient's disease and whether curable or incurable. Possibly as an inspiration to both ill and indigent, the city fathers named the new institution the House of Industry. At £60 per annum John Wilson and his wife, as superintendent and matron, and their daughter were engaged to take charge.

Simultaneously with this, in May, 1848, with council capital support of £50 towards rental and furnishings and a maintenance allowance of 2s.6d. per week per inmate, the Ladies' Benevolent society, a strong Protestant charitable institution, established an Orphan asylum, which shortly harboured some twenty of the surprisingly large number of orphans in the community.

In 1849, another cholera year fell with a crushing weight on the city's already shaky financial structure.

Until the late 1840's the government, now of the united Canadas, established in Montreal, had assumed a share of the burden thrust upon port towns by its immigration policy, maintaining local "emigrant" (properly, immigrant) agencies in season, operating local emigrant sheds and hospitals—in Hamilton situated on the bay front south of the later Stuart Street station—and contributing to the cost of operation of local boards of health. In 1848, with £400 still owing the city from the previous year, the government discontinued all financial aid, closed the Emigrant agency, and directed Dr. Dickinson, council-appointed emigrant physician, to close the emigrant hospital and transfer its patients to the care of the Hamilton board of health.

The year 1849 was a staggering one for the city. During the five-month shipping season Hamilton received 2,910 immigrants forwarded by the Chief Emigrant agent on free ticket, in addition to hundreds who paid their passage; provided the destitute with bread; maintained the emigrant hospital where 244 patients were treated; buried 66, and shipped hundreds hastily out of town to other communities. Many received private assistance. That the newcomers were largely destitute, many widows with small children, and others unemployable, added to the city's difficulties. Yet urgent deputations to Montreal and to the Governor-General brought only the curt reply that "should there be a surplus of the Emigrant Tax at the end of the season," Hamilton would not be forgotten.

Eventually the government offered compensation for the £700 which the city had by then expended. When the emigrant hospital was closed on November 18th and the remaining patients transferred to the House of Industry, the government offered hospital and furnishings as a gift to the city. Fortunately council discovered in time that acceptance of the building included taking over a large outstanding account owing to Mr. Tiffany for rent, and also implied willingness to assume any future expenses of immigrants to the port. The offer was refused.

As if to compensate for the ominous ending of the 1840's, the 1850's opened on a brighter note for the city. In November of 1848, the grim grey month of the year that most needed illumination, the city hall took a step forward when candlelight gave way to spirit gas and at a cost of five pounds, two globe lamps, with permission of the insurance companies, were installed in the hall. Up to this time candlepower had been the main indoor illuminant, with fish oil or candlelit lanterns and torches carried outdoors, and with social events planned by almanack for the full of the moon. Now candles were increasingly augmented by "burning fluid" and camphene—"and mighty dangerous things they were to handle," comments a bygone periodical. On the streets, lamps designed and manufactured in local tin shops and mounted on posts at the principal corners had been dimly lightening the gloom for six years, their motive power fish oil and camphene, the latter added to whiten and clarify the dull heavy light produced by fish oil alone.

Until the middle of the century this remained the *status quo*. By 1850, however, the bright white light of gas had begun to illuminate North America. Not only was gas more brilliant and cleaner but from estimates obtained in a survey of thirty-eight leading cities of the United States, gas cost materially less to light a community than did oil and candles. With the unbridled enthusiasm for progress which in general marked the middle nineteenth century, the corporation explored the possibility of building a gas plant under public ownership to supply the city with light. When this became a financial impossibility, leading citizens formed the Hamilton Gas Light Company,[7] and in eight months erected a plant on Mulberry Street to manufacture gas from coal, laid pipes, and placed gas lamps throughout the business district.

The gas company promised to have the town illuminated for Christmas but was only partially successful. The streets remained in darkness but stores, the town hall, the police station and many residences were lighted, the first private home in Hamilton to have gas being Dr. Gerald O'Reilly's big square brick mansion located on the northwest corner of King Street and Mary, across King Street from Dr. William Case's home.

From miles around people drove into town to admire the new illumination and its effect on stores and homes. On January 31st, 1851, with great éclat, some fifty street lamps were lit, with fire departments of Hamilton and Dundas celebrating the event with a parade and bands, followed by a "grand supper" at Young's hotel, courtesy of the Gas Light company.

At $4 per 1,000 cubic feet, the Hamilton company supplied its product at a price lower than any other in Canada. Beginning with 50 street lamps and 125 residence and business consumers, the company by 1857 had increased the output to more than 640 consumers and 290 street lamps and was able to reduce its rates to $3.50 per 1,000 cubic feet and still pay a dividend of ten per cent. At this price a small family, by exercising care, could light their home and cook with gas at 50 to 75 cents a week. So valuable did Gas Light stock become that only rarely did a share change hands.

Featured in an age of thrift, the company's contract with the corporation called for lamps to be lit one-half hour after sunset and extinguished one and one-half hours before sunrise, with no lighting on moonlit nights. As a concession, unusual to other Canadian communities except Toronto where lamps were lighted the year round, two extra nights of lighting per month were allowed for cloudy or rainy weather.

A constant source of fascination to children was the nightly lighting of the lamps. Singly and in small wondering groups, they followed the lamplighter and his ladder as he wended his way through the streets in the gathering dusk, setting his yellow tongues of flame alight. As fascinating and more impressive, even to their elders, were the gas fixtures of the town hall: in the council chamber a four-branch gas lamp suspended from the centerpiece, with two jointed bracket jets flanking the mayor's chair; a bracket jet for the clerk's office; and for the public hall two pendants, each with two branches and twelve jets apiece. In the beginning many people believed that the flame itself travelled along the pipes and could not understand why they remained cool to the touch.

With street lighting came improvement in the original rutted tracks and bordering footpaths of the early community. With pick and shovel, with oxen and chains, stones were dug out and stumps removed. Stumps were a particular hazard, on occasion causing serious injury to riders and occupants of vehicles in Hamilton streets. Until after the middle of the century mention of them occurs in council minutes. In the capital, York, so widespread was the nuisance that a Stump act was passed and later adopted by other communities whereby anyone found intoxicated in public might be sentenced to remove a certain number of stumps from the public way.

"After his 'community service,' " says Edwin C. Guillet,[1] the historian, "the culprit was usually very sober and very tired, and did not repeat his offence."

In the beginning roads and paths were maintained by the four ward pathmasters[8] with statute labour, an annual levy of road work (or its paid equivalent) required by law of every able-bodied man in the community. Initially roads were scraped, the worst hummocks ploughed down, the most treacherous hollows casually filled; gutters were dug to channel off the water seasonally flooding the majority of streets, including John and James, Main Street and King, and culverts were installed. Planked sidewalks, graded and gravelled roads, macadam: step by step the town progressed. Sidewalks varied according to the importance of the street: on James a sidewalk six feet wide laid crossways; on John a similar, four feet wide; on lesser thoroughfares three planks wide, lengthways; and barest utilitarian gesture, a two-plank-wide or even a single-plank footway.

In 1844 John Street was ordered macadamized, the first in the city, from King Street to the corner of R. J. Hamilton's front yard fence, undoubtedly to connect with the Port Dover Road, and planked from King Street to the bay. Not until 1847 was King Street graded, bridged against streams, and macadamized from the western city limits at Queen Street to Wentworth on the east, including the full width of the Gore, where the land dedicated to the city by George Hamilton added to the sixty-six feet of concession road allowance created a thoroughfare two hundred and thirty feet in width.

Except at the Gore, the street was cobbled a mere twenty feet wide, although certain long-visioned members of the community advocated that the width of King throughout its entire length should be what it was at James Street. Were this done, they contended, King Street would surpass in extent and beauty any other street of any city in Western Canada (Ontario) and in fact possibly North America, excepting Pennsylvania Avenue, Washington, D.C. "Imagine," they enthused,[9] "what a street, two or three miles in length, would be in such a city. Contrast it with the narrow dismal winding alleys of Montreal, New York or Boston, and you have the modern enterprise of the 19th century side by side with the limited sluggish spirit of the past."

Land was not dear in the mid-1800's and much of the length advocated lay through farm land, undeveloped land and swamp. Frequently civic-minded landowners gave street allowance for the advantage of having their property opened up. But a road two hundred and thirty feet wide! Such ideas, property owners cried, might be all right for these radical town planners, but conservative citizens needed to keep their feet on the ground. Thus so narrowly did Hamilton miss the asset of a Canadian Avenida da Liberdad.

What Hamilton streets lacked in breadth, however, they made up in activity. Horses, cattle, swine, dogs and geese pass in a continuous procession through council minutes: horses ridden furiously; teams and wagons rocking along main streets—James, most frequently—in an Upper Canada version of the Roman chariot race; runaways, wandering horses, impounded horses, and horses advertised and auctioned off . . . similarly cows, more placid, but deadly in gardens . . . swine, worst of all, rooting up turf, flower and vegetable beds indiscriminately . . . and annually a mad dog scare and all dogs chained.

A lively institution the local pound, breeder of animosity and outlet for grudges, since anyone who found a footloose animal could drive it to the pound and collect half the fine imposed. An unpopular citizen the poundkeeper. For the most part exasperated owners protested their fines but paid. Occasionally, however, one of sterner stuff at night removed palings from the fence or broke open the gate, permitting a general exodus and an empty enclosure to greet the morning's sun.

To the above vocal animal population, in streets eternally cluttered with construction materials and debris and lively with the buzzing of flies and chirping of sparrows feasting on horse droppings in the warm dust, add the commonplace sounds of humans going about their business: ladies in bonnets and dust-sweeping gowns waited on by obsequious merchants within the sanctum of their shops or at outdoor sidewalk displays beneath wooden canopies designed to attract the carriage trade; gentlemen suitably attired in stovepipe hats and cutaway coats; workmen in corduroy and homespun breeches or pants; and children, smaller replicas of their elders—and one has Hamilton downtown thoroughfares of the mid-nineteenth century.

Add impressive buildings, business and mercantile establishments and private residences, with a complete block of stone south of the Gore. Add too to the scents of summer, for final flavour, the identifying aromas wafting from shop entrances as one passes: the sharp astringent smell of new cambric, flannelette and cotton . . . malodorous fish . . . mouthwatering freshly baked bread . . . the sharp clean tang of oranges and the sensuous musk of overripe bananas . . . the oldtime grocery potpourri of coffee and spices, brown sugar, open tub pickles and strong cheese in the round . . . and a rancid whiff of cellar.

On January 17th, 1854, the streets were *en fête* for the most exciting event in the city's history to that date, completion of the Great Western rail line from Suspension Bridge at Niagara Falls to Windsor on the American border.

In 1837 council had requested citizens to illuminate their homes to signal passage of the Railway bill. Now celebrations went far beyond mere illumination. Main streets were decorated with flags, bunting and streamers, and at the northern intersection of King and James stood a triumphal arch erected by the local fire brigade.

Earlier, in November, 1853, the arrival of the first train on the first 43-mile leg of the Great Western line, from Suspension Bridge to Hamilton, had been appropriately celebrated. Special recognition had then been paid to Isaac Buchanan, wholesale merchant and later member of parliament for Hamilton, for his promotion of the railway, a poem, "The Iron and the Fire," being dedicated to him. Two verses are quoted:

"Hurrah for the straight, hard iron road!
For the fire horse swift and strong!
Hurrah, for the pond'rous chariot train
That fleetly speeds along.

Hail Canada! Thy fame, in part,
Is shadowed here today
When sounds the steam car's whistle loud
Round our Commercial Bay."

A month later, on December 17th, the Hamilton-London division had been completed,[10] and on the following January 17th the last spike in the completed main line was driven. At 2 a.m. on the 18th a train from the Falls carrying several hundred passengers en route to Detroit pulled into the Stuart Street station, to be met by hundreds of Hamiltonians who had been waiting its advent in neighbouring bars and were consequently well fortified against the chill January night and the half frozen ankle-deep mud of the streets leading to the depot.

Suddenly the clear icy air was shaken by an ear-splitting blast echoed by a hundred shouts: "The train from the Falls is in!" Contributing to the ensuing bedlam was the salute of the Rochester Brass Band which accompanied the American delegation and which now greeted the jubilant stationful of fanatics with the strains of "Yankee Doodle" and "Long Live the Queen." Complete strangers shook hands and slapped one another upon the back, offered drinks, or issued invitations to breakfast before the train pulled out for Detroit at six.

Sharp on time the wasp-waisted woodburner, piled high with fuel, chuffed its way out of the station and along the broad gauge (5′ 6″) tracks lined by thousands of spectators from Hamilton and the surrounding district. Thirty minutes later it was followed by a second "special," made up hurriedly to accommodate the passenger demand. Even with two trains of twenty-four cars, however, hundreds were left behind. Although there was standing room only, at each stop additional passengers crowded aboard until when the trains reached Windsor they disgorged one thousand celebrants.

Reception of the Canadian contingent, taken by ferry across the river, featured an artillery salute and participation in a giant parade which included vounteer cavalry and militia companies in resplendent uniforms, fire companies with their equipment, and numerous bands. The streets, decorated with arches of American and British flags and crowded with spectators, were brilliant with lights, with hotels and public buildings illuminated from top to bottom. In the freight house of the Michigan

109

Central Railway company, decorated with wreaths and festoons of ever-greens, with bunting and banners, two thousand guests sat down to an invitation banquet. Head table decorations included pyramids of flags and reproductions of a bridge and a locomotive flanking a Temple of Liberty. As many of the guests had neither eaten nor drunk for twelve hours, there being no food aboard the train, the manner in which the viands and champagne vanished was described as astonishing.

Even the reporters, present from eleven American cities as well as Canada, were impressed. Said one prominent American newsman: "The long rows of joyous faces, the blazing light," (every pane of glass in the huge building was illuminated) "the glitter from the profusion of glass and plate upon the snowy cloths, with the low hum of many voices con-versing, altogether presented a scene of magnificence seldom seen more than once in a lifetime."

In the numberless toasts which followed, the general sentiment of the times prevailed: the Mississippi is united to the Atlantic. East and west are bound together by ligaments of iron, the Hudson, the Niagara, the Detroit and the great father of waters. The voice of destiny and progress bears us onward. Young America comprises the earnest, the strong, the young blood which must go forward. Conflict lies behind. Together the lion of Great Britain and the eagle of the United States will unite in a friendly contest for triumph in the arts of peace.

At noon the following day the train left for the return celebration in Hamilton, carrying as many Detroit visitors as could crowd aboard. All were thoroughly inoculated with the mass hysteria which seized North America in the opening years of the railway era. If the rail line came to town, the community's future was assured; if it went elsewhere, the community was doomed.

Under the spell of this hypothesis it was possible for Hamilton city council in 1850, with an assessment of £61,359 and an annual revenue of less than £5,968, faced with major city works in streets and in sewer and waterworks systems, to subscribe £100,000 in Great Western railway stock.[11] Of this amount £50,000 was to be raised at once by debentures to be met on maturity by a special tax levied on the city—in addition to the annual rate—of 1s in the pound in 1851 and the following four years: 1s. 3d. in 1856-1860 inclusive; 1s 6d. in 1861-1865; 2s in 1866-1869; and in 1870 a tax of 6s 4d. in the pound.

Council's viewpoint was the optimistic one of administrations in gen-eral throughout the city's history: if council is faced with a problem, the farther ahead it can be projected, the less difficult it will become for a future administration to deal with it. In defence of the council of 1850, it must be stated that council considered that dividends forthcoming on Great Western company stock would considerably offset the city's obliga-tion in meeting maturing debentures.

As on the trip to Detroit the return journey was slowed by frequent stops to refuel at forest woodpiles where passengers tumbled out of the carriages to stretch their legs and possibly to help load the engine. At Hamilton a 21-gun salute welcomed the delegation. In a later procession which formed at the Gore and marched through the principal streets, the Artillery company, led by Captain Alfred Booker, and the police were followed by St. George's, St. Andrew's, St. Patrick's and the Highland societies, and these by local and neighbouring fire brigades, all accompanied by bands. Arm in arm marched Hamilton's Mayor James Cummings and the mayor of Rochester, followed by local magistrates and Hamilton city council, to be greeted from every window and balcony along the route by the fluttering handkerchiefs of the fair sex.

To accommodate all attending, two banquets were arranged: one given by the Fire Brigade, Hook and Ladder company, to six hundred at city hall, with Terrence Branigan, James Street baker, supplying the ample meal; the other provided by the mayor and corporation in the newly erected Mechanics' building, a hand's span to the north, where a further trainload of guests from Detroit and points west was welcomed. This more lavish affair was catered by Thomas Davidson, proprietor of the City hotel who would later take over the Royal, the city's most palatial hotel of all time. In spite of the leanness of the civic purse council appropriated £500 for the city's entertainment, £95 for the firemen's.

Amongst those specially chosen for honour at the above festivities, one was notably absent, Sir Allan MacNab, father of the Great Western, being confined to his bed with a cold. Prior to the banquets, however, a parade which included the Artillery company marched to Dundurn where a 21-gun salute was fired in the doughty knight's honour. In response Sir Allan appeared briefly on the balcony to receive the cheers and congratulations of the paraders, even his disillusioned creditors and his business and political opponents forgetting their grievances for the time being.

Not to be outdone by the municipalities it serviced, the Great Western company for its part climaxed the various celebrations with a magnificent Railway ball held a few days later in the Mechanics' Institute hall and attended, according to *The Spectator*'s Editor Smiley, by "fifteen hundred gentle knights and ladies fair . . . from all parts of the province and the United States . . . a display of beauty and fashion . . . gorgeous and dazzling."

Dancing was enjoyed from nine o'clock until dawn, with three suppers served, the first at midnight with covers laid for seven hundred, followed by two smaller seatings thus permitting six to seven hundred dancers to remain at all times on the floor above. In keeping with the times, each repast was followed by a long roster of toasts. When morning dawned the Great Western was well launched. All that remained for the city was to meet the interest charges on the debentures and the debentures themselves as they matured.

On December 3rd, 1855, the opening of the Hamilton-Toronto line of the Great Western completed that railway's network about the head of the lake. Four years later construction of the Great Western shops in the city to manufacture railway rolling stock, the first in Canada, established Hamilton as the main terminal of the line. Procured largely through the efforts of Allan MacNab ("Railways are my politics!") and of Jasper T. Gilkison, the shops not only provided a strong impetus to Hamilton's industrial expansion but also encouraged harbour development.

Since 1846, Hamilton Bay had been vested in the corporation and the city represented by a council-appointed harbour master, although permission to erect buildings along the waterfront still remained with the Governor-in-Council. In 1846, a second widening of the Burlington canal had permitted entrance of larger vessels to the port, and in response to this three years later Aeneas D. MacKay, shipping agent recently arrived from Scotland, had constructed at the foot of James Street the first dock of any size in Hamilton, equipped to handle the vessels the MacKay firm operated on the lakes. West of this on the waterfront the Great Western in the 1850's built a grain elevator, a stark grey monument to progress, while across the bay at the present La Salle park appeared Brown's wharf (not to be confused with Browne's two wharves at the foot of Hughson and MacNab Streets) built to accommodate the extensive shipping of the north shore area. Over the years the wharf came to be a fuelling centre for the wood-burning steamers of the day, in one year 50,000 cords of wood cut from the surrounding district being taken aboard vessels.

The port brought prosperity, but what it gave with one hand it took, as before, with the other. In 1854 again it brought the cholera, and of the three major or worldwide epidemics introduced into Canada, this was the most virulent, especially for Hamilton, reportedly the hardest hit community in the province.

Again the dead wagons creaked through the streets of the city, gathering the blackened corpses, many deposited outside their doors by the fear-crazed inmates within; again wound their slow way up York Street to the quicklimed burial pits. Now, however, the sandy rutted track to the old military burying ground had become the graded "Road leading to the Upper Bridge at Burlington Heights," flanked on the west by the new Burlington cemetery,[12] enclosed by a six-foot close board fence.

Day after day, week after week as the heat mounted, as the flies multiplied and as the stench of sewage and garbage grew more overpowering, the pall of death deepened over the city. Throughout the summer a dreadful contest developed, with hundreds of immigrants attempting to enter the city from the plague ships and an equal number of residents trying to flee to healthier inland communities such as Brantford which remained comparatively unaffected.

To keep immigrants from the city proper, ship captains were notified to discharge their passengers at the Railway depot wharf where the health officer and one or more of the city police supervised landings and hastened aboard trains all who could be forwarded. Refusing to enter the deadly emigrant sheds, hundreds of the newcomers slept without shelter in the surrounding fields.

In the city, shortages developed as farmers refused to visit the city with their produce and the market was deserted,[13] while certain proprietors closed their shops until fall. Medical health regulations grew stricter and out of them at this time one city institution was born, the city dump, resulting from council's direction to the board of health to obtain a proper place to deposit the filth and the dead animals found on city streets.

Throughout July and August the cholera raged and in the two months 552 died in the city. Tirelessly, through the relentless heat, members of the medical profession fought the epidemic, unmindful of personal danger, hastening from stricken house to house, working without rest or relaxation and frequently without food for hours on end. Especially notable for their devotion were Dr. Gerald O'Reilly; Dr. William Billings, first surgeon of the Great Western railway; Dr. Thomas Duggan, who favoured ale in treatment of the disease, and Dr. John G. Dunn who in conjunction with other measures preferred brandy; Dr. Henry T. Ridley, young in medicine and new in Hamilton, who would become during nearly half-a-century of service one of the city's most beloved citizens; Dr. E. Henwood, city physician and son-in-law of Dr. Case; and John Moore, health officer.

Equally heroic were Sisters M. Philip Lenaten and M. Philomene Sheridan of the Sisters of St. Joseph, then established some two years in their first small Hamilton convent at the corner of Cannon and MacNab Streets. Although they spent themselves in untiring service and came each day in close contact with the disease neither contracted it.

On one occasion the Sisters were summoned to the home of an elderly couple said to be stricken. Unable to enter the house the nuns broke down the door, only to find the two dead. Rude coffins were dumped in the street some distance away and these the Sisters dragged to the house and having prepared the bodies for burial placed them within. Until the dead cart arrived they waited and prayed. Then since the neighbours stayed indoors the two intrepid women helped the negro cartman carry the unwieldy boxes and hoist them into the wagon. Later asked if they were afraid, one replied, "We were too busy to have fear!"

On August 7th the city united in a day of fasting and prayer for the lifting of the scourge that afflicted it. Stores, churches, business houses— all were closed and the voices of children were stilled in the streets. By September, with cooler weather, the last visitation of the plague to Hamilton was ended.

The 1850's which had begun so auspiciously, however, had still another disaster in store for the city. On Thursday, March 12th, 1857, late in the afternoon, the regular Great Western railway passenger train from Toronto crashed through the swing-bridge spanning the Desjardins canal on Burlington Heights, shattered the ice forty feet below and buried itself in the frigid waters of the canal. Of approximately 100 passengers, 59 were killed and 18 injured, 17 of the dead and 5 of the injured being Hamiltonians.

Across the still frozen ice of the bay Hamilton citizens streamed from

113

the city to help in the work of rescue of the living and recovery of the dead. The night was moonlit and bitterly cold after a bright sunny March day. All that night and the following day rescuers toiled, many operating from rafts constructed on the ice for safety. Soon there was not sufficient room in the depot for the dead, although bodies brought up from the shattered coaches in the murky waters were identified and removed speedily by grief-stricken relatives and friends. Among the dead were children and infants, youth and age, the prominent and the humble, and the "stranger within the gate": "An old man," says the official record, "name unknown, drab overcoat, blue vest, red comforter, striped woollen mittens. In his pocket a bag of silver."

In her home, Wells' Cottage, on the Mountain, Eleanor Bull, wife of the Rev. George A. Bull (later, Canon Bull) of St. Peter's church, Barton, confined to bed with her first child and namesake, found herself unable to sleep because of the constant tramp of horses and lumbering of wagons passing on the Caledonia Plank Road outside. Not until later was she told of the wreck and that the wagons were moving to the scene to help transport the bodies of the victims.

The morning after the accident Hamilton schools showed a noticeable decrease in attendance. "My father," said Thomas Kilvington, later well known Hamilton florist and nurseryman, "forbade me to visit the wreck. He ordered me flatly off to school. Nevertheless several of us played hookey and headed for the canal. It was a long walk from Emerald Street where my family lived at the time. At last we got there and who do you think was the first person I met? My father!"

By proclamation of Mayor John F. Moore, March 16th was set aside as a day of humiliation and prayer. On this Monday all forms of business were suspended and public worship was held in the various churches, the largest interdenominational prayer meeting in the city's history to that date being conducted in Knox Presbyterian church, James Street, by the Rev. Dr. Irvine. On Sunday and Monday the city was shrouded in black and church bells tolled for hours as long funeral processions made their way to the cemetery on the Heights, a stone's throw from the wreck.

All were heavily attended. Hamilton's dead included the Rev. Alfred Booker, pastor of Park Street Baptist Church, the first Baptist congregation in Hamilton, which he founded in 1843; Captain James Sutherland, for whom the *Magnet,* later renamed the *Hamilton,* the first iron steamboat to sail North American inland waters, was built for the Hamilton-Kingston run; Adam Ferrie, Jr., eldest son of Hamilton's first mayor, Colin S. Ferrie, deceased the previous year; Alexander Burnfield, engineer of the ill-fated train; Mrs. P. S. Stevenson, wife of a Hamilton commission merchant and daughter of Sheriff Thomas; John C. Henderson, brother-in-law of C. J. Brydges, managing director of the Great Western railway; the Rev. Dr. Heise, German curate of Christ's Church; and ex-alderman Donald Stuart.

For days after the disaster *The Spectator* and other papers appeared in mourning, with columns bordered in black. So great was the public demand for information that in addition to increasing the number of copies of regular issues,[14] *The Spectator* printed six extra editions. On the Monday following the wreck nearly six thousand newspapers were mailed from the Hamilton postoffice to England via the S. S. *Persia*.

On March 24th the engine, the American-built Oxford, was raised from the canal. During fifteen days of exhaustive inquest it was determined that the accident resulted from a broken axle which threw the engine from the rails, shattering the bridge under the impact. Yet although canal waters were only twelve feet deep, not until 1873 were the forward trucks and the broken axle itself brought up from the bottom. One recommendation of the jurors is of interest: that trains should come to a dead stop before passing on this and all similar bridges.

12

Sewerage, Waterworks, and a Glass Palace

AFTER twenty years of urgent recommendations of committees, complaints, demands and lawsuits of citizens, and hopeful resolutions of councils, later rescinded due to lack of funds, Hamilton sewers became a reality in 1855, a year after the cholera epidemic which their earlier completion would undoubtedly have ameliorated. By legislation the city was authorized to borrow £50,000, the money being raised by debentures sold privately in London, England.

From the council pronouncement of May, 1850: "Resolved that the time has arrived for some provision of a permanent nature for sewerage in the city," to the report of the city engineer, William Hodgins, dated January 5th, 1855, outlining the progress of the main James and Catherine Street sewers, laid from the bay southwards, and the branch lines on John Street, King and Barton, the course of Hamilton's desperately needed public utility was beset with trouble. In this, sewers established a precedent maintained to the present.

At the end of September, 1855, with 11,384 feet of the total 15,080 feet of sewers completed, dissatisfaction with Mr. Hodgins' handling of the Upper James Street sewer, resignation by the contractor, George F. Lynd, of the Upper John Street contract, higher costs, and a cave-in of the brickwork of the completed James Street North sewer at Mulberry led to Mr. Hodgins' dismissal by council.

By December, 1855, all work on the sewers had halted; the contractors, Lynd and Mullen, had entered suit to recover their last estimate;[1] Mr. Hodgins refused to surrender not only documents relating to Upper James Street but sewer contracts in general; and citizens like Judge Miles O'Reilly were petitioning for bridges or footways over the open sewer excavations isolating their homes.

In March, 1856, G. F. Cockburn, at an annual salary of £500, was appointed civil engineer, architect, and provincial land surveyor for the city and board of school trustees, his duties to be performed at his own expense. Two weeks later the sewerage case was settled out of court by arbitration and work was resumed.

On September 1st Mr. Cockburn received three months' notice of dismissal. Controversy this time centred on the Barton Street sewer whose location was changed in the summer of 1856 to make it a main outlet instead of a branch. Passing along Barton Street eastward to Ferguson Avenue, the sewer ran north on Ferguson to the inlet there, then northeasterly along this to the point of discharge.

At this time Peter Ferguson was laying out his land in town lots and Mr. Cockburn, possibly hard pressed by his multiple duties, permitted him to stake out Ferguson Avenue without supervision or subsequent check. Unfortunately, in laying the line of sewer north on Ferguson, William Drennan, C.E., former assistant engineer for the surveying department of the Great Western and the Hamilton and Toronto railways, whom Mr. Cockburn had engaged, was equally casual.

Employed to take levels along "a line of stakes through a grass field north of Barton Street . . . to the railway," and finding the stakes unmarked, Mr. Drennan assumed without further investigation that they marked the centre instead of a side line of the proposed street. Before his error was discovered the excavation was well on its way. Later when Contractor Lynd submitted accounts for two excavations, irate taxpayers and council members demanded that Mr. Cockburn pay for the first from his own pocket.

On November 1st, 1856, William Haskins became city engineer. Not only was Mr. Haskins a competent engineer but he possessed also certain qualities either of endurance or *sang-froid* for he remained in office until 1896,[2] weathering the periodic outbursts of criticism which, in Hamilton at least, seem an adjunct of his office.

For his close attention later to the new waterworks pumping station at Burlington Beach, a special committee took him severely to task, claiming the attraction for Mr. Haskins was not waterworks but the gentle pasttime of fishing. Compounding his felony, moreover, the engineer had hired buggies at city expense and had taken as companion James B. Minty of the waterworks office.

With sewers a *fait accompli*, council turned to an equally pressing civic requirement, a waterworks system. As with Hamilton sewers, planning and pressure for waterworks dated from 1835 when tenders for their construction were called for and an award of five pounds paid a Mr. McPowers for the winning plan. Again, as with sewers, waterworks waited on municipal funds, and hundreds of wells, private and public, remained the source of water for household, commercial, industrial and civic purposes. Periodically the medical profession or Hamilton's health officer would warn of the danger of an epidemic in the existing fraternal relationship of wells, privies and cess pools, while the chief engineer of the local fire brigade would stress that with the available water a major fire could threaten the whole community.

Although a then crystal clear Lake Ontario lay at the city's door, suggestions for city water included sources as far afield as the River

Maitland, Township of Arthur; Lake Medad, northeast of Waterdown; and even the Grand River. Others advocated tapping the springs on the mountainside, thereby providing the secondary benefit of saving the city its seasonal floodings; diverting the Ancaster stream at the mountain top; and sinking an artesian well. In January, 1855, Mr. McElroy's plan for waterworks received first prize in a city-sponsored competition judged by Thomas Coltrin Keefer, chief engineer of the Montreal Water Board and a prominent consulting engineer, who now became associate engineer at Hamilton.

Although Mr. McElroy's plan featured water from Burlington Bay and a reservoir in Dundurn park, Mr. Keefer recommended that city water be pumped from Lake Ontario. Obviously the Montreal engineer mistrusted the bay as a future source of pure water; and gravity sources, while of sufficient capacity for the present city of twenty thousand, would prove inadequate, said Mr. Keefer, for the future fifty thousand or more of population he foresaw.

First unit in the waterworks system consisted of a 1,200-foot basin excavated on the lakeside of the Burlington sandstrip, just north of the earlier King's Head Inn. Today, filled in, this lies immediately west of the modern concrete swimming pool at Lakeland Beach. Built without intake pipe or connection with the lake, the 16-foot-deep basin depended on water filtering through the sand. From the basin the filtered water flowed by gravity through a large wooden pipe to the suction well of the pumping station some 2,000 feet inland.

From this well the pumping plant (today still standing on the east side of Woodward Avenue above Beach Road) lifted the water across country to Ottawa Street and from there south to the Barton storage reservoir on the mountainside. To bring water into the city proper a large distribution main was laid along Main Street to James, from which auxiliary mains were run for domestic and fire department purposes.

Authorized by an act passed by the legislature on June 19th, 1856, the new works were officially inaugurated by H.R.H. Edward Prince of Wales, later King Edward VII, during his 1860 visit to Hamilton. Following a state luncheon at the Royal Hotel on September 19th the party proceeded to the pumping station where young Adam Brown, water commission chairman, delivered an address and the prince turned on the steam in the two engines, whose wheels were covered for the occasion with red velvet.

Prior to this, however, two tests of the waterworks system had been made. On May 24th, 1859, before full completion of the mains, the pumping station was turned on at the fire department's annual parade held in Court House Square. So successful was this that a formal display was arranged on the Gore for June 2nd.

Invited to attend by the water commissioners were city officials, members of the annual Wesleyan conference then meeting in the city, and a thousand pupils of Hamilton's famous Central School, opened in May,

118

1853, as the first representative graded common school in the province. With the interest in youth notable throughout his near-century of life, Adam Brown chose the two head boys of Central to turn on the water. Under the intent gaze of their fellow students lining the north side of King Street and of the Fire Brigade under Chief Engineer Thomas Gray massed on the south, sixteen-year-old Johnny Gibson (later Major-General the Hon. Sir John M. Gibson, Lieutenant-Governor of Ontario) and George Craigie, grandson of Dr. William Craigie, turned the taps that shot a stream of water ninety feet into the air.[3] When firemen played two intersecting streams from hydrants across this geyser the delighted spectators greeted the tableau with shouts and cheers.

That the works constructed under direction of a five-man board of water commissioners were substantial and durable is beyond denial. The reservoir, now far inside the city, still holds its place and use on a mountainside scrolled with the intricacies of modern access roads, while the pump house and its machinery is a museum piece, unused since 1920, but still capable of running efficiently.

Described as resembling "a fortress without and a Greek temple within," with dramatic polished black steel columns and fluted rods extending from floor to ceiling, the waterworks plant with its three-foot stone walls lined with brick, flooring of three-inch-thick solid white oak, and with its imposing machinery was second in Canada only to that of Montreal. The huge "walking beams" and the pumps with their 22-ton flywheels driven by steam from four boilers were built by the John Gartshore Company of Dundas. Oldtimers can still recall the schooners that unloaded slab wood at Van Wagner's beach to feed the boilers. Looming to a height of 150 feet the chimney of the plant was a landmark visible for leagues to sailors on the lake.

From the standpoint of efficiency the water commissioners succeeded admirably. From the standpoint of economy and moderation in view of the widespread depression following the United States' crash of 1857, and the precarious condition of the corporation's finances, the commissioners were less successful. In 1860 the works had cost the city $900,000.

Faced with alarmingly rising expenditures for which by terms of the Waterworks Act council was responsible and yet over which it had no control (the commissioners having authority to issue city debentures for works construction without consulting council) the latter body had unsuccessfully sought transfer of waterworks management from the commissioners to the corporation. The waterworks were the crowning achievement of an era of civic extravagance which day by day was irrevocably reducing the once solvent city to bankruptcy. Behind the gay facade of festivities planned to celebrate the visit of the nineteen-year-old heir to the British throne, the civic machinery was grinding to a stop.

At a soup kitchen, maintained for the past three years, the line of the hungry daily lengthened. Daily the number of paupers applying for aid to Relief Officer Dawson increased. Charity was reduced to bread and firewood, and city labour—breaking stones—was doled out at 50 cents a day to labourers, 75 cents to foremen.

In 1849 the finance committee of city council in its annual report had soberly warned that the corporation's backlog of debt had reached the danger point and must be reduced. Succeeding committees had echoed the same admonition. They might as well have saved their breath, for each year's council, with complete dismissal of the future, piled debt upon staggering debt.

To the stock subscribed in the Great Western railway company was added £50,000 in shares of the Hamilton and Port Dover line, promoted assiduously by Sir Allan MacNab; £35,000 in the Galt and Guelph railway company; and £25,000 in the Preston and Berlin branch of the Galt and Guelph line. In addition, by-law tumbling on the heels of by-law:[4] 3,000 additional shares in the Hamilton and Port Dover railway; and a further eager subscription to the Great Western to enable it to purchase from Isaac Buchanan, who held the controlling shares, the charter of the proposed Southern railway, to remove "all possible rivalry and unwholesome competition forever."

By the late 1850's the Great Western's powerful opponent, the Grand Trunk railway, had been completed from Montreal to Toronto and was now invading southern Ontario, acquiring and building branch lines, and affording a threat to the city's hardly acquired position as headquarters of the Great Western and railway centre.

In its determination to promote and maintain this position by acquiring controlling stock in the above railways, the city pledged $900,000 in debentures, remarkable when compared with Toronto's investment of $440,000 in railway stock for the same period. One proposal Hamilton opposed: the successful motion of directors of the Great Western to present £5,000 to Sir Allan MacNab in appreciation of his efforts in obtaining the railway's charter.

In other ways besides stock subscriptions the railway fever affected Hamilton. Having become accustomed to spending and calculating the city's future on a grandiose scale, councils found it difficult to stoop to pinch pennies except where actual outlay of hard cash left no choice. Furthermore if the ambitious city was to maintain its position as provincial railway centre it must keep up with the more affluent Joneses, in this case Toronto, where mayor and council attended en masse a Railway ball and dejeuner; Rochester, especially friendly after the Great Western added a steamboat service to its line; and Oswego.

As a secondary result of this intercourse, council cast a critical eye on the city and determined to expand and improve the downtown area. To attract capital and provide a hoped-for source of badly needed income to the city, the corporation in 1857 purchased properties north of city hall, in many cases at highly inflated prices, expanded the market lot and erected stores for rental, at a nominal debentured £39,042.

Since this improvement increased the shabbiness of the Gore, which had progressed through dust bowl, parade ground and wood market to present consideration as a grain market, council of 1859 accepted the water commissioners' suggestion to ornament the Gore as a park, complete with fountains. As Isaac Buchanan and other citizens offered $1,200 towards railing the Gore, grassing it and gravelling the paths, the city escaped lightly by authorizing expenditure of £400, to include cost of fountains.

Lastly, Hamilton determined to build a Crystal Palace, patterned after the great glittering glass building erected in Hyde Park, London, England, by Albert Edward, Prince Consort to house the Great Exhibition of 1851. At this period provincial agricultural exhibitions were an important practical means of promoting agricultural knowledge. In 1859, through efforts of Sir Allan MacNab and the Hon. Isaac Buchanan, Hamilton not only defeated a bill before the legislature limiting the holding of provincial fairs to Toronto, Kingston and London, but capped this success by securing the 1860 exhibition.

As a setting for this, the city built the Crystal Palace on a site purchased from the Hon. W. H. Dixon, located between Florence, Locke, Sophia and Louisa Streets,[5] land which disclosed its origin by an old discharged mortgage in the abstract of titles, given by Richard Beasley to Messrs. Des Rivières, Blackwood and Company in 1819. Today the eastern part of the grounds is occupied by Victoria Park with its sports facilities for all ages, from playground area and wading pool, through tennis courts and baseball diamond with stands, to shuffleboard for older citizens.

Assisted by surrounding counties and municipalities the city built an ornate yet substantial glass-walled building surmounted by a dome and flanked by glass wings. From the great central hall below the dome, capable of dining hundreds, floating stairs led to an encircling balcony. Located about a hundred yards west of Locke Street, the Palace's main entrance faced east, with ground entrances for pedestrians opposite Little Main (now Peter) Street. Along King Street stood the stables, with entrance at the corner of King and Locke for stock and the farm implements and machinery, just beginning manufacture, which afforded one of the greatest attractions of early fairs. To provide for parking of that era an open carriage shed 180 feet in length was built. Locke and tributary streets were graded and plank sidewalks laid, while to ensure water a main was pushed through to the Palace grounds.

As the September 18th date of the visit of the Prince of Wales approached, council under Mayor Henry McKinstry assumed a strange dual role, on the one hand concluding arrangements for the forthcoming event, and simultaneously engaging in a desperate effort to repair the city's finances.

On August 20th council struck the rate for 1860 of 18 cents on the dollar, instead of the 20 cents recommended by the finance committee, or the 25 cents the latter felt was actually needed to meet the city's

121

obligations. As a body the finance committee resigned and was replaced by a new committee who elected Alderman M. W. Browne an unwilling chairman. At the same time a public meeting approved council establishing a rate of one cent in the dollar for the Prince's reception.

In the first week in September the president of the Gore Bank, which had seen the corporation through many crises, refused from that date to honour the chamberlain's cheques until the city's overdraft was reduced. On September 10th the mayor and council called a meeting of leading citizens and property holders who determined to return the tax rate to 20 cents, and to meet current obligations and provide work for the needy, to invite citizens to pay part of their taxes at once, with the amount each paid to be deducted from his later tax bill.

Into this supercharged situation a bomb was suddenly exploded. In mid-Atlantic, officials in charge of arrangements for the Prince's tour decided to cancel his planned three-day visit to Hamilton as they felt the mountain roads leading to Sir Isaac Buchanan's Gothic mansion, Auchmar, where Prince Edward and his staff were to be entertained, constituted a risk to the royal person.

With the Crystal Palace and Provincial Agricultural Exhibition to be opened, the waterworks to be inaugurated, three sapling elms to be planted in the newly fenced and landscaped court house grounds on Main Street,[6] henceforth known as Prince's Square, this change of royal plans to a brief station-stop was a calamity. Adding to the chagrin of corporation and civic leaders was the anguish of the fair sex who had assembled new and glamorous wardrobes for the official levée or the ball to be held in the recently opened and magnificent Royal Hotel.

In the midst of the prevailing consternation Adam Brown, wholesale merchant and leading citizen, stepped into the breach. Although only thirty-four, Mr. Brown had already acquired a reputation for civic mindedness and for Scottish sagacity and acumen in handling difficult situations. When the ship carrying the Prince of Wales appeared off Quebec, Adam Brown was waiting on the quay. His pocket held the keys of Arkledun, the John Street mansion of hardware merchant Richard Juson, and of Oakbank, the James Street combination Gothic revival and modified Loyalist stone residence of Mr. Juson's brother-in-law, spice merchant W. P. McLaren, who was also Adam Brown's brother-in-law, Mr. Brown's wife, née Miss Maria Z. Evatt, daughter of Captain Evatt, being a sister of Mrs. McLaren.

As the ladies of the two households were then in England, the homes were available with a minimum of dislocation. With the Prince accommodated at Arkledun and his staff at Oakbank, abutting gardens would provide easy private communication. When Sir John Rose, in charge of arrangements for the royal tour, was pleased to accept the substitution, offered with Adam Brown's genial charm, another city crisis passed.

Many years later Miss Elsie Buchanan, daughter of the Honourable Isaac and ardent mountain resident, rose in defence of John Street. "It was not the danger of the road," she protested, "that led to the proposed cancellation of the Prince's visit. My father was delighted to entertain any member of the family of his revered Sovereign, Queen Victoria, but when he learned that the house must be entirely given over to the Prince and his suite and his own family turned out, he objected."

The visit of Prince Edward was a tremendous success. The opening of the Crystal Palace and the exhibition was attended by forty to fifty thousand people, while on the night of the ball, seventy-five thousand crowded into the city. Flags fluttered from bunting-bright buildings and welcoming arches spanned the streets at strategic points, the most notable being one on the mountain brow, visible to the whole city, erected by Isaac Buchanan, beneath which the Prince would have passed en route to Auchmar.

Shortly the lights would go out in Hamilton streets but for the Prince's stay they burned brightly. Buildings blazed with gas or candles. As part of its illumination the Royal Hotel installed a great circle of lights with the words *Honi Soit Qui Mal Y Pense* in variegated colours, the whole surmounted by a brilliant crown, with a second crown on the Merrick Street wall done in lamps with tin reflectors.

It would seem that the youthful son of Queen Victoria enjoyed himself as much as Hamiltonians did. At the ball His Royal Highness danced every number, stopping only for supper for which seventy-five dishes had been prepared to tempt the royal palate. Not until 3.30 a.m. did the debonair Prince retire, having danced with all the partners arranged for him, and for his own part, one may be certain, with as many pretty girls as possible. It is of interest that members of the Prince's suite found Miss Kate Kerr of Brant House, daughter of Lt.-Col. William Johnson Kerr, M.P.P., and Elizabeth Brant, and granddaughter of Chief Joseph Brant, the loveliest woman present. The royal party noted also Kate's brother, William J. Simcoe Kerr[7] who succeeded his uncle, Chief Joseph Brant, as Ichkarihoken, or chief, of the Mohawk nation through his mother's line.

Prince Edward's visit may be said to have ended an era for the city or to have begun an era. Whichever it was, the visit stood squarely between the years of carefree spending, of calling the tune and leaving posterity to pay the piper, and the years when watchfulness and penny pinching became second nature, until eventually the learned lesson was again forgotten.

13

Common Schools vs. Ryerson and Central School

In no field in Canada West was there more acute need for improvement in the 1850's than in that of education. Private schools and the government-supported, yet high-feed Grammar schools of the day provided learning only for the children of the well-to-do. Where common schools were available, they were small, dark, poorly heated, unventilated and ill equipped. Text books were scarce and being British or American were largely unsuited to Canadian needs. Teachers were untrained, inefficient, underpaid or not paid at all. Nor, until the 1840's, was this considered unreasonable.

The Gore District council itself proclaimed that old men, cripples unable to work and low priced immigrants were quite competent to teach.[1] It remained for Dr. Egerton Ryerson to introduce the first semblance of order into the chaos of public school education in the province and lay the foundation of Ontario's educational system.

On December 5th, 1842, under the School Act of the previous year, Hamilton was divided into five common school districts. In support of schools in these districts the town was authorized to receive a division of the government fund allotted to the Gore District council, and to levy an assessment equal to the parliamentary grant.

Some two months later George Sunley, town assessor, reported to council that there were 1,760 children in the town within the ages of five and sixteen and of this number 402 were being taught in ten common schools by eleven teachers, male and female.

In April, 1843, Hamilton's share of the district school fund—£128.15.8—was received and divided by Mr. Sunley among the teachers in proportion to the number of children taught by each. Highest paid was W. M. Friar, 64 children, £20.5.8; lowest, Misses Wilmot and Elliott, who shared a room and 40 children, receiving together, £12.16.8; with Miss Moore, lowest single, with 25 children, £8.0.5. Following payment Mr. Sunley had a balance of 1s. 2d. This the board of police with commendable impartiality divided between the seven lowest teachers, giving two pence each.

On May 31st, 1843, the board of police appointed a temporary board of examiners to secure competent teachers, who alone would be eligible for engagement; advertised an examination for candidates at the police office; and set about acquiring a temporary schoolhouse in each of the five school districts.

On July 3rd the board of examiners—Rev. Mr. Geddes, Rev. Mr. Gale, Vicar General Dr. Rae, Miles O'Reilly, Rev. Mr. Osborne and Mayor G. S. Tiffany—reported that only four candidates had been found qualified to teach: Thomas Casey, Patrick Thornton (previously employed in Hamilton), Robert Kelly and Charles Ozen Counsell.

Three weeks later the board engaged the first school premises for the coming term, renting from Maurice Fitzpatrick at five dollars a month for six months a school room about 25 feet square with front and back doors, separate yard, proper privy, and a good well.[2]

From Mrs. Laura Campbell, situated on John Street adjoining the brick chapel, the board subleased for six months at one pound per month the upper part of the house except the rooms over the kitchen, with free ingress and egress through the kitchen door and adjoining stairway, and with privileges of yard, well and outhouses. Corporation privileged to remove partition or make alterations, if later replaced.

On Monday, August 7th, 1843, in accordance with the Common School Act of that year, five schools opened in Hamilton, with pupils paying in advance a monthly fee of 1s.3d. apiece, collected in the school room and recorded by the teacher. In addition the five school districts were taxed under the act one-half per cent of their assessment as a school levy. As the boundaries of school districts and city wards did not coincide, the teachers agreed that the public funds should be divided amongst them without reference to the number of children in each school district, thus avoiding an otherwise necessary reassignment of boundaries.

In view of the integration problems of the mid-twentieth century one might note that in 1843 the coloured community of Hamilton, of considerable size and largely situated on the Mountain on Concession Street from Sherman Avenue to 23rd Street, protested to the governor-general that coloured children were denied admittance to the town's common schools. Their plea for equal rights with others was concurred in and integration proceeded uneventfully.

On January 15th, 1844, the Rev. John Osborne was elected unsalaried superintendent of common schools for the town. On April 1st, following, having received no remuneration to that date from the preceding August 7th, Patrick Thornton appealed on behalf of the teachers for part or the full amount of their share of the school fund. In response council directed City Clerk Leggatt Downing to divide £38 among the five teachers, paying each £7.12.0. Not until year end was the staff further paid. On November 27th council announced the government grant for 1843 as

£112.1.8, to which the city added £48, making £160.1.8 to be divided equally among Messers. Thornton, C. O. Counsell, Langford, Carruthers, Langtree and Friar.[3]

Apparently the successive school bills enacted at this time caused considerable confusion and some disaccord as to the relative duties and responsibilities of the board of police and Superintendent Osborne. Previously school accounts for rent, cleaning, whitewashing, repairs, firewood and so forth had been met by the board in collaboration with the teacher whose duty it was not only on occasion to rent the school room but also to keep it in daily order and to arrive in time to shovel snow and light the fire. In addition the teacher was responsible for arranging for house-cleaning, including privy, repairs to the school room, and purchase of firewood.

By 1845 school trustees, first mentioned in July, 1844, for School District 2, were beginning to usurp the handling of school accounts, and the following year the disbursement of school funds and authority in educational matters in the city passed from municipal hands.

On November 1st, 1847, under the terms of Egerton Ryerson's Common Schools Act of the previous year, Hamilton's first city council appointed a board of trustees for the city, among them the Rev. J. G. Geddes, Rev. Mr. Gordon, Rev. Mr. Ryerson, Dr. Craigie, Major Bowen, and Rev. Mr. McKid. Two years later the school sections difficulty was solved by constituting the whole city as one school section, with the various wards its component parts, thus substituting one school board for the previous five and clearing the way for the building of a central school containing the higher branches of education, which might be combined with the existing District Grammar School.

Strongest advocate of the central school was Dr. William Craigie who steadfastly opposed plans for construction of common ward schools on five sites procured for them. When in 1850 construction of a central school was approved by the board, a rider recommended that no present funds should be spent on building ward schools.

A milestone in school buildings and in educational progress in city and province, the so-called Central School stood on Lot 15, Concession 3, purchased by George Hamilton in 1815 and sold to Peter Hunter Hamilton in 1823. On April 11th, 1851, for an outlay of £1,000 it became the first property in Hamilton owned by the board of education. The school itself stands on the former site of Mr. Hamilton's barn, beside the field in which Colonel Gourlay reviewed local militia during annual musters.

Occupying a high rise and covering a full city block of land, the first large graded school in British America[4] faced south, overlooking the site of the present city hall. Of stone, built in Italianate style, the twelve-room school was a substantial dignified two-storey building with a second-floor auditorium, capacious well lighted rooms and adequate heating and ventilating systems. Boys and girls occupied separate rooms and playgrounds but followed the same studies. Pupils gathered in the assembly room for opening exercises, then retired to classrooms—the first in Hamilton adequately equipped with proper furniture, blackboards, maps, globes and textbooks.

Although capable of accommodating over one thousand students, on opening day, May 2nd, 1853, less than two hundred enrolled. Coming weeks saw only a moderate increase in attendance. The school was pioneering Egerton Ryerson's new Normal School methods of public school education.[5] It drew bitter opposition alike from the District Grammar School, private schools catering to the well-to-do, and the primitive common schools whose untrained teachers were doomed under the advocated system. Creating additional hard feeling was Central's high cost, estimated by its first principal, John Herbert Sangster, M.A., M.D., at fifty to sixty thousand dollars, discontent over its erection in preference to ward schools, and sectarian, political and social dissension.[6]

For a year the staff, including Miss Annie Morrison (Mrs. James Cummings) and Benjamin Charlton, forgot that "such a thing as clocks and school hours" existed. In addition to regular and overtime teaching and other multiple duties, 22-year-old John Herbert Sangster met the angry parents who daily stormed the school to protest "the indignities practised on their children in sending them home to take a bath, change their linen, have their clothes mended, or put on shoes and stockings."

Well-to-do Hamilton associated common schools, said Dr. Sangster later, with "dirty, ill clad unkempt bare-footed children conspicuous for bad language and worse manners." This attitude had to be changed, for if Central was to succeed it needed to enrol the children of the city as a whole.

In enforcing the school's rock bottom standard of pupil admittance, "a wholesome person, cleanly and neatly, even if humbly clad," the staff received unexpected help. While many parents objected violently, some even appealing to board and press, the majority of poorer children, "seeing what was required, took the matter into their own hands," said Dr. Sangster, "and refused to leave home until properly attended to."

When in April, 1858, J. H. Sangster was summoned to Toronto by Dr. Ryerson to assume an intermediate post leading to headmastership of the Normal School, he left an established school system behind him. Not only was Central crowded "from basement to rooftree," but its overflow filled a primary school under two or three teachers in every ward in the city, all serving as feeders to Central and under management of its principal.

In addition night classes had been inaugurated, and union under a joint school board formulated with the District Grammar School, the latter opening in Central on August 1st, 1856. From this date stem the Hamilton public and secondary school systems as they function today, with a single board of education composed of elected trustees appointed by city council, and a representative of the separate school board.[7]

The success of Central marked the end of class privilege and class distinction in the field of learning in Canada West. An educational showpiece for the province, Central School became a foundation stone of Ontario's present system of education.

For teachers 1860 became a red letter year with the first teachers' salary schedule in Hamilton established. Starting at $200, annual salaries progressed to the $1,300 received by Central's principal, Archibald McCallum. The salary schedule appears in decimal currency, officially adopted by the corporation on January 1st, 1858.

Gradually Canada was assuming individuality. On May 20th, 1851, the first Upper Canada postage stamp appeared on a letter, the provincial governments in that year taking over their own postal departments, previously administered through Canadian deputies by the postmaster of the United Kingdom. For years the post had bred official dissension and public discontent with its slowness, irregularity and high cost. On May 6th, 1856, a handsome stone three-storey combined postoffice and postmaster's residence was opened on James Street, opposite Merrick, by Postmaster Edmund Ritchie. For sixteen years the provinces would retain control of postal matters until with confederation the department would be assumed by the new government at Ottawa.

James Street was developing. A block north of the postoffice, opposite Gore Street, Hendrie and Shedden, the Great Western's cartage agents, had established their freight depot and parcels' department, forerunner of Hendrie and Company (William Hendrie, Sr., and sons, William, Jr., and George Muir), railway and general cartage, located on West King Street at MacNab, with stables for the company's famous matched dapple grey Clydes and Shires, on Market Street between Bay and Caroline. The stables, complete with smithies, occupied a block, with company homes opposite on the north side of the street. At the height of its teaming era the Hendrie company operated three hundred horses and built its own wagons.

"For over half a century," said the late David M. Nelligan, "one of the early morning sights of the city was the long parade of Hendrie lorries, light and heavy, heading down Bay Street to reach the freight sheds on Strachan sharp at 7 a.m." On the return trip, so steep was the hill from Strachan to Bay that an extra horse or team was frequently hitched to the end of the whiffle tree to pull a full load of freight.

"At one time, there were many fine powerful horses in Hamilton and drivers loved to parade them on holidays. It was a wonderful sight. The horses realized it too. They were a bunch of show-offs."

Hamilton had always loved horses. Throughout the nineteenth century the sport of kings was one of the most popular pastimes in Upper Canada, with racing, steeplechasing and trotting races featured. Steeplechasing on the north shore of the bay and racing on bay ice were early featured in Hamilton. In 1831 the *Hamilton Free Press* records a three-day meet in November, with heats of one and two miles, for horses owned within forty miles of Hamilton. Stewards: Messrs. Peter H. Hamilton, John Law, William B. Sheldon, James Brown and Dr. Merrick; secretary,

J. M. A. Cameron. Within the community the earliest established race course was the Aberdeen Avenue track[8] near the later Hamilton Amateur Athletic Association grounds. Here in 1846 a 40-mile race was trotted, the winner Mr. Cotton's Jack on the Green.

Of these extended races where distance and stamina outweighed speed, the outstanding example in city racing annals was run in 1857 when Owen Nowlan's Old Spice defeated "H. W. Perry's gray mare" in a race from Hamilton to Brantford and return without stopping, for a prize of $250. Both Mr. Nowlan and Mr. Perry were livery stable proprietors and the race climaxed a notable public exchange of bragging. In the same year Mr. Perry's Bones and Mr. Van Norman's Red Bird ran a widely publicized three heats of one mile each, best two out of three, at $1,000 a side, with Bones winning two heats, best time 2:38. Oddly Red Bird trotted to harness, Bones to saddle.

Over the years Hamilton boasted many ardent horsemen, none more noted than William Hendrie, Sr., and his sons by his first wife, Miss Margaret Walker of Arbroath, Scotland, William, Jr., and his brother John. In 1863 at the Hamilton Spring Steeplechases held on Dennis Moore's property, Oaklands, on the north shore, John Hendrie, a great cross-country rider, rode his own horse, Doncaster, to victory and later his brother's Rifleman. Held in perfect racing weather, the meet drew some four thousand spectators three miles by steamboat from the railway wharf opposite, or five miles on foot or by vehicle around the head of the bay.

On May 24th, 1866, the then most outstanding racing event in Hamilton history occurred with the opening by R. R. Waddell of a new mile track on Main Street adjoining today's Gage Park. Besides celebrating the Queen's birthday, an important annual occasion, a grand race meet for trotters and runners was organized, which featured for the first time in Hamilton the running of the Queen's Plate.

In charge of arrangements for the meet was the recently formed Hamilton Riding and Driving Association, with Mayor C. Magill, M.P.P., president, and Messrs. William Hendrie, T. G. Furnivall and George Roach, stewards. For several years subsequently running and trotting races divided honours at the annual Dominion Day and fall meets at the new track which was well patronized by champion Canadian thoroughbreds, among them Dexter, champion world trotter; Luther B., owned by R. R. Waddell, "a great horse over the sticks", who won the Ontario Plate in 1868; John White's Terror, winner of the Dominion Plate, July, 1869; Garibaldi, St. Patrick, Whirlwind, Royal George and others.

"The race meeting of 1867," says Logan Stewart,[9] "gives first evidence of the true start to the running of the thoroughbred in a controlled manner with a system of handicapping." At this meet also riders were required to wear proper jockey costume.

In 1873 'Doc' Hannon, Canadian turf pioneer, leased the track for a successful meet, and the following year the Queen's Plate was again run at Hamilton. Public interest in the sport however had begun locally to dwindle and when Mr. Waddell closed the track it fell into dormancy for nearly twenty years until revived by the opening of The Hamilton Jockey Club in 1893.

There were other group sports equally popular in the 1850's and '60s. Probably lacrosse (inherited from the Indian), tug-of-war and horseshoe pitching were the first games engaged in by the pioneers. Records show that in 1846 lacrosse was played locally.

Cricket too was popular. In 1851 stationing of Imperial troops in the city gave the game a long lasting impetus. Cricket matches incited great rivalry between teams which numbered among outstanding players Allan N. MacNab; Miles O'Reilly; C. A. Sadleir, city solicitor; Robert Nixon, auctioneer and commission merchant; R. N. Law, barrister and council member; and Joseph and George Hamilton, sons of Peter Hunter, who served as first president of the Hamilton Cricket Club, located on Bold Street near his home. A man of parts, Peter H. Hamilton: one of the first chief magistrates in the city, an outstanding athlete, and one of the most popular men in Hamilton, without whose presence no game was complete. When regular troops were stationed in town Mr. Hamilton established a golf course for their officers to play on, and to provide ice for curling, dammed a stream.

As the century progressed, pastimes multiplied. In 1860 Frederick W. Gates, wholesale drygoods merchant, petitioned council for permission to erect a wooden building at the corner of MacNab Street and Maiden Lane (Jackson Street) as a club house for a racquet court.

Baseball was a favorite Hamilton diversion while still unknown to many American cities. Wherever there was a common there was a minor team, with majors contesting hotly for space in the Crystal Palace grounds: the Old Stocking Base Ball Club, the Maple Leaf, Atlantic, Standard, Eagle, Hop Bitters, and later the Baseball Association of the Hamilton Collegiate Institute. Council also loaned the horse ring to lacrosse, football and the odd cricket club.

In the 1850's yachting became so popular that the Royal Hamilton Yacht Club was founded in 1860 and a club house erected at the foot of Wellington Street. One of the earliest pleasure craft on the bay was the 54-foot *Range,* followed by H. B. Whipple's *Rivet* built in Renfrew in 1856, Judge Monck's *Cyprus* and Edward Sullivan's *Evangeline.* For those without private craft a succession of pleasure steamers plied the bay, operating between city wharves, Bay View and Oaklands Park on the north shore, and the Brant House and other holiday spots at the Beach. Among the earliest were the *Victoria, Little Lillie* and the highly popular *Little Mason* and *Maggie Mason.*

With winter, curling flourished on the bay. Until the first frame building was erected on Bond Street in 1861[10] curlers were entirely dependent on the weather. Storms, rough ice, biting winds and intense cold could postpone games for days and weeks. Yet intrepid zealots of the roaring game were not discouraged. In 1853 the Ontario (later Thistle)

Club was formed with 93 regular and three honorary members, and with three pairs of "stanes" purchased by the club and loaned generously until more accrued. Some four years later the Burlington Club was established, with the first contest between the two clubs held in February, 1857, the Ontario Club winning.

In 1858 the first bonspiel was held on Sherman's Inlet and its success, in spite of bad weather, led to similar annual events and to the first international bonspiel, played in Buffalo in 1865, with 26 Canadian and 23 American rinks competing.

Besides the bay, the Hamilton clubs played on outdoor rinks, with the Ontario Club curling for several seasons on a frozen creek (probably the stream dammed earlier by Peter H. Hamilton) near the site of the present Hamilton Thistle Club, successor in 1871 to the Ontario Club.

Four years previous to this the Hamilton Mechanics Curling Club (later the Hamilton Caledonia Curling Club) was established at the corner of Main and Catharine Streets, with four sheets of ice. Although rapidly expanding membership obliged the club to move to more spacious quarters on Victoria Avenue South, facing Young Street, not until 1899 was a two-storey brick club house erected, with four sheets of ice. A year later the present name, Hamilton Victoria Club, was incorporated.

The Mountain looked down on an ever-changing city. Even the longest lived of pioneers were vanishing: in 1852, James Mills, founder of the Mills family; in 1857, Peter Hunter Hamilton; and John Young, of Young, Weir and Company, wholesale merchants, whose imposing stone mansion, Undermount, on John Street South would become the nucleus of a great hospital.

In May, 1855, *The Spectator* lost its first editor, Robert Reid Smiley, who died of tuberculosis at the age of thirty-eight, shortly after completing his handsome brick and stone residence, Rose Arden, better known as "Smiley's Castle." Classical in design, the pretentious abode stood on the east side of Bride's Terrace, today East Avenue, at King William Street. Over a decade later the estate was purchased by James Turner who rebuilt the house in 1873. Its next owner was T. H. Pratt, drygoods merchant.[11]

Following the editor's death *The Spectator* passed briefly through the hands of John Smiley, Robert's brother, and William Gillespy, founder and first president of the Canadian Press Association, organized at Kingston in 1859. Five years after this event the now-pining publication was purchased by Thomas (later, the Hon.) and Richard White, able journalists, who restored it to editorial and financial repute.

In the outer world the Crimean War came and went, taking a small local toll of casualties and leaving as memento two Russian cannon, still extant in Harvey Park. Presented by the government in response to council's application, sparked by Major Alfred Booker, the guns were disembarked at the wharf in Hamilton in June, 1860, and teamed gratuitously to the Court House Square by Hendrie and Company and Edward Zealand.

Mounted on the Square, the cannon inspired great satisfaction until the following July 12th when one was fired in celebration of the day, whether with or without council's permission is uncertain. The discharge shattered all windows on the east side of the Square and brought indignant claims for damages from George Lees, flour and feed dealer, and Dennis Nelligan, hotelkeeper, both of John Street South. Council paid the claims, then to prevent a recurrence ordered the cannon plugged. In 1873 the guns were removed to the Crystal Palace, and upon its dismantling were transferred to the grounds of Dundurn Castle.

As the century advanced, the city added still another development. In the summer of 1849 three hospitals were operating in Hamilton: the new House of Industry, the old Catharine Street hospital and the Emigrant hospital on the bay shore. In July council closed the old hospital, and in November the Emigrant hospital, transferring their patients to the sole remaining House of Industry.

Comfortable and well built, the latter had one fatal drawback, its location. Close to the mountain, it lay in the path of quarry slides, and its attractive wooded two acres of grounds, selected to ensure hospital privacy, constantly tempted council.

In the summer of 1850 complaints and petitions obliged the corporation to erect at a safe distance from the community a powder magazine for explosives, then stored on merchants' premises. "In making choice of a site," say minutes of September 4th, "committee have had a proper regard for the safety of the inhabitants of the locality, security of the magazine, and convenience of those using it, and therefore recommend that a portion of the two acres on which the House of Industry is erected, be granted, as they conceive that when the lot is fenced, no more safe and secluded place could be found within the limits of the city."

When in December the existing pound became too cramped and dilapidated to hold its tenants—dogs, cats, horses, cows, swine, geese, ducks, hens and goats—council knew where to find a new site. Into the two acres at the base of the mountain went an enlarged pound. Three months later council consolidated the two operations by making John Wilson, superintendent of the House of Industry, the new poundkeeper, with the fees his remuneration.[12]

As if this were not enough, in the summer of 1851 the quarries above began to move in on the secluded pleasant plot. Like the camel which gradually usurped its Arab master's tent, the quarries in their first assault of waste metal (stone) down the mountainside merely breached the fence and put a nose inside. Immediately the hospital committee reported the attack to council and asked that quarry owners Alderman Robert McElroy and the Messrs. Scarth be required to repair the fence and remove the slide before serious damage resulted. During the ensuing year the hospital committee, a special committee, and an engineering survey

132

reported, warned and recommended with increasing urgency while council, with commendable tolerance, considered.

On August 18th, 1852, the quarries were in. Pressure of stone, reported the committee, had rendered the hospital untenantable and unfit[13] and inmates had been removed to the Barracks at the lake. In April, 1853, the latter was purchased for £1,250 and the following month the name City Hospital was first officially used, the caption, House of Industry, disappearing.

The City Hospital, later Macassa Lodge, a three-storey-and-basement brick building, had been erected in 1830 by Nathaniel Hughson as an hotel. Situated at the corner of John Street and Guise (or Guy), it was fronted by a full width double verandah commanding an uninterrupted view of Hamilton's active waterfront. Built lavishly, it had been an imposing structure for a town of two to three thousand population.

Until the railroad era the hotel, its fellows and the area in general flourished. In fact, close to the harbour and wharfs, Hughson's hotel attracted so much patronage that uptown hotels united to sponsor a bus service from the ships to Hamilton proper. The bus service had its effect. Gradually also as rail established its business centre uptown, the Port Hamilton core deteriorated. One by one hotels closed. Hughson's became a barracks for Her Majesty's regulars during the Mackenzie rebellion years, then a Customs House.[14] In 1842 it was lost to Nathaniel Hughson, the Younger, his father's spendthrift heir, on a foreclosed mortgage.

Accompanying the House of Industry to its new site, John Wilson and his wife remained as superintendent and matron. The position of city physician previously held by Dr. Hunter, was now filled by Dr. E. Henwood.

For nearly thirty years the City Hospital on the bay front served the city, latterly with increasing difficulty as population mounted from 16,000 in 1853 to 36,946 in 1882, when patients were moved to the newly erected City Hospital on the north side of Barton Street, still actively in use today and nucleus of the Hamilton civic system of hospitalization.

14

Bankruptcy and a New Economy

IN 1862 the disaster that had so long threatened the city finally overtook it. Unbelievably it was declared bankrupt. Unbelievably, since until the bailiff was actually in the house the city fathers refused to recognize that bankruptcy impended. Until the city's household goods appeared on the sheriff's block, council with the peculiarly blind optimism of the era maintained that the day of reckoning could be averted, that somehow, by some means the civic difficulties would be resolved.

Late in 1860 council had reluctantly reduced staffs (the police to a force of eight, including Chief John Carruthers); had cut salaries to bare subsistence level;[1] had watered relief to one-fifth its former moderate outlay, providing only bread and wood and that to certified cases; and had set the tax rate at 20 cents in the dollar.

Council's program was simple. When taxes came in, the corporation would pay twelve months' interest on the Gore Bank debt, and the interest on city debentures and city endorsed railway bonds held in England. With these payments met, council felt assured the Gore Bank would assist the corporation to any reasonable extent,[2] and the English shareholders would refrain from legal action to recover principal. Furthermore, council determined, the government must recognize the expediency of assisting not only Hamilton but other embarrassed municipalities by some measure of permanent relief. To this end the city sent a deputation to confer with twelve such communities.

In 1861 the Quebec legislature, considering it important for the country's image that Hamilton's interest debt be promptly met, advanced $75,000, a drop in the bucket, for which the city surrendered on deposit its Great Western scrip.

In 1862, still convinced that Hamilton's importance in the provincial and national economy, and its integrity in offering future settlements must bring recognition and help, the city appealed again to the government for relief and to the English stockholders for further postponement of overdue principal payments. Again and again by letter and delegation council appealed, explained and promised.[3]

The government refused to help however and the bondholders answered by obtaining injuctions and ordering in the sheriff. In addition the bondholders took legal action to enforce levy of a tax provided for in their agreement with the city: on the real and personal property of the taxpayers of Hamilton over and above all rates whatever. Added to the 1862 tax and water rate of 25 cents (not mills) on the dollar, the bonds tax would have resulted in a ruinous overall tax rate for the year, of 80 cents on every dollar of assessment.[4] As if this were not enough, the city's firm standby, the Gore Bank, through its president, Andrew Steven, not only refused further credit but demanded additional security for the $50,000 indebtedness already incurred.

In the bewildered days of 1862 confusion lay like an aura on the city, houses began to empty as their tenants fled to easier living, the lights went out in the streets to save the cost of lighting and the water was turned off in the fountains in Gore Park to save the expense of pumping.

On November 1st, 1862, a sheriff's bill advertised sale of the corporation's chattels: all city hall furniture, including the mayor's "throne"; all works department tools and equipment; all furnishings of the City Hospital and House of Refuge; and unbelievably, all fire engines and firefighting equipment.

Prior to this, to continue functioning, the city had attempted to purchase at a valuation its chattel property. When this offer was refused, Mayor Robert McElroy, who saw the corporation through its three worst years, appealed to all civic-minded citizens to bid in the furnishings and equipment necessary to enable the city to operate and to protect itself. Probably no auction sale in history ever brought lower prices or netted less to creditors than this, conducted unhappily by Bailiff William Milne, later governor of the gaol. As fast as items were bid in, principally by ex-mayor James Cummings, they were hurried on loan back to their former location, except for city safes which were stored in the warehouse of Isaac Buchanan and Company.

Still to be met by the city however was the staggering payment of $357,272.39, composed of $250,000 arrears in interest to bondholders, executions in the hands of Sheriff E. Cartwright Thomas, and the debt to the local Gore Bank. At this time Hamilton's assessment was $500,000. As the city was forbidden to issue further city notes or debentures, and the Court of Queen's Bench had ordered surrender of the collectors' rolls to the sheriff to be used in striking a rate to raise the amount of the executions he held, there seemed no possible escape from disaster.

Actually the solution was simple. Key to the situation lay in the assessment rolls. Without them the sheriff could not strike his rate and levy the tax as ordered. Quietly, without fanfare, young City Clerk Thomas Beasley disappeared from the city. With him disappeared the collectors' rolls from the assessment office.

The following day council was informed that Mr. Beasley had left town with his physician, Dr. Lewis M. Springer, and was now in residence at Sulphur Springs, near Rochester, a spa where Mrs. Beasley was already a patient.

That the 31-year-old city clerk conceived and carried out so bold a plan unadvised and unassisted seems doubtful. More doubtful when one considers two items in council minutes of November 24th, 1862: "Letter from Thomas C. Mewburn protesting against City Clerk leaving the City at the instigation of certain members of Council." And again: "Protest from Aldermen Holden and Lister, Councillors Mewburn and Mackelcan disapproving of the course . . . taken by Council in regard to the Assessment Rolls."

Councillor Mackelcan resigned, but he was at odds with most of the city. Mr. Beasley was considered a public hero and the only concern was fear that he had exposed himself to prosecution by removing the rolls from the city. Prior to his return however the rolls were discovered in a city safe on the premises of Buchanan and Company. Unfortunately for the city's creditors the Court of Queen's Bench had recessed before the discovery and the special levy had expired.

When Thomas Beasley returned he explained regretfully that in the confusion caused by his illness, which had resulted from worry over the city's financial situation, he had placed the rolls in the safe and forgotten all about it. On this note the matter rested. As to how the city paid its debts and resumed solvency, it did it the hard way, by refusing to spend an unnecessary copper. Example of the new regime are expenses authorized for the visit of the Governor-General Sir Charles Stanley, Viscount Monck, in September, 1862: "Cab hire, $40; grant, Fire Brigade, $40; crimson cloth for platform, $11.55; dinners for cavalry, $13.50. Total: $105.05." The dinner honouring the vice-regal party was given at Auchmar by the Hon. Isaac and Mrs. Buchanan, city officials being included.

In charity, payment for orphans sent to the Asylum by the city was reduced from 75 cents per head per week to 50 cents, retroactive four months; and farmers and employers were notified that children of eight and twelve years were available who were capable of earning their living and thereby relieving the city of their support.

With assistance of Sir Allan MacNab, Bart., who after a sojourn in England had been reelected to the provincial parliament and was now serving as Speaker of the legislative council, and of the Hon. Isaac Buchanan and Thomas Stinson, with Samuel Mills, M.P.P. (later Hon.), the three wealthiest men in Hamilton, and with the board of trade, terms were worked out for gradual elimination of the city debt. To meet current needs the city issued negotiable one dollar notes payable within the year. New long term debentures, carrying lower rates of interest, replaced those held by bondholders, and the latter accepted a 50 per cent discount on due coupons. Collection of arrears in taxes on non-resident land was pressed. And turning from its mercantile destiny the city made its first determined drive for industry, offering up to five years' exemption of taxes on new machinery, stock and buildings, special water rates and similar inducements to establishment.

Sir Allan was not to witness the city's recovery. For years he had suffered from gout. In 1856, in his farewell appearance at the end of two years as prime minister in the MacNab-Taché coalition administration,[5] he had been carried into the old parliament house on Front Street, Toronto, his lower limbs swathed in flannel and had addressed the house from a chair. As prime minister, MacNab had shown unexpected political flexibility. His government can be credited with settling the thorny issues of the clergy reserves in Canada West and seigneurial tenure in the Lower Province, and with signing the Reciprocity treaty with the United States.

Now he belonged to the past. In 1856, wearying of the leadership of this "last of the High Tories," his party had replaced "the fearless old Chieftain" with "the young Chief," his former first lieutenant, moderate and progressive John A. Macdonald.

MacNab had resigned and gone to England where he had been received more than once by Queen Victoria. It is reported that MacNab's advice led to Her Majesty selecting Bytown (Ottawa) as Canadian capital. Victoria had created MacNab a baronet and made him a colonel of the British army and her honorary aide-de-camp, while the exclusive United Service Club of London, England, elected him an unprecedented honorary member.

Undoubtedly MacNab's personality and appearance were prime factors in his winning such honours. While to his enemies he was a stubborn, arrogant, crafty, none-too-honest Scotch bully, to friends and family he was the handsome, well built, shrewd laird of Dundurn, whose natural geniality, love of practical jokes and a quality of devil-may-care added to his charm. MacNab was a super salesman, as witness his coup in Masonry.

Although he possessed at the time only a second degree, MacNab returned from a trip to Edinburgh with the warrant of the Grand Lodge of Scotland appointing him provincial grand master in Canada; two years later, having taken no further degree, with a warrant obtained in London he became district grand master for England of the Provincial Grand Lodge of Canada West, thus receiving a doubly endorsed appointment as provincial grand master before he became a master Mason.[6]

In 1860 Sir Allan said goodbye to England and his daughter Sophia Mary, wife of Viscount Bury (later the seventh earl of Albemarle), who had undoubtedly presented the laird of Dundurn to Queen Victoria. At that time comptroller of the royal household, the young viscount had been attached to the Canadian civil service when he and Sophie had been married in 1855. The wedding in the beautiful verandah setting of Dundurn, overlooking terraced gardens and bay, had been the social event of the year.

Sophie, raised in the Roman Catholic faith of her deceased mother,[7] had been married in two services, Roman Catholic early in the morning and Anglican at noon following arrival of Governor-General Sir Edmund and Lady Head, Colonel Baron and the Baroness de Rottenburg and numerous other distinguished guests in the chartered steamer *Chief Justice Robinson*. The Lord Bishop of Toronto, assisted by the Very Venerable Archdeacon of Kingston, uncle of the bride, performed the Anglican ceremony.

By 1862 the social functions Allan MacNab cherished were drawing to a close. Possibly the last was a public dinner held in February at the Royal Hotel in his honour and in appreciation of his recent happy escape from shipwreck on the *North Briton* while returning from England. Present were not only a host of Sir Allan's friends but many who on occasion had strongly opposed him.

On August 8th, 1862, Sir Allan Napier MacNab, Bart., died at Dundurn. Possibly no other natural death in Canada has ever attracted more public attention, argument, dissension, and invective. A lifelong and faithful adherent of the Anglican faith and staunch member of Christ's Church which he had helped build, Sir Allan on his death bed was declared converted to the Roman Catholic faith and so buried. So unexpected was the conversion that a group of Masons arriving to hold a Masonic service were said to have found a wake in progress and been forced to retire.

The religious animosity and intolerance of the era may be judged by a widely circulated cartoon which showed Sir Allan in his coffin being claimed on the one hand by the Anglican Rev. J. G. Geddes, Dean of Christ's Church, and on the other by the Most Rev. John Farrell, Roman Catholic Bishop of Hamilton, while in the background his satanic majesty, the Devil, awaited his turn. Supporting Dean Geddes was Dr. Craigie, Sir Allan's physician, who had affirmed his patient was comatose when the Roman Catholic rites were administered; behind Bishop Farrell, Sir Allan's Roman Catholic daughter and sister-in-law.[8]

The last-minute conversion became a *cause célèbre* when George Brown attacked Bishop Farrell bitterly in the Toronto *Globe* and the Hamilton *Times* defended him. A still-current story relates that scarcely had the laird of stately Dundurn drawn his last breath when Bailiff Best's man descended on the Castle to take up residence and ensure that no one spirited away the rich presentation silver or other valuables.

"To keep the man company in his grisly watch," said Francis Mac-Beth Woodburn,[9] "my grandfather, Charles Burrows, later editor of the St. Catharines *Evening Journal*, helped guard the body." During the night the two conceived an idea. If the old chief was to be buried with Papist rites, at least he should rest under Protestant colours.

The following evening, fortified by bottled courage, the watchers removed the name plate from the coffin, inserted ribbons they had brought, and replaced the plate. When MacNab was carried to the walled family graveyard of the estate, located on a wooded point overlooking Burlington Bay and was laid to rest between his two wives as his will directed, he took the insignia of the Orange and Blue with him.

To attend MacNab's funeral prominent figures in political, business and social circles from both provinces and the United States converged on Hamilton. As the hour of burial approached, hundreds of mourners gathered at Dundurn where many first heard of Sir Allan's conversion. When it became known that Roman Catholic rites were to replace the expected Masonic funeral, the majority of those present withdrew in a scene of considerable turmoil.

So involved were MacNab's affairs that Dundurn was tied up in litigation for years. On June 16th, 1868, the property was sold at public auction by Thomas N. Best and was purchased by Sophia (Mrs. D. A.) MacNab for $6,700. In 1871 she sold the estate for $20,000.[10] At this period Dundurn served for several years as home of the Upper Canada Institute for the Deaf and Dumb, with an attendance of fifty to eighty.[11]

Four years after Sir Allan's death abrogation of the Reciprocity treaty, signed during the MacNab-Taché administration, added to Canada's economic distress. If the United States hoped that the British provinces would accept annexation to save their trade, the States was mistaken. In Hamilton repeal of reciprocity propelled the city a further step along the path leading from a mercantile to an industrial economy.

In 1859, establishment of the Great Western railway shops had heralded a period of industrial expansion in the city. Initially rails and equipment for the line had been imported from England, with English "navvies" and mechanics brought in to do much of the work, many remaining as settlers.

Prior to their manufacture in Hamilton, locomotives had also been imported from England or the United States. At Hamilton, Stoney Creek, Winona and other points where the line ran near the lake, locomotives were unloaded from schooners, assembled by English mechanics, and were then used to haul ties and gravel. The two first locomotives on the Great Western, the *Canada* and *Niagara*, were built by the Lowell Machine Shops, Lowell, Massachusetts, and shipped to Hamilton by schooner. The succeeding two, the *Hercules* and *Samson* built at Schenecteday, New York, were followed by some twenty locomotives produced by the two firms. The first freight engines came from Bristol, England, and were named *Rhinoceros, Hippopotamus, Elephant, Panther,* and *Buffalo.* By the end of 1854 the Great Western owned fifty locomotives.

When Hamilton began to manufacture locomotives in the Daniel C. Gunn Shop, largely for the opposition Grand Trunk railway, they too were named, the first *Ham, Shem* and *Japhet,* followed by two wood-burning freight engines, *Achilles* and *Bacchus,* and two switching engines, *Boxer* and *Growler.* By the time the Gunn Shop ceased production in the early 1860s the Great Western Shops were building their own engines and giving them good Anglo-Saxon names: *Britannia, Scotia, Erin* and *Saxon,* the *Scotia* noted as the first engine to have a complete steel boiler instead of the previous iron. By 1865 the shop was turning out passenger locomotives of latest design, brass bound and highly polished, and named after individuals, as the *Adam Brown* and *William Weir*. The 1880's closed a colourful page in railway history when engines ceased to be named.

In 1863 the Great Western constructed the first rolling mill in what would be known as Ontario, a huge wooden building 120 by 135 feet, with enormous timbers supporting a slate roof so high it was lost in gloom, dust and cobwebs. The mill was built to reroll English rails which had proved inferior in quality and unable to withstand the rigours of the Canadian climate. ". . . sometimes in one day of intense frost," says the chief engineer's report, "twenty rails are broken, some in two places, by passing trains."

The 20-inch mill which rerolled the rails was run by an enormous vertical single-cylinder engine so sturdy in construction that it survived sixty-two years, giving faithful service until 1925 when it was replaced by an electric motor. Roughing was performed under one of the earliest steam hammers in existence.[12] Years after it had ceased to function, its great gaunt frame towered into the gloom of the dusty roof. In 1898, following a fire, it was removed. Reported to have cost $107,500, a staggering sum for that day, the plant employed about 130 men.

In the later 1870's, following introduction of Sir John A. Macdonald's protective tariff aimed at promoting the Canadian iron industry, the Great Western shop was leased by American businessmen from the iron regions of Ohio, to become the Ontario Rolling Mill Company. Uniting with the Hamilton Iron and Steel Company on Huckleberry Point, the combined works became the Hamilton Steel and Iron Company, nucleus of the later Steel Company of Canada Limited. Over the years its founders and their successors would write the story of steel in Hamilton: Richard Brown; A. M. and C. S. Wilcox; P. M. Hitchcock; C. E. Doolittle; W. A. Child who succeeded Henry Willard as secretary; D. D. O'Connor; and H. H. Champ, one of the city's best known business leaders of all time.

Under the city's new industrial policy, buildings and machinery of the Ontario Rolling Mill were exempted from taxation for several years, as were various new companies, or companies introducing new machinery: David Morton, soap factory, Emerald Street South, whose fine red brick home on the corner of Emerald and Main Streets occupied the present site of the Cathedral Boys' High School; L. D. Sawyer and Company, agricultural implement manufacturers, foot of Wellington Street, successors to C. McQuesten and Company, Dr. Calvin McQuesten having retired in favour of his nephew, Luther D. Sawyer, who later introduced the Masseys, to form the world-famous firm of Sawyer-Massey; Meakins & Sons, wholesale brush manufacturers and cabinet makers, who now commenced operations in lock and cabinet hardware manufacture; and Edward and Charles Gurney, iron founders, manufacturers of ploughs and cultivators and parlour, box and cooking stoves "of every size and new and fashionable pattern," who after becoming Gurneys and Carpenter (Alexander), reverted again in the 1860's to E. & C. Gurney Company, expanding into a four-storey building which would stand nearly a century.

Asking exemption for machinery to be employed in manufacture of glass were the proprietors of the Hamilton Glass Works, Nathan B. Gatchell, Lyman Moore, John Winer and George Rutherford; and in manufacture of cut and plug tobacco, the firm of Quimby and Tuckett. Starting alone in a small shop at Bay and York Streets where he manufactured and sold cigars and plug tobacco, George E. Tuckett in succession partnered David Rose, Amos Hill, Alfred C. Quimby, and John Billings, the latter constituting half of the famous T B trademark, known throughout Canada. In their day the firm's Cherub, Anchor, and clear Havana T B were the most popular five-cent cigars in the country. In 1880, with retirement of John Billings, Mr. Tuckett's son, George Thomas, and later his nephew, John E. Tuckett, joined the firm.

Already established were Sanford McInnes and Company, wholesale clothing manufacturers; Joseph Flint who operated the first saw factory in Canada, and Mr. Beech who handmade the first Canadian files, for fifty years maintaining a national monopoly because of superior workmanship; Young and Brother (William and Robert) who produced the first burners for coal-oil lamps in Canada, creating a land office business in the conversion of lamps to their burners; and Dennis Moore & Company, iron founders, manufacturers of stoves, tinware, tools and machines.

At the middle of last century we find familiar names: J. H. Aussem, manufacturer and retailer of fine French, English and American confections, whose catering services would launch generations of local brides; coal dealers, R. W. Dunstan, Daniel Dewey, and Thomas and James Myles; tobacconists C. A. and M. B. Birge; jewellers Thomas Lees and Caleb Van Norman; and undertakers John Blachford and Arthur E. Snelgrove, the latter on the Court House Square, with supplementary Upholstering and Home Furnishings to boot; and on James Street, the predecessor of today's Right House, established in 1847 by Irish-born Thomas C. Watkins and his brother John H., the oldest still functioning department store in Hamilton.

Strengthening the city's financial position was the formation in 1859, with local head office, of the Hamilton Provident and Loan Company which would function until its absorption in 1926 in the larger Huron and Erie Trust Company. Already Thomas Stinson's bank was functioning, and by 1860 Nelson Mills and his brother George H., ex-mayor, were engaged in a private banking business.

More than offsetting these gains however, was loss of the Gore Bank. During the depression, losses from defalcations and local business ventures and over-speculation in land and railways so adversely affected the bank that its notes were refused. In 1868 the corporation of the city of Hamilton, which had contributed to its downfall, withdrew its account. In 1870, after two reductions of capital stock, the bank reorganized, consolidated its shares and amalgamated with the Canadian Bank of Commerce which assumed the headquarters building.

Before this occurred one major and one minor event would affect the city: the Fenian raid of 1866 would cause a passing flurry of excitement, and the following year Confederation would bring the permanent and important changes of union, one being adoption for the upper province of the name Ontario.

Possibly the most significant effect of the Fenian invasion was the surge of patriotism it inspired throughout the provinces of British North America and the consequent increased enthusiasm for Confederation. The American Civil War had demonstrated the isolation and vulnerability of these provinces. The First Battalion, Incorporated Militia, had been disbanded. When British forces were withdrawn for war in the Crimea there remained a mere skeleton force of regulars to protect the province.

To meet this situation the Militia Act of 1855 provided for recruiting on a voluntary basis of a small body of active militia, to be equipped and trained ten days a year (twenty for cavalry) at public expense. In Hamilton a troop of cavalry, a battery of artillery, and two independent rifle companies were enlisted.

Later, public demand for a larger force resulted in recruiting additional rifle companies which on December 11th, 1862, were organized into the 13th Battalion volunteer militia (infantry), with the Hon. Isaac Buchanan officer in command. With $4,000 subscribed by the public, a drill hall was erected, the battalion parading for the annual muster on June 4th to the completed large wooden building on James North. Uniforms were scarlet of the line with regulation shako adorned with small white pom.

On the following September 1st, the drill hall witnessed a second impressive ceremony when Mrs. Buchanan presented the battalion with its regimental colours—royal blue with the number 13 richly embroidered in gold and the motto, *Semper Paratus.*

Three years later the battalion received its baptism of fire. During the night of May 31st, 1866, some 1,500 Fenians from Buffalo, under General John O'Neill, crossed the river from Black Rock and went marching off across country, "to capture and hold Canada in ransom to compel England to return Ireland to the Republic." Ahead of them, farmers drove their animals into woods or swamp. The attitude of the United States to this invasion of a friendly country from their shores was one of indifference.

In Hamilton on the morning of June 1st the report of a cannon from the drill hall and the clangour of an alarm bell informed the city of the invasion of the Irish extremists. Hastily the 265 volunteers of the 13th repaired to the drill shed. Of their number 150 were under twenty years of age and 80 had never practised with ball cartridge. But the battalion, now under Lt.-Col. Alfred Booker, a martinet in dress and deportment, had at least drilled and marched. Now cheered by Hamiltonians lining James and Stuart Streets they marched to the depot and embarked for the front.

At 6 a.m. on June 2nd, the force disembarked at Ridgeway, weary, hungry, thirsty and depressed, having had only one meal in the past twenty-four hours and an inedible issue of bread and herrings, no water on the train and no water flasks.

In the dusty road beyond the station the scarlet-coated 13th fell in behind the dark green ranks of the Queen's Own Rifles, earlier arrived from Toronto, 480 strong, and two rural rifle companies. It was a bright cloudless hot June day. For the first time many heard the ominous order: "With ball cartridge—load!" Biting off the end of a paper cartridge, the soldiers poured the powder into the barrels of their rifles and rammed home the heavy bullet. Lieutenant-Colonel Booker, senior officer in command, ordered the force to advance on the Lime Ridge Road and the men moved off in column of fours under a pillar of dust. Reserve ammunition, later vitally needed, was returned to Port Colborne by train for safety.

At the head of the 13th rode Colonel Booker, the only man mounted, while the rear was brought up by Major James Skinner, a tall bearded patriarchal man. Later the only humorous note in the Fenian affair was said to have been the extreme reluctance of Colonel Booker's steed, loaned by Major Skinner, to enter the mail van and go to war.

For the ensuing fiasco Colonel Booker was courtmartialed and while exonerated of charges of cowardice and desertion was censured for an error in judgment which led him at the moment of victory, with the Fenians retreating on both wings, to panic and order formation of a hollow square to meet non-existent cavalry. Colonel Booker resigned command in favour of Lieutenant-Colonel Skinner. A few years later he died in Montreal, some said broken-hearted. In all nine Canadians, all of the Queen's Own, were killed and thirty-one wounded. Severely injured were Lieutenant Percy Gore Routh, Hamilton, and sixteen-year-old George A. Mackenzie, son of the Rev. John G. D. Mackenzie, M.A., curate of St. John's Mission Chapel, on the southeast corner of King and Queen Streets.

A little known story of the Fenian invasion is of the march of fifty Delaware and Cayuga braves from the Grand River reservation to Hamilton, to volunteer to "go on the war path" shoulder to shoulder with their white brothers, "to drive back the enemies of Canady." Attired in deerskin jackets or old coats, wearing squirrel or coonskin caps, black felt hats or battered cloth caps, and with moccasins, "shoe packs" or leather boots and occasional "foot rags," the volunteers marched down the Port Dover Plank Road, to be challenged by the astonished Home Guard sentinel stationed at the mountain brow.

When permission was received from headquarters, the warriors, the younger braves gaudy with war paint, advanced down the mountain into the city, carrying their various arms: muzzle-loading muskets complete with powder horn, stout war clubs and powerful bows and flint-tipped arrows. Wiser in the ways of war than their white brothers, they carried iron rations of parched corn and dried rabbit meat.

At the drill hall the Indians were officially welcomed and their leader informed that the Fenians had withdrawn across the Niagara on June 3rd. After being wined and dined the volunteers were taken on a tour of the city. Then with their tobacco supply amply replenished and with army rations for the return journey, they left with a last promise which their descendants would redeem in World War I: "Well, if you ever need us, just send a runner to the Injun bush. We'll be right behind him."

After the "Fenian Bother" there would be nearly five decades of peace for the city, broken only by the local enlistments, the distant excitements and alarms of the South African War at the century's turn.

Already the calamitous '60's were brightening, with the lighting of city streets symbolizing the general improvement in city conditions. For six months Hamilton had functioned under a nightly blackout, in which only the city hall had been lighted, and police station and engine houses allowed one lamp apiece. Lamps had been dismantled and stored. When they were returned to the streets, although lighted only till midnight, the city breathed a sigh of relief. With the invention by William and Robert Young of a burner for coal-oil lamps, street lighting was converted to oil for four years, 1862-66, after which the city resumed gas until the advent of electricity.

Before the city paused, with Confederation, to take stock of itself, it had again certain pages to close. In 1863 Dr. William Craigie died, and the following year Thomas Stinson, the banker, was buried from his handsome stone mansion set in wide lawns and bright garden beds in the then highly residential area on the east side of Queen Street, north of York, opposite the imposing residence of the late Colin C. Ferrie.[13]

In the city two other deaths in this decade would silently turn a leaf in one of the most romantic love stories in Canadian annals.

In his book, *Overture to Victoria*,[14] McKenzie Porter tells with a candour previously impossible, the story of the union of Edward, Duke of Kent, fourth son of George III and father of Queen Victoria, and his lovely countess, the charming Alphonsine Thérèse Bernadine Julie de Montgenet, Baronne de Fortisson, known to Canadians through nearly ten years of residence in Canada as Madame Julie de St. Laurent.

For the twenty-seven years that Edward and Julie lived together, so obviously happy and compatible was their relationship and so modest, discreet and socially impeccable was "Edward's French lady" that the couple was received openly in court circles in England, and in Quebec by the social arbiters of the capital.

Following the death in childbirth of Princess Charlotte, daughter of

144

the Prince Regent and heir presumptive to the British throne, the Duke and Julie separated, to permit the marriage for dynastic reasons of the Duke to Victoria Maria Louisa, daughter of the Duke of Saxe-Saalfeld-Coburg. On May 24th, 1819, in Kensington Palace the infant Alexandrina Victoria was born, the future Queen Victoria, greatest of British monarchs. Eight months later her father, aged fifty-two, died of pleurisy.

That there were children born to Edward and Julie there seems no doubt. Nor is there doubt that the couple, unlike Edward's brothers with their liaisons, for some reason were determined to conceal the existence of their children, consigning them to various foster parents, while they yet maintained them generously and rewarded those who reared them. Since, in addition, following the death of the Duke, all records of his connection with Julie disappeared, proof of descent becomes very difficult.

If documentary evidence is missing, by accident or design, there exists however a solid background of private and public tradition, unusual circumstances, physical resemblances, unexplained wealth and possessions, and special preferments which dovetail with historical facts to indicate that one of the world's outstanding romances, in one of the world's most fertile periods, was not barren.[15]

For a century and a quarter tradition has established to the satisfaction of Hamilton's "400" a link between mountaintop Barton Lodge and the British royal family. About Isabella Hyde, wife of John Lionel Whyte, who inherited the estates of his brother, Colonel James Matthew, and about her daughter, Emily Esther Elizabeth, who married Colonel William Gourlay in 1850, clung an aura of romance and mystery which in Victorian days set whispers circulating behind fluttering fans.

Wealth; an extensive estate whose rigid entail to the female line persisted unbroken for over one hundred years; the astonishing resemblance of Emily to Queen Victoria, her reputed half-aunt; visits and acceptance at St. James' court of Isabella and her daughter; unusual and beautiful household furniture, paintings, silver and jewels, and a library of rare first editions of such eminence as to be consulted by Sir John A. Macdonald; trained servants from England who remained a lifetime—such factors have satisfied Hamilton upper circles for generations of a royal connection never claimed nor referred to publicly by Isabella or her descendants.

Church records show that Isabella Hyde was born in 1791, the year of Edward's and Julie's arrival in Quebec from Gibraltar by British warship. Possibly her birth occurred aboard this warship during its May-June voyage, as a younger brother's is said to have later occurred. Possibly too the infant was consigned immediately to the Couvent des Ursulines, Quebec, a theory which would provide a logical explanation of Anglican Edward's historically recorded interest in the convent, attributed to his love for Roman Catholic Julie, and of his lengthy visit and inspection, followed by a donation of two hundred and eighty pounds, on December

20th, 1791. Reliable Quebec historians have claimed that secrets of the Kent-St. Laurent union lay locked in church registers.

Later, says family history, the child was reared in Hyde Hall, Jamaica, and in Knightsbridge, where Julie resided following her return with the Duke to England.

Family legend maintains that the Whyte family was selected by the Duke of Kent, and rewarded with plantations in Jamaica, to provide husband and protection for Isabella; that James, prior to Victoria's ascension to the throne, left his honourable post as one of His Majesty's privy council and a justice of assize in Jamaica to establish an estate in the wilds of Upper Canada that would maintain Isabella's line for futurity. Time may prove that other siblings were settled in Upper Canada.

For over a century the story has been a romantic page in city history. When Edward Prince of Wales came to Hamilton in 1860 he visited Barton Lodge. Princess Louise, daughter of Queen Victoria, and her husband, the Marquis of Lorne, Governor-General of Canada, paid their respects to the Gourlays, as did Prince Arthur, Duke of Connaught. "All these," said a descendant, "the Duke of Devonshire, Baron Rothschild, Des Barats, all signed their names with a diamond on a library window. As children we knew each signature. All are gone, lost in the fire that gutted the house in 1930."

"On the mantel at Barton Lodge," wrote an intimate friend of Mrs. Gourlay's daughter, "I saw many times a small silver casket which contained a lock of 'dear Albert's hair' and an accompanying letter bearing Queen Victoria's signature. 'Dear Albert,' of course, was Prince Albert, consort of Victoria.

"When I married I was given as a wedding gift a Spode cup and saucer in the royal blue pattern and bearing the royal crest. The cup, which is priceless, could have come only from royalty. Barton Lodge possessed a whole service, used regularly."

Today only the memory of the past remains. Yet Hamiltonians still recall the family carriage and its liveried footman, with its brass sparkling in the sun, its jingling harness and prancing horses. And seated within, the gracious dignified woman, daughter of Isabella Hyde, Emily Gourlay, who looked enough like Queen Victoria to be her sister.[16]

15

Confederation, Fire Fighters, and Police

ON JULY 1st, 1867, the birth of the infant Dominion was celebrated. That the celebration was in great measure due to its being a holiday was of little moment.

The Confederation of the British North American colonies was largely the work of the statesmen who conceived it, bore it through a difficult and hazardous pregnancy and finally triumphantly delivered the new-born federation. To the workman in the city and the man behind the plough the problems of union, of Canadian geographical and Canadian racial cultures were as vaguely understood as were its benefits.

What the average man understood and accepted was the leadership of the dynamic fathers of Confederation—in Canada West Conservative John A. Macdonald, knighted when he became the first prime minister of the new Dominion, and the fiery editor of the Toronto *Globe*, "Clear Grit" George Brown.

Probably the greatest popular enthusiasm for union existed in Ontario, yet in many parts of the province it inspired only moderate interest. On the whole Hamiltonians were prepared to approve it. Already the swing of the civic pendulum was unmistakably from commerce to industry. By allaying the unrest and suspicion which had retarded development of the colonies, by unifying the country and linking it by rail, Confederation, it was felt, could not fail to improve trade and business in general.

"The bridal of the provinces," reports Editor Thomas White in *The Spectator*, "like all other weddings, was celebrated by the peal of merry marriage bells."

The day started early. At six o'clock in the morning the gay chiming of the church bells was augmented by the crackle of firecrackers and roar of artillery as the Hamilton Field Battery under Captain McCabe fired a salvo of forty guns from Eastern Park, site of today's Barton Street jail.

"Flags waved from every housetop," reported the *Spectator*. "Red, white and blue bunting was stretched across the streets, laurel and ever-

147

greens clustered round verandahs and balconies, while from window, housetop and gallery the fairest flowers of our city blushed not unseen, and added grace and beauty to the scene."

Highlight of the day was the parade from the Gore through various downtown streets, finally out York to the Crystal Palace. In the lead marched the volunteer fire brigade, three hundred and ten strong, under Chief Engineer Matthias W. Attwood, the various department machines gaily decked with flowers; the juvenile Royal cadets armed with wooden guns; the city's carriage-borne school trustees; and following on foot Principal Archibald Macallum of Central School attended by four hundred students waving flags, singing and cheering for the Red, White and Blue.

Since Mayor Benjamin E. Charlton (vinegar manufacturer), council and city officials were to bring up the rear of the parade, the civic watering carts were out at dawn in an all-out blitz on the soft summer dust that blanketed Hamilton streets at this period. The horse-drawn, dumpy little cisterns on wheels had done their best but by late morning under the hot July sun dust again filled the nostrils and powdered marchers and spectators alike.

Undaunted, the parade unrolled its length. Behind the students marched the trades of the city with displays—iron moulders, butchers, shoemakers; a Canadian oil cart drawn by six horses; and outstanding in floats, the Wanzer Sewing Machine Company's wagon filled with pretty girls dressed in delicate colours and wearing diadems inscribed Ontario, Quebec, Nova Scotia and New Brunswick.

Marking the day, a new steamship service was inaugurated between Hamilton, Oakville and Toronto with the first large vessel in local waters, the side-wheeler *Rothesay Castle*, a recent blockade runner in the American Civil War, making the trip in two hours and a half, return fare one dollar.

When the run did not pay, the *Rothesay Castle* reverted to the Atlantic coast. In 1877 she was rebuilt, renamed the *Southern Belle* and returned to the Hamilton run by George E. and David Keith. Later an upper deck was added requiring a compensating system of blocks along her hull to prevent her capsizing in a heavy sea. Following removal of the *Belle* from this run a small steamer, the *Hastings,* replaced her, succeeded in 1888 by the popular *Macassa,* built on the Clyde and brought over on her maiden voyage by honeymooning Captain Charles P. Hardy.

Linked with Confederation also was the appointment of Samuel Mills, M.P.P. since 1849, to the Senate, and the first experiment in lighting by electricity in Canada. By the use of carbon pencils George Black, manager of the Montreal Telegraph Company, established in 1847, created quite a brilliant Confederation night display in the window of the telegraph office on James Street South opposite the Gore.

Confederation was a fitting time to assess city development. In 1858 Hamilton's population had reached 27,500. Two years later it had fallen to 19,000, and after a brief rally, in 1864 nosedived to 17,000. Now it had climbed again to 21,485, mute evidence that the corporation had weathered the storm. By 1873 population would reach 30,201 and the debenture debt, $147 per capita in 1864, would be reduced to $82.

Having set its financial problems on an established course, council turned its attention to neglected municipal services. In 1866 the Board of Health resumed activity. Under threat of an impending epidemic James McCracken, high bailiff and health officer, with an expanded department staged an all-out city-wide clean-up campaign which included public education and participation, and which happily replaced several "public necessaries," including one on the market, long the target of bitter public complaint.

Roads and sidewalks were repaired and extended; sewers and water mains further developed and domestic and industrial connections increased in number. Waterworks began to return an appreciable revenue. Real estate values improved. From 1873 to 1878 a widespread depression would slow the local economy but with its finances on a sounder basis the city would progress for the next quarter century at a moderate but steady pace. Until the gay Nineties Hamilton would show practically no debt increase. Revenue would pace expenditure and the tax rate would hover about seventeen mills.

On July 1st, 1867, the Hamilton Fire Brigade consisted of a hook and ladder company, one hose and three engine companies.[1] Following one of the complete disbandings and reorganizations by which the volunteer force on occasion purged itself of deadwood and incompatible personnel and/or emphasized its protests to council over impossible firefighting conditions, the brigade was low in strength. A decade earlier, following such a shuffle, the force had stood at eight companies, with five hundred and eighteen officers and men.

A voluntary force composed mostly of young men with the necessary strength, stamina and daring, and requisite civic-mindedness to protect city property in which few held a share, the firemen of early days not only served without remuneration but frequently purchased engines and equipment with their own funds and money they solicited. Their return was the thrill and distinction of their calling; exemption, after a certain period, from statute labour and jury duty; a potent dram at the site of the fire; and a uniform including at various times cap and belt, red shirt, light blue coat, and white staff and badge of office.

While willing hands still propelled equipment to a fire, a standing award was offered for the first teams on hand to draw the water tanks to the conflagration.

At the shout of "Fire!", the clamour of the fire bell or later the fire telegraph alarm, firemen dropped their work (if in the shop forfeiting pay without reimbursement) sprinted at top speed to the engine house, dragged their unwieldy equipment to the fire and without pause engaged the raging, wood-glutted foe. At night the brigade's juvenile torch bearers

149

lighted the way. It was the pride of every company to be first at the blaze and have the first stream playing on the fire.

Even when fire engines of gradually improving type were acquired —the engine from Q. Lemoine, Quebec, throwing water 125 feet, and the Perry engine of Montreal having been milestones—the bucket brigade still operated. Prior to establishment of the city's waterworks system, water was provided for firefighting by some twenty tanks and wells throughout the city, kept filled by contract, their locations indicated by finger posts. Householders were required to keep a barrel of water always on hand. In addition, premiums were paid for water delivered to a fire, at one time the first barrel of thirty-two gallons bringing a bonus of one pound.

Following city incorporation, an incentive was offered the firefighters themselves, the first engine reaching a fire being awarded 10s., while each company received a bonus for company funds of 1s. 3d. each for members in attendance.

By Confederation, Hamilton had an Engine house in every ward in the city,[2] thus removing the earlier hazard of arriving at a fire with engines and equipment which had stood unprotected in the open since the preceding fire and were largely unfit for use. Exception had been the engine sheltered in the foundry of Fisher and McQuesten, James and Merrick Streets, which John Fisher had built and presented to the city.

It speaks well for Hamilton's volunteer fire brigade that in the half century following the conflagration of 1832 the city had few major fires. This also in spite of various outbreaks of arson, so grave that rewards of four hundred dollars for convicting information were offered; council petitioned parliament for power to designate "Watch Light" districts in the city and to impose a special tax on their residents to provide protection; assistant bailiffs were sworn in to attend fires; and citizens formed vigilance squads to patrol the streets.

Of serious fires most unfortunate was the 1859 gutting of the frame and roughcast St. Mary's Cathedral, since fire insurance on the twenty-one-year-old building had lapsed. However, at a public meeting in the Mechanics' Hall, presided over by Mayor Henry McKinstrey, the city subscribed so generously that a new cathedral of patterned red brick and stone, located slightly west of its predecessor, at the corner of Park and Sheaffe Streets, was dedicated by His Lordship Bishop Farrell on May 21st, 1860.

In 1855 a major fire wiped out the foundry of Fisher and McQuesten, causing the death of two firemen and serious injury of a third. Crushed by a falling wall were Lawrence Bowers and William Wood. Miraculously, William Omand, rescued hours later from beneath the mass of baking stone, survived the ordeal.

Possibly the most popular fire with the firefighters in Hamilton's history was the big burn at the Gompf brewery, foot of John Street. The fire in the brewhouse, noted for the excellence of its "suds," broke out on February 13th, 1875, at six p.m., just as tired workers were returning home from a day's labour.

The following evening, still weary from their battle at Gompf's, the firemen gathered for their annual meeting, to which the brewery had suitably contributed its thanks. With the 6.30 a.m. whistle of the Great Western shops in mind, the boisterous meeting broke up at 1 a.m. As the firemen streamed out into the icy night air they were greeted by the loud, strident clang of the alarm bell in the city hall tower, an unusual four-storey square structure displaying a clock face on each side below the bell cupola.

Behind the hall the Nicholson block, at the junction of Market, MacNab and York Streets, was ablaze. The fire was fought in bitter cold which froze the water thrown on the building, sheathing it, adjacent premises, the street and firemen in ice. Not until the following noon was the fire quenched in the icicle-tombed ruin.

Most spectacular of all fires in Hamilton seems to have been the holocaust that destroyed the five-storey warehouse of D. McInnes and Company, merchants and manufacturers, on the southwest corner of King and John Streets, site of today's Post Office building. Head of the firm, Senator Donald McInnes, then owned and occupied Dundurn Castle. First discovered at 5 p.m., August 1st, 1879, the fire raged throughout the night and after being quenched, twice broke out again. So fierce was its suction that two blocks to the north burning shingles fired the roof of the Methodist Episcopal Church. In the blaze three men lost their lives.

The McInnes fire marked the beginning of Hamilton's modern fire department. Until 1863 no hint of commercialism intruded on the post. Then William Inkson, who followed Hugh Boyd, asked for but did not receive remuneration. More fortunate, his successor, James McCabe, was voted $100 and first received the title, Chief of the Fire Brigade. In 1868 the city council established an annual salary of $100 for the post, John P. McKenna becoming the first formally paid Chief.

Connecting link between the old fire brigade and the new was Mr. McKenna's successor, Chief James Amor. During his ten years of office the ever popular fire horse joined the department, council granting $500 to purchase three horses and harness, thus gladdening small boys' hearts for generations and adding a colourful page to city history. When Fire Chief Alexander W. Aitchison next took office, on January 14th, 1879, revised regulations ushered in the modern fire department.

In the twin department of police service, a similar development occurred. Prior to the Municipal Act of 1849 the force had consisted of a High Bailiff, Assistant Bailiff and two constables who policed the town and in addition discharged the duties of health officer and inspector of streets and sidewalks. For round-the-clock service the constables in turn slept in the unheated, and at times unlighted Engine House on King William Street. Although the Municipal Act called for a constable in each city ward, council did not increase the force until 1853 when a wave of depredations in the city led to public outcry for a night patrol and four men were borrowed from the special force established by the Great Western during the lawless and violent period of railway construction. The following year, with disbandment of the railway detachment, the four were added permanently to the city force, two being assigned to attend the arrival and departure of the steamships.

During the lengthy service of High Bailiff James McCracken, 1852-1877, the police force took form. Following Chief Constable John Moore's resignation, John Carruthers was appointed Chief Constable, to become Police Chief Carruthers during his twelve-year term of office. In 1865 Chief Carruthers was dismissed by council in favour of Captain W. H. Nicolls.

The Parker gang, led by burglar Joe Parker and a notorious Hamilton gambler, Jim Jeffery, led to Chief Carruthers' downfall. Although several crooks were captured by Hamilton police, so bold did the gang become in their robbings and beatings of householders that Detective Armstrong of the government police was called in.

Robbed repeatedly, the wholesale drygoods firm of F. W. Gates and John O. Macrae and the retail drygoods establishment of John Peacock verged on ruin. Detective Armstrong lined up the gang and their hideout. When Chief Carruthers, instead of sending police, entrusted the surprise arrest to Bailiff McCracken's untrained men, resulting in Parker's escape, public outcry, sparked by Mr. Gates and Mr. Macrae, led council to replace the chief.[3]

In turn Chief Nicolls and Deputy Chief Herman F. Ahrens were discharged in 1868 for malfeasance in office. In considering this bit of history one must remember that city councils for decades frequently discharged civic officials—as witness city engineers—only to relent later and rehire the same individual. Succeeding Chief Nicolls was Chief Ralph Davis, in turn followed by Chief John Henery. When the latter became governor of the Barton Street gaol in 1875, Matthew Logan, a member of the detective department formed in November, 1865, took his place.

By Confederation the Hamilton police force, including the High Bailiff, numbered twenty-one men and consisted of a police magistrate, chief of police, sergeant, detective and sixteen policemen. It was governed by a three-man board of commissioners, first established on August 16th, 1858, composed of recorder (judge), police magistrate and current mayor. The growth of the department had not been steady. In the lavish Fifties the force had neared thirty and boasted four sergeants. In 1858 it had levelled off at twenty-six, to run into the depression decade two years later and be slashed by council to a force of eight.

Through the years of unlighted streets when empty pockets and hungry stomachs bred crime, when salaries dwindled and duties increased in proportion to decrease in staff, the local police coped with a city that exhibited its full share of the period's unrest and lawlessness.

Murder, arson, burglary, assault—all these the darkness aided—larceny, horse stealing, jail break, the minor crimes, and vandalism which damaged cemetery, private homes and public properties, uprooting some twenty trees in Gore Park in the heart of town. So wanton was the destruction in the Gore that council moved the gas-globed drinking fountain, presented by Mr. Archibald Kerr, outside the fence on James Street and replaced the four corner entrance turnstiles with iron gates to be unlocked only on special occasions when police attended.

In the old council minutes one finds laconic entries: "Expenses approved for James McCracken in arresting pickpockets at Suspension Bridge (Niagara Falls) . . . Vote of thanks by council to Chief of Police Nicolls for his energy and ability in arresting Henry Parker, also known as 'Bristol Bill'." A noted bank burglar, English Bristol Bill and his accomplices escaped to the United States after an unsuccessful attempt to rob the Galt town bank while a town ball was in progress. Having previously featured in major bank steals in New York and Pittsburgh, Parker found the States too hot and slipped back across the border, to be spotted and nabbed by Chief Nicolls.

Considering this and similar items one regrets the loss to the community of Chief Nicolls' services. When minutes also show the authorities considering dismissal of Chief Davis and laying court charges against Police Magistrate James Cahill, successor to Magistrate Armstrong, whose death in 1863 terminated sixteen years in office, and find that various fire chiefs were also summarily removed, it becomes evident that public servants of the early corporation walked insecurely.

To the 1870's belong three important developments related to the police department: erection of a new gaol, new Registry office and new Court house.

As early as 1852 the question arose of a combined gaol for the counties of Halton, Wentworth and Brant and the city of Hamilton. By 1870 the cells of the King William Street station had become totally inadequate. Having considered and discarded a plan to construct cells in the basement of city hall, it was determined jointly with the County of Wentworth to erect a new county gaol in Hamilton to serve the city and replace the temporary detention cells in the court house, with the city paying sixty and the county forty per cent of capital cost. As a site fourteen acres of Eastern Park, lying between Elgin Street and Ferguson Avenue on the north side of Barton, was chosen.

Although tenders were accepted for erection of the gaol in November, 1871, and Scotch stonemasons were well advanced with their work the following year, not until May 1st, 1875, was the three-storey sandstone building occupied.[4] On June 5th, 1875, the account of C. Armstrong and team, $6 was paid for "moving from the Old to the New Gaol," while the first year's tender for foodstuffs dates from July 1st, 1875.

Much of this delay resulted from the inability of city and county to agree on division of capital and maintenance costs of the undertaking, matters as minor as cost of hospital diet and advertising courts causing infinite argument. When no agreement could be reached, arbitrators were appointed and when their arbitration proved unpopular, new arbitrators to arbitrate the arbitration. Regularly too the principals determined to separate, the county once sending a bill to the legislature demanding its freedom from wedlock, and being refused. When the final clause was written, the county would seem largely to have profited, but whether from superior shrewdness or more stubborn tenacity is hard to say.

Prior to moving in the prisoners it was discovered that while the gaol stood untenanted the locks of the cell gates had rusted so that they had to be removed and oiled. Built in the Italianate style of the period, to plans of Deputy Sheriff William Milne, the gaol accommodated sixty male and six female prisoners. A formidable building, it possessed walls three feet thick, concrete floors, stone-lined cells and six basement dungeons for solitary confinement. Twenty-foot walls surrounded a gaol yard 60 feet by 100. A carriage house later housed the gallows. The following year the grounds were laid out in shrubbery and flowers. About the walls, on some adjacent pasturage, John Taylor's cows cropped contentedly.

Hard on the heels of the gaol came the county Registry office in Prince's Square, completed in 1876, a long low white brick, stone trimmed building designed by Architect A. H. Hills and erected to the west of the old Court house.

In 1877 a new Police court and cells, furnace heated and gas lighted, was constructed at the old stone two storey Engine house on King William Street, near Mary, to supplement facilities in the Court house, now woefully inadequate.

When the county determined to replace the Court house with a larger, functional building, court space was rented in the Police court. In 1877 the cornerstone of the third Court house was laid with full Masonic ceremonies. Among the speakers was John W. Willson of Winona, whose father, the Hon. John Willson, M.P.P., had laid the cornerstone of its predecessor.

Designed by Architect C. W. Mulligan and built by John Hancock and Eli Van Allen, the Court house was considered Architect Mulligan's *tour de force*. Of stone in Italianate style, tending with its complicated frosting to baroque, the tower-crowned, many windowed county building added a touch of late sixteenth century French civil architecture to nineteenth century Hamilton. Unlike its predecessors, the new Court house had no gaol accommodation except two lock-up cells for temporary detention. On September 15th, 1879, the new building was opened by the Governor-General, the Marquis of Lorne.

For a brilliant state ball and drawing room given by city and county and attended by members of the government, bar and bench and the province's leading citizens, the Court house was handsomely adorned with standards of flags and massed flowers, except for the imposing, domed main court room, considered sufficiently embellished by its softly gleaming walnut wainscoting, carved furnishings and judge's bench.

With nineteenth century delight in elaborate formality, the fortunate élite invited to the ball contrived the most elegant costumes possible. It was therefore a shock when *The Spectator* the day before the ball advised its readers that the "full dress" of the invitations was not required but that "ordinary walking or morning costume" was permissible. "Such dress," said *The Spectator*, "as a person uses attending church."

Again county insistence had won, the change being made, it was said, on demand of Warden Thomas Stock, a virile personality, who had never owned nor worn formal attire and saw no reason at this date to change his habits.

That Warden Stock was in the minority is proved by press reports of the ladies and their attire. *The Spectator* commenced, "Ranged on either side of the Princess Louise and the Marquis were the ladies of the city including Mrs. Gourlay and her daughter Evelyn, Mrs. Fuller" (wife of Right Rev. T. B. Fuller, D.D., Bishop of Niagara), "Mrs. Aemelius Irving, Mrs. Isaac Buchanan and others."

At the first meeting of Wentworth county council, an ornamental fish pond before the Court house was ordered filled in. Today its site is occupied by the striking monument presented to the city by the late Mr. and Mrs. Stanley Mills commemorating, "the United Empire Loyalists[5] who . . . largely laid the foundations of this Canadian nation as an integral part of the British Empire." The pioneer family group was designed and executed by sculptor Sydney March of the famous March family of Farnborough, Kent, England, sculptors of the Canadian war memorial on Parliament Hill, Ottawa.

In the year the third Court house was opened, the Hamilton Law Association was founded with sixty-five members, its aim to create and maintain a law library for members. First president was Aemelius E. Irving, Q.C., M.P.; vice-president, Thomas Robertson, Q.C., later the Hon. Mr. Justice Robertson of the Supreme Court bench; treasurer, Alexander Bruce; and secretary, R. R. Waddell. In 1888 the office of president passed to Edward Martin, K.C., succeeded by Francis Mackelcan, K.C. The famous B. B. Osler was a founder, as were Sir John M. Gibson, Thomas C. Haslett, Stephen F. Lazier, Charles Lemon, John Crerar, and J. B. Teetzel.

Over the years many members have been elevated to the bench: the late Archer Martin, chief justice of the Supreme Court of British Columbia; Russell W. Treleaven, Q.C., justice of the Ontario Supreme Court and grand master of the Grand Lodge of Canada, Province of Ontario; the late Reid Bowlby, Q.C., and C. W. G. Gibson, Q.C. Sir Lyman Poore Duff attained the distinction of becoming chief justice of the Supreme Court of Canada. With service on the bench of the Wentworth county court one finds the late Judge W. F. Schwenger, Judge Theo. L. McCombs and Judge J. A. Sweet, among others.

Missing from the opening of the third Court house was High Bailiff and Health Officer James McCracken, whose place as bailiff was taken by Thomas Beasley and as health officer by John W. James. In place of Robert W. Kerr, whose death in 1872 ended nineteen years' service as city clerk, Alexander Stuart attended.

On September 30th, 1873, the corporation had officially attended the funeral of the Most Rev. John Farrell, D.D.; and the following year that of the Hon. Samuel Mills, donor to the city of Harvey Park adjoining Dundurn on the west, and of the land and funds to build All Saints' Anglican Church, situated on the southeast corner of King and Queen Streets, opposite the brick farmhouse of pioneer James Mills. On this site George T. Tuckett later built his towered Italianate brownstone mansion now incorporated into the present Scottish Rite Temple. Surviving Senator Mills was his widow, née Miss Aurora Holton, daughter of Janna and Brisies Holton, and several of their eight children whose marriages led to connections with many well known city families: Cawthra, Young, Gage, Woodruff, Davis, Freeman, Stares, Birge and McKay.

Of all deaths in the Seventies the one that attracted most public attention and avid interest was the brutal and bizarre slaying of Nelson Mills, fourth son of James.

A shrewd businessman, Nelson had converted his land into rental properties on a lesser scale but in similar fashion to his brother Samuel who built row upon row of workingmen's homes. Among his tenants Nelson numbered Michael McConnell, a butcher on the James Street market who rented a house and ten acres of land on Concession Street, today's Aberdeen Avenue. Then southern boundary of the city, the street was noted for citizens' complaints concerning the piggeries crowding it and the cows, goats and other animals which pastured on the adjacent mountainside.

In January, 1876, McConnell (remarkable for an oddly shaped head resulting from an old fracture above the left eyebrow, which he considered a distinction) owed fourteen dollars on his rent which he refused to pay until certain improvements were made on the property. On the morning of Wednesday, January 5th, Nelson Mills had a distress warrant served on the house and Mrs. McConnell hurried to the market to inform her husband. Without a word McConnell pulled off his butcher's apron, drew on his blue coat over his grayish waistcoat and checked flannel, white collared shirt, slipped a butcher's knife up his sleeve and departed muttering he would see who was boss.

Followed by his alarmed wife McConnell strode the six or seven blocks to Nelson Mills' white stucco home standing on the southwest corner of Queen and George Streets behind an ornamental iron fence. Ringing the bell he asked the coloured maid for her master. While she was absent, enquiring, Mr. Mills approached, walking north on Queen.

Shouting, "Here he is!" McConnell rushed to meet him. Disregarding his wife's pleas, he drew his knife and stabbed his victim in the head. Twice the injured man escaped, caught up stones and threw them at his attacker, and twice was set upon and furiously assailed.

156

After the last attack McConnell stood for a moment staring at his prostrate victim, then shook his head and walked coolly away, wiping his knife on his sleeve. At the corner he met his victim's father-in-law, Andrew Gage. "He did it to me," said McConnell, "and now I've done it to him!" Without haste he walked up Queen to his home on Aberdeen. As he washed his hands of blood Detective James C. Macpherson arrested him. Nelson Mills died the following Sunday.

Michael McConnell's trial before Judge Moss was the last murder trial in the old stone Court house. In spite of a plea of insanity by the prisoner's counsel, John Crerar, supported by testimony of experts, Crown counsel James Shaw Sinclair assisted by the celebrated B. B. Osler obtained a verdict of guilty and McConnell was sentenced to be hanged on March 14th, 1876.

Over the years the second Court house had participated in several murder trials and hangings, the hanging of John Mitchell on June 7th, 1859, for the slaying in anger of his common-law wife being the last public execution in Hamilton. Staged on Jackson Street behind the Court house, the hanging was watched avidly by hundreds who crowded surrounding rooftops to peer into the high-fenced gaol yard, while other hundreds thronged the streets below, eager to taste death safely secondhand.

If not public, the execution of Michael McConnell was certainly not private. After a sound night's rest and a moderate breakfast, McConnell was joined by three spiritual advisers and later by the sheriff, several reporters, the bailiff and others. Upon arrival, the masked executioner pinioned the prisoner's arms, calmly assisted by the latter, and the assemblage marched to the scaffold. Upon the scaffold the group was joined by the deputy sheriff, two justices of the peace, Governor Henery of the jail and the jail turnkeys.

After reading the execution order the sheriff asked the prisoner if he had anything to say.

"It was not my intention," replied McConnell, "but since I see so many here I think I am justified in expressing a few of my sentiments.

"I am placed here in a very solemn position which I say from my heart I never deserved. If I am the murderer of Nelson Mills, I never planned or contrived it. If a little moderation on Mills' part had been shown it would have saved us both. I was his tenant for four and one-half years. Fourteen dollars was the full amount and he knew I was worth more than that.

"If he had given me even a week it would have saved all the trouble. That is the sum and substance of the matter. I lost my temper. I hope from my soul that it will be a warning to all men to exercise moderation in all their transactions. I have no hard feelings in going to my doom. I am quite cheerful. I hope I leave no enemies."

The prisoner then affectionately kissed the Rev. J. C. Smith and shook hands with everyone on the scaffold, beginning with the sheriff and ending with the hangman, remarking to the latter, "I do not know you but I forgive you."

McConnell knelt on the platform as the hangman adjusted the black cap and began to pray. The rope was placed about his neck and he asked that it be drawn tighter.

With evident emotion the Rev. Mr. Smith offered a prayer, then began slowly and solemnly to repeat the Lord's Prayer, McConnell and all present responding. At the words, "Lead us not into temptation but deliver us from evil" the bolt was drawn and without a struggle Michael McConnell was dropped eleven feet into eternity. Fourteen minutes later the gaol surgeon, J. W. Rosebrugh, M.D., pronounced him dead.

The murderer's death was a strange contrast to the violence of his crime. When the black cap was removed there was no sign of struggle or pain on his features or in his firmly set mouth. Death, said the doctors, must have been instantaneous.

16

Churches, Horse Cars, and Access Roads

IN 1875, Hamilton's population topped 32,000. The city had twenty-four churches and seven chapels and missions covering eight denominations besides Wesleyan, Epicopalian, New Connexion and Primitive Methodist and British Methodist Episcopal.

Said Mabel Burkholder, "Along a five-mile stretch of present Highway 53 stood four Methodist churches and four cemeteries: Bowman Church, known as the local cradle of Methodism; Garner's, also called Zion and the White Frame Church; the White Brick Church; and Shavers' Church,[1] now Bethesda. They called it 'Methodist Row'."

Methodism was the religion preached by the hardy circuit riders, a vital faith peculiarly adapted to pioneer conditions. "It was a lively religion," said Miss Burkholder. "It appealed to the lonely, hard working settler. And its ranks were constantly recruited at revival camp meetings. In the 1860's, when the population of Hamilton stood at 25,000, one-fifth of this number was Methodist."

Said Mrs. Frank Leland, wife of the American consul at Hamilton during the 1880's, "As a church going community I have never seen the equal of this city." She might also have added, "As a church building community." By the 1890's the Baptist congregation of the mother Park Street Church under Rev. Dr. William Stewart had built the James Street Baptist Church, a large, handsomely designed stone edifice at James and Jackson Streets, still strong and vigorous today in its ministry. In addition, missions had been established throughout the city which would later grow into McNab Street, Hughson Street, Trinity, Stanley Avenue and Wentworth Street churches.

At the corner of Main Street and West Avenue stood the Anglican Church of St. Thomas, erected in 1869 by a congregation previously worshipping in a stuccoed frame church on Emerald Street North. A dignified, square-towered stone church, the new St. Thomas' helped serve the Protestant section of Corktown. Gradually also about the city other Anglican churches were rising: St. Luke's, St. Mark's and St. Matthew's, St.

George's and St. Peter's, several of their rectors achieving notable recognition: Canon R. G. Sutherland, B.A., Canon F. E. Howitt, Rev. Thomas Geoghegan, Rev. J. W. Ten Eyck, Rev. (later the Venerable) George Forneret and Canon Samuel Daw.

One of the oldest churches in the city was the Congregational Church, housed first in a handsome frame building on the southeast corner of Hughson and Henry (Cannon) Streets built during the pastorate of the Rev. David Dyer. Following a later schism between the church and its fellow churches, the congregation was dissolved and re-formed and a new brick church erected under the guidance of the Rev. Thomas Pullar.

Organized in 1853 as the Hebrew Benevolent Society Anshe Sholom of Hamilton, with a site purchased for a cemetery, the Jewish reformed congregation of Anshe Sholom was incorporated ten years later. In 1880 a synagogue was built on Hughson Street South, with Edmund Scheuer its first president. In 1873, under the leadership of Mrs. Herman Levy, the Deborah Ladies' Aid Society, said to be the oldest Jewish women's philanthropic group in Canada, was formed. In 1887 Beth Jacob congregation was founded, its president Kalman Cauman, with a synagogue erected the following year.

Parallelling the city's religious growth was its educational expansion. In 1875 Hamilton's school system consisted of Central School, nine primary schools and a Grammar School opened in 1866 at the corner of Main and Caroline with John M. Buchan as principal. Under the School Act of 1871 the name "Grammar School" was replaced by "High School." In September, 1897, a new combined Central Collegiate Institute and Ontario Normal College was opened on the former Richard M. Wanzer property bounded by Hunter and Stinson Streets, Victoria and West Avenues, the Caroline Street High School being then converted into a public school. Principal of Central Collegiate was R. A. Thompson, B.A., with J. B. Turner vice-principal; of the Ontario Normal College, Dr. J. A. McLellan, M.A., LL.D., principal, and R. A. Thompson vice-principal.

Following passage of the Roman Catholic Separate School Act of 1885 and establishment of a formal Hamilton separate school system, St. Mary's and St. Patrick's Schools were built. In charge of the Sisters of St. Joseph, who had conducted classes in the convent since its opening, the schools had a master for senior boys, two of the earliest being James B. Looney, St. Mary's, and John McKenzie, St. Patrick's.

In 1860 a two-room school, St. Vincent's, was opened, which at a later date was conducted by the Ladies of Loretto. The subsequent two-room St. Lawrence School, replaced in 1900 by a new six-room building, was also taught by the Sisters of St. Joseph. During the episcopate of His Excellency Bishop Crinnon the Sacred Heart Model School for the practical application of advanced studies was built in 1882.

In addition, in private tuition Hamilton boasted the celebrated Wesleyan non-sectarian Ladies' College, incorporated by act of parliament,

August 15th, 1861, whose principal was the noted educationist, Mary Electa Adams. The college was housed in the elaborate 150-room premises of the former Anglo-American Hotel. Of the imposing board of directors Edward Jackson was president; Dr. Calvin McQuesten, vice-president; Joseph Lister, treasurer; and Rev. S. D. Rice, secretary. So favourably was the college known that it drew students from all parts of Canada and the United States.

Serving the Mountain during this era was the small red brick Mountain Union Mission, familiarly known as "The Mission," which for years doubled as an undenominational Protestant church and school. Flanked by open meadows, its view from Concession Street was unobstructed to the brow. A typical Ontario one-room little red school, School Section No. 4, Barton, on Sherman Avenue south of Mohawk Road, served the Burkholder settlement. On the west end mountain, the Union School in 1874 replaced the original log school house. In the 1870's a Rymal, David Sykes, taught in the school and three later generations of Rymals attended.

East of the city the wooden Red Hill School stood on a red clay bluff which still gives its name to its successor, annexed by the city in 1949. A crude building with roughly planed pine boards nailed to the wall as a blackboard and chalk made from the nearby creek's red clay, the school yet attracted an average attendance of one hundred and paid its teachers five hundred dollars a year.

In many ways the city was changing. Wooden balconies before shops were vanishing in favour of canvas awnings. As early as 1847 Hamilton, Toronto and Buffalo had been linked by telegraph service but at a cost which limited use to the press and business houses. Twenty years later however the Dominion Telegraph Company was sufficiently well established to seek permission to erect poles on city streets, inaugurating locally the street blight common to late nineteenth and early twentieth century North American communities.

A decade later telephone poles augmented the telegraph, Hugh Cossart Baker II, president of the Hamilton District Telegraph Company, applying on February 4th, 1878, to the city for permission to erect poles to service the first telephone exchange in the British Empire.

A versatile man of many interests, Mr. Baker had seen a telephone demonstrated at the 1876 Philadelphia Centennial Exposition and had heard Alexander Graham Bell tell of the first long distance telephone call in the world, one-way from Brantford to Paris, Ontario, on August 10th, 1876. With customary decisiveness Mr. Baker determined to establish a telephone department in his telegraph organization. By replacing signal boxes on the telegraph circuits with telephones he produced the first commercial instruments of their kind in Canada. His test on August 29th, 1877, was the first occasion in Canada on which more than two telephones operated commercially on one circuit.

For years Hugh Baker had been playing chess by telegraph with two friends, Thomas Chilton Mewburn, father of the later Major-General

S. C. Mewburn, K.C.M.G., and Charles D. Cory, insurance company manager. Now three telephones apiece were installed in the three homes to permit those present to converse and listen.

After private testing a public demonstration was made, guests including the Hon. Adam Hope, George Black, manager of the Montreal Telegraph Company, Joshua G. (Josh) Buchanan and George Mainwaring, editor and reporter of the *Hamilton Times*. So successful was the test that by December of that year forty telephones were listed in the Hamilton exchange.

On June 28th, 1878, the Hamilton District Telegraph Company was incorporated with a capital of three thousand dollars and the following shareholders: Hugh C. Baker, $2,500; and George Black, C. D. Cory, George Patterson and Thomas H. Wadland, a young telegraph operator who became company manager, $125 each. On January 19th, 1880, the name of the company was changed to the Hamilton Telephone Company. On the following April 29th Mr. Baker received a charter for a Canada-wide telephone company and named it Bell Telephone Company of Canada. On July 8th, 1880, he sold his Bell Telephone Company charter and his business to the recently formed Bell Telephone Company of Canada.

Originally located in the basement of 8 Main Street East, in the Kronsbein block, the Bell Telephone main office today is one door west. From the simple telephone of 1878—a receiver moved from mouth to ear —today's instrument has become so highly complex that subscriber dialling around the world is now possible.

Between the advent of telegraph and telephone poles on city streets, the tracks of the first public transportation system made their debut. In 1873 Lyman Moore, druggist, and his brother-in-law, Dr. Lewis Springer, with J. B. and T. B. Griffith substantial shareholders, obtained a charter to operate a public transport system, with two miles of track to be in operation by January 1st, 1875; cars to be drawn by horses or mules at not more than seven miles an hour; and adult fares five cents, children's three.

On May 11th, 1874, the first horse-drawn car left the barns at MacNab and Stuart Streets, rolled south on James to King and turned east to Wellington Street. Later in the year the single track was extended east to Wentworth Street, south to Main, and east on Main to Prospect Street, the city's market gardening and nursery area. To return, the driver unhitched and transferred horse or team to the other end of the car.

In 1875 a second route was opened, south on James to Herkimer, west to Queen Street, with a switch at Queen to make the return trip. Later this route was extended north on James Street to the wharf. The following year saw cars travelling west on King Street to the Crystal Palace at Locke, returning and running out York to Dundurn, a route later extended to the first gate of the cemetery. Mainly single, the Philadelphia rail track had occasional stretches of double for passing. At certain

162

points switches were installed to reverse the service as on Barton Street at Wentworth, on the run east from James. In 1881 a trackless grooved turntable was installed at busy King and James Streets to turn the cars driven on it. Three years later cedar block paving was laid throughout the downtown area.

From eight cars requiring some fifty horses and as many men to operate, the line gradually expanded until in 1892, when electrified, between twenty and twenty-five cars were in service. Cars came in two sizes, the smaller drawn by a single horse, the larger by a team. Although work teams hauling loads frequently operated between the rails, teams drawing cars were hitched with one horse between the rails, the other offside, a set-up which cost the company an extra eighteen inches of road bed maintenance on each side, but which the hazards of turning corners rendered necessary. Instead of a name to identify routes, earliest cars depended on colour—vivid scarlet, green and canary. Later, with added lines, routes were indicated by side boards on the cars painted in various Scotch tartans. At night variegated running lights were carried fore and aft.

For company horses additional barns and stables were established from which fresh relays were trotted by hostlers to changing points on the line. On an unseasonably hot day in September, 1884, records show horses were changed every hour.

Strictly utilitarian, the horse cars boasted few comforts especially in winter. The first vehicles were unheated, with open entrances and exits. Passengers facing one another in zero weather on the unpadded, car-long wooden benches could only shiver deeper into their voluminous wraps and seek comfort for tingling toes in the layer of pea straw on the floor, regularly sifted for dropped fibre fare-tokens, similar to today's five-cent piece. Later a small coal-burning Jumbo was installed in each car. Light was provided by two coal-oil lamps, left front and right rear.

From an open platform outside, exposed to summer storms and winter blasts, the hardy driver handled the reins, watched the fare box on the wall beside the entrance, gave transfers, and responded to the stop signal of the suspended bell-cord.

"In warm weather," said William A. Gray, "for holidays and special occasions at Dundurn open two-horse cars were used requiring a motorman and conductor to operate. Days, say, when Billy Stroud, the father of baseball in Hamilton, played his International Baseball team with its stars, Pete Wood, Mickey Jones and Billy Andrus."

When the Hamilton Street Railway was inaugurated, western city limits lay at Paradise Road and eastern at Wentworth Street. Static on the west, the eastern limit moved in 1891 to Sherman Avenue, in 1909 to Ottawa Street, and in 1912 to Kenilworth Avenue.

Beyond the city limits at Wentworth Street, and even from Emerald eastward, Main Street was largely occupied by extensive farms complete with truck gardens, apple orchards and vineyards. Beyond Wentworth the wooden sidewalks ceased and a path bordered the roadway. On these rural estates, behind high iron fences or clipped hedges, stood commodious mansions shaded by stately elms and maples, perfumed with lilac and syringa, and colourful with roses and oldfashioned flowerbeds.

In the factory behind the David Morton home at Emerald Street, Victor, the first wrapped soap in Canada, was scenting the neighbourhood. To the east Peter Grant (Grant Avenue) occupied property extending to Wentworth Street. With Joseph Middlewood, Mr. Grant owned the Spring Brewery, established in 1838, famous for its ale, porter and beer. Later on the site of Grant's orchard, on the northwest corner of Main and Wentworth, where the horse cars turned, Hazell and Son, and later Hazell and Dawson, grocers, catered to the élite of Main Street.

East again, where later Presbyterian St. Giles Church would stand on Holton Avenue, on market land previously held by Thomas Kilvington, Warren and William A. Holton set out nurseries from Main Street to King. Beyond the toll gate east of Burlington Street (Sanford Avenue) stood Thomas Barnes' imposing Carrick Lodge, reached from Main Street by a deep semi-circular drive curving through wide lawns, which later became town lots and rows of houses. From the ridge of the watercourse that bisected Main Street at Barnesdale, Thomas Barnes took thousands of loads of moulding sand to the Steel Company of Canada.

Before the home of Sheriff James T. Middleton, marble manufacturer and merchant, the car line ended, short of the sixty-four-acre farm of the late Robert R. Gage, barrister, (today's Gage Park) then laid out in vegetables and fruit. The horse cars stopped at all the big houses on Main Street and if a passenger were elderly the driver left his car and gallantly saw her to her door. Reciprocating favours, Mrs. Luke H. Parker, wife of the organist of Centenary Church, in cold or stormy weather always took coffee to the driver. Another convenience offered, in a pre-telephone day, was a stop at Arthur Peacock's butcher shop (still family operated)[4] on the northwest corner of King and Wentworth Streets, while husbands delivered their wives' daily orders.

When Dr. Springer defeated R. R. Waddell for South Wentworth in the provincial house, in 1882, the street car company on election night serenaded the H.S.R. manager with a brass band at his home, the former Horning homestead, later to become St. Peter's Infirmary.

On Main Street by that time lived the Galbraiths, Eastwoods, Mitchells, Murtons and Beasleys; Brennens, lumber and construction; Browns, whips and hides; the Hoodlesses, McCaulays, Truesdales, Sweets, Allans, John Gages and Blandfords; and Messrs. Robertson and Turnbull, partners in Robert Duncan and Company, successors to George Barnes and Company, James Street North—today, under W. Lester Turnbull, the oldest continuing books, stationery and accessories firm in Canada.

The settlement of Main Street East was representative of the city as a whole. Between 1870 and 1900 Hamilton's population more than doubled, advancing from just under 25,000 to nearly 52,000.

164

To accommodate this growth, lines of new streets spread below the mountain, consolidating older sections and opening up new surveys. Following the streets came sewers, water mains and gas lines. Later and not too speedily, the dust and mud of the streets gave way to cedar block or macadam paving, plank or stone curbing, and wooden sidewalks or asphalt.

Of the multiple problems of growth—need of new schools, a new city hall, additional trunk sewers to accommodate the root spread of pipe lines, and extension of the water works system to meet the consumption increased from a daily average of 3,810,947 gallons in 1890 to 4,973,848 in 1900—none was more pressing than that of access roads.

Because of Hamilton's situation access had always presented peculiar problems. In the latter years of the nineteenth century the only passable roads were the universally disliked toll roads, privately owned and maintained. To the east of the city where concession roads Main Street and Barton were built eastward to connect with the King Street Indian trail from Niagara, all approaches were controlled by toll roads.

First built was the King Street Road, Highway 8, constructed by the district council from Wentworth Street, Hamilton city limits, to a point east of Stoney Creek. When in 1849 the city petitioned for the opening of Barton Street eastward, to provide residents of north Barton and Saltfleet Townships with access to the north end of the city, without the long trip south to King Street and return within the city, the district council refused regretfully but firmly, unmoved by the argument that the city was entitled to the opening of all crown thoroughfares (concession roads).

"In macadamizing the road," said the district council, "[they] had determined to compel all parties travelling to the city from the east to use their road and thus contribute towards its support and payment of the debt incurred in building it."[5]

Eventually the road was sold to David Williamson who in turn sold it to the Barton and Stoney Creek Road Company, headed by Albert Edward Carpenter.[6] When the Main Street Road was later opened two miles easterly from Wentworth Street by another company, Mr. Carpenter bought the stock of this also. Consolidating the two roads, he placed a toll gate where Main Street (now Queenston Road) and King Street still intersect east of Stoney Creek, and gates on King and Main Streets east of Sanford Avenue.

Meanwhile, to afford communication between King and Barton Streets, the city, in 1855, opened Barton Street to the city limits at Wentworth Street and Wentworth Street itself from Barton Street to the mountain.

When Barton Street east of the city at last was opened by John Dickenson, what more natural than that Mr. Carpenter, with Andrew Gage, should obtain control? As operated by the Hamilton and Saltfleet Road Company, Barton Street extended from the city limits to east of Winona where it joined Highway 8 by a short southerly connection. As Mr. Carpenter's company now also owned a section of the Lake Road, north of Barton Street, which followed the lakeshore past the Van Wagner property to Stoney Creek (now vanished under erosion), he literally controlled all eastern entrances to the city.

On April 12th, 1893, prior to the opening of the Hamilton Jockey Club, on Barton East between Ottawa Street and Kenilworth Avenue, the city purchased from the above two companies for four thousand dollars "those parts of the toll roads of Barton Street, King Street and Main Street lying within the limits of the city,"[7] i.e., from Wentworth Street to Sherman Avenue. Toll houses and gates were moved outside city limits, one placed at the Delta junction of King and Main Streets commanding both thoroughfares.

Although city and county in 1895 appointed joint committees to confer on the abolition of toll roads in both city and county, pay roads persisted until the 1920's.

On the west, city approaches were equally costly to the wayfarer and even more difficult. West of Garth (Dundurn) Street, King Street dropped into Beasley's Hollow where it crossed a stream on a ramshackle bridge. Dark and eerie, the valley was a favourite ambush of footpads, said to lurk in a cluster of caves honeycombing the cliffs north of the later Norman Slater Company plant, today Slater Steel Industries Limited. On high ground west of the Hollow, opposite today's Westdale Tripartite School, stood a toll gate, with the Dundas Road and the cut-off to Ancaster also tolled.

If Hamilton's east and west access roads proved troublesome, however, they were far outdistanced by the north and south routes.

Prior to the building of the High Level bridge, traffic across the Heights followed the old ordnance low road which ran along the east side of the promontory and turning right, crossed the early natural outlet of the marsh on a swing barrel bridge at the Valley Inn to pick up the road to Toronto. Near the present Wolfe Island a left fork of the road climbed the Heights and descending near the later Lilac Garden of the Royal Botanical Gardens, crossed the marsh on a military pontoon bridge to join the town line road (between East and West Flamboro) which led to Waterdown, Dundas and Guelph.[8]

For more than a century, over these roads and the Indian-trail Waterdown Snake Road, also leading from the Valley Inn, passed all of the city's important northwest traffic. When roads were impassable or bridges down, market returns fell to such an extent that the market clerk begged for a rebate on his fees. Only with construction in 1931-32 of the Longwood Road low-level extension, and in the 1960's of the thirty-million-dollar Chedoke Expressway (Highway 403), were new access routes opened to the west end of the city.

To the present, five High Level bridges have spanned the Desjardins canal since the Canal Company in 1852 paid the Great Western Railway Company approximately $65,000 to cut a channel through the Heights and fill in the old outlet with a railway embankment. Above the new channel the Canal Company built a one-span suspension bridge on the high level, while the Great Western constructed a swing bridge to permit passage of vessels. While the cut was intended to expand ship traffic to Dundas, the nuisance value of the bridge reversed this in favour of the port of Hamilton.

Over the years the suspension bridge and its successor, an insecure wooden truss bridge, involved the city in a rash of accidents and suits, some as serious as the death by drowning of three children. When the toll roads began to lose money from decreased traffic, the city in 1869 made a loan to the Hamilton and Milton Road Company and granted it permission to collect tolls within city limits on the Heights in return for erection of a satisfactory bridge over the canal and extension of its toll road into the city to the eastern end of the ordnance lands.

On stone piers the road company erected an "entire iron bridge," approved by the city engineer and by George Lowe Reid, chief engineer of the Great Western. When this was replaced in 1896 by its $60,000 successor, the toll roads were closed and Burlington Heights entered its modern phase.

As with the eastern toll roads, one finds names here recurring constantly in road companies: the Hon. Samuel Mills, Miles O'Reilly, F. W. Gates, Archibald Kerr, S. W. Ryckman, Peter Carroll and R. R. Waddell.

At the time the iron bridge was building on the Heights, a new access road, the Jolley Cut, was being hacked out of the mountainside across the city. James Jolley hated tolls. To circumvent the toll houses on the steep John Street Road running to the mountain top and south to Caledonia, and William Strongman's road angling southeasterly across the mountain face from John Street to Concession, Mr. Jolley gave land, raised funds, and circulated a petition to city council asking permission to build a road commencing at Concession Street and "descending the mountain at Wellington, thence westerly along the quarries, intersecting John Street at Mr. McInnes' residence."

That was before Donald McInnes sold his pinnacled stone mansion on the mountainside, Rock Castle—erected and first occupied by Alexander Carpenter, of Gurneys and Carpenter—and in 1872 purchased Dundurn Castle. Standing immediately north of today's Hairpin Turn, Rock Castle was typical Gothic with its steeply pitched roofs and clustered chimneys, its pointed arches and mullioned windows. For generations it was part of Hamilton's gracious age.[9]

It took four years to chisel Jolley's road with its notorious Extremity Point[10] out of the mountain's rugged limestone and shale, to line and grade it. In 1873 Mr. Jolley deeded land and road to the city with two conditions: that the corporation maintain the road in repair and keep it toll free.

The road was a longtime ambition. Born in Scotland in 1813 and brought to Montreal at the age of seven, James Jolley had opened a

167

modest saddlery shop in Hamilton in 1843. Following marriage with Sophia Burgess, daughter of James Burgess, well known local musician and owner of mountain property extending from Wentworth to Sherman Avenue, Mr. Jolley had built a mountaintop home, Bellmont (the later Dale Community Centre) to give his delicate wife the mountain air recommended by her physician, Dr. Gerald O'Reilly—a prescription so effective that Sophia lived to be ninety-four.

Between his home on Concession Street and his shop on John, James Jolley beat a trail down the mountainside. Neighbours used the same path. Even farmers travelling to market carried their produce down Jolley's path and lugged their groceries and purchases up the same rugged ascent to save paying tolls. By the 1860's, however, Mr. Jolley had outgrown the path. Business had prospered. James wished to drive his horse and carriage to work and to service in the Church of the Ascension below, on the corner of Maria and Upper John Street. Since this offshoot of Christ's Church, built of mountain limestone on land donated by Richard Juson, had opened for service in 1851 under Rev. John Hebden, M.A., the Jolley family had been devoted members.

The day the board of works graciously accepted the Jolley Cut for the city was a happy occasion for both corporation and mountaineers. Less felicitous was the day in 1882 when Mr. Jolley after endless appeals, warnings and threats, promised legal action unless the Cut, now almost obliterated under landslides of mud and rocks from the cliffs and metal debris from the quarries, was returned to public use.

The city promised immediate action and presumably to some degree satisfied the mountaineers since proceedings were halted. The city's reprieve however could have been only temporary. After eight decades of perennial repairs; after being rerouted, widened, regraded and paved in 1953 at a cost of $850,000; and five years after this again cut back, banked and guard-railed for an additional $100,000, the road from John Street, Hamilton's "million dollar baby," in 1962 was still slipping and sliding down the mountainside.

The problem of seasonal and flash floods over the mountain at James and John, aggravating the natural problems of mountainside and upper city roadways and sewers, the city largely overcame in 1878. After an abortive attempt to channel the water westerly and discharge it over the mountain at Queen Street, the city about-faced and constructed the Mountain Drain (familiarly, the City Ditch) which diagonalled easterly from the head of James Street to discharge over the escarpment at Buttermilk Falls. In its course it crossed the farms of men intimately concerned in mountaintop history: James Jolley; George F. Webb, shrewd businessman, extensive property owner, contractor, and president of the company which in 1906 would purchase the east end (Wentworth Street) incline, built seven years earlier; George E. Mills, contractor and brick manufacturer; Adam Inch, staunch Conservative, reeve of Barton township and lifelong mountain resident, and a director with John Milne and Joseph

Morris of the Hamilton Mountain Park Company (president, Rev. Samuel Lake) which built the east end Hamilton Mountain Incline railway; J. Jardine; and B. H. Hughson.

Since the City Ditch ran by gravity and descent was one foot in the mile, its normal movement was slow and sluggish. In part it followed a natural watercourse. Built when mountaintop settlement was sparse, the drain was originally intended only for storm overflow. Later it became a trunk sewer carrying both overflow and sanitary waste, with a connection in 1909 at Sanford Avenue to carry the waste down the mountain to the city sewer. The same year pipe was laid on streets in the area. The first sewers above the escarpment, therefore, forerunner of today's mountaintop underground labyrinth, occurred about Wentworth Street north of Concession, a comparatively well settled development even then, with numerous small wooden houses and a few larger homes.

Over the years the City Ditch maintained its dual capacity, in spite of recurrent bitter complaints of citizens and arguments with county council. In 1931 dual pumps, storm and sanitary, were installed in three pumping stations at Wentworth, Sherman and Gage Avenues, which largely separated storm water from sanitary waste, discharging the latter into city sewers and speeding the former along the Ditch to pollute natural watercourses.

Not until after the last world war was the Mountain Drain discontinued, the ditch filled in and its right-of-way lost in the headlong rush of wartime housing and new subdivisions.

17

All Around the Town

THE history of Hamilton's mercantile antecedents is written in the imposing mansions of the latter nineteenth century which in a more spacious
age stood isolated and aloof on the lower wooded slopes of the mountain.

Built in a day when prestige items were the impressiveness of a man's
home and the smartness of his carriage and liveried coachman, as today
three cars, a pool and a plane, the houses stood in sculptured, tree shaded
grounds, frequently covering a city block. Conservatory and *porte-cochère*,
a fountain playing in a lily pool, garden statuary and a tennis court were
acceptable adjuncts.

Arkledun, built in the 1840's by Richard Juson, hardware merchant,
and later occupied by Edward Browne, wharfinger and coal merchant; by
James Turnbull, general manager of the Bank of Hamilton,[1] the city's
premier financial enterprise; and by E. D. Cahill, barrister . . . Idlewyld,
built by Reginald Kennedy, father of Reginald Aemilius Kennedy, president and manager of the *Hamilton Times*, who occupied the residence for
years . . . Italianate, towered stone Ballynahinch, corner of Aberdeen and
James Street, popular residence of Edward Martin, Q.C., now converted
by its final owner, Samuel Hensen, to Hensen Park apartments.[2] . . . Ingle-
wood, believed designed by the outstanding architect, William Thomas,
for Archibald Kerr, dry goods importer, and later occupied by John
Stuart, president of the Bank of Hamilton; by W. D. Long, wool merchant; and by the late W. J. Southam, vice-president and managing
director of *The Hamilton Spectator*, a distinguished Gothic villa whose
unusual interior beauty has been largely maintained in its conversion to
multiple living. . . .

Elmwood, home of Senator Andrew Trew Wood, who represented
Hamilton for eight years in the Canadian House of Commons, founder of
the firm of Wood, Vallance and Company, in the 1890's probably the
largest hardware company in Canada; later occupied by his son, the late
William Augustus, father of the twins A. T. and B. R. Wood; subsequently
acquired by the Sisters of St. Joseph, and converted into a nurses' resi-

dence, Marygrove, with part of the rolling lawns to the south becoming Mountain Boulevard, today St. Joseph's Drive. . . . and high above James Street, secluded in stone-walled, wooded grounds extending from Duke to Robinson, Anisfield, the turreted home of Robert Thomson, wholesale lumber merchant, popularly known as The Castle, today fallen to a sorry fate as apartment dwelling and service station. In these and like impressive settings the city's premier families enjoyed the community's most gracious era.

"Our home," said the late Miss Caroline Crerar, daughter of John Crerar, K.C., and granddaughter of Senator Adam Hope, "was Merksworth. Lovely grounds and beautiful trees. In the house was a huge drawing room, forty feet long, enormous dining room, library, powder room, vast kitchen—took minutes to walk from the kitchen to the front door. Sitting room and storage room off the kitchen. Bells in the kitchen for every room. Fireplace in every room, too. We always had three maids: cook, upstairs and downstairs maids, laundress, gardeners."

She paused, small, slight, vivacious. "Growing up was a wonderful experience," said the sandy-haired alert ex-president of the Ontario Liberal Women's Association. "Going to Miss Walton's private school here, to Europe for finishing, then coming out. A huge reception in the afternoon, with friends of the older generation pouring. At night a ball. All at home of course in those days. For dances the orchestra played in the hall. Linen covers were brought down from the attic for the dining room and drawing room floors and laid and waxed. Supper was in the billiard room on the second floor: turkey, roast beef, tongue, hams, salads, trifles, pyramids of macaroons. Aussem catered."

In the big houses at the turn of the century everybody knew everybody. Boys went to Upper Canada College or Ridley. Men wore evening clothes and white gloves to a dance, and bachelors repaid hospitality by calling at the various homes on New Year's Day and by giving the annual Bachelors' ball.

"Then there was the Garrick Club ball," said Miss Crerar. "Held in the Grand Theatre. The dance floor was laid above the seats and we sat in the boxes. My father founded the Garrick Club, you know. It was the first Little Theatre in Canada. They gave plays in autumn and spring and people who now join the Junior League joined the Garrick Club. It was important. It folded in 1914.

"We had other amusements too. There were euchre parties and straight whist and musical evenings. When you went out for the evening everyone had to perform. At one time I recited *Enoch Arden* with Dr. Hewlett[3] at the piano. We went all over Ontario. Once we performed at Mrs. Sanford's home, Wesanford, when she opened it for a benefit."

Social drinking at the century's turn differed from today. Men did their hard drinking apart from the ladies. Cocktail parties were unknown. "At New Year's," Caroline Crerar said, "you served sherry and coffee and wine. At dances we drank lemonade and coffee. Wines at dinner. Tea in the afternoon. Some afternoons there was tea in the garden and straw-berries." The swift vibrant voice paused nostalgically. "Tea and straw-berries in the garden—it seems like another world!"

On the fringe of the great houses flourished another settlement, lustier, as distinctive and as self-contained.

On the flats and commons and the lower slopes of the quiet green mountainside cropped by the tethered family cows and goats, east of the Hamilton burial plot and west of Wellington Street, mushroomed the humble, self built cottages and shanties of the Irish workmen who helped lay the shining rails of the finally enfranchised[4] Hamilton and Port Dover railway up the mountain. Interspersed among them were the larger and more pretentious homes erected by competent builders. All were bright with poppies, peonies and morning glories.

At the southwest corner of Ferguson Avenue and King Street a station sprouted. On Ferguson Avenue near Barton appeared a freight shed, roundhouse and shops. At the foot of Wellington Street the railway added a grain elevator and wharf. In 1877 a line spun out across Burlington Beach, adding a new dimension to lakeside cottage life. It also spiced the slow lazy summer days with interest.

"The great event of the day," recalled a onetime beach cottage owner, "was the 'double header' which went steaming past with its long tail of cars. All along the beach children ran to wave and dogs to bark."

The beach was not the only area affected by the railway. As a residen-tial street Ferguson Avenue protested vigorously at being selected as route of the new line. Nevertheless, reports an account of September 14th, 1872, "Last Friday evening, the first engine of the Hamilton and Lake Erie rail-way ran from the Great Western track onto the new line and cautiously felt its way nearly as far as King Street. On Saturday it was constantly being run up and down the line as far as rails were laid, and today began its work by drawing carloads of ties and rails . . . to the place to be laid. Engine and tender have been nicely ornamented and painted and named *Lucy Turner*, in honour of the daughter of James Turner, president of the road.

"The locomotive is a perpetual source of wonder to the lads in the vicinity who congregate and follow it about, much to the annoyance of the engineer. Even the young ladies along Ferguson Avenue sit outside in the morning sun and discuss it and the prevailing gossip. It will not be long until the novelty of the iron horse running up the face of the moun-tain may be seen by Hamiltonians."

While Irish, many well-to-do, had emigrated earlier to escape religious and political interference, and were well established in the city, the resi-dents of Corktown largely fled the devastating potato famines of the 1840's and '50s. As Cobh, port of the city of Cork, was a leading embarkation point it seems probable that Corktown was named for the last Irish city homesick eyes had rested upon.

Young Street was its main street and its capital and social centre was

Liberal "Dude" Sullivan's grocery and liquor store, first at Walnut and Augusta Streets, then on the corner of Young and Cherry Street (Ferguson Avenue). A heavy-set, dark haired man with a black handlebar moustache and a fancy for clothes, Mr. Sullivan was for years the all-powerful political boss of the area centred north of Young and east of Catharine Streets, in the so-called Corcoran's Court. Here in the earliest days of Corktown were concentrated the wakes, the weddings and christenings, the cock fights, election celebrations and occasional dance whose echoes carried awesomely into the outer city. Following Dan Sullivan's death the saloon became Gurrie's Hotel, later the Corktown House.

If from the first generation of Corktown came policemen, shopkeepers, gardeners and railroad workers, the second and third sent "such a file of young people into the priesthood and convents," said Robert J. Hanley, well known sports editor of *The Hamilton Spectator*, and himself from Corktown, "that their conviction and devotion was a wonder for the whole archdiocese . . . Mother Thecla and Mother Marguerite served a span of eighteen years as superiors of the community of the Sisters of St. Joseph. From the Paddons, Fords, Sullivans, Doyles, Simpsons, Curtises, Morriseys, O'Briens, McCowells and Donovans came sons who went into Holy Orders."

In other fields besides the church Corktown's sons and daughters made their mark. Jack Caffery won the Boston marathon; "Mickey" Jones made the big leagues in baseball; "Mush" O'Heir, Bill Moore and Tom Wren were football greats; while Johnny Williams became a top jockey of his day. To the stage, Corktown gave the celebrated Julia Arthur, "one of the Lewis girls." William J. Warnick served as superintendent of the railway Corktown helped build. And in the civic field Mayors Alex McKay and John Peebles hailed from Corktown, as did Fire Chief Robert Aitchison, killed when his buggy racing to a fire collided with the statue of Sir John A. Macdonald.

On Catharine Street South, in a large landscaped family mansion, The Willows, lived Judge Miles O'Reilly, after whom O'Reilly Street was named, and his granddaughter, Judge Helen Gregory MacGill, who shaped social history with the reforms she instigated in Ontario, California, Minnesota and British Columbia. Of Corktown also were the staunch German Burkholder, Mueller and Blatz families, the latter two producing outstanding educationists in Dr. Victoria Mueller and the late Dr. William E. Blatz, an internationally recognized authority on child development, author, lecturer and television personality. And an ardent son of Corktown is James G. O'Neil, former editor of *The Hamilton Spectator*.

In the 1890's Corktown began to lose its real identity with the coming of the freight yards and freight sheds to the mountainside and the laying of a new line of track intersecting the first and cutting the old ward in four.

By that time the city too had changed. On the site of the old city hall stood an impressive brownstone pile with four-foot-thick walls supporting pinnacles and a clock tower above arched and colonnaded entrances.[5] On the north side of Main Street, immediately east of Centenary Church, a spacious red brick building housed the newly established Hamilton Public Library, opened on September 16th, 1890, under librarian R. T. Lancefield, largely through the determined efforts of Sir John M. Gibson, the Hamilton Association, and the board of education. Completed in 1886, a handsome red stone Post Office and Customs stood at King and John.

A new Christ's Church, now the Cathedral Church of the Diocese of Niagara, recently established with the Right Rev. T. B. Fuller elected Lord Bishop, had been erected under the leadership of the newly appointed Dean Geddes. At the foot of the Mountain, too, a second Church of the Ascension replaced the first, gutted by fire in 1887, only the spire and bells presented by Mrs. Richard Juson escaping. On the corner of Wellington and Maria Streets the McLaren Mission, built by Mr. and Mrs. W. P. McLaren to house a Bible class that outgrew their home, Oakbank, enjoyed week-long activity.

From Dundas the blunt-nosed small steam-operated cars of the Hamilton and Dundas Street railway were shuttling into the city and back, past Ainslie's wood and along Aberdeen, Herkimer and Main Streets (connecting links, Queen Street and MacNab) to their eastern terminus at the Hamilton and Northwestern railway depot at Ferguson Avenue. For some reason the Dundas "Dummy"—regulated to a rattling clip of six miles an hour within the city, ten without—inspired a unique amused affection in all.

"On a hot summer day," chuckled the Rev. Calvin McQuesten, brother of the late Hon. Thomas B. McQuesten, "the Counsell boys used to butter the rails on MacNab Street, on the rise below Hunter Street." His grin belied his eighty-odd years. "It was great sport! When the wheels hit the butter they'd spin round and round and the driver would get mad and shake his fist. Of course no one was in sight. But we all had a peep-hole, from behind a bush or tree or around the corner of a house."

Said another Hamiltonian: "I remember my grandmother telling of Dundas theatre parties that used to come in on the Dummy to attend the Grand Theatre,[6] a highly social event then. Women wore elaborate evening gowns and wraps, their escorts tails and toppers. With their satin-lined capes and their canes men looked very gallant, said grandmother. Following the theatre everyone went to the Royal for supper, after which the Dummy returned them to Dundas."

In the fabulous north end of the city, in a community largely Irish Catholic, theatre did not rate in the social scale with church suppers, socials and family gatherings. Picnics too were popular, with the Crystal Palace and Dundurn vying with Burlington Beach, north shore Bayview with its horse-operated incline, and Oaklands, and following its opening in 1915 by the Hamilton parks board, chaired by George Wild, Wabasso

174

Park. On its fifty-five well wooded acres, the park offered full picnic facilities including a spacious pavilion and refreshment stand; children's play area with forty swings and a merry-go-round; a bathing beach; and strong drawing card for the sports loving north-enders, a five-acre athletic field and adjacent softball field. Sports of all kinds, including cockfighting and fisticuffs, ranged high in north end favour but so also did romantic moonlight steamer excursions.

"People speak of the north end," said the late Alderman Frank Dillon, dean of council, noted for his fancy waistcoats and his knobheaded cane, "meaning the area north of Barton Street. They are completely in error. Above the bridge, over the Canadian National railway tracks, and below the bridge were two totally different districts with different problems. There was jealousy between them. 'Below,' the north end, was concerned with the bay; 'above' was not.

"To the north end," said the portly 'Little Senator' who had represented the area for twenty-five years, "the bay was an asset never fully appreciated by the rest of the city. It provided work. It was the old swimming hole and old playground combined."

Work lay in the shipbuilding yards: owned among others by Captain John (Boston) Malcolmson; Captain Archibald Robertson; H. L. Bastien, who started life in Hamilton as a contractor building houses and ended building yachts and launches for the Canadian and American markets; Thomas W. Jutten who came to Hamilton in 1871 as an immigrant boy of fourteen, to become a leading boat builder, member of city council and mayor; James Massie who after three successful decades sold his business to James A. Thompson who later specialized in racing craft; James Weir, at the foot of Wentworth Street; George Askew, whose named burned into the boats he built became a trademark of excellence; and indispensable to all these, Robert Soper, sailmaker, tent and awning manufacturer.

By the late 1890's boat building was turning towards pleasure craft. By then George Webster's trim *Volante*, Mr. Ambrose's *Samoa*, Thomas Dalton's *The Nancy*, F. E. Kilvert's graceful *Psyche* were all a-wing, along with ex-alderman Judd's *Mona*, the *Acacia*, *Alfie*, *Rhoda*, *Spray* and others. To house them Kerr's Boat Livery was established in 1910 with 50 much needed boat lockers.

Before the end of heavy shipbuilding the bay witnessed an historic launching. On Thursday, July 21st, 1892, the steel hull of the steamer *Arabian*, manufactured by the Hamilton Bridge and Tool Company, was scheduled to slide down the ways. About 3 p.m., bright with flags and pennants and with decks crowded with the venturesome, the 180-foot, 1,200-ton *Arabian*, largest ship launched to that date in Ontario, was tapped free of her wooden supports. From the sunmisted hills across the bay the sharp mallet strokes and preliminary toots of tugs and steam yachts echoed faintly back. The crowds thronging surrounding wharves and bay front hillsides cheered.

The ship did not move, although heavy battering rams were improvised, jackscrews were placed beneath her, a powerful tug broke four heavy hawsers, and the crowd aboard ran fore and aft to vibrate the hull. At 6.30 Captain J. B. Fairgrieve postponed the launching to Saturday and the 2,500 spectators dispersed.

When the crowds assembled on Saturday for the announced 3 p.m. launching, they were too late. So great had been the Thursday throng that the company had feared for the spectators' safety. On Saturday the hull of the *Arabian* was raised, the ways abundantly lubricated, and two powerful hydraulic jacks installed. Sharp at 2 p.m. the supports were knocked out and immediately the bull voice of Fire Chief Aitchison roared, "She's going!" Little Rita Fairgrieve cried, "*Arabian!*" and swung the ribboned bottle and the christened *Arabian* glided smoothly into the water. When the crowds reached the harbour the big craft, pennants flying, was circling majestically in the bay.

Even in winter the bay provided employment. Many north-enders worked for D. R. Dewey and Son, and the Magee-Walton Ice Company, cutting huge blocks of ice and floating them along a channel to the conveyor which carried them into the icehouse for storage.

"Up to 1914," said James Smith of Wood Street East, "bay water was wonderful. Swimming was our greatest sport. Then I left Hamilton. When I returned in 1922 they were talking pollution. I got a job cutting ice that year, the last year bay ice was cut, except for some small firms on the north shore.

"The bay drew the ships and the ships brought work. My father, Andy (Dutch) Smith, was a boss stage man in charge of a gang of stevedores unloading sailing vessels around the turn of the century. He worked for the John Rogers Coal Company, and later for Thomas and James Myles. Father owned eight horses. He unloaded the ships at the John Street docks, hauled coal to the company's yard and teamed it to customers. Coal was $4.50 a ton screened.

"To unload a ship then, large buckets or baskets were lowered into the hold, shovelled full, hoisted to the top by block and tackle and dumped into two-wheeled carts. Two stage men stood on deck and guided the buckets over the side while a hoist boy led the horse operating the block and tackle back and forth across the wharf. When I was eight or nine, I began two years as hoist boy."

A foreman with William Muirhead's civic Streets and Sanitation department, Mr. Smith briefly interrupted his work of speeding the city's garbage to the dump. But first he waved the garbage truck on its way. "We work to a tight time schedule here," he said. "I'll pick them up in the next block." He reverted to the coal loading.

"The men could unload a ship in a day. At the end of the day they were so black that it took a whole bar of soap and the bay to get a man clean. They scrubbed and played tag on the dock and tossed one another into the water. Finally it became cheaper to ship coal by rail and that ended the coal ships."

"It was a hard life but it had compensations. Father and his cronies used to catch snapping turtles in Coote's Paradise, with big hooks baited with meat and set overnight. They'd catch two or three every time. At home they'd cut them up in the big yard that lay between the house and barn. They'd throw in vegetables, sometimes a chicken, sometimes a rabbit or two. George (Rabbit) Hill, the blacksmith, lived behind Wood Street on Catharine and he raised rabbits. After dark someone would jump the fence and grab a couple and into the stew they'd go. Then they'd invite George to the meal. 'That's good. That's real good!' he'd say. 'It should be, George,' someone would yell. 'It's your rabbits!' It was good, too, cooked on a wood or coal stove while the men groomed and bedded down the horses. Every man on the coal boats knew mother's turtle soup."

The foreman looked down the east end city street of well ordered symmetrical brick houses baking in the hot July sun—each behind its tidy handkerchief of lawn, each with its emptied garbage containers primly at the curb. If a can gets tossed on its side, a telephone is likely to record the fact in the Streets and Sanitation department in City Hall. Sixty years before this land had been a cultivated farm. Thoughtfully Mr. Smith wiped his forehead. It was a long and a very short distance back sixty years.

"Afterward, they'd turn the horses into the yard and father would stage a cockfight in the barn. In Pennsylvania, U.S.A., they wrote a book about father and his cocks. He took them all about the country on the circuit, Buffalo, Reading, through the Alleghenies. He had twelve to fourteen main of chickens. They go by weight, you know. A cock has to weigh in at the weight of his adversary. Father always carried more than he needed to ensure the proper weight.

"Sometimes we'd get word a party from the west end was coming down. Real top drawer, as they say now. Women with them, too. All dolled up in finery and furs. Father always held the match in the parlour then. Of course cockfights were against the law but father had a sure protection against police. One of his horses would kick the stars out of the sky, another was bulldog breed; once he got his teeth in he'd never let go."

Unique also to the north end were the glassblowers: those who worked out of town, returning when summer heat interrupted their task, and those employed in the local Burlington and Hamilton Glass Works, the latter operated by Rutherford and Company, a wild rough and tough band, but good natured, sport and fun loving.

No other area of the city had the characters of the north end: "Collar Button" Kelly; weakminded handyman Tom ("Bumble Bee") Stafford, also known as "Lousy Tom," who went mad if anyone buzzed at him; Kitty Lewis who endlessly roamed the town, chewing tea; giant, fiery-tempered Dick Roach, brother of Paddy, whose motto was, "Fight first and argue afterwards;" Tom Cross, who lived on the bay, supporting himself on what he took from the bay, and finally died in the bay although he boasted it was not big enough to drown him; and "Long John"

Murphy, proprietor of the Modjeska House, unofficial mayor of the north end and a noted owner of game chickens.

From the same lively area came physicians, barristers, and clergy; champion tug-of-war teams; baseball and football greats; and Denny and Jerry Donohue, Charlie Furlong and William Wark of the Nautilus Club who won the senior fours in Boston at the National Association regatta in 1885. This was five years after formation of the Canadian Rowing Association. Rowing in Hamilton however preceded this by years. In 1870 the Hamilton Rowing Club was formed. In the second annual report, given in September, 1872, by Colonel Alex H. Moore, second vice-president, a membership of 117 is reported, with 88 paid-up members. H. A. Stinson was treasurer.

In 1877 west-enders Harold Lamb, Robert Hobson and S. G. Mewburn raised funds to build and equip the Leander Club on pilings at the end of Bastien's wharf, while the following year the Nautilus Club, composed largely of glassblowers, was founded. With current Black Diamond crews the above clubs provided many powerful racers during the next two decades, Hal McGiverin, A. E. and R. B. Ferrie, E. E. Kittson, Insole and John Murphy, T. H. Stinson and John Jeffrey being internationally known. To a considerable degree Hamilton successes in continental competition were owing to the slim shells turned out by local builders, especially H. L. Bastien and James H. Weir.

In 1895 the Leander Club expired, its members turning to the new sport of cycling. The Nautilus Club followed suit and sculling lapsed. Later, after the turn of the century, the Hamilton Rowing Club was organized through the efforts of R. T. Steele, to be succeeded by the present active Leander Boat Club.

When the *Macassa* and *Modjeska* ceased to run in the late 1920's, the "great gay days of the old North End" belonged to the past. Gone too were the moonlight sails and the lights of the Royal Hamilton Yacht Club at Burlington Beach dancing in the dark canal waters. *En fête* for a Friday night dance the clubhouse had appeared like a brightly lighted liner moored between moonlit lake and bay. Japanese lanterns, dancers, an orchestra playing The Pink Lady, laughter and the tinkle of glasses, stars and a pumpkin harvest moon—all the props of romance had been present.

It was a unique age . . . an age of gaiety . . . of innocence, in a manner of speaking . . . the last age of isolation and privacy the world was to know.

In Hamilton it took with it when it went Robert McElroy, mayor during the city's bankrupt years; the Hon. Isaac Buchanan; Joshua G. Buchanan, uniquely individual city editor of the *Times,* socially popular, an entertaining companion with an unlimited store of reminiscences, and a man noted for his daring practical jokes, who was accidentally drowned in the canal basin at Dundas while returning from the Rockton fair with Editor H. F. Gardiner of the *Times;* and Right Rev.

178

Peter F. Crinnon, D.D., Bishop of Hamilton, who had served the diocese in erection of St. Patrick's Church, and purchase of sites for St. Lawrence Church and Holy Sepulchre cemetery.

With the era vanished the Mechanics' Institute whose assets, due to financial difficulties, were sold at public auction in 1882; and the Crystal Palace, condemned and razed in 1891. Obversely, by 1892 the first city inclines were seesawing up and down the mountainside at James Street. In 1895 a gaping trench, south of Hunter Street and west of James, proclaimed the tunnel of the Toronto, Hamilton and Buffalo railway, with the first train, Toronto to Welland running December 30th, 1895. And in 1899 the east end incline opened for service, with the Hamilton Street railway running a cross-town transfer line from King Street to the head of Wentworth Street.

18

Hospitals and the Medical Profession

By the year 1873 history at the City Hospital was repeating itself: once again the hospital was beginning to stretch at the seams. By purchasing additional land, adding to the building and improving its heating, the institution at the foot of John Street was kept in operation until 1878 when the hospital committee called for tenders for a new site.

For $4,600 four acres of farm land were purchased in (Hon.) John H. Cameron's survey on the north side of Barton Street East, lying between Wellington, Victoria and South Streets. Not until November, 1880, however, were tenders circulated for the new buildings. On October 25th, 1882, patients were removed from the old to the new City Hospital.

Last resident physician in the John Street hospital and first in the Barton was F. E. Woolverton, M.D., who with Drs. John A. Mullin and E. Graves Kittson had assisted the architect and hospital committee in planning and overseeing construction of the new buildings. Following fencing and landscaping, the fountain then standing before the Wesleyan Ladies' College was installed before the main entrance, to become for years a flower-bright hallmark of the institution until hospital expansion forced its removal. Today the fountain's pedestalled upper basin, brimming with petunias, graces the postoffice grounds at mountaintop Hannon where it was located by Mrs. Lyle White, postmistress, who discovered it lying discarded at the rear of the hospital.

Described as "equal to anything of its kind in Canada," the new hospital of red and white patterned brick was built in Italianate style and consisted of a four-storey main building parallelling Barton, with a central tower and two detached brick wings extending southward and connected with the main building by open corridors.

With its cheerful well lighted wards; adequate ventilation and heating, the latter provided by central fireplaces, back to back as in English hospitals; water closets; gas lighting; speaking tubes; and dumb waiters, the City Hospital was creditably modern for its time.

Certainly it was a far cry from the John Street institution as described by the famous Dr. William Osler who acted as *locum tenens* for a month in the absence of the resident physician, Charles O'Reilly, M.D., C.M., receiving for his services twenty-five dollars and a pair of elastic-sided boots too small for Dr. O'Reilly. "In those days," Dr. Osler recalled, "the inmates of the hospital were primarily rats, streptococcus and patients."

The opening years of the Barton Street hospital were timed to epochal advances in the field of medicine. By disclosing the role played by the microbe in nature, Louis Pasteur founded the science of bacteriology. Pasteur opened the door to animal and laboratory experimentation, to solution of the problems of disease by scientific research. Pasteurization, inoculation, vaccination: these were the shock troops in the dawning battle of preventive medicine. Anaesthesia in 1846, Lister's theory of antisepsis, William Roentgen's X-rays, and in 1882 Koch's discovery of the *tubercle bacillus,* enabling tuberculosis to be overcome: step by step the battle was engaged.

In this new era in medicine, Hamilton was fortunate in having among its medical practitioners Archibald E. Malloch, M.D., who followed graduation from Queen's University by serving as house surgeon to Lister in the Glasgow Royal Infirmary when the latter was developing his antiseptic technique. In 1870 Dr. Malloch introduced antiseptic surgery in City Hospital, its first use in America, it is believed.

By the 1890's the day of antiseptic solutions had arrived, of rubber gloves in the operating room and sterilized instruments. There however asepsis halted. Correct surgical garb consisted of dark clothing with preferred frock coat, although one noted surgeon wore always a favourite smoking jacket, another an old tweed coat.

Associated with Dr. Malloch in medicine were members of the Hamilton Medical and Surgical Society,[1] organized in 1863, in part to promote an efficient library and to further unity and harmony among its members. The society was responsible for nominating the medical staff of City Hospital, then admitting only public patients. Over the years, appointment of this staff became a source of dissension which split the Medical Society into two opposing camps and eventually caused its demise.

With Dr. Malloch, Drs. James Leslie, James White, Samuel Cummings and H. S. Griffin did most of the hospital surgery. A prominent medical specialist was Dr. A. B. Osborne whose resignation in 1886 as city physician led to appointment of young Dr. Ingersoll Olmstead. During two terms of office Dr. Olmstead reorganized City Hospital methods and administration, and to provide desperately needed trained nursing personnel, in 1890 organized a Nurses' Training School, with Miss Carrie M. Bowman head nurse.

Before his resignation in 1893 to accept a post with the University of Pennsylvania, Philadelphia, Dr. Olmstead introduced the first operating suite in the hospital and city. At this period well-to-do and rurally situated patients were largely treated in their own homes, with surgery performed on kitchen or dining room table, frequently under adverse conditions. From this time forward, as hospital facilities advanced and roads and transportation improved, more and more surgery was performed in local hospitals.

To celebrate Queen Victoria's diamond jubilee the small occasional operating room at the end of Ward III—full length of the ward away from hot water and heat for sterilizing — was replaced with a three-room operating suite built in conjunction with a private ward, Jubilee V, for surgical patients, with a circular operating theatre skylighted by a glass dome, later razed in 1930. The wing incorporated the best features brought back by Dr. Olmstead from a tour of European hospitals. When it opened in 1898 successful pathologist Dr. James W. Edgar had succeeded Dr. Olmstead.

With the end of the century came the opening salvos of the South African War which oddly revived the Hamilton Medical Society. Before leaving for the front with the Canadian contingent, Col. A. B. Osborne, M.D., at a farewell dinner appealed to fellow practitioners to end the dissension which had terminated the society. As a result the society was reorganized, first president being the late James White, M.D., father of Dr. Thomas E. White,[2] in practice today. Following continuous expansion, the society was again reorganized in 1933 and incorporated as the Hamilton Academy of Medicine, with over two hundred members. Today it has 511. Executive Librarian-secretary is Miss Margaret W. Ball.

Commenting on practice in the early years of the twentieth century, Dr. Harold Martin says:

"Contrary to the present layman's trend to patronize young specialists versed in latest techniques, patients preferred a well established practitioner. Consequently younger men had a hard time getting started unless they went into practice with an older doctor. I began in 1917 as assistant to Dr. George S. Bingham who was dedicated to his practice, working Christmas Day, New Year's and Sunday afternoons. Sunday calls were highly popular, helping a patient fill a dull day. About 1910 doctors began to eliminate Sunday hours. The doctor took patients as they came; there was no office nurse. In my early practice my wife stayed home religiously to take calls."

Dr. Elizabeth Bagshaw, year of 1905, who began a still active practice in the city the following year, described early transportation. "When I began practice," she said, "doctors used 'shank's mare,' the street car, a bicycle, or a horse and buggy. In those days street car service was better than it is now. Also the city was smaller and more compact and patients in the doctor's locality, requiring less time to reach them."

Many doctors rented horses from liveries. Some owned and stabled their horses on their own premises, as Dr. George S. Rennie and Dr. William Arrell. Dr. Bingham had a coachman. So had Dr. Samuel Cummings who was driven in a brougham, a hard-topped closed carriage with an elevated driver's seat.

"Dr. H. S. Griffith," said Dr. Martin, "northeast corner Main and Walnut, where the Silhouette Club now stands, drove a dapple gray; Dr. Thomas Wickett, a roan; Dr. A. B. Osborne, early psychiatrist, drove a cob with a docked tail; Dr. W. J. McNichol, father of today's Dr. J. W. McNichol, always drove a plug of a horse; Dr. Olmstead, a chestnut high-stepper. I can see him yet swinging down Victoria Avenue, wheeling in at the side entrance and tying up his horse in the driving shed beside the ice house.

"It seems only a day," said the gray-eyed man behind the desk, "and yet they are all gone. Dr. D. G. Storms, too, on the southeast corner of Main and Bay, on today's City Hall property. He cut quite a dash in winter in a yellow cutter with a high curved front, a fur cap and a big buffalo robe." Dr. Martin smiled. "One thing is certain, you'd never find a doctor with a black horse. No medical man would dare drive one!"

Even more unusual was the troika outfit brought from St. Petersburg, Russia, by Senator William Eli Sanford. Drawn by three bright bay horses abreast, the centre horse beneath a belled arch, the troika flashed musically through the snowy streets.

On April 12th, 1898, the late John Moodie, merchant, founder of the Eagle Knitting Company,[3] introduced the first horseless carriage to Hamilton and Canada. Noiseless, except when braked, the one-cylinder Winton, costing a thousand dollars, resembled a heavy phaeton with pneumatic tires. Neither devotee nor scoffer could foresee that the new perverse gasoline or steam propelled motor vehicle with its duster-clad driver would prove the most potent single factor in the twentieth century in shaping Canada's economic way of life.

Twenty years earlier Mr. Moodie had brought the first English hard tired gearless velocipede to the city. With a front wheel almost six feet high and a back wheel one foot low, the so-called boneshaker was mounted by climbing two small steps, then pedalling furiously to prevent overturning.

By the 1890's the safety bicycle with a coaster brake and proper gears had replaced the velocipede, and the bicycle built for one, two or even three was as much a part of the gay Nineties as the knickerbocker suit for both sexes which it necessitated. It was a carefree, happy era and the bicycle contributed to its gaiety. On the roster of the flourishing Hamilton Cycle Club are names of many leading Hamiltonians.

By the time the Cycle Club was succeeded by the Hamilton Automobile Club the new century was well launched. The late Col. J. R. Moodie and W. G. Walton had acquired Wintons and the late S. O. Greening a steam-driven Locomobile. Within the next five years cars multiplied to a point where legislation was demanded for their control. Part of the difficulty lay in gearing down to the maximum seven miles an hour speed limit. Finally ten miles was granted but it was required that a car stop upon approach of a horse and vehicle, and the motorist dismount and lead the horse past the car.

To protect their interests and enjoy in common the pleasures of motoring, nineteen motorists met in the Royal Hotel on April 29th, 1903, and founded the Hamilton Automobile Club, first of its kind in Canada. Officers elected were S. O. Greening, president; J. R. Moodie and S. E. Malloch, vice-presidents; and James Moodie, secretary.

A month after formation of the Hamilton club the Toronto Automobile Club was organized, to be merged three or four years later into the Ontario Motor League of which the Hamilton club became one of the founding sponsors. In 1913 the Hamilton club also helped promote formation of a national organization, the Canadian Automobile Association, which celebrated its golden anniversary in 1963. Throughout its existence the Hamilton club has maintained the dual purpose of protecting the motorist from unfair legislation and governing its membership in the interests of society.

By 1910 the automobile was making its impact on the medical profession.

"About 1911 or '12," recalls Dr. Elizabeth Bagshaw, "I bought a car. It had three coal-oil lamps, two carbide headlights, brass trimmings, no doors, buggy top, plain glass windshield, and a non-removable crank. Sometimes it cranked, sometimes it didn't. One night as I came home at dusk a police officer stopped me at King and James. 'Lady,' he said, 'you haven't your lights lit.' I replied, 'I don't smoke so I haven't matches.' He lit them.

"There was constant trouble with tires," said the woman who in 1954 was awarded the rare honour of life membership in the Ontario Medical Association, and is also a member of the Canadian Medical Association, the Hamilton Academy of Medicine, and the Canadian Federation of Medical Women. "Tires weren't removable. You had to take off the rim, patch and pump up the tube and replace the tire. I learned to change my tires."

The Nineties had taken a way of life with them. Something of frills and femininity, something of masculine gallantry was gone forever. In their place there evolved a more tailored, more functional era, as typified by the new female ability to change tires. A more sober era, too, its tempo set by the end of the Boer War and return of Canadian veterans from the front, followed by the death of Queen Victoria.

The veterans had met a rousing civic reception in the drill hall, with a welcome from Mayor J. V. Teetzel and bands playing, "When Johnny Comes Marching Home," "Soldiers of the Queen," and finally, "Home Sweet Home." The Women's Wentworth Historical Society, chartered in 1899, had also entertained the soldiers at their newly acquired Mary Gage Battlefield House, site of the battle of Stoney Creek.[4]

Preceding the death of Queen Victoria, on January 22nd, 1901, prayer services were held in city churches, in Christ's Church Cathedral the congregation kneeling to sing, "God Save the Queen." Following announcement of her death by Mayor John S. Hendrie, the city was draped in crêpe. City council bought two thousand yards of costly foulard and shrouded city hall, fire halls and police stations. Public buildings went into purple and black, city newspapers were banded in mourning, and flags fluttered at half mast. Women adopted deep mourning and men wore black ties and arm-bands. Schools closed two days before the Saturday burial, observed in the city with memorial services, closed shops and the dread tolling of bells everywhere.

As a memorial the women of Hamilton raised funds and erected the bronze statue of the queen which stands at the western end of the Gore.

With the Edwardian era came new changes for the city. The first cement sidewalks were laid, and city limits moved eastward along Burlington Street to accommodate new industry. In 1903 the International Harvester Company of Canada Limited, having amalgamated with the Deering Company, constructed the largest implement works in the British Empire, and under Superintendent George L. Rice shipped its binders, mowers, drills and hayrakes in trainload lots to western Canada, South America, Australia and Russia.

Among its employees at this time, International Harvester numbered certain well known Hamiltonians, among them blond Irish-Canadian Robert (Bobby) Kerr, track great, whose remarkable career as a runner climaxed hundreds of victories and new records (some still standing) with a 1908 Olympic championship in the 220 yards; Douglas Dumbrille who achieved a place on the legitimate stage and on screen; and Chester S. Walters, mayor of Hamilton, 1915-16, who became Dominion tax commissioner in Ottawa, and subsequently, 1935-55, Ontario treasurer and controller of finance.

Across Wilcox Street, east of the thriving Harvester plant, another giant industry, the Steel Company of Canada Limited, was born on June 22nd, 1910, through merger of five Canadian companies, two in Hamilton —the Canada Screw Company and Hamilton Steel and Iron Company. Faced with the powerful competition of the steel industry of the United Kingdom and United States, a merger of the Canadian companies was organized by W. M. (Max) Aitken, later Lord Beaverbrook, from which evolved the largest basic steelmaking plant in Canada. Charles S. Wilcox, first president; Robert Hobson and R. H. McMaster, second and third; and William Southam, John Milne, Cyrus Birge, and Lloyd Harris, M.P.: these among others created Stelco.

In spite of the American depression of 1911 and 1912 the advantages of consolidation permitted Stelco to expand the Hamilton plant, enabling the company to meet successfully the heavy demands of World War I. As the war progressed the first coke oven battery was built. With reconstruction and deepening of the Welland ship canal, Stelco added a coal and ore dock to Hamilton's expanding industrial waterfront.

Southward, just north of Barton Street, where the two-storey home, Woodland, of Robert Land, Jr., had once been reached by a drive circling east from Wentworth, another industry stood in the green shadow of

Woodland Park. By 1914 the Canadian Westinghouse Company, Limited, which had made a modest beginning in the city in 1896 as the Westinghouse Manufacturing Company, had built the first railroad airbrakes in Canada; begun manufacture of the first electrical equipment in Canada to utilize alternating current, including the first turnover toaster; and had engineered and manufactured the first Canadian 110,000 volt transformers and circuit breakers for Niagara power development. Paul J. Myler, Francis A. Merrick and J. H. Kerr: in the beginning these were Westinghouse men of stature.

The destruction in a storm of the Great Western railway bridge over the Desjardins canal set opportunity knocking for Benjamin Greening and his half-brother Timothy, recently arrived from Manchester, England.

The fallen bridge contained a wealth of wire; the Great Western railway was then erecting traffic signals at all stations; and the Greening family for generations had engaged in the manufacture of wire. In 1858 Benjamin was commissioned by the railway company to convert wire from the suspension bridge into wire strand, manufacturing over forty miles. He was then engaged to make strong wire web for locomotive engines.

Under the name Victoria Wire Mills, Benjamin Greening and Company were first in Canada to manufacture wire rope, wire cloth and wire screens. Following Benjamin's death his son, Samuel Owen Greening, became president of the firm which in 1889 was reorganized as the B. Greening Wire Company Limited, with John Maw as superintendent.

With the death in 1911 of S. O. Greening and succession of his son, President Harry B. Greening, the firm ended the Victorian era by discontinuing manufacture of its highly ornamental wire work flower stands, garden arbours, and so forth, to begin the making of armour-clad wire rope, under Frank James Maw, head of the wire mill.

A man of wide interests, H. B. Greening was an accomplished musician and a speed boat enthusiast who built the first motor boat engine in Canada. Multiple racing victories included capture at Detroit in 1928 of the Sir Thomas Lipton trophy for the North American motorboat championship. Prior to World War II Mr. Greening helped found International Airways, today a part of Canadian Pacific Airlines.

Before that war's predecessor, the late Clifton W. Sherman established a new steel foundry, Dominion Steel Castings, Limited, in Hamilton, which later as Dominion Foundries and Steel Limited (Dofasco), would become one of the city's leading industries. In December, 1912, the foundry poured its first heat of steel.

In its early years, Dominion Steel cast locomotive frames, axle boxes and mud rings for the Canadian Pacific railway. At that time experienced steel foundrymen were rare in Canada, earliest crews being imported from the States, with a heavy turnover of labour. Before World War I wages ran fifteen cents an hour for unskilled labour; seventeen cents, semi-skilled; and twenty-two cents, skilled. The night gang might run to a thirteen-hour shift. Annealing ovens were fired with coal and one fire-man, John Sadler, could shovel twenty tons of coal every night.

"Little wonder," says Milford Smith, business editor of *The Hamilton Spectator*, "that lunch boxes were giant size. Many new Canadians carried a flask of 'red dog' made at home. The men snuggled down beside the forty-foot annealing ovens in winter to eat their midnight meal, undisturbed by lack of a washroom, although a man coming off shift 'spit black.' Many of the day gang however would walk south through the fields to the Driving Park Hotel on Barton Street to rinse their throats with a five-cent glass of beer." Where sheep then grazed on the Chapple farm north of Barton, neat rows of workmen's houses would later stand, and the red gumbo roads that mired under rain would be surfaced against city traffic.

In 1920, following the end of the war, Dofasco diversified into flat rolled steel and fifteen years later began production of the first tin plate in Canada. Today Dofasco estimates that fifty per cent of Canadian canned goods are contained in company tinplate.

Uniquely, when Dofasco celebrated its fiftieth anniversary, the original team that built the company was still with it—Frank A. Sherman, chairman of the board; Arthur G. Wright and Fred A. Loosely, vice-chairmen; and D. F. (Dofasco Dan) Hassel, vice-president-personnel—except for Clifton W. Sherman, founder, who died in 1955. Current president is F. H. Sherman.

The Great War changed the economy and tempo of Hamilton. Already the end of the century had brought its changes. Miles O'Reilly was gone. In 1899 Dr. William Case II died in his ninety-sixth year. In the closing months of the century Alexander David Stewart, former city police chief, 1880-1886, alderman and mayor of Hamilton, 1894-95, who had sought a glittering fortune in the gold fields of the Yukon, found instead a lonely grave. One of a party which included R. H. Cresswell, James (Baron) Irvine, the Tiger football player, and W. H. Tallman, Stewart died of hardships and scurvy.

A distinguished figure, of imposing physique, highly social, fond of sport and holding office in numerous clubs, Stewart was one of Hamilton's most colourful civic figures. Appointed crown prosecutor by the federal government, he prepared and successfully conducted the case against Louis Riel and other leaders in the North West rebellion, and attended Riel's execution. During his term of office, which followed that of Chief O. McMenemy, an efficient detective and faithful and indefatigable officer, Chief Stewart reorganized the force and improved police methods, increased the detective force from two to four men, instituted a rogues' gallery and a museum, to which the Royal Canadian Mounted Police donated Riel's leg-irons, and is credited with introducing the first horse-drawn patrol wagon service in Canada.

Strangely, some four years after A. D. Stewart's death, his successor in office, Hugh McKinnon, 1886-1895, would find a northern grave in

Dawson City. In other ways the two men resembled one another. Chief McKinnon was six foot three inches in height, weighed over two hundred pounds, had Stewart's handlebar moustache, and as a government detective had been connected with many of the outstanding criminal cases of the province. An all-round athlete, Hugh McKinnon won hundreds of medals and cups in contests in North America and Europe, holding the heavyweight championship of the United States and Canada for five years, and retiring undefeated in 1879. In 1901 he was sent to the Yukon by the government to combat illicit liquor production and importation. On December 12th, 1903, he died of a heart attack.

With the new century the police force expanded to between forty and fifty men. Under Chief Alexander Smith, 1895-1915, the modern detective department originated with Detectives Donald Campbell, later inspector; David Coulter, later chief, 1924-1935; John Bleakley, who died prematurely; and John Miller, later provincial inspector of detectives. In 1895 the county concluded sale of the Barton Street jail to the city.

Four years later, for $50,000, the city acquired Dundurn Castle from the Hon. Donald McInnes. Reserved in the sale, as still property of the MacNab family, was the burial plot on the point north of Tecumseh Street which had been maintained by Sophia (Mrs. A. D.) MacNab,[5] sister-in-law of Sir Allan, until her death on April 19th, 1891.

Following Sophia's death her niece, Mrs. Mary Stuart Daly, daughter of Sir Allan, with her daughter Mrs. Caroline Sophia French offered the burial plot to the city for $2,500, provided the city erect a monument to Sir Allan and assume perpetual care of the plot. This offer was refused by the parks board and its chairman, George Wild, who was convinced the city could obtain the land for less.

On May 24th, 1900, Dundurn Park was officially opened by Mayor J. V. Teetzel in the presence of a throng of Hamiltonians and visitors which overflowed the grounds.

The day commenced with presentation of a towering 150-foot steel flagstaff on the Gore extension. On behalf of the Canadian Club this was presented to the city by its president, A. E. Manning, and past president, Kirwan Martin, assisted by Charles (later Col.) C. R. McCullough, founder in 1893 of the Canadian Club movement.[6] Following acceptance by the mayor the red ensign was unfurled by Mrs. Teetzel.

Beginning with a monster parade the day then took the usual course of public celebrations, then and now. Said the press the following day:

"It was a wild day and wilder night." . . . "Thousands of visitors took a ride on the Hamilton and Barton incline and viewed the city from the mountaintop." . . . "The street railway had fifteen cars on York Street all afternoon and evening but it was impossible to handle the crowds there or throughout the city, although trailers were used all day." . . . "The Gore illuminations were greatly admired by visitors, as were the Dundurn fireworks."

Following the opening of Dundurn Park, Samuel Weaver was installed as caretaker in the gatehouse, and Mrs. Clementina Fessenden, widow of Rev. E. J. Fessenden, Anglican clergyman, was appointed curator of the Castle. First woman in the city to hold such a position, Mrs. Fessenden owed her appointment to the generosity of Stanley Mills, son of Nelson Mills and Cynthia Elizabeth Gage.

An active clubwoman, dedicated to public service, and an ardent imperialist, Mrs. Fessenden is best remembered as founder of Empire Day (the day preceding May 24th, Victoria Day) which she advocated devoting to patriotic observances and teaching in Canadian schools. From a small beginning in 1897, the movement spread throughout the Empire, in 1917 sixty-four flags of the British dominions being massed in St. Paul's Cathedral, London, England, in a great Empire Day celebration.

In recognition of her endeavour the first Hamilton chapter of the Imperial Order of the Daughters of the Empire, organized in 1900, the year the order was founded, was named Fessenden chapter. This was changed, however, in 1902 to Municipal chapter of Hamilton. First Regent was Mrs. J. V. Teetzel. One of the first projects of Fessenden chapter was the purchase of new colours for the 13th Regiment upon its return from South Africa, the presentation being made by H.R.H. Duke of Cornwall and York (later George V).

In 1904 natural gas, which had been discovered in the counties bordering on Lake Erie a decade before, was brought to the city. Securing a charter and franchise the Ontario Pipe Line Company Limited now offered natural gas in competition with the Hamilton Gas Light Company's manufactured product, at considerably lower rates. Nine years later the Ontario Pipe Line Company bought out its competitor and assumed control as today's United Gas and Fuel Company of Hamilton Limited.

In the city the new gas illuminated the era of the bungalow with its wide over-hanging eaves—forerunner of the ranch house of the 1950's— and its deep porch usually supported by piers made of boulders . . . of Mission furniture and Mission coloured art glass lamps suspended from the ceiling . . . of elaborate cast iron and brass beds, hall racks of golden oak, and cuckoo clocks . . . of bamboo and wicker . . . the day of the post-impressionists, the futurists, the cubists . . . and of the new Sunday supplement and equally new comic strip to accompany the Sunday roast— "Little Nemo," "Buster Brown," "Mutt and Jeff," and in 1911, "Bringing Up Father," whose socially ambitious Maggie and corned-beef-loving Jiggs struck so universal a chord that it was translated into twenty-seven languages.

"Bringing Up Father" was two years old when Hamilton celebrated a premature but enthusiastic city Centennial (August 11th-16th) presided over by John Lennox, a leather goods merchant. Unique features were the "tens of thousands of coloured lights festooned in trees in the Gore, Dundurn Park, the Court House Square, city hall, and cricket grounds;" the garden party given by Stanley Mills at his residence, Glenfern, entrance fee being fifty years' residence in the city; opening of the Exposition by a native-son lieutenant-governor, Sir John M. Gibson;

and the Midway, centering on Market Square, complete with trained elephants, boxing kangaroos and performing dogs and horses, with girlie shows, sideshows, and shooting galleries, and with refreshment booths selling the popular ice cream cone invented in 1904 at the St. Louis World's Fair by a resourceful Armenian concessionaire who ran out of dishes for ice cream, substituted waffles and found he had a "sell-out." Featured, too, was the three-storey four-bedroom house built in a day in Britannia Park,[7] completely furnished and equipped for occupation, won on a 25-cent beans-in-a-bottle guessing chance.

If today's solid citizens are tempted to cavil at modern youth's hoop-la, they might well consider the centennial's final evening pyjama parade from the Waldorf Hotel (Connaught Sheraton today) to Gore Park, for which the city's leading male citizens donned their gaudiest night attire. Paraders included Dr. J. Edgar Davey, future M.O.H.; Ewart (Red) Dixon, Tiger running back; Dr. R. A. Thompson, principal, Collegiate Institute; 'Addie' Richardson; W. D. Wishart; Harry Stares, Mus. Bac., with the 91st Regiment band; Fire Chief A. B. Ten Eyck; Mayor John Allan; and in voluminous night shirts, Controller Bird and Walter McMullen, sports editor of *The Herald*.

Nor dare too much be said about modern a-go-go. Certain melodies of 1913 vintage will undoubtedly move oldtimers to nostalgia: "Trail of the Lonesome Pine," "Put On Your Old Gray Bonnet," "Hail, Hail, the Gang's All Here;" for the unabashed sentimentalist, "Oh, Where Is My Wandering Boy Tonight?" and "Darling, I Am Growing Old;" and for the subliminal depressive, whose numbers are increasing significantly today, "The Curse of an Aching Heart," with its wail, "You Made Me What I Am Today."

On the other hand there was the sprightly, "Father, Shake Your Feet for Your Ears Are Dusty" and "Moses Loves Me," the latter, reports the press, harmonized by the crowd at midnight under the leadership of "Pigs" Olmstead, of Bismarck, better known as "Uppy the Oyster":

'Moses loves me, yes I know,
Very much obliged to Moses.
He washed me as white as snow,
Dirty little job for Moses.
Pretty girls now walk the streets
Too sweet to blow their noses,
Blisters on their tiring feet,
Blow their noses, Moses.'

In certain streets roped for dancing, the waltz and two-step were certainly evident. But neither was as popular as the grizzly bear, the turkey trot, or the tango.

To encourage an *entente cordiale*, males carried feather duster "ticklers" to tease the fair sex and the latter reciprocated by wearing headbands inviting, "Kiss Me, Kid, I'm Kandy."

19

Further Hospitals and a Bevy of Murders

BY 1914 the city had spread to Kenilworth Avenue on the east, although it still stood at Paradise Road on the west and stayed north of Concession on the mountain. Within these bounds, however, settlement was advancing rapidly. In 1880 Hamilton's population had stood at 35,000; in 1890 at 44,653; in 1900 at 51,561; by 1910 had risen to 70,221; and four years later had soared to 100,808.

"That was a period of peak immigration into Canada," said Hamilton citizen Hon. Ellen L. Fairclough, federal Minister of Immigration in the Diefenbaker government from 1957 to 1963. "There were no restrictions on immigration at that time. In 1911 the wave began rolling with 300,000 immigrants. The next year we hit the second all-time high with over 375,000 and in 1913 made the Canadian peak with 400,870. The cause? Political unrest and war rumours, allied to land grants in the Canadian west, then just opening up. Mind you, this immigration was not all European. A considerable number of immigrants came from the United States. American immigration to Canada was common at the beginning of the century. Today it is a different matter."

As before, one of the first areas affected by the city's increase in population was its hospital services.

By 1914 the original City Hospital had expanded into a full-fledged institution with added maternity ward, isolation wings, outdoor department presented by Mr. John Billings, children's wing, and augmented staff and service facilities. In 1902, during the mayoralty of her son, the late John S. Hendrie (later Lt.-Col. Sir John, K.C.M.G., C.V.O.), the late Mrs. William Hendrie, Sr. had presented a nurses' residence; and William Southam[1] and Mrs. Southam had given the Southam home for advanced cases of tuberculosis.

Unfortunately as the City Hospital matured, city demands, intensified by immigration, increased, and older parts of the hospital deteriorated. Although St. Joseph's Hospital, founded by the Sisters of St. Joseph and opened on June 11th 1890, with 25 beds, was now operating with 50;

St. Peter's Infirmary, instituted by Rev. Thomas Geohegan, was accommodating patients with chronic disorders; and the Mountain Sanatorium had opened in 1906 for treatment of the tuberculous, the city was still unable to meet the mounting demand for hospital beds and treatment.

In April, 1917, on a site acquired four years earlier, the Mount Hamilton Hospital of 100 beds was opened by His Excellency the Duke of Devonshire. It contained a maternity floor, operating room for minor surgery, and nurses' residence.

In the previous year, 1916, the Sisters of St. Joseph had added a wing of 75 beds to their hospital at the head of John Street. Originally the home of John Young, the building had been acquired by Bishop T. J. Dowling, D.D., as an episcopal residence but instead had been converted into a hospital under direction of Mother Superior M. Philip Lenaten. In 1894 addition of St. Ann's wing had increased hospital capacity to 50 beds, surgical and medical, while the opening of an obstetrical department in 1912 had broadened its scope.

In 1911, the Sisters purchased Postmaster Adam Brown's home on Alma Avenue and converted it into a nurses' residence and training school, the first class graduating in 1914. The house was sold with the romantic provision that a small fountain on the grounds should remain intact, this being the spot, according to Mrs. William Hendrie, on which her father, Adam Brown,[2] proposed to her mother, Mary Kough.

Until 1922 the Adam Brown house remained the nurses' home. It was then replaced by a modern nurses' residence and school, Undermount. Two years later the department of obstetrics was transferred to Casa Maria, the onetime home of George H. Bisby, wool merchant; and St. Monica's ward for children was opened.

In 1890, St. Peter's Infirmary was founded by Rev. Thomas Geohegan, first rector of St. Peter's Church, to answer the need of male sufferers from chronic disorders who were unacceptable in hospital because of the length of their stay. Without funds but with a passion for work and an indomitable spirit, Mr. Geohegan formulated a plan and selected the old Springer homestead on the earlier Horning estate[3] to incorporate into it.

Originally one-storey, the red brick Springer home had been transformed by a second storey into a dignified and commodious residence topped by a large cupola and with a wide veranda supported on paired columns. Its price, with four acres of land, was $9,000, with a down payment of $1,000. Assisted by Right Rev. Charles Hamilton, Bishop of Niagara, and a dedicated group of clergy and laymen, the money was raised and household furnishings collected. The first year, thirty patients were treated.

In 1893 St. Peter's Home for Incurables, the second in Ontario, was incorporated, its matron Miss Lucie Chowne, an English trained nurse formerly matron of the City Hospital. Miss Chowne had offered her services gratis for a year and remained seventeen, 1890-1906, six without remuneration, the remainder at a small salary. She died in 1907.

Burlington Skyway Bridge from the north shore. (Tom Bochsler.)

Ore carrier entering Hamilton Harbour via Burlington Canal. Harbour Commission land and Pier 29 in foreground, with Burlington Skyway and towers of vertical lift vehicular and railway bridge behind. (Phil Aggus & Son.)

Cargo liners at Hamilton Harbour Commission terminals. Middle right, H.M.C.S. Patriot, headquarters for Canada of the Royal Canadian Naval Reserve. (Tom Bochsler.)

Busy port scene at Hamilton Harbour Commission wharves. (Hamilton Spectator.)

Oxygen steelmaking plant at pioneering Dofasco. Furnaces have a 150-ton capacity and operate on a 45-minute cycle; actual steelmaking time is about 22 minutes. (Dominion Foundries and Steel Limited.)

Great Lakes ore carrier unloads at Dofasco docks. Stockpiles of coal and iron ore will feed company's hungry blast furnaces. (Dominion Foundries and Steel Limited.)

Night-time view of three of Stelco's four blast furnaces. (The Steel Company of Canada.)

Engineering building, McMaster University. (Tom Bochsler.)

West block, Central Secondary School, originally the Hamilton Technical Institute. In 1966, Central's east block became an experimental matriculation school, accommodating Grade 13 students only. (Hamilton Spectator.)

"Shack," Mountain Sanatorium, built in 1910 with open wings. (Hamilton Health Association.)

Year-round Chedoke Civic Golf Course and Ski Run, operated by the Parks Board on site of earlier Hamilton Golf and Country Club. (Hamilton Spectator.)

Modern St. Joseph's Hospital. (Lloyd Bloom.)

First Methodist Church, 1868-1913. On this site the first church in Hamilton was erected in 1824. (Frank Wright.)

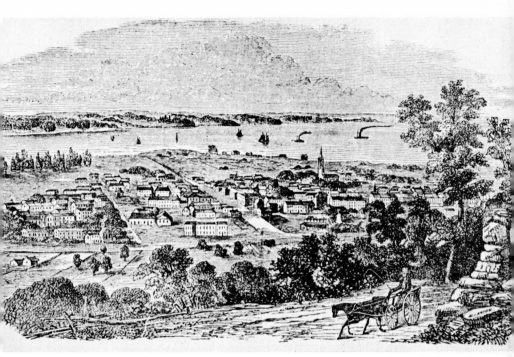

Hamilton in 1845. (Hamilton Spectator.)

Present-day Hamilton, seen from the Mountain. (Tom Bochsler.)

Hamilton's largest, most modern complex, Terminal Towers. (Panda Associates, Toronto.)

Future Civic Square with York Street in background. (Murray Jones and V. Karklins, City Engineering Department.)

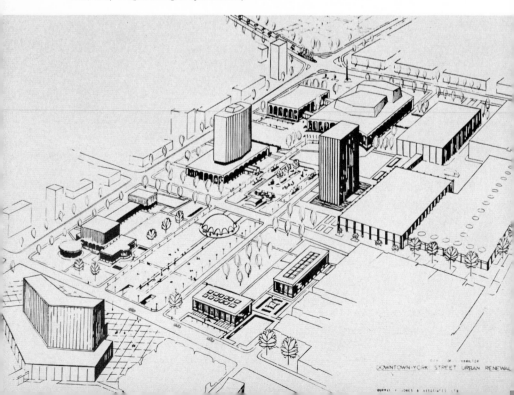

For years the home ran on a minimum budget, supported by a modest grant from the provincial government, fees paid by city and county for patients referred, donations and bequests, and funds raised by devoted workers. Cows and hens were kept to reduce expenses. Patients paid only what they could afford. Yet by 1915 St. Peter's was free of debt, although both county and city had discontinued referring patients, the county opening Wentworth House of Refuge in 1912, and the city having located its aged and infirm at the John Street North Hospital. The city substituted a small grant.

During these years, private funds provided for expansion and improvements, for installing regular hospital equipment, adding a sunroom, new bathrooms and diet kitchen.

Far to the west, above the escarpment, the Mountain Sanatorium, operating under the Hamilton Health Association, was opened in 1906 by Governor-General Earl Grey. Since the opening occurred prematurely, to coincide with Earl Grey's visit to Hamilton, buildings were not completed, and the first patients, four male and four female, were accommodated in two tents set up in the orchard of the 98-acre William Macklem farm, donated by the wealthy wool merchants, W. D. Long and G. H. Bisby. First physician-in-charge was Dr. A. D. Unsworth.

This was two years after J. H. McMenemy, Hamilton relief officer, had tried tent treatment for tuberculosis, placing his young daughter and two other girls in a bell tent on the Mountain brow. The successful founding of the Mountain Sanatorium was due to the efforts of Mr. McMenemy and Mrs. Lyle, wife of Dr. Samuel Lyle, B.D., pastor of Central Presbyterian Church, the Local Council of Women,[4] instituted in 1893 by Lady Aberdeen during her sojourn in Hamilton prior to Lord Aberdeen's term as governor-general, and the I.O.D.E., founded to carry on patriotic work during the Boer War.

The first purely local anti-tuberculosis association in Ontario, the Mountain Sanatorium grew from two frame shacks housing twelve male and ten female patients to the largest tuberculosis sanatorium in the British Empire, with a bed capacity of 750.

The Hamilton Health Association consisted of a men's advisory and fund raising board and a ladies' auxiliary administrative body. Mrs. P. D. Crerar, then regent of Municipal chapter, I.O.D.E., served as president of the women's board until her death in 1919. Equally faithful were vice-presidents Mrs. Robert Evans and Mrs. William Southam. Samuel Barker, M.P., a well known political figure of the day, was president of the men's board, with William Southam secretary-treasurer. To ensure an adequate supply of linen for the young institution, Mrs. Crerar established a new chapter, St. Elizabeth, whose sole duty this would be. When St. Elizabeth came to celebrate its sixtieth anniversary in 1966, it would find its members had raised $116,000 for Sanatorium linen.

By the time Dr. Unsworth resigned in 1908, to be succeeded as medical superintendent by Dr. John Howard Holbrook, the first permanent building, the Grafton Infirmary, gift of Col. J. J. Grafton and his brother, J. B. Grafton, of Dundas, was in use. For nearly forty years the short, slight medical superintendent, a dedicated man with an in-built dynamo of energy, guided the Sanatorium through its growing years, developed its techniques in combating the "White Plague," and promoted its interests in the city.[5]

To the east of the Sanatorium, on the brow, a provincial institution was also expanding. Erected on 100 acres of heavily wooded property, in part purchased from Isaac Buchanan, ex-M.P., and Mrs. William Gourlay, the Asylum for Inebriates was completed in the fall of 1875.

Of red and white patterned brick with stone trim, set upon coursed stone and topped by a mansard roof, the asylum housed 200 patients and staff. Its erection resulted from determined lobbying by temperance advocates for a place of detention for the alcoholics of the day.

When the expected dipsomaniacs failed to appear, J. W. Langmuir, inspector of prisons, urged that the asylum be assigned to the insane, whose numbers overflowed existing institutions and gaols into private houses. On March 17th, 1876, the building, under superintendent Dr. Richard M. Bucke, was opened for the chronic insane and 210 patients were transferred from Toronto, Kingston and London asylums. A year later Dr. J. M. Wallace replaced Dr. Bucke.

In 1879 wings increased the asylum's length to 550 feet, and a three-storey addition was built in the rear. At this time eight counties were assigned to the hospital. In June, to meet demand, basement housing for 27 patients was added.

In this year also the unsatisfactory system of sewage disposal by collecting and treating waste in tanks blasted out of the rock before the main building—with raw sewage overflowing down the mountainside—was abandoned and connection made by pipe with city sewers. The vexatious problem of water supply was solved by a special pumping station, which was erected at the corner of Queen and Markland Streets.

When Dr. Wallace retired in 1888 because of ill health and Dr. James Russell took office, the Asylum for the Insane at Hamilton was officially declared best in the province. Additions had provided East House for the criminal insane and accommodation for 300 added patients. A flight of wooden steps now led to Queen Street below.

In 1892, following a disastrous fire, a 200,000-gallon reservoir, a fire hall and hose tower were erected, with a powerful steam pump to ensure adequate pressure. The new century saw an infirmary and operating room built; a skating rink installed; and substitution of electricity for gaslight. With additional property purchased, by 1914 the asylum owned 529 acres, housed 1,312 patients and served eleven counties.

In May, 1907, Dr. Russell resigned and was replaced by Dr. Walter M. English who in turn would serve twenty years before being succeeded by Dr. J. J. Williams.

This was the era of social philanthropy, when ladies drove to meetings in their carriages, fashionably attired, gloved and hatted, dainty parasols raised against the sun, and urchins watched wide-eyed as the coachman handed them down. Yet these same prominent matrons provided comforts for the children of the Orphan Asylum and battled their way through awesome Sanatorium mud to carry aid to the fledgling institution isolated by storm at the end of a lone farm lane.

The era, still, of diphtheria epidemics, of smallpox, scarlet fever, and typhoid which annually crowded hospital wards and corridors. In 1871 an epidemic of scarlet fever caused eighty deaths in four months. In October, 1915, seven cases of black diphtheria in Strathcona School resulted in three deaths. Standard treatment for typhoid at this time was to place the patient in a bedside tub of water and ice, keep him there ten to fifteen minutes, repeating every three hours until his temperature abated. Pneumonia was treated with mustard plasters as a counter irritant, and mounted inexorably to a crisis, following which the patient either died or recovered.

The era, this, of twelve-hour duty for nurses—in April, 1937, eight-hour duty was first introduced — with fourteen and sixteen hours in epidemics; of low iron back-breaking beds and straw ticks which covered the floor with litter. After the death of a patient the tick was emptied behind the driving shed and refilled. Later felt mattresses were introduced, a wonderful innovation, to be replaced in 1913 by hair mattresses.

"In the early 1900's," recalled a nurse, "we still had gas jets. At night we carried lamps, and before rubber heels arrived, wrapped our feet in flannel bandages which sometimes caught on floor splinters and came undone."

Important as health and medical developments might be, there was more general interest in William J. (Billy) Sherring's winning the 26-mile marathon in Greece in 1906; the Alerts bringing home the first official Grey Cup to Hamilton in 1912, with the Tigers, who had begun play in 1872 under the well known yellow and black, repeating the feat the next year; the disagreement between the parks board and Mrs. French in 1909, the board's renewed refusal to purchase the MacNab burial plot leading Sir Allan's irate granddaughter to remove the fifteen bodies from the plot and re-inter them in Hamilton and Holy Sepulchre cemeteries — separating Sir Allan from his first wife and son, his parents and brother, and breaking his will[6] — preparatory to selling the plot as a gravel pit, a threat scotched by city by-laws; or the several murders which enlivened the scene prior to World War I.

Beginning in 1899 with the Parrott matricide on Steven Street — in which a drunken son axed to death an equally drunken mother, the only redeeming feature of the sordid affair being the release of the inoffensive husband, teamster Benjamin Parrott, Sr., from the life of misery he had been led — four murders occurred in a decade. Hanged for his crime, "Crazy Ben" Parrott earned the distinction of being the last murderer buried in the Barton Street gaol yard. Surprisingly, seven medical men attended the execution: Drs. Balfe, Cockburn, M. E. Gillrie, Wallace, White, Baugh and Bauer. An autopsy disclosed that Parrott's brain weighed two ounces over normal. "Good proof," announced the physicians, "of no insanity in the murderer's make-up."

Four years later, the murder of popular Constable James Barron, father of Walter (Wally) Barron, great Tiger lineman, while patrolling his beat on Catharine Street North, was never solved. Constable Barron was shot as he attempted to corner an unidentified prowler. The murder brought demands to arm the police who had not carried revolvers since a policeman had shot and killed a suspected intruder in the Victoria Hotel some twenty years earlier.

A revealing sidelight on police equipment prior to flashlight, walkie-talkie and call-box derives from a query of Mayor W. J. Morden and the police commissioners as to why police were not equipped with lanterns on their beats. "The men do not like them," replied Chief Alexander Smith. "The oil from the lanterns spoils their uniforms."

When Chief Smith substituted the horse-drawn "paddywagon" for the earlier hand-propelled two-wheeled cart, "the wheelbarrow," a patrol station on Napier Street was built to house the wagons. In 1907 they were moved to the rear of Central police station and the former patrol station, today a fire hall, was closed. Prior to World War I the first motor vehicle was introduced into the department. When the Sherman Avenue station was built in 1910 and the east end division opened — then one of the most difficult in the city — David Coulter, who had driven the paddywagon before becoming a detective, was made inspector. In the detective department was Harry Sayer, a well groomed, dark haired and dark moustached former constable, who served as detective, senior detective and deputy chief before his premature death at forty-nine.

About this time two more of Hamilton's rousing roster of murders occurred.

On October 10th, 1905, a dark haired, well dressed, pregnant girl was discovered gagged and shot in James Marshall's bush on the Mountain. Although the girl and her presumed murderer had been seen, neither was ever identified.

"My mother, Mrs. James Johnston, saw them pass on the road," says Mrs. R. Gladstone Woolley,[7] née Elsie (Essie) Johnston of Upper Paradise Road. "He was walking a few steps ahead of her. My father and brother, working in the field, saw them too. My brother watched them go into the bush. At noon when he and pa came home for dinner he rode his bicycle down past the bush but then had a funny feeling and didn't go in. The man was stout, wore a black christy and carried a raincoat.

"The next day when three boys gathering sweet chestnuts found the body they came running to our house, scared to death. My brother wanted to go and look but pa wouldn't let anyone near the woods until Constable George Nichol arrived."

196

While the body of the murdered girl lay in Blachford and Son's funeral parlour police estimated that 10,000 spectators viewed it. Description of clothing and jewellery, from good American shops, was broadcast widely and for seven months the case was kept open. Although rumours abounded, it remained unsolved. "If the police didn't know who did it," observed one resident, "it was said that others did. But the girl was dead. Why create more unhappiness? Best leave things as they were."

Of all Hamilton murders, however, the one that vied with the renowned Dick case in rousing widespread public and press interest in the inquest was the unsolved daytime shooting of young Ethel Kinrade, eldest daughter of Thomas L. Kinrade, principal of Cannon Street public school, and owner of considerable east end property, inherited in part from his father, after whom Kinrade Avenue is named. A generous family, the Kinrades frequently fed transients or gave them food tickets.

Following lunch on February 25th, 1909, Mr. Kinrade had left for school. Mrs. Kinrade had departed to visit the police station to report an attempted break-in the preceding evening and ask for protection that night. At home the sisters, Ethel and Florence, after clearing away the lunch dishes, were dressing for a walk.

Reassured by Inspector McMahon that the comfortable red brick home with double veranda at 103 Herkimer Street would be watched, Mrs. Kinrade was proceeding homeward when a crowd about a bulletin in a newspaper office window attracted her. To her horror it announced the murder of her daughter.

As far as could be judged from Florence's conflicting stories, by open windows and footprints in the snow, she answered the doorbell to confront a man of medium build, with light hair, a brown moustache, wearing dark clothes and a felt hat, who first demanded food, then money. Running upstairs to get ten dollars from her dresser drawer she called to Ethel to lock herself in her room, but hearing shots, "like the house going up," realized that she had not done so.

Although her bedroom window faced the street and opened on a balcony, and she threw it wide, Florence did not call for help, attempt to escape, nor lock herself in. Instead she returned downstairs, gave the man the bill, entered the parlour and climbed out of the window. She was pulled back by the intruder, ran through the kitchen into the back yard (although a side door gave access to the street) crossed to the low back fence, where a mound of snow offered easy escape, stood momentarily with her back to it, then returned to the house, pushed past the man who was still standing in the hall and crossed the street to tell a neighbour, "Ethel is shot, six times!"

Seven bullets had been fired into Ethel's body, "with unparalleled malignancy," declared the crown, since medical testimony showed some fifteen minutes had elapsed between bullets fired into the brain and into the heart. Whether Florence saw her sister shot or when or where she first saw the body could not be ascertained.

At the inquest conducted by Dr. James Anderson, which lasted fifty-six days, with fifteen sessions held mostly at night, George Tate Blackstock, K.C., famous criminal lawyer was engaged as crown investigator to assist S. F. Washington, Q.C., crown attorney of Wentworth County. George Lynch-Staunton, K.C. (later Senator), assisted by Thomas Hobson, represented the Kinrade family.

Mr. Blackstock's gruelling examination, while it did not secure an arrest and charge, elicited some unusual facts.

Pretty Florence, a trained and well known concert singer and soloist in Hamilton churches, had been engaged some months earlier to sing at a church in Richmond, Virginia. In the confused abstract of the Richmond visit were strange lines and designs: revolver practice by Florence as a safeguard for the journey; a vaudeville engagement in the south; a mysterious Miss Elliott who had paid Florence's travelling expenses but whose address she did not know; correspondence with an American matrimonial agency although at the time she was engaged to a young divinity student, Montrose Wright; a love affair and promise to marry an American actor, James Baum; a veiled and unhappy stay in Virginia Beach; and mail and a gift brooch intercepted by her mother and Ethel following Florence's return home.

Although clairvoyant Anna Eva Fay, appearing in Hamilton at that time, "saw" the murder weapon under the sidewalk near the Kinrade home and a revolver was indeed found, it was a new weapon, unfired, clearly a hoax.

Neither murder weapon nor cartridges were ever located. Nor was a motive established. Unanimously the family testified to its harmony and unity but this evidence was at variance with general gossip, which whispered of jealousy of Ethel as her father's favourite, to whom he entrusted the task of collecting rents on his properties.

Mr. Blackstock's relentless examination was described by leading lawyers as worse than the "sweat box." To combat it emotional Florence "forgot" or swooned.

As interest in the inquest mounted to fever pitch the Kinrades moved to a Toronto hotel, and people travelled over one hundred miles to attend the hearings for which queues formed early in the day. The final session attracted some fifty pressmen. The verdict found that Ethel Kinrade had been shot by a person or persons unknown and requested the crown to continue its investigation in view of "the unreliability of some of the evidence produced."

Shortly afterwards, Mr. Kinrade resigned as principal and the family left the area. Florence married Montrose Wright, who gave up his theological studies in favour of law. In 1918 he died of pneumonia in Calgary, leaving his wife with two small children to support. Returning to the stage Florence Wright attained a certain measure of success. In the 1920's she played Hamilton. Later she settled in California. Long before this the crown had closed the case.

One significant sentence was never explained. Informed by telephone at school that his daughter had been murdered, Thomas Kinrade hastened home, not knowing which daughter until he entered the house and saw Florence in hysterics being attended by Dr. McNichol. Nearby stood Detective John W. Bleakley.

Mr. Kinrade was obviously distracted. "I have expected something like this," he cried, "for a long time."

Then he saw the body on the stretcher. He lifted the oilcloth covering. "It is Ethel," the father said and, stooping, kissed her.

20

War and Industry

THE first world war came and went and while it was in progress there was nothing else in existence and when it went, as all other things before it, it was forgotten.

In the beginning there was a great rush to enlist, to "get into the scrap" before the war was over. The 4th Field Battery volunteered to a man for overseas service. In three days the unit was up to war strength; in a few more, was under canvas at the Jockey Club; trained at Valcartier; sailed on the *Grampian*; and on March 2nd, 1915, was in action in France.

Under the command of Lt.-Col. Henry Picton Van Wagner from 1883 to 1897, the 4th had attained a high state of efficiency, winning many coveted prizes for markmanship and manoeuvres. Succeeding him, Col. Sir John S. Hendrie, Lt.-Col. William O. Tidswell, and Col. Henry G. Carscallen in turn assumed command, Colonel Carscallen taking the battery to France. Serving under him were Capt. Harry D. G. Crerar, who would win fame later as commander of the First Canadian Army in the 1944 invasion of Europe, and Capt. W. I. S. Hendrie. From the time it arrived in France the battery, renamed the 11th, played an active role, at Ypres winning the title, the "Fighting Eleventh."

Leaving even before the 4th, the first contingent out of Hamilton was composed of ex-members of British and Canadian regular forces, "old soaks" enlisted to form the Princess Patricia's Canadian Light Infantry.

In the first world war, militia regiments did not provide whole battalions under their name for war service. Instead, regiments were called on for contingents from which the *ad hoc* numbered battalions of the Canadian Expeditionary Force were formed. By December following the declaration of war, the 13th (now the 13th Royal Regiment, permission to add "Royal" having been granted in 1910) had forwarded three contingents and provided forces to guard local strategic points.

In 1912, when the 13th Royals celebrated its 50th anniversary, the regiment had reached an all-time high in mustered strength and in general proficiency and marksmanship. Much of this was due to John M. Gibson, who had followed Lt.-Col. James Skinner as C.O. from 1885 to 1895, and who in addition to being a distinguished lawyer, legislator[1] and financier, was also an internationally famous rifle shot who had represented Canada frequently at Bisley, in 1879 winning the Prince of Wales' prize. Although he had retired from command twenty years before, being succeeded by Lt.-Cols. Alexander H. Moore and Frederick Ross, it was Colonel Gibson who came to the regiment's rescue when cancellation of the government grant to non-permanent active militia involved the 13th Royals in 1915 in financial difficulties. Until the end of the war Sir John paid the regiment's bills out of his own pocket.

In August, 1914, the song, "It's a Long Way to Tipperary," already popular in England, was introduced to Hamilton at the old Grand Opera House by George Evans and his Honey Boy Minstrels. A month later Lt.-Col. Ross announced it as a new marching song of the 13th.

In August, 1914, headlines were optimistic: GERMAN RETIREMENT APPEARS IMMINENT. Two months later the end seemed even nearer: ALLIES OFFICIALLY REPORTED TO HAVE MAINTAINED OFFENSIVE AGAINST GERMANS FOR TWO WEEKS.

Nevertheless, new recruits were sworn in and regiments held manoeuvres on the Market Square. Nightly, speakers of the Hamilton Recruiting League urged the city's youth into khaki. They included Sir John M. Gibson and S. F. Washington, K.C., both of whom would lose a son in the war,[2] and Pastor Peter W. Philpott, who with his wife had opened a mission in 1896 in a small saloon on Hughson Street North, graduating four years later to the old burlesque and vaudeville Star theatre, on the corner of Merrick and Park Streets.

Here on Sunday, compliment of Webber Bessey, Star owner, the tall, broad-shouldered, handsome ex-blacksmith sandwiched his crowded gospel services between the week-day appearances of George M. Cohan, Rose Sydell's London Belles, and "Sliding Billy" Watson and his "Beef Trust." In the Star the Rev. Mr. Philpott raised funds to begin building the Gospel Tabernacle, later the Philpott Memorial Church which for many years he crowded to the doors.

In 1914 the cornerstone of the Royal Connaught Hotel was laid, with the building opened two years later; the Tobey store advertised with its men's suits and overcoats, "nobby new lines of Astoria shoes, indeed with 'Knobby' toes, $4-$6;" a concrete highway was being constructed to link Hamilton and Toronto; city consumers of electric light increased from 6,500 to over 10,000; and in December George H. Summers' popular stock theatre on the Mountain, east of the east end incline, punctuated a decade of entertainment with a fire whose flames illuminating the night sky were visible throughout the city.

By 1915 headlines were changing: HUNS' SUB ACTIVITY EXTENDED . . . ATTACKS LAUNCHED BY WARSHIPS OF THE KAISER ON FRENCH CITY OF

DUNKIRK. On May 7th, 1915, without warning, the British liner *Lusitania* was torpedoed off the Irish coast with over 1,000 lives lost. Hamilton casualties included James M. and Mrs. Young who were returning from visiting their son, Lt. James V. Young, in hospital in England with wounds.

Son of John Young, James M. contributed largely to the development of Hamilton's textile industry. With his brother-in-law, R. A. Lucas, he founded the Hamilton Cotton Company, becoming president. He was president also of the Imperial Cotton Company and director of the Dominion Belting Company, both of Hamilton. An ardent sportsman, Mr. Young was president of the Hamilton Squash Racquet Club, and a director of the Hamilton Golf and Country and Tamahaac Clubs. He was president, too, of the local Red Cross, in which both he and Mrs. Young had taken an active interest.

TWO THOUSAND SONS OF CANADA FALL AT YPRES . . . THOUSANDS ANSWERING WAR CALL IN LONDON, GREAT ARMY RECRUITED. In November, 1915, Lt.-Col. H. D. Fearman, C.O. 13th Royals, transferred to the 120th City of Hamilton Battalion, to become known as the 13th Overseas Battalion, and took more than 1,200 officers and men to France. For successfully leading the first daylight trench raid ever attempted, Lt. Bertram O. (B.O.) Hooper, popular manager of the Bank of Hamilton, won the Military Cross. At a later date, Lt.-Col. Hooper assumed command of and brought home the 20th Battalion. Twice wounded during the war, Lt. (later Lt.-Col.) Colin W. G. Gibson, son of Sir John, won the M.C., the Order of Leopold (Belgian) and the Croix de Guerre (Belgian).

Until Col. R. A. Robertson, of the 13th, established Hamilton's recruiting centre in the Armouries[3] and organized mobilization, enlistment for the C.E.F. was conducted separately by militia units. Frequently paymasters arriving from headquarters with funds for new recruits found enlistment far exceeded their docket. On occasion enlistees, instead of pay and boarding allowance, received $5 only on account.

When even patriotic landladies began to evict soldiers for arrears of board, Lt.-Col. S. C. Mewburn secured the Mountain View Hotel as temporary quarters until the city should erect barracks on the John J. Scott property, purchased in 1912 as an east end park. Located between Lottridge and Trolley Street (Gage Avenue), King Street and Barton, the property consisted of farmland which had earlier belonged to James (Delta Jim) Gage and upon which the Gage home and outbuildings still stood, being retained from sale and occupied by the Gage family—the later highly contentious Hall of Fame.

For over a year the Mountain View housed Depot Canadian Mounted Rifles, raised from Ontario cavalry units in general. A five-storey building of native stone topped by a peaked observation tower and a tall flag pole, the Mountain View, proprietor Webber Bessey, was El Dorado to the troops, with good meals, hot and cold baths and comfortable beds. The move in December, 1916 to the brown frame bunkhouses of Scott Park was made reluctantly.

In addition to barracks, Scott Park housed non-commissioned officers' quarters, an equine hospital for the cavalry horses, and a military isolation hospital of forty beds. Intersecting the drill and parade ground a rutted wagon track marked the line of unopened Cannon Street.

Long after the rigours of training were forgotten soldiers would recall the treats and parties and entertainments at different city churches, clubs and private homes; the occasional swim at the Y.M.C.A. on James Street South; the regimental church parades led by Capt. Rev. George Pugsley; the old Gage Avenue schoolhouse, mess of the C.M.R. officers, later destroyed by fire; and bitter winter nights on duty at Stelco and Dominion Foundries, guarding them against sabotage.

By 1916 shortages were becoming a factor of civilian life. While rationing, as in World War II, did not occur except for meatless, heatless and butterless days, which restaurants were required and householders in honour pledged to observe, there were the same foods in short supply: foodstuffs required by the armed forces and Great Britain, goods imported by sea, and shortages due to removal of workers from food-producing fields.

To help offset these deficiencies citizens planted victory gardens on home lots, and spearheaded by churches, the Kiwanis Club of Hamilton and other service organizations, cultivated waste plots in and near the city. Civilians employed their holidays working on farms, in canning factories, behind counters and in the western harvest fields. The women of the city, operating through the local branch of the Red Cross Society, through churches, clubs and organizations, big and small, established a record in canning, packing and forwarding vegetables and fruits equalled only by their shipments to the troops of dressings, knitted goods, bed and wearing apparel, and comforts.

Housewives baked their own bread; bundled their newspapers for salvage; and saved fat for the manufacture of explosives.

The war gave the world Rosie the Riveter. Thousands of women of all ages, many of whom had never before entered a factory, joined the ranks of the lunch pail worker who begins his shift by punching a time clock.

In the green twilight of a late March evening of 1916 the first overseas draft of Depot C.M.R.—Hamilton officers Lts. Stewart C. Chambers, Walter (Spike) Howell and Erroll Boyd — marched from Scott Park to the Stuart Street station, spurs jingling on Hamilton streets that some trod for the last time. At the station Acting-Mayor Booker (Mayor Chester S. Walters being on active service leave) and a great throng waited to see them off for Halifax and H. M. Transport No. 4103, the former White Star *Olympic*.

Mayor Booker was becoming proficient in farewell addresses. Hamilton's 91st Highlanders had already sent two contingents overseas, the first under Major H. L. Roberts and Capt. (later Lt.-Col.) Frank

Morison, the second commanded by Lt.-Col. John I. McLaren and Major (later Col.) W. R. Turnbull who led the unit at Ypres and in the terrible Somme fighting.

The 91st belonged to the new century, formed following agitation by local Scottish societies — Sons of Scotland, St. Andrew's and the Hamilton Gaelic — for a Scottish regiment, and formally gazetted on September 16th, 1903, on a four-company basis. Prime movers in the project were Col. J. R. Moodie; James Chisholm, barrister, first paymaster; and Lt.-Col. (Hon. Justice) William Alexander Logie, first C.O.

On May 24th, 1904, Hamilton witnessed the first march-out of the regiment in full Highland costume—feather bonnets, scarlet doublets, and green kilts and sporrans swinging to the drums and the bagpipes. Presented by Municipal chapter, I.O.D.E., the 91st received its colours from Lord Aylmer. In June, 1905, now eight companies strong, the 91st was allied with the Argylls of Stirling to become later the Argyll and Sutherland Highlanders. Under Bandmaster (later Capt.) Harry Stares the Sons of England band became recruits. On March 13th, 1907, Major W. H. Bruce took command *vice* Lt.-Col. W. A. Logie, assuming command as lieutenant-colonel in 1914.

Of the many officers of the regiment who gave outstanding service overseas in various units, only a representation may be named: Col. Harry Hatch who commanded the Argyll and Sutherlands after the war, and later the 4th Brigade; Capt. (later Col.) Lionel H. Millen, C.O. of the 19th at war's end who returned the battalion to Canada; Major David McKeand, of Tiger football fame, winner of the M.C. while with the 58th in France; Lt. R. R. Moodie, popular C.O. of the 205th (Tiger) Battalion; and Honorary Capt. Ferdinand (Fred) Hamilton, regimental quartermaster, grandson of Peter Hunter Hamilton, who had recently cooperated in a notable hoax played on the city.

During preparations for the 1913 Centennial Mr. Hamilton had been visited by Fred Cloke of Cloke and Sons, booksellers and stationers, who was looking for a picture of Mr. Hamilton's grand-uncle, George Hamilton, founder of the city.

Fred Hamilton regretted there was none in existence.

"We're publishing a Centennial history of the city," explained Mr. Cloke. "We need one as a frontispiece. You wouldn't have another photograph," he suggested, "that we could use?"

Fred Hamilton produced the family album.

When later the Centennial volume appeared,[4] it carried the now well-known picture of a silk hatted, bearded, handsome man holding a cane, which for fifty years has represented the late George Hamilton. In reality the picture was a likeness of the founder's nephew George, son of Peter Hunter Hamilton.

"The story was too good to keep," said Frank Moore who knew Fred Hamilton well. "He thought it was a great joke. As proof he showed me the original picture from which the print was taken. It was a daguerreotype *carte de visite* size. Photography under Daguerre," explained Mr. Moore, "dates from 1839 and George Hamilton died in 1836."

Throughout the final two years of the war headlines were little comfort to the allies: OPENING OF GREAT GERMAN OFFENSIVE FROM ARRAS TO LA FERE, BRITISH RETIRE ON WIDE FRONT . . . GERMAN SUBS SINK 19 SHIPS OFF U.S. COAST . . . AIR RAID ON DUNKIRK, LONDON AND THE EAST COAST OF ENGLAND, PARIS BOMBED.

Beneath this cloud, life went on its way. In keeping with earlier policy the city continued to extend favourable settlement terms to industry, offering even more attractive long term reductions in tax rates, coupled to low plant and property assessment. To these concessions were added the advantages of electric power, first delivered to the city in 1897 from De Cew falls by the Hamilton Electric Light and Power Company; and improved rail and water communication.

During 1910 and 1911 the T. H. and B. railway had built the Hamilton industrial belt line which looped through the north end of the city, throwing off spurs to various plants. Highly popular, this became one of the railway's best sources of revenue.

Prior to the war also, the port of Hamilton embarked on a continuous program of expansion and development under the Hamilton Harbour Commission, inaugurated by the federal government in 1912.[5] Revetment walls were constructed and land reclamation undertaken. In the 1920's new docks and a second warehouse extended port facilities.

In response to the above inducements, projected glowingly by the chamber of commerce, the city gained the Otis Elevator Company; the Grasselli Chemical Company of Cleveland, forerunner of Canadian Industries Limited (CIL); the Frost Wire Fence Company Limited, general manager, Harry L. Frost, which in 1937 would be absorbed by Stelco; and the Canadian Drawn Steel Company Limited, which pioneered for Canada production of cold finished steel bars.

To meet growing demands of Canadian railways for rolling stock, the National Steel Car Corporation erected a plant and in December, 1912, produced its first freight car. In 1919 the company was reorganized and Robert J. Magor elected president, succeeding Sir John M. Gibson. In 1942 R. S. Hart assumed the presidency.

Lastly, the Hamilton Bridge Works Company Limited, founded in 1863, in the railway era, to construct bridges, now under direction of J. S. Hendrie, president, R. M. Roy and W. B. Champ, underwent expansion to permit the manufacture of components necessary to Canada's war-vital shipbuilding program.

In a different field the Chipman, Holton Company Limited, founder, W. A. Holton, became in 1902 the city's first hosiery manufacturer, knitting plain cotton stockings for women in brown and black, an introduction to the later diverse range of colours and patterns, in cotton, wool, rayon, nylon and other synthetics.

When one adds to Chipman, Holton the city's earlier established yarn sales and textile mills and the later T. Eaton Knitting Mill, dating from 1916, the Mohawk Mills of 1932 — president, Harold G. Smith, O.B.E. — which produced Botany yarns for the trade, and the National Hosiery Mills, former makers of Phantom hose, Hamilton's title of Ontario textile capital, held for several decades, becomes understandable.

Of necessity, the upswing in industry created activity in real estate. New plants meant increased employment which in turn spelled more homes, and since the new factories lay far to the north and east, an opening of new surveys.

"In 1906," said the late Thomas Crompton, real estate broker, "there was nothing east of Wentworth Street but open fields. When F. B. Robins and I started the Crown Point subdivision, centred on today's Ottawa Street, people thought we were crazy. Crown Point lay a mile and a half east of the city, there were no conveniences, no roads worthy of the name, for sidewalks only of a few hundred feet of planks that washed away in the rainy season, and the land was clay, greasy and sticky as paint. We always kept rubber wading boots for prospects to wear in spring and rainy weather."

Although a lot carried only a down payment of five dollars, and price of a good lot and frame house on Ottawa Street was $750, very few prospects bought. Some who did buy lots paid only one dollar down. Then working after the day's shift, they would build a small eight by ten shack, tar-papered.

"We had a cheap frame store," said Mr. Crompton, "built on Ottawa Street to serve the area. The only water was a spring-fed horse trough at the corner of Barton and Ottawa Streets. People came with pails from half a mile."

For boys Crown Point was a paradise. Along the bay shore, Gage's Inlet lay just north of the Jockey Club, Harvey's at the end of Harvey's farm lane leading now into the Steel Company. Inlets seemed specially made for boys, their reedy waterways a magic door to nature's secrets. In the inlets boys caught fish and frogs and gathered watercress, in adjacent woods they harvested walnut and hickory nuts, and at Schumacher's German boarding house on the northeast corner of Sherman Avenue and Burlington Street they could exchange these commodities for rare, prized cash.

When shrewd J. Walter Gage, dean of Hamilton real estate promoters, bought land a mile and a quarter further east, at present Tragina Avenue, and laid out Rockwood subdivision, Crown Point's battle was won. In 1910, in one month 310 lots sold. When William Carroll, founder of the famous chain of grocery stores, bought the southeast corner of Ottawa and Barton for $1,750 cash, and erected his seventh store, the cornerstone of the Ottawa Street shopping district was laid.

War slowed the real estate boom, general throughout the city, to a steady unspectacular growth. Not until 1919 would local realty enjoy another land office year.

In the meantime, on September 18th, 1915, the Royal Hamilton Yacht

Club, then under Commodore Samuel Vila, was totally destroyed by fire . . . Dr. James Roberts, M.H.O., who replaced Dr. Walter F. Langrill in 1905 when the latter became medical superintendent of the City Hospital, was granted indefinite leave of absence for overseas service. Strangely both physicians would hold their posts until 1940 when Dr. Langrill would retire and Dr. Roberts would die in office . . . In 1911 at a five-day air meet held on Beach Road at O'Heir's Field the ultimate thrill for 1,500 entranced spectators was J. A. D. McCurdy's sensational flight to Toronto in 32 minutes, travelling "the tremendous distance of 45 miles without touching the ground and in part over Lake Ontario, and attaining the frightful speed of 60 miles an hour." McCurdy also ascended to the record height of 3,000 feet and came down blue with cold which is understandable, early planes having instead of a cockpit a bicycle seat slung into the framework. In 1915 Proctor and Gamble Company, Limited, announced erection of a million-dollar plant in Hamilton.

In 1915, at a meeting of watchmakers and jewellers in Hamilton, daylight saving was endorsed by George H. Lees and Norman Ellis. A daylight saving bill introduced into the House of Commons was defeated but the first gun in a long campaign had been fired.

More successful was Sir William Hearst, lifelong temperance advocate, whose Conservative government passed the Ontario Temperance Act barring the legal sale of beer and liquor in licensed hotels, thereby channelling sale of alcohol into the hands of bootleggers and speakeasies. In Hamilton it introduced the flamboyant era of Rocco Perri, self styled "King of the Bootleggers," and Bessie Perri, his common-law wife.

The war was entering its most crucial stage. On August 29th, 1917, the Military Service Act of the Robert Borden government enforced conscription. In Hamilton between 10,000 and 11,000 men in all enlisted with the C.E.F. With the fighting units went hospital and ambulance corps. In the 1890's Col. G. S. Rennie, C.M.G., had organized the 12th and 19th Field Ambulance Corps of the Army Medical Corps, serving as C.O. of both, with the 19th later taken over by Major R. Y. Parry. When Colonel Rennie transferred to the artillery, Col. G. D. Farmer took command of the 12th, Lt.-Col. J. Edgar Davey of the 19th, both seeing overseas service.

Lt.-Col. R. H. Labatt, Brig.-Major H. L. Roberts, Col. Armand Smith, Col. Thomas Morrison, brother of future Mayor William Morrison, Brig-Gen. Sir Edward Morrison, C.M.G., K.C.B., D.S.O., the former Eddie Morrison, cub reporter of *The Hamilton Spectator*, and Capt. Harold A. Cooch, future president of the Canadian Westinghouse Company—it is impossible to mention more than a fraction of the local officers who fought in World War I, or even to begin to mention the equally gallant enlisted men.

Of those who did not return only a few must represent the many: Major Gordon H. Southam, son of William Southam, Lt. William V. Carey, Lt. Harry Adie, Lt. Warren Biggar, son of ex-mayor S. D. Biggar, and Lt. Cameron D. Brant, great-grandson of Chief Joseph Brant.

At home the city suffered losses, too: Prof. James Johnson, leader of the Scottish Rite Cathedral choir, for forty years the well-loved music master of city schools; Police Chief Alexander Smith under whom the force reached a high standard of discipline and morale; and "Kit" — Kathleen Blake Coleman, wife of Dr. Theobald Coleman and mother of Mrs. John Gartshore—premier newspaperwoman of the day, for twenty-one years woman's editor of the Toronto *Mail* and special correspondent abroad for outstanding events, including the Spanish-American War in Cuba. Kit was the first president of the Canadian Women's Press Club, founded in 1905, with a Hamilton branch established in 1927, largely by Bessie Gowan Ferguson.

On November 10th, 1918, Kaiser Wilhelm II crossed the Dutch border into exile. On November 11th the last shots of the war were fired at Mons. From Hamilton 2,000 soldiers had died.

ARMISTICE SIGNED . . . GERMANY HAS SURRENDERED . . . KAISER ABDICATES

When the news of peace reached the city just before 3 a.m., factory whistles and bells pealed the glad tidings. Long before daylight great crowds moved to the heart of the city where Mayor Booker proclaimed a holiday — a superfluous formality. Floats used in the previous Saturday's Victory Loan parade turned out again in a mile-long procession swelled with decorated cars.

On the Gore, Bandmaster Harry Stares' band played the national anthem, "O God, Our Help in Ages Past," and "Rule Britannia," and the people sang. Later at the Court house Bruce A. Carey led massed choirs in a thanksgiving service. At noon a human fly climbed the Bank of Hamilton building, and in court Magistrate George F. Jelfs, successor to Magistrate Cahill, released twenty-two prisoners without sentence. Doctors gave "prescriptions" to all who applied so that everyone might celebrate fittingly in spite of William Hearst.

Only the poets did not celebrate. Before he died in action Canadian Lt.-Col. John McCrae wrote:

"We are the Dead. Short days ago
We lived, felt dawn, saw sunset glow,
Loved and were loved, and now we lie
In Flanders fields."

And Siegfried Sassoon: "How many dead? As many as you wish, Don't count 'em; they're too many. Who'll buy my fresh corpses, two for a penny?"

And from a Hamilton poet, Quartermaster Sergeant Norman Stapley, a prayer: "When war's last thunder dies and we who made the thunder, cleanse our hands."

A prayer unanswered, since the opportunity would never come to Q.M.S. Stapley to cleanse his hands of a war that carried him with it into the great beyond, where who knows how long its thunders will roll.

21

Radial Age

Postwar Hamilton possessed a flavour distinct to itself. The social scene had changed and with it the early emphasis on birth and breeding, with wealth a welcome but lesser asset than family. Ownership of land no longer carried its former prestige. Where the family founder had set his impressive domicile on a square block of land, his son or grandson reserved a modest property and divided the remainder of the block into profitable town lots. Now with the postwar era a new industrial element, largely American, began to infiltrate Hamilton's social scene, the first lazy ripple of the North American twentieth century "big company" cult.

In other ways too industry was making an impact. Absorption in 1882 by the Grand Trunk railway of the Great Western, and the subsequent removal of the general offices to Montreal, repair shops to Woodstock, and terminals to Toronto, shattered Hamilton's ambitious dream of becoming the rail and financial centre of Ontario. The McInnes fire is said to have started the exodus of Hamilton's wholesale mercantile houses. In the 1890's financial head offices one by one moved from the city.

On the other hand, industry during this period was taking root and expanding, with labour increasing its influence in all areas. "Lunch pail town" and "strike city" have been two sobriquets as commonly applied to Hamilton as "the ambitious city." Not until after World War II, with the growing influence of McMaster University and the outcry of new citizens against the cultural sterility of the community, would Hamilton show interest in changing this image of itself.

From a fragmentary beginning in the 1850's and development of craft unions in the 1880's, growth of the labour movement in the city progressed slowly but steadily until World War II, when organization of the city's steel mills in the 1940's sent it surging ahead. In 1906, Hamilton's first major strike, and one of its most dramatic, involved the Hamilton Street Railway, when 180 employees walked out to enforce demands for an increase in pay rate, then eighteen cents an hour,[1] and union recognition.

"When officials of the line," says an account, "brought in strike breakers, the strikers stoned and rotten-egged the cars, and when their aim was not too good, the buildings along the route. Shots were fired."

Finally Mayor S. D. Biggar called for troops. On the evening of November 24th, before a wild mob of ten thousand, the Riot Act was read from city hall steps by Wentworth County Sheriff J. T. Middleton, attended by the mayor and Police Chief Smith. In the ensuing forcible clearing of the streets, police charged with batons, troops with bayonets. Two hundred persons were injured, one rioter was jailed for two years, several were committed for trial. Later the Ontario Railway Board decreed that wages remain the same but the company recognize the union.

By the time of the strike, the H.S.R. had undergone two important changes: electrification and change of ownership. "In 1892," says W. J. McCulloch, personnel manager of the street railway, "a power house was built on the bay front on Guise Street where bay water could be converted into steam for power. With electrification the first iron rails were replaced by steel. Service began in July."

New trucks were brought in on the Grand Trunk railway to the Ferguson Avenue station, lifted onto the street railway tracks at Ferguson and King and towed to the Stuart Street barns. Here they were outfitted with horse-car bodies with added vestibules and scoop fenders, and completed with motors, electrical appliances and wiring. The first car on a test run was pulled by four horses. As it moved up James Street crowds gathered to watch and shouting small boys raced this ultramodern product of the new electrical age. The timid refused to use the cars.

In 1913 the H.S.R. constructed a double-track extension on Burlington Street from James Street to Kenilworth Avenue, south to Main then west to meet the existing line at Sherman Avenue. "This was the initial belt line," said Mr. McCulloch, "followed by the belt line along Barton Street."

The change of ownership of the H.S.R. in 1900 resulted from the organization of the Cataract Power Company of Hamilton Limited, chartered on July 9th, 1896, to develop electric power at De Cew Falls, near St. Catharines, Ontario, and transmit it thirty-four miles to Hamilton. The long distance transmission of power was the dream of Irish-born John Patterson and his fellow company directors: Sir John M. Gibson, John R. Moodie, John Dickenson and John W. Sutherland. Opposing their theory was the accepted belief that power could not be transmitted by wire farther than twelve miles.

Over the years the De Cew Falls generating station, famous as the "cradle of hydro-electric power in Ontario," has stood as a monument to the "five Johns." One of the earliest high-head hydraulic developments in Canada, the station began operation in 1898. Built to serve Hamilton, it supplied power to communities along the Welland canal and the escarpment, to Brantford and Oakville.

At the turn of the century, the Cataract Company's system of power was based on purchasing electric motors and leasing them to manufacturers who paid for the power used. In the 1890's steam was the motive force in all plants and factories in Hamilton. To overcome local opposition to hydro-electric power and prove it would cost less than steam power, the Cataract Company accepted for the first year the average annual amount of the customer's coal bills. Although coal was only six dollars a ton, Cataract proved its point and also made money.

First Hamilton company to change to the new power was the Canadian Coloured Cotton Mills, C. O. Dexter, manager, later under A. E. Adam known as Canadian Cottons Limited. It was followed by the later established Imperial Cotton Company Limited, manager, Spencer Turner, assistant manager, W. S. Burrill.

Electricity did more than illuminate and set the dynamos of industry humming. Power ushered in the colourful era of radial passenger and freight transportation, when electrical lines, raying out from Hamilton, webbed the surrounding countryside, uniting hitherto isolated communities by their large, comfortable, shrill-voiced cars.

In 1896, the Hamilton Electric Radial Company, John Patterson's dream, began operation from Hamilton to Burlington, and later to Oakville, from a terminal at the corner of James and Gore Streets. So popular did the line prove that the Grand Trunk discontinued service to the canal. Oldtimers still recall nostalgically the exuberant parties the radials carried to Dynes' Hotel on the beachstrip to enjoy the famous dinners of the house — fish, turkey, wild fowl and game.

Opened two years earlier, the Hamilton, Grimsby, and Beamsville line and the freight it carried became an important factor in the city's economy. In 1931, prior to the onslaught of highways, industry and settlement, the Niagara peninsula produced 4,055,000 six-quart baskets of peaches alone. In Hamilton the Aylmer and Simcoe Canning Companies and Wagstaffe's Limited, with its jams and jellies, expanded rapidly. Equally benefited was Norton Manufacturing Company, which in 1887 had introduced the first automatic line of machinery in Canada for manufacture of packers' cans, forerunner of today's American Can Company of Canada Limited, familiarly "Canco."

The opening of the Brantford and Hamilton Electric railway on May 21st, 1908, completed local radial construction.

In 1899, the Cataract Power Company changed its name to the Hamilton Electric Light and Cataract Power Company Limited, and the following year took over the Hamilton Street Railway and the Hamilton Radial Electric Railway. In 1903 the company was incorporated as the Hamilton Cataract Power, Light and Traction Company Limited.

In 1907 the Hamilton Terminal Company was organized, and erected the Terminal building on King Street at the southeast corner of Catharine, and in the same year the Dominion Power and Transmission Company Limited was incorporated.[2] Although uncompleted, the Terminal building was opened for business on November 18th. Recognized as one of the most modern and elegant electric railway stations on the continent, the three-storey and basement Terminal belonged to the new era of cement construction and height, being designed by architect Charles Mills to permit later expansion to skyscraper proportions. Of concrete, with steel-reinforced beams and columns and fireproof vitreous brick, the building was supported on underground walls four feet thick, with brick wall sections at the King Street entrance six feet in thickness. Floors of similar reinforced cement and brick construction, set with 22-foot slabs were designed to withstand a heavy carrying load.

In the best Edwardian tradition, interior walls were dadoed ten feet high with Italian marble, and woodwork was of quarter-cut oak. Outside two great Byzantine columns flanked the entrance. In the rear was the radial terminus.

Until the 1920's the radial era flourished, but towards the end of the decade cars were gradually replaced by buses. First of the interurban routes to close was the Dundas line, the track being sold to the T.H. and B. railway as a freight line. On June 30th, 1931, the last car ran on the Brantford-Hamilton system and the radial age ended. Cars went to the junk yard, tracks were torn up and the Terminal was converted into a bus depot and office building.

A year before the demise of the radials the D.P. and T. Company that operated them ceased to exist. Until 1911 the company had had a monopoly on electric power in Hamilton and, as frequently happens in such cases, the city suffered. Council records abound with disputes with the H.S.R. over the latter's refusal to service new parts of the city, to keep the line's right of way in repair, and to maintain company payments as agreed upon.

In the field of street lighting there was widespread dissatisfaction also. Not until ratepayers approved a city by-law authorizing council to contract with the Hydro Electric Power Commission of Ontario, which had followed the Cataract Power Company in power production at Niagara, did the D.P. and T. Company change its policy. It then offered to light Hamilton streets at $47.50 per lamp per year, instead of the prevailing rate of $85 per lamp.

Although Mayor T. J. Stewart was pro-Hydro, so strong was the D.P. and T. in the city, where stock was widely held, that only after a bitter battle and the election in 1911 of his successor, Mayor George H. Lees, and a majority of city representatives on a straight Hydro platform, was a contract reached with the commission. The same year a plant was constructed to distribute electrical energy, beginning operation on January 1st, 1912. In 1914, when the city's contract with the D.P. and T. Company expired, Hydro assumed all power requirements for the community. With a gold key, the recently knighted Sir Adam Beck switched on the power that has illumined Hamilton ever since.

In October, 1915, the Hydro Electric Power Commission of Hamilton was established. Sixteen years later Hamilton Hydro took over the distribution system of the D.P. and T. Company, purchased the preceding year by the H.E.P.C. of Ontario, including all shares of the H.S.R.

Strangely interwoven with and paralleling the history of the D.P. and T. Company, which financed it, was the life story of a popular local playhouse built at the same time as the Terminal building. Facing north, the theatre was reached from King Street by an arcade along the west side of the Terminal. Bennett's was a vaudeville house, but acknowledging the infant moving picture industry, it ended its program with a picture — a Bennettograph.

New competition in entertainment had appeared on the horizon, the nickelodeon, forerunner of today's motion picture palace. Frequently housed in a converted store dressed in secondhand theatre trappings, the nickelodeon offered a silent one-reel melodrama, a short-short comedy and song slides for audience participation. With the show went a pianist and sometimes a crooner, the whole costing the nickel which gave the house its name. So popular was the nickelodeon that even churches began to show discreetly selected pictures, and established theatres lowered their prices. The Royal, King Street West, offered a two-hour show of six reels, for five cents, afternoon and evening; Griffin's, high-class films, the lower floor, 10 cents, with seven rows at twenty cents, balconies, five cents, and Friday, amateur night.

When vaudeville died, Bennett's changed its name to the Temple and turned to stock; briefly became a motion picture house; then reverted again to stock. The theatre was popular with Hamiltonians who approved of its light green and red décor, crimson plush seats and curtains in the brass-railed boxes, and its plaster floral wreaths swung by plump cupids. With troupers it was noted for its excellent quarters.

Oddly, the same modern invention that supplanted the radials ousted the theatre. Leased by Wentworth Motors Limited, the Temple was opened in 1926 as an agency for the sale and repair of Ford cars. During the process of dismantling and rebuilding, an unknown hand inscribed the epitaph of the house on the call-board where actors had clustered to read their bulletins: "Temple Theatre. Born, 1907. Died, 1926."

Eventually cinema and the motor car, which made Toronto available, also eliminated Hamilton's landmarks, the Grand Opera House and the Star. Following World War I, however, the Grand offered Hamiltonians theatrical fare now unobtainable short of Toronto: elaborate musicals such as Chu Chin Chow; opera; Al Jolson and black face minstrels; and Captain Merton Plunkett's Dumbells, fresh from entertaining troops in the front line.

By the 1920's in Hamilton in other fields besides theatre a booming economy had replaced the stabilization of war years. In addition to a backlog of repairs, extensions and additions were required by an again expanding population. From 107,826 at the end of the war, Hamilton's population rose to 154,701 in 1932, at which figure it remained static for nearly a decade. Contributing to this surge were annexations which increased city area by over twenty-six per cent, from 7,130 acres to 9,694, those of 1928 and 1929 — in part extending city limits south to Fennell on the mountain — offsetting the initial effects of the crash of 1929 and the severe depression which followed.

Of necessity expenditures, current and capital, rose sharply. In 1919 the current outlay per capita was $33.99; in 1924, $51. From 27 mills in 1918, the tax rate climbed steadily to 35 mills in 1920. Faced with growing postwar unemployment, need of greater revenue, and an understandable reluctance to increase the tax rate further, council compromised by raising assessments under a new and more scientific method of equalizing property values. By this means the tax rate was reduced one and a half mills while the per capita tax rose by $5.64, netting the city in revenue some $787,000 above the preceding year. In 1922 the tax rate was again 35 mills, then levelled at 33 for years.

With like rapidity capital expenditure increased, the total net debenture debt advancing from less than 10½ million dollars in 1919 to over 17 million in 1924, an increase per person from $94.74 to $141.20. With the exception of the disastrous railway boom years of the 1860's,[3] never had civic expenditures and debt climbed so alarmingly as in the period of 1919-1924.

Works department costs, board of education and separate school board, parks board and annexation were main consumers of the tax dollar. In annexed areas requiring servicing, some 869 acres lay west of Paradise Road between Main Street and the Dundas marsh, the present Westdale, annexed in 1914. To increase property values in this area the age-old line of King Street was diverted from its course through Beasley's Hollow, to wind through the later Westdale shopping area and rejoin Highway 8 to the west.[4]

To meet the heavy increase in city water consumption City Engineer E. G. Barrow, who had succeeded William Haskins in 1896, installed a new force main running from the Beach pumping station along Barton Street to James Street, with supplementing branch mains. To Mr. Barrow's administration also belongs the James Street reservoir, built 243 feet above lake level, with a capacity of 2,500,000 gallons. Following its construction, the Barton reservoir was cut off and reserved for emergencies. With its grassy hilltop crater of clear, still water reflecting the surrounding circle of whispering pines, its pine-needled path and its violets purpling the meadow below, the Barton reservoir was a favourite walk of early east-end Hamiltonians. To the west on the mountainside stood the large, gabled red brick residence of the superintendent of the waterworks department, with immaculately kept grounds and flower beds.

In 1910 the Gartshore pumps, now half a century old, were supplemented by electrically driven pumps installed in new buildings. In 1919 an additional electric pump and a steam turbine pump were added. When these were followed ten years later by three new electric pumps and a diesel engine generator set to furnish standby power, the old steam pumps were retired.

Similarly the air lift, constructed about 1910 at the foot of the mountain at Wentworth Street to provide water for mountaintop settlement, was later abandoned when the Ferguson Avenue repumping station was replaced with a new building, new electric pumps were installed, and an 80,000-gallon storage tank, with connecting main, was erected near the top of the Jolley Cut.

By the 1930's the waterworks system for the lower city was largely established. As early as 1889 the lowering of the lake level, today a major problem, had necessitated supplementing the filtering basins with an intake pipe. In 1901 the basins were doubled in size and a second larger pipe laid into the lake. By 1927 two steel intake pipes of sufficient capacity, length and depth to avoid winter ice blockage and surface pollution had been constructed. When these were directly connected by conduits to a screen house and suction well, the outmoded filtering basin was permanently abandoned. By laying additional mains the city was then divided into three pumping areas, low, middle and high level, and the distribution system extended into the newly annexed east end of the mountain.

During these developments citizen discontent with the works department, then functioning under Andrew F. Macallum, 1909-16, led to a public enquiry conducted by Judge C. G. Snider which resulted in the dismissal of several members of the department.

A decade later, in 1924, trouble flared again when an assistant cashier in the city treasurer's department absconded with some $50,000 of civic funds. In the long ensuing investigation by Judge John Gordon Gauld widespread laxness and dishonesty were found in the departments of city treasurer, tax collector, city accountant and city auditors. Judge Gauld credited this in part to political influence exercised in filling municipal positions and to underpayment of clerks holding responsible offices.[5] Certain officials were dismissed, other employees prosecuted. Only the absconding cashier was never returned to justice — again, it was rumoured, because of influence.

Unfortunate as these affairs were, the resultant upheavals helped lay the foundation of modern city administration, the council undertaking a complete reorganization of the treasury and accounting departments and renovation of the tax department.

The term of City Engineer W. L. McFaul, who succeeded E. R. Gray, 1916-23, and who would hold office until 1959, included the depression. "In depression days," said the short, now comfortably rotund but still peppery ex-city engineer, "relief labour was used. The works department employed approximately fifteen per cent of the relief labour in the city. Rates ranged from 49½ to 55 cents an hour but when they reached 55 the board cut them back to 50. Each man got 24 hours of work—3 days— every 3 weeks.

"In 1931," he said, "we built a new reservoir at the south end of Mountain Avenue. Fourteen million gallons. It's still in use. To protect it we covered it over and built a park above it."

With the new reservoir in use the James Street reservoir was abandoned and in the teeter-totter of the years the old Barton reservoir was returned to the system.

"Our next move," said the white-haired engineer, "was a water purification plant, opened on March 17th, 1933. It was a prestige item. Also it was the beginning of the modern waterworks system. Our next big move was servicing the mountain area and the west end beyond Mc-Kittrick bridge.

"In my term of office we supplied Westdale with sewers, water mains and roads; had two bridges built over the Grand Trunk in 1922 and '23 and the High Level bridge in '32; built the circle around York Street and Longwood Road to bypass the bridge over the canal; and opened Longwood through to Main Street and then south, past the Canadian Westinghouse plant which was only a foundry and lamp division until World War II. Then came the Valley Street Road."[6]

The water purification plant succeeded by six years chlorination of city water. "For two weeks," said Mr. McFaul, chain-smoking with unbelievable rapidity, "we chlorinated and said nothing. Then we announced it and immediately the telephones began ringing!"

Chlorination was in step with medical health practices and services which began with the new century. In 1907 Hamilton was the second city in Canada to establish medical inspection of public schools, Dr. James Roberts being engaged as inspector. A year later the first school nurse, Emma J. Deyman, was appointed. In 1910 pathologist Dr. W. H. Tytler equipped and organized the first city laboratory in City Hospital, to serve jointly the public health department and the 300-bed institution. Doctor Tytler was followed by Drs. E. Fidlar and F. B. Bowman, and in 1914 by Dr. William J. Deadman, who would hold the post, with leave for war service, until April, 1956. In addition to hospital laboratory examinations, city water was examined bacteriologically twice a day, and all milk sold in the city was tested for the health department.

In 1908 the appalling death rate from *cholera infantum* among infants in City Hospital had led Dr. Roberts to ask city council for a grant to bottle clean milk for bottle-fed babies. When council refused, funds were guaranteed by the Victorian Order of Nurses for Canada through its Hamilton branch,[7] organized in 1899 under auspices of the Local Council of Women to provide professional home nursing at graduated fees.

By using milk from a tuberculin-tested herd and sterilizing utensils and bottles (but not the milk itself) the death rate from *cholera infantum* in 1909 was reduced thirty per cent, a figure justifying continuation of the procedure. In 1911 this was taken over by the Babies' Dispensary Guild, organized for this purpose. Until Guild headquarters were established at

12 Euclid Avenue, daily clinics were held at the outdoor department of City Hospital.

Endorsed by such leading citizens as Archdeacon Forneret, Rev. W. H. Sedgwick, George Hope, H. H. Champ, and Dr. J. Heurner Mullin, the B.D.G. became one of the city's principal charitable institutions,[8] its aim to promote the health of children of the poor under three years of age, with older children referred to the family physician. Long lists of subscribers appeared in the daily press. First Guild president was Gordon J. Henderson, with R. R. Moodie, secretary, and H. W. Wilcox, treasurer, assisted by Drs. D. G. Storms, J. P. Morton, James T. Rogers and J. R. Parry. An active woman's board also operated. First devoted nurse supervisor, who died in office in 1915, was Miss Helen N. W. Smith.

Shortly, a cluster of baby buggies proclaimed Guild clinic days. By 1914 four nurses were engaged, with an average 220 to 240 patients a day under care, and the Guild had returned to the hospital for greater space; home visiting was adopted, calls averaging 500 a month; additional city clinics numbered five by 1916; and infant supplies were sold at cost, infant equipment loaned and thousands of bottles of milk a year delivered at half-price, eight cents a quart.

In June, 1924, the Guild moved into its own new building on Victoria Avenue North. In the annual report, Dr. J. Edgar Davey lists a staff of fifteen medical men, fifteen volunteer workers and five nurses. During the year 1,493 children had been cared for and clinics had been established within easy walking distance of any city point.

Meanwhile the city health department was expanding. In 1916 the first home visiting nurse, Miss I. Ramsay, was appointed and dental clinics, advocated for years by the Local Council of Women, were established in the schools. In 1918 three additional public health nurses were added to the staff, their services required that fall for the first of three annual epidemics of influenza, which resulted in thousands of cases and hundreds of deaths in the city from the disease.

In 1919 alone 6,268 reported cases occasioned 332 deaths. When all normal medical and nursing facilities proved inadequate to handle the multitude of sick, civilian volunteers were enrolled to assume routine hospital duties and assist in nursing in the temporary tents and billets, such as Scott Park barracks, set up to supplement hospital accommodation. From this period in some cases, as the Hamilton General Hospital — renamed from City Hospital on June 25th, 1919 — stemmed the permanent women's auxiliaries, without whose devoted labour hospitals would find it difficult to function.

In 1921, the city's first health centre was established in the Hamilton Public Library building on the north side of Main Street West. Miss Annie B. Boyd was appointed first superintendent of nurses with a staff increased to eight the following year. The department's Well Baby clinics were set up, largely in city churches, and the local branch of St. Elizabeth Visiting Nurses' Association formed.

In 1922, Dr. J. Edgar Davey was appointed school medical officer. During the year the city suffered an epidemic of diphtheria, with 747 cases and 32 deaths, and for the first time diphtheria immunization was administered in city schools. Developments of 1924-25 included city mental health clinics under Dr. G. S. Glassco; a sight saving and a lip reading class; two teachers to instruct handicapped children in their homes; and medical inspection extended to secondary schools.

In 1928 these developments were implemented by the compulsory pasteurization of all city milk, and in March, 1932, by the opening of the city's first incinerator, located on property later acquired by the Steel Company of Canada.

By 1934 duplication of services led to amalgamation of the B.D.G. with the department of health and school medical services, the Guild ceasing to function individually. In this same year Dr. Davey became assistant M.H.O. and director of school medical services, succeeding to the post of M.H.O. in 1940, following the death of Dr. Roberts. A year later Dr. L. A. Clarke was appointed assistant M.H.O.

The schools for which these services were instituted had multiplied in the new century. In 1900 the city was made up of six school districts, each under a headmaster, with twenty public schools, including the Boys' Home School and the Girls' Home School, 170 teachers and a yearly attendance of nearly 9,000 pupils. In addition the city possessed the new Collegiate Institute and Ontario Normal College, and the private Hamilton Business College, established in 1882 by R. Eugene Clemens. There were seven Roman Catholic schools with an attendance of 2,000, including the six-room Holy Angels' School, converted from the palace of Bishop T. J. Dowling, D.D., the adjacent eight-room St. Mary's, with two classrooms assigned to continuation classes, and Loretto Convent, with private tuition for resident and day pupils under direction of the Ladies of Loretto. In 1885 the Ladies first taught under the separate school board.

By 1900 kindergarten classes had been established in each school district. In 1896 the teaching of sewing was begun, following several years of pressure by the Local Council of Women, led by Mrs. John Hoodless, for introduction of household science and manual training in city schools. The following year, when the Trades and Labour Council supported the demand, the board of education approved a grant to enable a number of public school students to attend a domestic science class in the Young Women's Christian Association building, opened in May, 1889, in the former residence of Dr. Edwin Henwood, 7 Main Street West,[9] as a residence for women workers. In 1901 the domestic science class numbered 75 students, at 75 cents apiece, and in 1903 some 300 with $1,000 paid by the board, a triumph for the earnestness of purpose and ingenuity of the Y.W.C.A. ladies who not only established the Y.W.C.A. but also conducted the domestic science course.

So excellent was the course that in 1900 it became the Normal School of Domestic Arts, fully supported by the province, a training school for teachers as well as students. Following establishment in 1902 of the household economic course at McDonald Institute, Ontario Agricultural College, Guelph, the Normal School was moved there. By that time domestic science was being taught in the Collegiate Institute, with two centres established in the public schools in 1904, and others later added. Not until 1908 was manual training started, with A. E. Wilcox and A. J. Painter as instructors.

In part, this delay had resulted from the closing of the Teachers' Normal College at Central Collegiate in 1907 and opening of the Normal School on Strathcona Avenue the following year. Realizing the growing importance, especially in an industrial city such as Hamilton, of technical training adapted to requirements of pupils who intended entering the trades or industry, and with the hope that such a course might decrease the alarming number of drop-outs at the age of fourteen, the board of education replaced the Normal College with the Hamilton Technical School.

Standing immediately south of the Collegiate and connected with it, the new brick and brownstone building faced on Stinson Street. In addition to technical training and domestic science departments, it also housed the Hamilton Art School — principal, Samuel John Ireland, 1888-1903 — now operated by the board, the city having discontinued its former $3,000 annual grant. Principal of the Technical School, which opened in September, 1909, was J. G. Witton, B.A., B.Sc.; instructor in household science, Miss I. W. Strong; with D. P. Brown, drawing instructor.

Later the well known Hamilton artist, orator and pungent personality, John S. Gordon, A.R.C.A., headed the Art School. Upon retirement in 1934 he was succeeded by his wife, the former Hortense C. Mattice who had taught in the school since 1916. As an artist, the late Mrs. Gordon, A.R.C.A., was noted for her championship of modern art trends, her encouragement of young artists, her ability as a critic, and her tremendous zest for life. Associated also with the school as teacher before she became art director, for twenty years, of Westdale Secondary School was the well-loved Ida G. Hamilton.

At first slow in accepting the concept of technical training, within ten years of its opening Hamilton had outgrown the Technical School. In 1919 a new Hamilton Technical, strongly endorsed by the Board of Trade, Trades and Labour Council, and Manufacturers' Association, was opened on Wentworth Street North. Renamed the F. R. Close Technical Institute in honour of Mr. Close, a longtime school trustee, the highly modern technical institute, with a second unit completed in 1922, cost more than one million dollars.

By 1920, city primary schools had increased to twenty-five, with an average attendance of 14,316, and separate schools to twelve with 5,000 attending. Actually these figures are misleading as two schools were destroyed by fire during this period and one sold for demolition. There was also a heavy building program of additions to existing schools.

Studying the list of new schools, two facts are evident: the eastward push of the city, all but the Earl Kitchener School on Dundurn Street being in the east end; and the war influence evidenced in their patriotic naming, Queen Mary, Lloyd George and Memorial. In the following decade the city honoured members in the field of education — Dr. W. H. Ballard, public school inspector, George R. Allan, George L. Armstrong and A. M. Cunningham, school trustees.

Schools of this later period show a significant development. While five appear in the east end, four others, all annexed, are located on the Mountain, three are west in the city, and one north. Growth throughout the city therefore is becoming general. On the Mountain the southward movement has passed Queensdale Avenue and reached Fennell.

During the 1920-30's three outstanding educational events occurred in the city: establishment in 1923 by the provincial department of education of the Ontario Teachers' Training College for technical teachers, adjacent to the Hamilton Technical Institute; and the building of Delta Collegiate on Main Street East in 1924 and Westdale Secondary School (later Westdale Tripartite) in 1930, the former required when passage of the Adolescent School Attendance Act in 1919, raising the compulsory school age from 14 to 16 years, increased city secondary school enrolment from 1,226 in 1918 to 3,668 by 1924.

Offering collegiate, technical and commercial departments, Westdale Tripartite was one of Canada's largest and best equipped schools of the day. Exclusive of equipment it cost $1,524,130 with $40,000 added for site. Gone was the day when a school such as the Queen Victoria, a three-storey-and-basement showpiece of patterned red and white brick, complete with cupola and bell tower, might be built for $34,637, upon a site in central Hamilton costing $6,400.[10]

When in 1930 the Central High School of Commerce was erected on Sanford Avenue and all senior and junior commercial classes moved to it, Wentworth Street North was definitely established as the technical and commercial educational centre of the city.

Meanwhile the separate school system was expanding and establishing its own educational centre. Two-room St. Ann's on Sherman Avenue, taught by the Sisters of St. Joseph, was replaced in 1914 by eight-room St. Ann's, quadrupled but still slight neophyte of the thirty-four room St. Ann's of 1961 with its thirty-three teachers and 1,265 pupils. A new St. Patrick's on East Avenue was followed by St. Mary's Lyceum, equipped with a spacious lyceum, an art-modelling room, and the first separate school domestic science centre in Ontario offering a course regulated by the department of education.

By 1920 lay women teachers and the Sisters of Notre Dame had joined the staff. Introduction of the Christian Brothers of Toronto however was unsuccessful and was discontinued. At this time St. Vincent's School was equipped for commercial classes, and in 1928 the present handsome stone Cathedral Boys' High School was erected at the corner of Main and Emerald Streets. The school functions under a private board of governors, the Separate School Act allowing only junior high (grades nine and ten) to operate under the separate school system. In 1955 Cathedral Girls' High School was built on the north side of Main Street, slightly to the east, thus forming with St. Patrick's School to the west an active separate school education centre.

Over the years the separate school board increased from three to sixteen members. Dean of trustees was J. J. O'Connor, 1913-1964, with fifty-one years of service.

In 1930 an outstanding event occurred in the Hamilton educational field with the transfer from Toronto to Hamilton of McMaster University. From a restricted site, 250 feet square, on the campus of the University of Toronto, McMaster moved to a large beautifully situated property, since extended from 103 to 230 acres, in west Hamilton, bordered by tracts of parkland of the Royal Botanical Gardens.[13] The Gardens had originated in the 1920's as the brainchild of the board of park management under leadership of the Hon. T. B. McQueston and of C. V. Langs, Q.C. — chairman of the board for 26 years.

With a dream of establishing a vast park system and also of creating a botanical gardens at the western tip of Lake Ontario, a location peculiarly suited to it, the parks board, spark-plugged by Mr. McQuesten, had over the years acquired lands, parcel by parcel, by purchase, by gift, and sometimes by arrears of taxes. From these lands they now made a site available at an inviting figure to the university. Furthermore, the parks board assisted in landscaping McMaster grounds, developing with relief labour the beautiful sunken garden at the entrance to the university from Main Street.

With its transfer to Hamilton, sufficient resources to establish the university in its new setting and provide for its maintenance and expansion were forthcoming from graduates, members of Baptist churches, and Hamilton citizens.

"The first ten years of McMaster's life," said the late Chancellor George Peel Gilmour, "[was] spent in the cultivation of mutual friendship. . . . It takes time for roots to grip new soil, and for mutual confidence and respect to develop. It speaks well for both university and city that a small university college (for that is what McMaster essentially was before 1930) should have moved and gained new friends and new strength so quickly. The new partnership," he added, "has been a gain too for Hamilton because an industrial city needs cultural life encouraged within it, and to have its interests varied. There is no more natural leadership in such a matter than a university."

The Second World War interrupted McMaster's growth and in the postwar period absorbed its energies in the education of veterans. In 1948 non-denominational Hamilton College was established and affiliated with McMaster, assuming science departments and research. In 1957 the university determined to become a non-denominational private institution,

221

surrendering the right of self-government under religious auspices but opening the door to government aid. At this time University and Hamilton Colleges were united. To continue the university's historic Baptist connection, McMaster Divinity College, devoted to theology, was now incorporated and affiliated.

The reorganization opened exciting vistas. In a five-year construction program the university added an engineering building, Canada's first on-campus nuclear reactor, a student centre, divinity college, science building, first half of a library, and extended the physical science building. Equally important was the expansion of graduate studies and research, especially in the nuclear field, and the rocketing growth of the university extension department. In 1947 Mrs. J. Edgar Bates was appointed Dean of Women.

In 1948 chemistry Professor Henry George Thode introduced the late Dr. Charles H. Jaimet to the untapped potential of nuclear medicine. From study of radio-isotopes would come improved methods of diagnosis and treatment of cancer and heart disease using nuclear tools. For work in this field, in close collaboration with St. Joseph's Hospital, Dr. Jaimet became the first physician in Canada certified by the Atomic Energy of Canada sub-committee to administer radioactive materials to patients.

22

Works Department, Health, and Schools

In the first half of the twentieth century the numeral nine seemed to possess unusual local significance.

In 1909 municipal government underwent an important change with the board of control coming into existence. For the past seven years the city, since 1875 divided into seven numbered wards each electing three aldermen,[1] had been administered by a standing committee of seven aldermen responsible for finance, legislation, railway, printing, assessment, and reception. They served without salary. In 1909, determining to centralize the city's administrative authority in a smaller, more competent and more responsible body, council proposed a four-man board of control whose members would each receive $1,200 annually, with consequent obligation to devote more time to city business. The electors approving, in 1910 four controllers by general vote, three aldermen per ward, by wards, and a mayor for a two-year term were elected.

Before the following election city wards had been increased to eight and the number of aldermen per ward reduced to two, giving the city its existing form of government: mayor, board of control of four members, with the mayor as chairman making five, and a council of sixteen aldermen. Standing committees were reduced to five members, and the administration in general streamlined. The next major change was in 1960, when wards, without being increased in number, were realigned to extend from the mountain to the bay, producing a notable upheaval at the polls the following election.

Following the end of the First World War, the year 1919 ushered in the city's second major period of growth. Reversing this, 1929 brought a stock market crash of phenomenal proportions, widespread financial ruin, and a worldwide depression that devoured life savings of thousands.

In Hamilton, industry cut back production, laid off or put workers on part time, and reduced wages. Bread lines grew. Not only did the rising tide of unemployment increase demands on the civic purse but it reduced city income by increasing tax arrears which climbed from $7.32 per capita in 1930 to $19.25 per capita in 1934.[2] By the latter year government relief contributions (two-thirds of the total amount of direct relief spent by the city) reached $1,603,318.

Between 1919 and 1929 the roaring Twenties achieved an aura which evokes the same indulgent nostalgia as the gay Nineties. Even today uptempoed tunes of the Twenties like "Yes, We Have No Bananas," "Don't Bring Lulu," and "Ol' Man River" set hips swinging.

Era of the Bright Young Things, of short skirts, straight lines and bobbed hair, of pennant-waving college youth in coonskin coat, of flapper, flivver and the debutante slouch, the Twenties was a period of high spirits and high jinks between war and depression, its trademarks jazz, bathtub gin and the Charleston. The romantic era of Greta Garbo and Rudolph Valentino, of Charlie Chaplin, of the cloche hat, the long tapered cigarette holder and perfumed cigarettes, of the emergence of the female leg for the first time in centuries, and to offset this the highly modest covering of the previously well exposed bosom.

The 1920's saw the first movement to the suburbs. Under the newly coined slogan, "Own your own home!" which swept the country, modest adaptations of château, châlet and English country house appeared in outlying prosperous subdivisions. Unlike the suburban ranch house flood of the 1940's and '50's, these homes were individualistic, each differing from its neighbour across the boundary privet hedge. French doors opening on vistas, multiple-pane leaded glass windows, panelled rooms, modified square plan, projecting second storey, half-timbering — each featured its own version of picturesque charm and irregularity.

In Westdale, where streets radiate like the spokes of a wheel from a central shopping hub of stores and business houses, on Oak Knoll Drive, Mayfair Crescent and Mayfair Place bordering on the lovely wooded ravines of the Botanical Gardens, on Whitton Road, Dalewood Crescent and Forsyth Place, such houses date from the 1920's and City Engineer McFaul's laying of sewers and water mains and opening up of streets.

For forty years the subdivision would continue as one of Hamilton's finest residential areas, a circle commercially self-sufficient, fending off depreciating industry and high-rise apartments, priding itself on its cultural conjunction with McMaster University, and deriving realty benefit from the green sweep of the landscaped campus. In turn Westdale formed a fitting backdrop to McMaster.

Throughout university expansion following adoption of its non-denominational standing, this remained the mutually satisfactory *status quo*. In the 1960's, therefore, it would stun Westdale to discover that its erstwhile friendly associate had developed brobdingnagian tendencies and threatened first depreciation then final absorption of its choicest residential area.

That Westdale's early boast of becoming the educational centre of the city should come true beyond its conception, and that this development should adversely affect Westdale itself has an element of irony. Long before the 1960's and the skyrocketing expansion resulting from Mc-

Master's medical school, teaching hospital complex, Westdale had established its claim.

In 1930 Westdale Secondary School had opened under three well known local educationists. Quiet unassuming Benjamin L. Simpson, principal of Delta Collegiate, became principal of Westdale's collegiate section. A star kicking backfielder with the Hamilton Tigers, who had led the team to a Canadian championship in 1908, lanky Ben Simpson was also adept at soccer, baseball, cricket, golf, curling, track and field. At Delta his high school football teams had won for the collegiate both Ontario and Canadian interscholastic championships. Dallas W. Bates, whose predicted brilliant career was cut short by his death in 1946, was in charge of Westdale's technical school. Principal T. W. Oates was appointed to the commerce department.

With the George R. Allan public school opened on King Street West in 1927, a child could now progress from kindergarten through university within a mile radius. In 1949 Dalewood School on Main Street was completed, supplementing with a smaller edition Westdale's large auditorium and stage, used by the city in general for the staging of plays, concerts and other productions.

In addition Westdale possessed in its immediate vicinity the city's only private school for boys, Hillfield, founded in 1901 as Highfield by the late John H. Collinson, M.A., under sponsorship of Sir John S. Hendrie, the Hon. J. M. Gibson and other prominent Hamiltonians.

For over half a century the mountain had looked down on the gray stone Gothic mansion with its gabled walls and numerous chimneys, which John Brown, wholesale general merchant, had erected. Later another merchant, Hon. (Senator) James Turner, senior partner in the firm of F. F. Dalley, had purchased it. During their Hamilton residence, Lord and Lady Aberdeen had occupied the gracious house that stood on present Ravenscliffe Avenue, slightly west of Bay.

Commencing with some 50 boys, Highfield had increased this number by 1918 to 120, with 20 to 30 boarders. It had also established an enviable reputation among private schools in Canada, especially as a preparatory school for entrance to Royal Military College, its cadet corps, affiliated with the R.H.L.I., setting a high standard. During World War I, 265 Highfield old boys served with the allied forces, 37 losing their lives. In 1918 the school was razed by fire, only the exceptionally fine Gothic entrance and the quadrangle of stables and quarters at the rear escaping.

Today only one of these buildings remains. Converted to modern living, this is occupied by Schenectady-born Lester F. Merrick, retired assistant manager of the Canadian Westinghouse Company, who attended Highfield as a boy, and Mrs. Merrick. Daughter of Mrs. W. C. Hawkins, founder in 1931 of the pioneer Birth Control Society of Hamilton, now the Planned Parenthood Association, Mrs. Merrick is an executive member and longtime worker in the organization, whose physician is Dr. Elizabeth Bagshaw.

Reopened as Hillcrest in 1920 by Rev. C. A. Heaven and located in the Dr. James Russell home, northwest corner of Main and Queen Streets, the school, though cramped for space, functioned successfully until 1929. Then on a site on the south side of the Dundas Highway, given by Major Colin W. G. Gibson,[3] Hillfield, an independent country day school for boys, was erected under combined Highfield and Hillcrest governors. Headmaster was Arthur F. Killip, M.A., and vice-principal, Rev. Cecil A. Heaven.

Today Hillfield, which became a college in 1959, with its then head-master, Col. John P. Page, B.A., E.D., as first principal, has entered on a new phase. When expropriation of part of the school property for the Chedoke Expressway forced another move, the board of governors combined forces with Strathallan School for Girls, a private institution founded in 1923 by Miss Janet Virtue and Miss Eileen Fitzgerald, to erect a million dollar coeducational college complex.

"This will be the first time," said Miss H. M. Pearce, headmistress of Strathallan in 1960, "that a girls' and a boys' school have occupied the same grounds, shared the same facilities, yet have retained their individual identity in so far as education is concerned."

For a quarter-century after Strathallan's opening, Scottish-born Janet Virtue, one of the outstanding educationists of the city, served as its principal. Miss Virtue was acclaimed not only for the scholastic standards she set but for the successful development of each pupil's individual physical, social and cultural potential. For years she served as secretary of the Women's Wentworth Historical Society. When she and Miss Fitzgerald retired, an educational trust fund was formed to maintain the school.

By 1960 Strathallan needed a new setting. The school's two converted private residences on Robinson Street were now nearly ninety years old and enrolment had expanded from an initial 75 pupils to over 190. On April 23rd, 1963, when Ontario's Lt.-Gov. J. Keiller MacKay officially opened the new Hillfield and Strathallan Colleges on the southwest corner of Garth Street and Fennell Avenue, Strathallan's enrolment topped 200 and Hillfield's surpassed 350.

Although the new colleges are built in traditional English courtyard style, the buildings are definitely contemporary. The two colleges share gymnasium facilities; hall and stage for morning prayers, assemblies and dramatics; dining hall; and administration building. In charge of this new experiment in education are Col. John P. Page, headmaster, and Mrs. R. S. Bruce, headmistress.

Possibly everyone in a lifetime forms an attachment for some school. Even today, fifty years later, Katherine Marks, now Mrs. Frank S. Pana-baker, wife of one of Canada's outstanding artists, warmly recalls her youthful days at the Misses Grant's private school in the Hamilton of that era.

"It is June, 1909, and the leaves of the big maples on Bay Street are still in spring green. In front of Mrs. F. S. Malloch's home the organ grinder and his red-jacketed monkey are tinkling out a tune and we wait for the last note before hurrying in the side door of the big brick house on the northwest corner of Bay and Markland Streets. Inside the doorway are glass cases of rock samples gathered by Col. Charles C. Grant, father of Miss Violet and Miss Alice. We are rather afraid of him because of his bushy whiskers, his black geologist's sack always slung over a shoulder and the small hammer with which he goes tap-tap-tapping at rocks on the mountainside.

"Up the dark stairway we climb, past Miss Violet's door and the more advanced scholars on the second floor to Miss Alice's room. Through the gable windows we can see the tops of the trees. Against the south wall extends a long desk before which we sit on benches in a row. The east wall bears a large blackboard, and on the west stands Miss Alice's desk with a heavy pointer, a 'backboard' and a ruler upon it.

"These instruments of discipline are well and painfully known to us. A squeaking slate pencil brings a sharp crack with the ruler on the knuckles. A late pupil is set on the dunce stool with a dunce cap on his head. During the last class the backboard, a large rounded back with handles, is passed and we take turns holding it and sitting stiffly erect.

"Prize giving is that afternoon so we dress in our Sunday clothes. There are piles of books on Miss Alice's desk and parents are present. Miss Alice gives a short speech followed by recitations by some pupils. Now the prizes are given out. Suddenly my name is called and I receive a prize for Writing and Good Conduct — a book, His Little Daughter, a sad tale of an orphan.

"It is over. As we run shouting up the street the waffle man appears at the corner of Aberdeen and Bay Streets. His cart is pulled by a fat horse and a delicious odour wafts out. We try to reach him before the Highfield pupils in their green and white striped blazers swarm down like locusts. It is too late. The boarders are there first and the waffle man works feverishly to supply the hungry horde."

There were other private schools. The Alexandra school for boys and girls conducted by Miss Angelina Murphy and her assistants, Misses May Murphy, Kate Gunn and Alice Burton, was housed in one of an attached row of tall narrow brick houses with double drawing rooms and steep stairs, that stood at the southwest corner of John Street and Charlton Avenue on land now occupied by the maternity wing of St. Joseph's Hospital.

Tall, tailored and severe in starched shirtwaist and long skirt, with a pince-nez through which she could paralyze an offender, Miss Angelina had only one apparent weakness, a love of rings which glittered and flashed on her fingers at all times.

On King Street West, between Ray and Pearl, stood the oldest continuing private girls' school in the city, which would celebrate the centenary of its founding on September 16th, 1965. Invited by Rt. Rev. J. J.

Farrell, D.D., Loretto Academy, Mount St. Mary was established by the Sisters of the Institute of the Blessed Virgin Mary.

Originally the residence of the 16th Regiment, the academy was transformed for its hoop-skirted charges with chapel, dormitories and classrooms. In 1892 a large five-storey wing was erected, with dormitories for the resident students, living rooms, classrooms and music rooms.

By 1928 enrolment at Loretto had reached 300, necessitating further expansion which led to a new wing in 1933, a core of the early building alone remaining. Only older Sisters and pupils would recall the wistaria that hung in lilac profusion on the east wall, the summer house hiding the ancient well, and the white statues of the Holy Family on the lawn, mirrored in the music room windows.

One other school must be mentioned. In a spacious red brick residence on the northeast corner of Hughson Street and Forest Avenue, Kingsthorpe Day and Boarding School for girls was operated by Mrs. M. T. Kitchen, headmistress, with her sisters, Misses Louisa, Elizabeth and Jean Turnbull, and Mrs. A. M. Brouse as assistants. A superior school, forerunner of Strathallan, Kingsthorpe had a large attendance in all grades. Unlike Strathallan it did not feature sports.

Kingsthorpe did however feature "musicales" staged by pupils of Miss Ellen Ambrose — a small bright wisp of a woman — on Sunday evenings after tea in its spacious drawing room and a play in French at Christmas attended by admiring parents.

"Today," says Dr. G. Roy Fenwick, from 1922 to 1935 genial director of music in Hamilton schools, "television, radio and recordings bring us much of the greatest music of the past performed by the world's great artists. Fifty or sixty years ago we had to make most of our own music, and if our knowledge of musical literature was limited and our performances not up to professional standards, at least we were not merely hearers but rather doers of the great art.

"The music I recall from my earliest days was mostly vocal and choral. Hamilton had not yet felt the effects of the influx of European immigrants which began about the turn of the century. The city then was almost entirely populated by people from the British Isles where a singing tradition has always been strong. Besides this, I grew up in an atmosphere of vocal music. My mother, Maggie Barr, was one of the best known concert and church sopranos of her time, and our friends were music lovers. One was J. E. P. Aldous, well known organist and teacher, who succeeded Dr. C. L. M. Harris as director of the Hamilton Conservatory of Music."

Hamilton's oldest continuing school of music and leading artistic centre for nearly seventy years, the conservatory opened in 1897 at the southeast corner of Hunter and MacNab Street, in the residence of Yorkshire-born Dr. C. L. M. Harris, who first won Canada-wide recognition as conductor of the highly successful Harris Orchestral Club. As President of the Associated Musicians of Ontario, conductor of the Hamilton Choral Society, organist and choirmaster of St. Paul's Presbyterian Church, examiner for music and advisory member of the University of Toronto, a member of the Hamilton String Quartette (with John and Edward Bartmann and Arthur Ostler), and director for eleven years of the conservatory, Dr. Harris' musical contribution was outstanding.

In 1899 the conservatory moved to new quarters in the former Hamilton School of Music building, southeast corner of Main Street and Charles, later to become the Stafford House, on the site of today's City Hall. Recital facilities were lacking however and five years later the present building on James Street South was erected, the architect — who also designed the present large and handsome Classic Hamilton Public Library on Main Street West, opened on May 5, 1913 — being A. W. Peene, brother of Miss Lilli M. W. Peene, an original faculty member of the conservatory.[4]

Today it is difficult to appreciate the enthusiasm shown in the city for music and kindred arts during the era preceeding radio, television and motor access to other centres. To the present the flame lighted by the late Miss Ambrose still burns brightly in the Duet Club. Commencing in 1889 with ten of her former students at Strathallan, whom Miss Ambrose paired in duets for mutual support, by 1932 the Duet Club was producing an annual concert considered the outstanding musical event of the season, and in 1964 celebrated its seventy-fifth anniversary with a buffet supper for a membership of 300.

Believed to be the oldest continuous ladies' music club in Canada, the Duet Club has won a special niche in city history. Many of the community's oldest families have been included as members and officers. In 1960, at its seventieth birthday party, twelve past presidents formed a chorus: Mesdames Stanley E. LeBrocq, Harold S. Beddoe, W. Eric Griffith, Charles E. Bull, Vernon T. Carey, H. Maxwell Morrow, Corbett E. Whitton, George Allan, Herbert A. Main, Caswell R. Green and William J. Deadman.

First president was Miss J. Katherine Macdonald, followed by Miss Alice Cummings and Mrs. J. Heurner Mullin. Among subsequent presidents the late Mrs. T. Jack Lees has been honoured for outstanding service by having the Eleanor Callaghan Lees scholarship established in her memory. The club presented, among other Hamilton artists, Mary Y. Syme and David Lee, pianists, Olive Barlow Blakely, contralto, and Mimi Johnston, soprano.

From Thomas Littlehales, who lived in a big house on Park Street North beside the gas works which he managed, came the Philharmonic Society which began as a family ensemble and expanded into the orchestral Jubal Club. Four of Mr. Littlehales' six children adopted music as a profession. When John Edmond Paul Aldous of Paris, France, took over the Jubal Club as conductor in 1885, he renamed it the Philharmonic Society. Under the baton of Dr. C. L. M. Harris this became the Harris

Orchestral Club, reorganized after fourteen highly successful years as the Hamilton Symphony Orchestra.

As early as the last century the German element in the city contributed to the community's musical development through the local Germania Club, organized in 1871 and incorporated ten years later, under respective presidents William Bartmann and Fred Schwarz. This was no ethnic group but descendants of the large number of Pennsylvania Germans among the founding fathers of the city. In 1891, from August 18th to 21st, the Germania Club sponsored the Eleventh Peninsular (Michigan) Saengerfest, attended by twenty visiting societies from Ohio, New York, Pennsylvania, Michigan, and Ontario, accompanied by their choirs, soloists, and bands. Germania Club officers responsible included Lorenz Roehm, president, William Nieghorn and Charles Schwenger.

Outstanding in the overall program was a promenade concert in the Gore by visiting bands and the XIIIth under bandmaster George Robinson; an evening concert in the drill hall with a chorus of six hundred voices directed by Walter H. Robinson, son of George,[5] with C. L. M. Harris' orchestra of sixty instruments. Also, following a convention meeting and welcome in city council chamber by Mayor David McLellan, there was an imposing street parade from the Gore to Dundurn, organized by Police Chief McKinnon and Fire Chief Aitchison. A banquet in the Crystal Palace rink, a grand ball at Dundurn Castle, and a finale of aquatic fireworks climaxed the song fest.

Thirty years later the first Hamilton Eisteddfod, promoted by Welsh music lovers under the chairmanship of Thomas Lewis and with Rev. Canon John Samuel as musical adviser, proved so successful that it became an annual event.

Culture was not confined to music alone. By 1907 the Hamilton Conservatory had expanded its musical syllabus with instruction in drawing and painting, language classes in French, German, and Italian, fencing, elocution and ballroom dancing, and was offering a Mus. Bac. degree, a teacher's diploma course, and a correspondence course in theory.

When Dr. Harris resigned a year later, J. E. P. Aldous of the Hamilton School of Music, who had served as organist with various city churches, was appointed musical director, with Dr. W. H. Hewlett and Dr. Bruce A. Carey forming a triple administration.

"Hamilton," said Dr. Fenwick, "has been blessed with several musical families, Ambrose, Beddoe, Anderson, Lomas" — also, Howard, Clark, Filgiano, O'Brien and Nelligan — "to mention only a few, whose members played an active part in its cultural life. One of the most talented was the George Carey family—Bruce, Edith (Mrs. Fred Smyth), Clara (Mrs. George Allan), Vernon T., and Bertha (Mrs. H. Maxwell Morrow), with dainty Estelle Carey, The Little Thrush of Broadway, a cousin, and Mrs. Olive Filman, known on stage as Dorothy Hunting, an aunt. All had exceptional talent."

After ten years with the Hamilton Conservatory, tenor Bruce Carey resigned to become director of music in city schools. A tall handsome man with a "gay personality as vibrant as his pitch pipe," Mr. Carey possessed a contagious enthusiasm which made his schoolroom visits a delight to his pupils.

Before accepting a position in 1922 as music director of Girard College, Philadelphia, conductor of the Bethelehem, Pennsylvania, Bach choir, and a member of the advisory board of the Philadelphia orchestra, Mr. Carey performed two last services for Hamilton. In 1905, working with members of the Erskine Presbyterian Church, he founded the Elgar (later Bach-Elgar) choir which won international recognition and over the years did much to uphold the city's musical reputation. In 1913, with Charles R. McCullough and Russell T. Kelley,[6] he formed the Rotary Club of Hamilton.

Among the challenges Bruce Carey met successfully was training probably the largest choir ever handled by one man, the 6,300-voice Festival chorus of the Philadelphia Sesquicentennial International Exposition of 1926, accompanied by bands he also led. In 1936 Moravia College, Bethlehem, Pa., awarded him a degree of Mus. Dr.

When English-born Dr. Hewlett took charge of the Hamilton Conservatory, following Bruce Carey's departure, he received the title "principal." An organist of note, Dr. Hewlett designed the organs in many local churches. He conducted the Hamilton Symphony orchestra and from 1922 to 1935 the Elgar choir. When he left the conservatory in 1939 the square jawed, dark haired musician had become a vital figure in the community, well liked for his dry humour, vast store of puns, and love of teaching and travel.

During his term the late Cyril Hampshire, Hamilton's dean of organists, had to combat the effect on the conservatory of the "slump thirties" and the war years. In 1944, when he resigned to become music director of the board of education, his place was taken in succession by Reginald Bedford who left to act as principal of Bedford Music Studio; Reginald Godden, pianist; and Lorne Betts, composer, whose works are heard regularly on Canadian Broadcasting Corporation radio networks. In 1959 Harold Jerome, organist and choir master with several city churches, assumed office. Mr. Jerome is well known in the city for his work in helping establish the annual Westdale Kiwanis music festival which, with the subsequent Concert of the Stars, seeks out, promotes, and presents youthful talent of the district.

Today James Street remains much as it was when the conservatory was built, with small shops and residences to the north graduating to the big important houses towards the Mountain. At that time there was no railway bridge underpass and consequently all entrances on James Street South were at street level.

There has been certain demolition to accommodate the seven-storey Medical Arts building, erected in 1930 to become an important medical nucleus in the city, eight years after the McGregor-Mowbray clinic on

Main Street East was established by surgeons James Kenneth McGregor, M.D., and Frederick Bruce Mowbray, M.D.; the Professional Arts Building of 1959, whose tenants include the Hamilton Chamber of Commerce; the Undermount office building; and Alexandra Square, a 15-storey office tower and landscaped plaza, with two levels of underground parking. These last three buildings are the redevelopment project of Angelo, Richard, and Nicholas Cutaia whose father, Anthony Cutaia, owned the grocery store which occupied the site of the Professional Arts Building.

Largely, however, the big houses have been transformed from residential to business, commercial, and professional use. Mrs. Charles D. Grantham's fine stone mansion has functioned since 1950 as Grace Haven, the Salvation Army's latest shelter for unwed mothers. On the west side of James, at Markland Street, the handsome Georgian mansion built by the late Harry L. Frost, after serving as the United States official consular residence, once occupied by American Vice-Consul Clay Merrell and Mrs. Merrell, is now headquarters of the Canada Life Assurance Company Limited. With the house, from its consular days, Canada Life inherited thirteen bathrooms.

Immediately south of the conservatory, between Bold and Duke Streets, a row of ten attached stone houses which in the early decades of the century were largely occupied by medical practitioners—Drs. John P. Morton, J. K. McGregor, Pryse Park, John R. Parry, Gerald O'Reilly, Jr., Gerald S. Glassco, G. E. J. Lannin, and T. S. McGillivray—are now converted into smart boutiques.

Gone and carrying with it over a half-century of memories is the Alexandra, Hamilton's last big dance hall. Acquired in 1909 and first operated as an ice rink by John M. Webber, successful Hamilton lumberman, hardware merchant, and tobacconist, the Victorian building later became a popular roller-skating rink, and in the First World War a joint relief work centre. Purchased in 1919 by Frederick J. Hicks, it featured over the years as winter garden, academy, dance hall, roller rink and convention hall.

An integral part of Hamilton life where many Hamiltonians found romance, the Alexandra changed with the years from gas lamps to electric light, from a Hammond organ to name bands. Cab Calloway, Woody Herman, Vaughan Monroe, and the Dorsey brothers played there, as well as local bands such as Nick Stoutt's, Len Allan's, Morgan Williams' and Jack Faregan's. The history of the dance hall parallels the century. "There were times," said Mr. Hicks' daughter, Mrs. Margaret Marshall, who operated the Alex after her father's death, "when we had capacity crowds six nights a week. But that was before radio, let alone television."

In 1960 the Alexandra turned to rock 'n' roll. Big stars such as Duane Eddy, Bobby Vee and Bobby Curtola packed the old hall with standing-room crowds of 1,000, but in between attendance lapsed. Today's teenagers feel no loyalty to a dance hall, and adults and young people today do not dance to the same music. "To youngsters now," said Mrs.

Marshall, "any music but their own is square. They go for weird and way-out steps like the Cheyenne, Charley Brown, Madison, hucklebuck, and twist and to most adults such music and dancing lacks appeal." So in April, 1964, for the last time Ron Wicken's band played the old favourites for the oldtimers: "Sweet and Lovely," "Ain't She Sweet?", "Muskrat Ramble," and "Harlem Nocturne."

After the Alex was razed its site served as a parking lot. Similarly, in 1959, the outmoded Terminal building was demolished — its massive brick and ferro-concrete walls and steel-reinforced floors air-hammered out of existence — and the site used as a car park. Also, in the mid-1950's the Turner building on the northwest corner of Hughson and Main Streets, onetime home of the *Hamilton Review* founded about 1905 by Mark Lynch-Staunton, was razed and converted to a lot. Today all three lots are rebuilt, the Alex site occupied by Cutaia Alexandra Square.

Completed in 1966, Terminal Towers on the Terminal lot is Hamilton's largest downtown structure. Covering a full city block, the British-owned $12,000,000 complex houses a 240-room, eight-storey hotel tower, ten-storey office tower, and a twelve-storey apartment tower mounted on a five-storey podium of arcaded shops, magistrates' courtrooms and facilities, and indoor parking space. The podium roof contains a swimming pool, wading pool, patio and pedestrian areas, and on this level convention accommodation including a hall to seat 1,000 or dine 500 to 600.

On the central Hughson Street site a $2,000,000 ten-storey office building now houses the head office of United Gas Limited, whose natural gas distribution system serves Hamilton and fourteen neighbouring communities. Distinguishing "The Gas Building" is an illuminated roof-top sculpture of the company's symbol, a gas flame. Features of the new building are a basement auditorium capable of seating 200, and heating and air conditioning systems using natural gas.

Today's service of a growing complex of municipalities, extending from Oakville, Burlington, and Stoney Creek north to Milton, Georgetown and Acton, and west to Dundas and the Flamboros, marks gas company expansion since growth of the city following the First World War outran the supply of available natural gas and led to installation of coke ovens to produce artificial gas. Coke was also manufactured to help overcome the constantly recurring shortages of hard fuel of the period.

When a by-product coking plant equipped with a battery of twenty-five coke ovens was put into operation early in 1924, the venture proved so successful that the number of ovens was later increased to sixty. A large dock was constructed at the foot of Depew Street to permit delivery of coal for the ovens. This valuable addition to harbour facilities enabled coal companies to import coal by water instead of rail.

With Hamilton's exciting new design for a civic square, the York Street entrance, north end rehabilitation, and mountain top planning, the problem of parking becomes a vital issue. As a problem it is of comparatively recent vintage. Prior to World War II, parking garages uptown, mostly converted stables, accommodated regular customers, otherwise curbside parking sufficed. On March 31st, 1947, the first parking meters, 325 in number, were installed on city streets, to be filled with coins by the curious a week before being put into operation. In 1957 the first public parking lot was opened on the southeast corner of John and Rebecca Streets. The first traffic signal in the city was erected at the Delta in 1925. Not until 1956 were automatic signals adopted at King and James.

Contemporary with these developments was the conversion of the H.S.R. — purchased in 1946 by Francis Farewell, president of Canada Coach Lines, Limited — to modern bus and trolley coach service. In 1947 P. A. S. Todd succeeded George E. Waller as general manager. In 1960 the city of Hamilton purchased the H.S.R. and its then subsidiary, Canada Coach Limited.

23

The Second World War

On September 1st, 1939, Hitler invaded Poland and on a bright sunny fall Friday, war came for the second time to the city within the span of a single generation. First casualty of the conflict was ten-year-old Margaret Hayworth, daughter of Mr. and Mrs. John Hayworth, who died of injuries received when the liner *Athenia* was torpedoed barely five hours after Britain's declaration of war on September 3rd.

On September 1st five commanders of Hamilton garrison units received the same curt telegram: "Mobilize." In the first ten days of the war 1,500 Hamiltonians enlisted, a number that would climb to 20,000 before peace was declared, with one-fifth of that total killed, wounded, or missing. The first Hamilton unit to sail for England was the 1st Divisional Petrol Company, Royal Canadian Army Service Corps, which embarked at Halifax on December 10th, 1939, under command of Major (later Lt.-Col.) S. H. Coombes. Twelve days later the Petrol Company was followed by No. 5 Field Ambulance, Royal Canadian Army Medical Corps, commanded by Lt.-Col. (later Brigadier) G. R. D. Farmer, whose father, Col. G. D. Farmer, had taken the same unit to England in 1915.

According to Second World War usage, having provided a first battalion for overseas, militia units enlisted a second to replace the first. In the First World War training had been hurried. In the second there was plenty of time to train.

Under Lt.-Col. T. W. Greenfield, E.D., the Argyll and Sutherland Highlanders of Canada (Princess Louise's) trained at Nanaimo, British Columbia, and Jamaica. They arrived overseas in July, 1943, to become part of the 4th Canadian Infantry Division, and went into action a year later in Normandy under Lt.-Col. J. D. Stewart, D.S.O., E.D. Among its heavy casualties the battalion lost Lt.-Cols. Frederick E. Wigle, O.B.E., D.S.O.; I. M. R. Sinclair, O.B.E., M.C., V.D.; and A. J. Hay, a war-time C.O. Commanding the regiment's 2nd (Reserve) Battalion was Lt.-Col. H. D. Fearman, D.S.O.

Arriving earlier in England than the Argylls, the Royal Hamilton

Light Infantry (W.R.), formerly the 13th Royals, under Lt.-Col. (later Brigadier) W. Denis Whitaker, D.S.O. and bar, took part in the action at Dieppe. On the beach a non-combatant, Major John Foote, who had joined the R.H.L.I. in 1940 as padre, won the Victoria Cross for conspicuous bravery in rescuing wounded under fire.

Reinforced in England the "Rileys" served in northwest Europe after D-day under Gen. H. D. G. Crerar, D.S.O., M.C., commander of the 1st Canadian Army. When the war ended, their casualties, like the Argylls, numbered between two and three thousand.

The oldest Hamilton garrison unit, the 11th Battery, Canadian Field Artillery, was mobilized in the Second World War as the 11-69 Battery of the 12th Field Regiment, R.C.A. (N.P.A.M.), under command of Major J. P. Phin, E.D. Later it again became the 11th and following training moved overseas in July, 1941, with Major W. J. Brigger in command. Recalled from retirement, Lt.-Col. George T. Inch, M.C., V.D.,[1] took over the regiment until July, 1942, when Lt.-Col. Phin assumed command, with Major D. M. Wilson taking the battery into action in Normandy. On a bitter December morning in 1945 Lt.-Col. J. A. Hornibrook brought the 11th home.

In both World Wars the 40th Field Battery, R.C.A., mobilized in the office of *The Hamilton Spectator*. Under the late Major Gordon Southam it was known in the First War as the Sportsman's Battery and included such well known figures as Mayor Chester S. Walters, Andrew Frame and Conn Smyth of Maple Leaf Gardens fame. In the Second War Major Frank J. Keen, later the city editor of *The Hamilton Spectator,* took the battery to England. In November, 1943, the 40th went into action in Sicily under Major L. Hemsworth, and later fought up through Italy into the south of France. The first Hamilton unit to arrive home in the Second World War, the 40th under Major David Keogh received a tumultuous welcome.

The city had fought and won its own battles. Men and women, munitions, food, armaments, clothing, merchandise, hospital equipment, and medical supplies — in an unending stream men, women and goods moved to the war fronts. Moreover, men and women had to be trained and housed, munitions and equipment manufactured, food produced and processed, garments sewn or knitted. Existing plants were converted to war production, and when necessary, expanded. New plants were government built — as the Longwood Road building of Canadian Westinghouse (president, John R. Read) which made weapons as diversified as bomb sights, anti-aircraft guns and torpedo engines.

Having supplied shells, gun carriages, and railway cars for France during the First World War, the National Steel Car Corporation brought experience to the second conflict. From 1939 to 1945, twenty million shells rolled off company assembly lines, as well as forgings, gun mounts, tank parts, universal carriers and steel truck bodies.

Building an aircraft plant at Malton the company also constructed

Lysander reconnaissance planes, Ansons and other training planes, and parts of fighters. In 1942 the plant was expropriated by the government and became Victory Aircraft, the later A. V. Roe of Canada Limited.

From the accelerated production of the giant steel mills to the all-out effort of the smallest operator, every industry in the city played its part in multiple ways. Curtailing manufacture of civilian clothing, textile mills turned out uniforms for the forces, and personal equipment ranging from suspenders to gas masks. In another phase, Harold G. Smith, who left the presidency of Mercury Mills to found Mohawk Mills, was awarded the O.B.E. for wartime service as knit goods administrator for the Wartime Prices and Trade Board, serving under Frank L. J. Selden, prices and supply representative of the Central Ontario region. A body instituted to prevent inflation by controlling prices and regulating trade, the W.P.T.B. eventually covered all commodities and services, including realty rentals.

No commodity was more essential to the war effort than rubber. The Firestone Tire and Rubber Company of Canada Limited, incorporated in 1919 by Harvey S. Firestone, built its first Canadian plant on broken-front waste marsh land, east of Kenilworth Avenue and north of Burlington Street, purchased from James Gage. First president, E. W. BeSaw, was succeeded in 1932 by William H. Funston who turned over the office in 1957 to T. M. Mayberry.

By the outbreak of war, Firestone had progressed from four types of fabric and cord high pressure tires, solids and inner tubes made of crude rubber imported from Malaysia, to tire cord fabric, gum impregnating processes, and balloon tires. In 1939 Firestone geared its production to war. Military tires became a priority. Bullet sealing fuel cells for aircraft, army "bogey" wheels for tanks and Bren gun carriers followed. By the war's end Hamilton Firestone was the largest producer of tank track wheels in the Commonwealth.

In January, 1941, an order banned civilian purchase of tires, casings, and tubes, except for essential use by doctors, nurses, police, and fire departments, and buses. Taxicab owners, stores, milk, bread and coal companies had to depend on reconditioned tires or do without. All tire sales required proof that purchase was essential.

To one branch of the service, the Air Force, Firestone products were of vital importance. In the air Canada made phenomenal strides in World War II. Under the joint Commonwealth Air Training plan by which airmen from twelve countries, including Canada, Great Britain, New Zealand, Australia and the United States, were trained, over eighty flying schools were built and operated throughout Canada. Hamilton was ringed by schools — R.C.A.F. stations at Jarvis, Hagersville, Brantford and St. Catharines, and at Mount Hope, a small community seven miles south of the city, No. 33 Air Navigation school (R.A.F.). For five years trainees of the C.A.T. plan, in their gray-blue Canadian and British and dark blue New Zealand and Australian uniforms, were an important factor in city life. Of the 22,500 servicemen a month who clattered up the steep stairs of the active service canteen, chairmanned by Mrs. Gerald W. Wigle, and located south of the Gore near James Street, the majority were air force personnel.

Following the war Mount Hope was established as a permanent R.C.A.F. station and airport. Today, municipally owned, it becomes part of one of the liveliest chapters in community history, the story of early flying and the Hamilton pioneers who gained international reputations in their field.

Probably the first birdman in the city was youthful Jack Burton whose optimistic glider launching from the mountaintop carried him to hospital. At the first 1911 air meet in Hamilton where Canadian pilot J. A. Douglas McCurdy defeated American Charles F. Willard by flying a speedy 35 miles in 36 minutes, a second flier came to grief, British flying instructor J. V. Martin's dive into the swamp off the Beach Road incidentally providing a future noted Hamilton airman with his introduction to flying. For dismantling and carrying out parts of the downed Farman machine, eleven-year-old Robert Dodds and his brother each received a dollar. Officially, commercial flying in the city was inaugurated by Dundas-born Jack V. Elliott who reportedly traded a fast racing car in 1922 for a Curtis Canuck; qualified at Borden as pilot and air engineer; with war surplus parts built two additional machines in a workshop on the bay front at MacNab Street; and began promoting air mindedness by offering short flights at a small fee.

At a flying field on the mountain and later on the Niagara highway, hundreds gathered on Sunday afternoons to watch the planes. With the Red Lake gold rush of 1926 aviation began to pay off. Elliott shipped two machines to Hudson, twelve days by dog team from the mining area but only two hours by air, and ferried prospectors in and out for $1,000 one way. He was appointed postmaster and Elliott airmail stamps are a collector's item today. Later he amalgamated with Fairchild as Elliott-Fairchild Air Service.

The following spring with five planes he opened the Beach Road airport and private flying school, using the old Ghent homestead as club-house. The first in Canada, the school received entrants from all parts of this country and the United States. Miss Eileen Vollick, the first Canadian woman to obtain a flier's license, was a pupil.

On August 24th, 1927, the first official air mail for Hamilton was received at the field. Flown by pilot Earl Hand, the mail was met by Postmaster John A. Webber[2] who arrived by horse and buggy. Followed by a crowd of spectators Mr. Webber advanced down Beach Road to watch the seaplane land on the bay and taxi up the lagoon east of the Firestone plant. Following its receipt the postmaster telephoned the post office announcing the arrival and amount of the mail.

When Jack Elliott sold his fleet of twenty-one amphibians, cabin planes and scout machines in 1928 to International Airways (president, R. O. Denman, D.C.M., M.M.), he was known across Canada. His countrywide barnstorming had resulted in his charting many of the routes and landing fields later used in aviation.

Another, less successful, service had been instituted in Hamilton by Mr. Elliott. On May 20th, 1922, Herbert Slack, owner of Wentworth Radio and Supply Company, went on the air with radio station CKOC, third station in the province. Two years later *The Hamilton Spectator* took a first step in the same field with station CHCS, sharing CKOC's wavelength, and broadcasting nightly newscasts and Sunday church service. The following year Elliott opened station CFCU from a studio on King Street West. Both CHCS and CFCU were later discontinued while CKOC flourished.

Shortly after sale of his business Jack Elliott moved to Owen Sound. In Hamilton his place was taken by the Hamilton Aero Club, started in 1927 by several first war pilots and chartered in 1928 with Major Robert Dodds, M.C., founder and first president. Occupying the old Stewart Park on Beach Road, a few fields from Elliott's site, the Aero Club began functioning with two machines loaned by the government. With the R.C.A.F. officially created only on April 1st, 1924, the need for trained pilots led the government to donate a plane for each machine purchased by the club and to pay $100 for each pilot graduated. By the year's end the club was able to purchase a new Gypsy Moth, with the government matching this and also paying for several pilot graduates.

In 1929, when the Hamilton Municipal airport was opened on the east side of Parkdale Avenue between Main Street (now Queenston Road) and Barton, Aero Club members numbered 133, with 52 taking instruction. Its executive included president, Lloyd H. Smith; vice-president, Beamer W. Hopkins, later chief magistrate, police commissioner and president of the Hamilton citizenship court, airman in the First World War and air commander in the second; secretary, Marshall J. Lounsbury; treasurer, William H. Acres; and a director, the late Samuel S. Foley, M.B.E., later regional director of air services for Ontario. In charge of instruction was Robert Dodds, a First World War member of the fledgling Royal Flying Corps — the later R.A.F. — who was rated by *The National Geographic*[3] as among the top twenty British airmen of the war, credited with destroying eleven enemy planes in aerial encounters. For "conspicuous gallantry and devotion to duty" he was decorated by King George V.

A joint effort of Hamilton and International Airways Limited, with the Hamilton Aero Club assisting, the 200-acre airport was hailed as an outstanding example of community foresight and cooperation. It was opened by the Hon. G. Howard Ferguson and Mayor William Burton, a feature being the institution of airmail service by Canadian Airways, the first Hamilton mail leaving the airport on Friday, June 7th.

In 1929 International Airways was absorbed by Canadian Airways Limited, which later became Canadian Pacific Airlines, and the office moved to Montreal. As bookkeeper went a small active smiling woman, Jean Cowman, who in her many years of aviation service would become known to pilots from Montreal to Medicine Hat for her cheery salutation and the proffered cup of coffee. Shortly Jean returned to Hamilton as assistant secretary of the Hamilton Aero Club and weather observer. Until June, 1932, when the thrifty Bennett government cancelled all airmail delivery in Canada except in the far north, Jean Cowman teletyped the local weather from the field each morning. During the war she served with Air Force Headquarters Staff, Ottawa. Almost two decades later Hamilton would have a permanent official weather reporting station established by the R.B.G., with conservationist W. J. Lamoureux as weatherman.

From the beginning, Municipal airport, selected without consulting air force authorities, was plagued by undrainable red clay soil which turned to blinding dust in summer and seas of mud in spring and fall, and developed cracks and crevices in all seasons. Although Tarco runways were laid in 1931 and improved lighting installed, trouble persisted. In 1951 the airport was abandoned, the land turned to housing.

"Had the Municipal airport been strategically located," said an old-timer, "and possessed of terminal port requirements, Hamilton might well have had an active terminal airport today, for Toronto lagged in this field for some time."

In 1944, the Aero Club, in common with other flying clubs across Canada, was given an instructional contract by the government under the C.A.T. plan and moved to Pendleton. Two years later, following the end of hostilities, it resumed operations at Mount Hope as the Hamilton Flying Club. In 1929 Robert Dodds had left the club to take a position with Canadian Airways as director of airmail service between Montreal and Detroit. In June, 1930, he entered government service at Ottawa, and was shortly appointed director of civil aviation in charge of airways and airports, a post he held until retirement in 1958.

Like the Hamilton Aero Club, No. 19 Bomber Squadron, R.C.A.F.— later No. 119 (BR), replaced in 1942 by 424 Squadron—had been founded largely by veterans of the R.A.F. of 1914-18, with Sq. Ldr. D. U. McGregor, M.D., a prime mover. In 1938, upon his retirement, 119 was taken over by Flt.-Lt. Norman S. McGregor, D.F.C. Other officers had included Flt.-Lts. Royden Foley and W. J. Peace, D.F.C., and F.O. Fenner Douglas, with Capts. W. J. Tice and H. A. Peacock as medical staff.

In 1940, the 119 was posted first to the west, then to the east coast. In October, 1942, it was replaced as the City of Hamilton Squadron by 424 (Tiger) Squadron, formed at Topcliffe, Yorkshire, England, with Wing Cmdr. (later Air Vice Marshal) Henry M. Carscallen, D.F.C., a Highfield College old boy, appointed C.O.

Following more than thirty operational raids against European targets, the 424 was moved to Tunisia to engage in sorties against Italian strong points; in 1944 it returned to European action; and on October 15th, 1945, was stood down. Under command of Wing Cmdr. Douglas H.

Wigle the squadron was reformed on April 15th, 1946, as an R.C.A.F. auxiliary squadron.

If in Canada the air force became a concomitant of the Second World War as it never had in the first, this was also true of the navy. Since U-boat slaughter began, as we have seen, with the declaration of war, the need of naval volunteers to man the seaways was immediate. Eighty per cent of the total enrolment in the Royal Canadian Navy came from the Royal Canadian Naval Volunteer Reserve, formed in the 1920's. Moreover, R.C.N.V.R. recruits possessed a basic training which enabled them to put to sea within days of their arrival at coastal ports.

In Hamilton, an R.C.N.V.R. unit with a complement of fifty was commissioned in May, 1923, under Lt. R. Howard Yeates, 1923-29, and Lt. H. Lloyd G. Westland. Unit Headquarters was a tall brick building, the old Thomas Reid machine works, MacNab Street North — technically H.M.C.S. *Star*, the unit's training ship.

"To go through the front door," says an account, "is crossing the gangway and going aboard. To leave is to go ashore. Inside the door hangs a bronze bell on which a naval rating rings out the watch every half hour. Second floor is upper deck, top floor the quarter deck. Only officers step on the quarter deck and they always salute when they reach it, possibly because it is the symbol of authority. In the wardroom naval officers are privileged to remain seated when drinking the toast to the sovereign, although they stand at functions ashore.[4] In the old days of wooden ships, ceilings of wardrooms were so low that tall officers cracked their heads every time they stood up. Hence the rule was abrogated."

In 1936 under Lt. Westland, 1934-37, H.M.C.S. *Star* slipped her moorings and moved down the roadstead to the former Dominion Vinegar works, Stuart and MacNab.

Seven years later Ellis Corman, M.P., Wentworth, announced the federal government's intention to erect new naval barracks on the Hamilton waterfront in Eastwood Park. At that date forty-seven per cent of convoy work in the North Atlantic was being borne by Canadian ships, officered and manned by men of the Canadian navy. The Hamilton *Star* (III) was the first entirely new establishment in the navy's inland flotilla of training ships. When she was commissioned in a deeply impressive naval ceremony on October 18th, 1943, ranking naval officers, government dignitaries and city officials attended in honour of the ship's record and the 5,000 officers and men she had sent to sea. On the wide parade ground, which separates the ship proper from the barracks block in which men in training eat and sleep, the white ensign was raised on H.M.C.S. *Star's* 70-foot mast. Adding a poignance to the day's events was announcement by the Hon. Angus L. Macdonald of loss of the Canadian destroyer, *St. Croix*, with practically all her crew.

Preceding the ceremonies aboard ship, dignitaries including Lt.-Cmdr. John McFetrick, C.O. of the *Star*, Col. the Hon. C. W. G. Gibson, minister of national revenue, and Mayor William Morrison, K.C., were entertained at the home of Clay Merrell, American vice-consul, after which they inspected the Red Cross packing plant engaged in providing weekly food parcels for Canadian and British servicemen in P.O.W. camps, for whose successful management Harold H. Leather[5] was honoured with an M.B.E. They were then conducted over the 200-bed Hamilton Military Hospital on Gage Avenue North, the former King George School, by Major G. H. Ryan, acting C.O., who had succeeded Col. Leeming A. Carr, the latter having taken No. 13 Canadian General Hospital to England two months earlier.

By 1943, the freezing of retail prices of goods, services (including wages), and rentals, under an overall ceiling, with drastic government controls of production, consumer purchasing, credit buying and consumption had been amplified by coupon rationing. Beginning with gasoline rationing on April 1st, 1942, sugar rationing had followed, then tea and coffee, with meat added on May 27th, 1943.

In 1944 Italy capitulated. On May 8th, 1945, in Berlin, representatives of the German High Command signed the instrument of unconditional surrender of the German forces. In the triumphal march into Berlin Lt.-Col. A. F. Coffin, D.S.O., Argyll C.O., led the composite Canadian Berlin Battalion, with Argyll pipers and drummers playing the marchers into the fallen city.

The following September Japan surrendered. JAPS ACCEPT ALLIED TERMS, shouted *The Hamilton Spectator* in four-inch type. WAR OVER!

"Let us give thanks," urged Hamilton Mayor Samuel Lawrence, speaking with little prescience of the future, "that we can again live in a world of peace."

The future would bring changes to two branches of the service in Hamilton. On January 20th, 1953, the Royal Canadian Navy announced a separate command for the R.C.N. (Reserve) and based that reserve in Hamilton, transferring the headquarters staff from Ottawa. Under the new set-up, the R.C.N. (Reserve) was given separate command and made directly responsible to the chief of naval staff as an integral branch of the navy.

First commander of Canada's twenty-two naval reserve divisions was Cmdr. Kenneth F. Adams, C.D., formerly commandant of the R.C.N. barracks at Esquimalt, whose headquarters were established in the converted upper storey of the barracks block of H.M.C.S. *Star*. Chief of Staff was Capt. A. G. Boulton, D.S.C. Three years later the flag officer and headquarters of the naval (reserve) divisions, under Lt.-Cmdr. F. H. Pinfold, were moved to H.M.C.S. *Patriot*, built for the purpose next door to the *Star* on the same base.

In 1964, in line with general defence reductions, naval reserve divisions were cut to sixteen. Today C.O. Naval Divisions is Cmdr. P. D. Taylor.

On their base at the foot of Catharine Street across from the *Star*, the Royal Canadian Sea Cadet Corps *Lion* and Navy League Cadet Corps

Cougar (younger boys, 11-15) have operated as a major youth training centre since 1948. Set up under the auspices of the Navy League of Canada, the Boys' Naval brigade dates from 1919. In 1943 R.C.S.C. *Lion* was formed, followed later by N.L.C.C. *Cougar*. Shortly a new cadet centre will be erected by the Navy League of Canada.

When the defence reductions of 1964 closed the R.C.A.F. station at Mount Hope, the 424 City of Hamilton Squadron was disbanded and its colours deposited in Hamilton's new City Hall, then four years old. Into the romantic past faded an era of Hamiltonians: Howard Gordon —retired editorial staff member of *The Hamilton Spectator* and husband of Gladys Gillan, talented stock actress and director of amateur plays— who downed six German planes in World War I and flew against the fabulous Baron Richthofen and his 'Circus' of crack German pilots; the late Gerlacus (Gerry) Moes of the Netherlands, consulting engineer, who organized and managed the elementary flying school at Mount Hope during the Second World War; W. J. (Bill) Peace, presently a fruit farmer, and Hugh B. Monaghan, Burlington executive, First War Handley-Page bomber pilots with the Royal Navy Air Service.

The era of Capt. Eric M. Coles, in the First World War transferred from the 1st Central Ontario Regiment to the R.F.C., and returned to the C.E.F. at war's end, subsequently vice-president in charge of engineering, Canadian Westinghouse Company, air devotee lost with his wife over the Pacific; Wing Cmdr. George A. Roy, D.F.C., overseas C.O. of 424 Squadron and P.O.W., son of Hon. Philippe Roy; Cmdr. Edward B. Hale, D.F.C., who followed some four years' service in anti-submarine Atlantic patrol with twenty-three combat missions in Korea, and later served at Fontainebleau, France, as chief of plans and policies for Allied Air Forces' central European headquarters; and Charles Augustus Lindbergh, great-great-great grandson of pioneer Robert Land,[6] who in May, 1927, made the first non-stop Atlantic flight from New York to Paris.

Today Hamilton Civic airport, taken over by the city upon government withdrawal, provides facilities for the R.C.A.F. Association, the Hamilton Flying Club, Emergency Measures Organization, private and company planes, and Air Cadet groups whose Canadian president is Lt.-Col. Robert F. Inch, M.C., post-World War I C.O. 3rd Machine Gun Battalion. Colonel Inch, onetime alderman and chairman of the Hamilton Law Association, is the second local national president of the 25-year-old Air Cadet youth training league, the post having previously been held by M. Banker Bates, Burlington, retired president of Life Savers Limited.

The manager of the Hamilton Civic airport is Glenn R. White, operator of a flying school, Peninsula Air Services, who retained the position he had held since 1948.

243

24

Labour, Lawrence,
and a Look-back

THE elevation of Sam Lawrence to the mayoralty was a measure of the
progress in the city of the trade union movement from the pioneer days
of the Nine Hour League, formed in 1871 to establish a maximum nine-
hour working day, Parliament's recognition of unions as legal bodies in
1872 with the Trade Union Act, and the founding of the Trades and
Labour Congress of Canada, also in 1872.

When the Knights of Labour, a secret United States society, moved
into Canada in the 1880's, Hamilton's preponderance of Old Country
workmen experienced in and devoted to the trade union movement led to
the first assembly being organized and the first general assembly meeting
being held in Hamilton. On November 12th, 1888, the first proposal to
form the Trades and Labour Council was made in Hamilton in the old
Central Labour hall on John Street South by Daniel J. O'Donoghue,
known as the "Father of the Canadian labour movement" because of his
half-century of organizing workers.

On December 3rd the Hamilton Trades and Labour Council was
formed, its first president William Derby of the Knights of Labour.
With surprising foresight the council advocated the establishment of
government machinery for settlement of labour disputes and a govern-
ment-supervised system of apprenticeship with advisory boards representing employer and employee. It protested child labour and cordially
supported the Women's Christian Temperance Union in its "efforts to
encourage sobriety and temperance among the working classes." Local
mouthpiece of labour was the *Labour Union*, later the *Palladium of
Labour*. In 1902 the T.L.C. banned the Knights of Labour from
affiliation.

When the late Samuel Gompers set about organizing Canada into his
federation of organized U.S. Trade and Labour unions, the later
American Federation of Labour (A.F.L.), strength of the trade union
movement in Hamilton made the city a key centre.

From the pioneers of the labour movement have come workmen's compensation, bargaining rights, and vacations with pay. Allan Studholme, M.P.P., 1906-19, and Hon. Walter R. Rollo, Minister of Labour in the Drury cabinet, 1919-23, were forerunners of such men as Sam Lawrence, John and George G. Halcrow, M.P.P., Hugh G. Sedgwick, and Hon. Humphrey Mitchell, M.P., 1931-35 federal Minister of Labour.

In honour of Allan Studholme, labour's "Grand Old Man," the Allan Studholme Memorial Labour Temple was built and opened on Catharine Street North in 1923, largely through the effort of the late Harry J. Halford, musician, alderman, controller and dean of the local labour movement. The cornerstone was cut by Sam Lawrence.

"Sam Lawrence," said James Stowe, president of the Hamilton and District Labour Council, upon whom McMaster University recently conferred an honorary doctorate, "was a lifelong friend and champion of workers. He honestly earned the title, 'Mr. Labour,' by which he will always be remembered." From 1922 until his retirement in 1956—except for four years spent as provincial C.C.F. member for Hamilton East—Sam Lawrence held civic office as alderman, controller, mayor, 1944-50, and again controller. He died in 1959. A son, Hamilton's Chief of Police Leonard George Lawrence, appointed in 1951, and a daughter, Mrs. Lloyd Priest, survived him.

The passing decades brought significant changes in the labour picture. In the 1930's the American C.I.O. moved into Hamilton and was responsible for the aggressive organization of the 1940's which brought into existence the United Steelworkers, Rubber Workers, Textile Workers, United Electrical Radio and Machine workers, and the Auto workers. These became affiliates of the Canadian Congress of Labour (C.C.L.).

On November 6th, 1941, the Hamilton Labour Council was officially formed. In June, 1956, it merged with the Hamilton and District Trades and Labour Council to form the present council, whose first officers were James Stowe, president, and Reginald Gisborn, M.P.P., vice-president.

Mayor Samuel Lawrence succeeded William Morrison in a mayoralty which had progressed from depression to war. Throughout this period and until 1948 city expansion ceased. Replacing normal residential growth, materials and manpower had gone into building camps for the armed forces; into vocational and industrial training schools set up to replace the skilled and semi-skilled workers constantly absorbed by the forces and industry; and into housing to accommodate these workers and their families. In the former Libby-Owens Glass works, southeast corner of Kenilworth Avenue and Beach Road, which was remodelled and equipped at a cost of $2,000,000, a wartime trade school was established, with housing for 2,000 men and 240 instructors near the plant.

In 1948, having served their original purpose, the Trade school buildings were sold privately and the wartime houses moved to provide speedy settlement in recently annexed areas, south of Main Street and west of Paradise Road (Dow and Cline Avenues), and on the Mountain east from Wellington and from Sherman to East 36th Street.

"On the Mountain," said F. J. Veale, B.Sc., city building commissioner, former Tiger player and coach, "they were interspersed among existing houses. There were two styles, one-storey and one-and-one-half storeys. You can still spot them."

For the 1946 inauguration, Mr. Lawrence invited as guests the city's six surviving ex-mayors, who dated back to Col. John I. McLaren, 1909-10, and in a brief flashback recalled events of each administration.

Expanding on Mayor Lawrence's theme, during two wars and an intervening depression, how had the city progressed?

In his term, Colonel McLaren had opened Burlington Street, a task made more difficult by the inlets gashing its length. Later those inlets would become dumps for city garbage. From Catharine Street where Eastwood Park, named after John M. Eastwood, editor of *The Daily Times*, is laid out on filled land, clear to the beach strip, the bay front today is largely man-made. From F. W. Fearman Company Limited, on Brant Street, successors to John Duff and Son, pork packers, and from the Canadian Westinghouse Company on Birch Avenue and Wentworth Street north to the bay, marshland was filled in with garbage. While the city built land with refuse, however, industry reclaimed land by pumping sand and silt from the bay, gaining fill together with deeper wharfage.

In 1909 the Hamilton Council of Knights of Columbus was formed, with Michael J. O'Reilly first Grand Knight. Four years later the Knights acquired Dr. D. G. Inksetter's handsome three-storey brick residence on Jackson Street West, which served as club headquarters until purchased by the corporation in 1958 as part of the site of the new City Hall. In 1959, new club rooms were opened on Queenston Road.

Dating also from this period, the Billiken Club in 1906 began its service to the Hamilton Health Association and Mountain Sanatorium initially in the battle against tuberculosis and later, following decline in incidence of this disease, in the wider hospital field assumed by the H.H.A. Fifty-five years later four of the original Billikens—Mesdames F. R. Martin, Gordon Powis, W. J. Watson and Miss Strathmore Findlay—were still members of the renamed Samaritan Club. Its activities now include the Samaritan luncheon bazaar (an annual social event of the city which nets some five thousand dollars a year); operation of the San Shop, marketing the work of the patients; and latterly organization of canteen services throughout the H.H.A. institutions.

The Hamilton Playground Association was also established during Mayor McLaren's term of office. It was formed largely through the efforts of Mrs. Frances Woolverton, wife of coroner Algernon Woolverton, M.D., assisted by the Local Council of Women and labour groups, to provide children with supervised play. Upon reorganization in 1931 as the Hamilton Playgrounds Commission, seventeen supervised playgrounds had been established throughout the city. In 1918, John J. Syme was appointed superintendent, commencing a term of devoted service which would last thirty-three years, winning him the title, "dean of Canadian

246

recreation." In his work with youth Mr. Syme also helped organize the local Boy Scouts, actively participated in the Y.M.C.A. Leaders' Training Institute, and during the depression years organized and administered a program of recreation for the unemployed, widely copied throughout Canada.

Enlisting with Mayor Chester S. Walters for war service had been another popular Hamiltonian—the turbine-engined *Turbinia*, which had joined the local fleet in 1904. Many a homesick letter during the war told of a Hamilton serviceman glimpsing the rolling old *Turbinia* running the enemy gauntlet in the English Channel. Prior to the war the local excursion steamers had changed hands several times, one owner being the Hamilton Steamboat Company, formed in 1889, with T. B. Griffith, president. In 1913, the *Macassa, Modjeska,* brought from the Clyde by Capt. Hugh Fairgrieve, *Turbinia* and *Corona* became the property of the newly amalgamated Canada Steamship lines. In 1927 the *Macassa* and *Modjeska* were sold, the *Macassa*, rebuilt and renamed the *Manasoo*, foundering in an epic gale in Georgian Bay a year later while carrying a load of cattle that shifted and broke her back.

No other Hamilton mayor ever gained more raised eyebrows, head-shakes, and laughter from ratepayers than Charles Goodenough Booker, 1917-20. Coupled with this, however, was a genuine affection, liking, and respect for him and his administration which led the same ratepayers to return "honest Charlie" four times at the polls. Warmhearted, jovial, unconventional, and completely democratic, Charlie Booker had that rare touch that made him a boon companion to the Prince of Wales, later Edward VIII. Upon landing on his second visit to Canada, one of the first questions H.R.H. asked of reporters was, "How is my good friend, Charlie Booker of Hamilton?"

At his first election, contested by Thomas S. Morris and W. H. Cooper, Booker was not even considered to be in the running. While a bitter mud-slinging campaign was waged, with temperance an issue and the papers taking sides with the two chief candidates, Booker went quietly about the city, shaking hands, smiling, and quoting apt bits of poetry.

"There was no radio in 1917," said Frank J. Keen, former city editor of *The Hamilton Spectator*. "Someone suggested flicking lights throughout the city to announce the result of the election—one flash, Cooper elected; two flashes, Morris. Then as an afterthought, 'If by any chance, Booker, then three flashes.'

"When the first flash came everyone held his breath. Then came the second flash and 'Morris is in!' they yelled. 'He's beaten Cooper!' Then came the third flash and the whole city was dumbfounded. They couldn't believe it!"

A tailor who should have known the niceties of dress, Mayor Booker did not hesitate to attend a formal function in morning coat, striped trousers, and tan shoes. He proved that he was quick-witted, however, during the Prince of Wales' visit to Hamilton in October, 1919. On

247

leaving City Hall for the official drive through the streets, the mayor, forgetful of protocol, preceded his royal guest into the open-topped motor car. Appreciating his error, he then opened the door on the far side, hastened around the car, and made a dignified entrance behind H.R.H.

Throughout the day, to the utter horror of Hamilton's elite, Booker was heard to address Edward as "Princey." That the Prince did not object seems proved by his exchanging watches with the mayor during the civic dinner that evening — a swap corrected the following morning by a tactful aide-de-camp.

The loss in 1918 of his son, Lt. Stewart C. Booker, on active service was a blow from which Hamilton's most colourful first magistrate never fully recovered.

"Thomas Jutten," said Mayor Sam, "reorganized city hall and modernized its administration during his 1923-24-25 term." Mayor Jutten was closely connected with the north end and its development, the North End Improvement Society being credited with his election as mayor. Opposite his boatbuilding establishment and his home, on the east side of Wellington, at the end of a long wooden bridge spanning marsh land, stood the Victoria Yacht Club, of which he was president.

"All the time he was mayor," said Charles Watson, superintendent of garbage collection in William Muirhead's department, "Jutten practically lived on the city dump, for we were filling in the east side of Wellington Street. Stench and rats and dump fires. The mayor could have moved out. He stayed and took it with the other northenders."

In Mayor Freeman F. Treleaven's mayoralty, 1926-27, an outstanding event was the celebration in June, 1927, of the Diamond Jubilee of Confederation. Highlights of the week were a colourful Confederation pageant; a Confederation dinner at which the speaker, Miss Charlotte Whitton of Ottawa, thrilled her hearers with her patriotic fervour; and the unveiling by Governor-General Viscount Willingdon of the fountain erected in Gage Park to the memory of Robert Russell and Hannah Jane Gage by their daughter, Eugenie Helen.[1] Prior to this event Lord and Lady Willingdon were greeted by 3,000 enthusiastic school children at Scott Park, the customary reviewing arena for visiting dignitaries, where King George VI and Queen Elizabeth would appear in 1939; Princess Elizabeth and the Duke of Edinburgh in 1951, and again, in 1957, as Queen Elizabeth and Prince Philip.

Since plans which go wrong are those most frequently recalled with enjoyment, the unveiling of the Gage fountain will be long remembered.

The day had been carefully planned. A platform held the vice-regal couple, civic officials, and local notables. To the south of the fountain, in a roped enclosure, sat several hundred guests admitted by ticket. About this static core, on the well groomed lawns and among the bright flower beds, the public crowded.

Following earlier events, C. V. Langs, parks board chairman, was to speak briefly, concluding with a request that Lady Willingdon receive

248

flowers to be presented by young Jane Treleaven, the mayor's daughter. His Excellency would then declare the fountain unveiled and simultaneously T. B. McQuesten would casually raise his handkerchief, at which signal an alerted attendant would turn on the fountain.

Unfortunately, well before Lord Willingdon's program participation, a guest on the platform took out his handkerchief and to general astonishment the fountain sprang into full play, just at a moment when the summer breeze gusted from the north, thoroughly spraying guests in the enclosure before the water could be shut off.

When the program resumed, Mr. Langs announced the presentation of flowers and Lady Willingdon graciously indicated her acceptance. An embarrassing pause ensued. There were no flowers. Laughing heartily, Lady Willingdon asked that Jane be presented to her. Later at tea in the clubhouse the errant bouquet arrived.

It would seem parks held considerable place in Mayor Treleaven's regime, for on June 10th, 1926, on a lovely spot overlooking the Dundas marsh and the later land-and-water sweep of the Royal Botanical Gardens,[2] Mrs. Treleaven had unveiled a bronze-tableted boulder to mark the site of the old military and cholera cemetery.

Until the 1960's the cemetery would remain undisturbed. With the building, however, of the $30,000,000 Highway 403, with its intricately engineered system of overpass, underpass and clover-leaf, approach and service roads, the cholera cemetery disappeared. When Interchange No. 3 bisected the Heights the bones of the dead were lifted, coffined, and reinterred with religious rites in the cholera section of Hamilton cemetery.

The combined regimes of Jutten and Treleaven were a time of beginnings and of endings. In 1924 the Bank of Hamilton, established primarily to cultivate a local field and now outgrown, amalgamated with the national Canadian Bank of Commerce . . . The Oliver Chilled Plow Works of Canada Limited sold its plant to International Harvester . . . All plots having been sold, the Anglican portion of Hamilton cemetery was conveyed to the city . . . The United Church of Canada was founded by the union of Methodist, Congregationalist and a majority of Presbyterian churches, an initial step towards the Anglican-United Church union proposed in 1965. . . .

The residence of George E. Tuckett, manufacturer of the popular Marguerite cigar, on the southwest corner of King and Queen Streets was reconstructed and converted into the Scottish Rite Cathedral, dedicated in May, 1923. . . . In the same month Governor-General Lord Byng of Vimy unveiled the Cenotaph erected in Gore Park extension by the Canadian Club of Hamilton to the memory of the war dead of the First World War.

In the mercantile field, the internationally famous Mills' china store was founded by Robert Mills and his son Herbert in 1924 . . . And three years later in the former Arcade premises on James Street North, A. Y.

Eaton officially opened the T. Eaton Company Limited, as an outlet in part of the Eaton Knitting Mill of Hamilton, operating on John Street North under Col. W. F. Eaton.

Even in a city partisan to sports, 1927 was an outstanding year. Through the efforts of Russell W. Frost, Alexander G. Muir and Seppi DuMoulin the Leander Boat Club was revived and moved into new quarters at the foot of John Street.[3]. In appreciation, on July 30th the Leander 150-pound eight (coxswain, George Cline, coach, Robert Hunter) won the eight at the Royal Canadian Henley Regatta. In 1931 Ernie Whelpton took the Dominion 140-pound singles crown at Henley, and then with Douglas Laurie won the doubles, ushering in a decade featuring Bob Pierce and other top Leander oarsmen.

At the regular May meeting of the Lions Club, formed in 1920, the champion track team of Central Collegiate Institute, headed by coach Capt. John Richard Cornelius,[4] and team captain, Johnny Fitzpatrick, sensational sprinter, were guests. The team this year, said Captain Cornelius, had cleaned up everything in high school competition both in Canada and the United States, with the help of M. M. (Bobby) Robinson, former sports editor and now assistant city editor of *The Hamilton Spectator*. Principal A. W. Morris of Central announced that the school's rifle team had again captured the Canadian Rifle League trophy.

In the same month Delta Collegiate riflemen, under instructor H. E. Parker, B.A., won the Ontario championship in the Dominion marksmen's competition with a score of 1,398 out of a possible 1,400. Victor Pickard set a new Canadian record in the pole vault. Russell T. Kelley's Hamilton Lacrosse team, formed in 1921 and future winner in 1933 of the Canadian championship Mann Cup, was drawing enthusiastic crowds to watch the game's "wild contests of the gutted sticks." Hamilton's round-the-bay road race, revived by the Hamilton Olympic Club in 1926, was selected by the Canadian Olympic committee as the official Canadian marathon trial, to be run September 17th, 1927. One of track and field's most faithful supporters, Albert Victor (A. V.) Smith, life member of the Hamilton Construction Association, an early bike racer and runner, began forty years of service to the club, officiating in every possible capacity.

While 1927 was not outstanding in senior rugby in the city, in both 1928 and 1929 the Tigers, captained by Francis R. (Pep) Leadley, fantastic drop kicker, captured the coveted Grey Cup from the Regina Rough Riders. Among Bengal greats of that period were Harry Batstone, punter "Huck" Welch, Frank McKelvey, Ken Walker, kicker Bert Gibb, snapback Ernie Cox, ball carriers Frank Turville and Jimmy Simpson, towering Dave Sprague, a devastating runner, and Brian Timmis, "The Old Man of the Mountain," believed by some to be the greatest player in Canadian football.

When the 1920's passed they took with them some of the city's foremost citizens: scholarly William P. Witton; Dr. Walter G. Thompson, dentist and all-round sportsman; Matthew (Matt) Hayes, the 400-pound proprietor of the International Hotel, James Street and Barton, international bookmaker, known in New York as the "Diamond Jim Brady of Canada," philanthropist, gourmet and gambler; F. F. Macpherson, B.A., principal of the Hamilton Normal School, who introduced the League of Nations Association to Hamilton and became first local president.

And finally, in his one hundredth year, Hamilton's "Grand Old Man," Adam Brown, whose survivors included his sons, William Evatt, father of William Arthur Brown, one of America's foremost magazine illustrators; Sir George McLaren Brown, European general manager of the C.P.R.; and his daughter, Mrs. William Hendrie of Gateside House, who in latter years has replaced her father in her multiple services to the community.

Holding office in the depression years of 1930-33, John Peebles was responsible for an intensive program of government-assisted "make work" projects.

To Mayor Peebles' term must be credited two outstanding events in city railroad history. On May 31st, 1931, the Canadian National railway, successor to the Grand Trunk, abandoned the nineteenth century station on Stuart Street, with its typical stiff flowerbeds and white stoned "HAMILTON," and built a modern station east of James Street.

In the same year, to eliminate existing street level crossings, the T.H. and B. railway undertook a grade-separation plan which included building the James Street subway. In December the first train crossed the subway. Two years later the modern T.H. and B. station of Queenston stone was completed, its stark architectural design initially inciting derisive protest.

Facilities of the new terminal were shared by the C.P.R. which in 1897 had acquired a right-of-way on the T.H. and B. line from Toronto to Buffalo. At that time the C.P.R. had proposed coming into the city with a common right-of-way for all rail lines and a union station on Cannon Street, east of John. Waiving any money payment by the city, C.P.R. president W. C. Van Horne had asked only a free right-of-way and station grounds. When his offer was rejected by council in favour of another route, the C.P.R. made terms with the T.H. and B. and the city lost union line and station.

"When William Morrison, 1936-43, came to office," said Mayor Lawrence, "the treasury was all but bankrupt, city debt high, tax collections low. Because of the depression, services, salaries, and wages were reduced. All of these items Mayor Morrison saw restored, while at the same time the rate of interest on loans was reduced to the lowest in city history."

By 1948, Hamilton's population had begun the postwar climb which has continued to the present. From 1930 to 1940, population increased from 143,129 to 154,915, an average growth of a mere 1,000 a year. By 1948 it had reached 179,995, increasing the average annual gain to some 2,800. Between 1948 and 1949, however, city population mounted

251

to 189,921, a gain for one year of almost 10,000, the result of annexation in Saltfleet, postwar European immigration—further reducing the earlier high Anglo-Saxon percentage in the city's labour force—and the first crop of postwar babies. In 1951-52 the city added almost another 10,000 to its population and in 1956-57 over 10,000 (225,638-236,531), annexations in Barton contributing to these jumps. Otherwise it has averaged a yearly increase of 5,500 to reach in 1966 a population of 283,099 for Hamilton proper and 395,189 for greater Hamilton.

Probably the most significant event in Mayor Sam Lawrence's term of office was the unique and costly steel strike of 1946, which with concurrent strikes in Canadian Westinghouse and Firestone laid off two out of every eleven workers in the city.

Commencing July 15th and lasting eleven weeks, the Steel Company strike was noted for its high feeling, bitterness, and violence. Following federal action instituted by Labour Minister Humphrey Mitchell, aimed at keeping the steel plant in operation, non-striking workers were permanently quartered in the plant, with supplies, shipped in by water, running the gauntlet of picket boats.

The strike belonged to the reconversion period of price and wage control following the war. While its causes were diverse and intricate, and laid according to personal sympathies at the door of labour, management, the federal government, Labour Minister Mitchell, Chairman Donald Gordon of the Wartime Prices and Trade Board, or the Steelworkers' union (C.C.L.-C.I.O.), the immediate cause was a $5-a-ton increase in the price of steel allowed by Mr. Gordon to the steel companies and not shared with the workers.

At strike's end, Stelco workers accepted thirteen cents an hour increase, with ten cents retroactive to April 1st, plus vacation benefits, instead of the ten-cent increase offered prior to the strike by the company. In wages, strikers and community had lost $1,500,000; the company, in extra wages, free board, free cigarettes and supplies, $3,750,000; and other local industries and trades in sympathy strikes, lay-offs and lost production, an incalculable amount.

Since Stelco is a family plant the strike featured the bitterness of civil war, with families divided and neighbour battling neighbour. Behind, it left a trail of court cases covering intimidation, assault, destruction of property, and arson. Two local personalities emerged from it: Mayor Sam Lawrence, advocate of labour: "Because I was a union man before I became mayor, and I shall be a union man when I am no longer mayor"; and slight, attractive Controller Nora Frances Henderson,[5] advocate of the rights of citizens in general, upon whose motion a special meeting of city council was called on August 8th to consider requesting provincial police aid in obtaining passage for Stelco workers in and out of the besieged plant and following which police were summoned to protect council members from mobbing.

"I am not a stooge of management," denied Nora Henderson. "I have never welched on labour. I have always been a consistent friend of the little man and little woman. What I am stressing is that the fundamental liberties of a citizen are being denied to a very large number of our citizens in this community."

"The *Review*," says *The Hamilton Review* of August 16th, "proposes to go on record as stating that Nora Frances has more guts than anyone we have seen at City Hall for a long time. The Editor of the *Review* would not have walked down the front steps of City Hall after Thursday's council meeting. Nora did."

Further comment from the *Review* came long after the five hundred provincial and mounted police asked for by Chief Joseph R. Crocker on August 23rd had come and gone; after H. G. Hilton, Stelco president, had mailed surprise ballots to all employees for a vote on return to work; and after Nora Frances Henderson had resigned in 1947 from the municipal field she had graced for sixteen years to become executive secretary of the Ontario Association of Children's Aid Societies until her premature death on March 23rd, 1949.

"As a devout socialist," said an editorial of December 23rd, 1949, "Mayor Lawrence brought his conscious participation in the class struggle into a field of public affairs where it did not belong, and by so doing failed many times to stand forthright and impartial as representative of all sections of the community."

Labour Leader James Stowe does not agree. "There is no doubt," he says, referring to the strike, "that Sam Lawrence's action at that time averted what could have been a very serious situation. He showed his greatest power at that time."

To Sam Lawrence's era belongs one of Hamilton's perennial mysteries: the disappearance of Rocco Perri, international bootlegger, now suspected of having been involved in narcotics, bank robberies and murder. A penniless Italian immigrant who had entered Canada from the United States in 1903, Perri and Bessie Starkman (wife of a Toronto bakery driver) had risen from extreme poverty to bank accounts in the Twenties in Bessie's name exceeding $500,000. Customers to whom Perri admitted selling as many as 1,000 cases of 60-proof whiskey a day (at a profit of some $40 a case) ranged from Mickey MacDonald, Canada's public enemy No. 1, to cabinet ministers and wealthy socialites.

Perri maintained a legal front. While Canadian and United States residents were forbidden to drink liquor, Ontario breweries could manufacture it for export. Perri arranged legal shipments to Cuba and Puerto Rico, then diverted them to lonely stretches of shoreline. The garden of the seventeen-room mansion the Perris bought at 166 Bay Street South was said to be honeycombed with a system of underground storage tanks. Nor was he alone. The hasty departure from the bay of the high-powered craft of a well known Hamilton boat builder was always wisecracked as meaning the latter was on his way to pick up a shipment. Rocco became a philanthropist, giving freely to Protestant, Roman Catholic and Jewish charities. He subscribed $30,000 to the "drys" to fight a liquor plebiscite, money well spent, since their successful campaign saved his business.

In 1930 Bessie Perri was shot in the garage of the Bay Street house as she returned home from an evening out with her husband, a murder possibly arranged to remove Bessie's reputed stranglehold on Perri profits. Her funeral to the Ohev Zedek cemetery on the Caledonia Road was the most flamboyant Hamilton had ever witnessed. Spectators by the thousands lined the route to glimpse the fifteen cars of flowers that followed the hearse bearing the $3,000 silver trimmed casket, with Perri as chief mourner in a limousine with safely drawn blinds. Pickpockets, already in the city for the British Empire games, enjoyed a field day.

Following two apparent attempts to eliminate him in 1938, by bombing his home and car, Rocco was interned as an enemy alien from 1940-43. On Sunday, April 23rd, 1944, while visiting a cousin in Hamilton he complained of a headache, took two aspirins and a cup of coffee and went out for a walk. He was never seen again. The theory is that Perri —like the missing revolver that killed Ethel Kinrade—lies in a cement shroud at the bottom of Hamilton's convenient bay.

Perri belonged to the passing era of local gangsterdom. Already across the pages of the press the more vicious shadow of the bigtime international mobs was falling. Canadian police deny that the American underground reaches across the border. Yet in Hamilton alone, eight out of thirty-two unsolved slayings since 1947 follow gangland patterns.

25

The Jacksonian Era

MAYOR LLOYD DOUGLAS JACKSON, B.A., 1950-62, was elected to office in 1950 by a heavy vote and overwhelming majority. In his first and later inaugural addresses he promised a new administration "without ideological or political bias and without influence by any vested interests or pressure groups capable of delivering bundles of votes for pre-election pledges."

The operation of the city was a business, stated the tall, broad-shouldered dignified owner of a baking industry employing some six hundred persons. It would be conducted with dignity and decorum, and operated by the people's elected representatives in the interests of the citizens as a whole.

Furthermore, discarding the smalltime policy of sidestepping major expenditures by "alleviating, stalling, postponing, and thus cramping the growth of the city," the new mayor aggressively called for adequate expenditure for necessary facilities and for early consideration of a five, ten or even fifteen-year program aimed at developing a big, fast growing city to its highest potential.

By 1950 city annexation had moved only one concession, slightly over one-half mile, south of the Mountain brow, while the city below the escarpment had expanded five miles, or ten times the Mountain gain. Yet because of the restricted nature of the plain, the city's expansion east and west netted the community an actual increase in size of only 11,000 acres in over a century—from 3,050 acres assessed in 1846 when incorporation as a city occurred, to 14,057 acres in 1950.

With 1950, however, the stagnation resulting from the Second World War and its aftermath, and the cautiousness towards capital expenditure of the Lawrence regime was ended. In the decade following 1950 the swelling population wave in the city proper broke the southern barrier, swept up over the top of the escarpment and started towards Lake Erie its southward roll of multi-coloured rooftops and business blocks. By 1961 it had covered 3.33 miles. From 7,600 in 1943 the mountain population

255

grew to 77,300 by 1963, well over one-quarter of the city's total 269,500.

In the city below the Mountain, this new lusty cuesta growth was paralleled by thrusting suburbs to east and west: street upon street, survey on survey of smart compact functional homes, sky-climbing tinted concrete apartment houses, abstractly designed churches, and new steel-boned, fire-resistant schools, bright with acres of fibreglass and rainbow plastics.

By the end of the first year of the Jackson administration, the pattern had been established: capital improvements in works and sewers, including work on the giant Fennell Avenue trunk sewer on the mountain; extended and improved services in these fields and in the department of streets and roads into outlying and annexed areas; widespread reorganization in civic management, including establishment of a property maintenance department; and a beginning on a long term solution of mountain access roads.

In addition, since the regime of the music- and garden-loving mayor would be noted for encouragement of recreational and cultural aspects of the city, the year saw the building and opening of Eastwood swimming pool, a venture so successful that three new pools, Inch, Coronation and Parkdale, complete with buildings and artificial ice, were opened in 1953, Eastwood at this time also expanding to include artificial ice. In the same year travelling playlots, which could be set up in any suitable spot, were undertaken to serve fringe areas of the city.

During his thirteen years in office, longest in city history to date, the mayor also encouraged and promoted industrial expansion; low rental public housing, as exemplified in east end Roxborough Park and Mohawk Gardens on the Mountain; an attack on the city's growing traffic problems; recognition of downtown degeneration and beginning of urban redevelopment; joint use of schools for related purposes; and a program of beautification sparked by a 1953 visit to England.

In buildings his era produced Hamilton's new City Hall, County Court House, Art Gallery, Macassa Lodge for elderly people; a much needed sewage treatment plant; and the market ramp garage. He instigated the restoration of Dundurn Castle by Professor Anthony Adamson of the University of Toronto, which became the city's Canadian Centenary project.

In his City Hall column in the *Spectator*, Tom F. Mills wrote: "Mayor Jackson came to typify the abandonment of parochial politics in favour of big city vision. He revamped City Hall departments and fire and police departments as well. His Worship did not do this all alone—the names of Warrender, Fairclough, Parker, MacDonald and others come to mind—but his was the hand at the wheel.

". . . More than ever before Mr. Jackson persuaded able men and women to serve on civic boards and committees . . . On the social scene the Mayor, frequently with Mrs. Jackson, represented the city at ceremonial functions with an enviable ease and dignity."

256

Undoubtedly an important factor in the success of Mayor Jackson's administration was the council which accompanied him into office, predominantly youthful, yet with enough longterm members to provide ballast—as the late Aldermen Hugh F. Brown, Q.C., and Frank G. Dillon, and Controller S. Leslie Parker, still in office.

Outstanding in promise was young and personable Alderman John A. MacDonald, whose civic career carried him in three years into the board of control and to head the polls. It was a misfortune of the present municipal elective system that in twice ill-advisedly contending for the mayoralty, Controller MacDonald should be lost to the civic scene.

It was MacDonald who headed the enquiry into management of the works department which resulted in the W. S. Darling and Associates' report advocating a division in responsibility and reduction of the fifteen sections in the works department, then all answering to the city engineer, W. L. McFaul.

Emphasizing postwar expansion of the city, the Darling report paid tribute to McFaul as one of the most competent municipal engineers in Canada, then concluded, "Despite this, the department has grown too large for a one-man operation," and advised separation of a new department of streets and sanitation from engineering.

In the ensuing reorganization of the works department to eight sections, replacement of outmoded and dilapidated buildings and equipment, and programming of the new division, "Alderman Jack MacDonald," said Tom Mills, "in the role of young Dr. Kildare, was chief surgeon."

From the setting up in 1952 of the department of streets and sanitation under Frederick H. Ferris, stems the city's modern garbage collection system; the street cleaning system with alternating and restricted street parking; and today's vastly improved trimming, care and replacement program for the city's thirty thousand trees, developed by city arborist Gordon A. McNair and his successor, Harry Rumble, under William Muirhead, commissioner of streets and sanitation, who shortly succeeded Ferris. To the new department too was given snow removal and sanding, and minor sidewalk and road repairs.

Even without these sections, city engineering faced a gargantuan task in installing the sewers, water mains and roads necessary to convert annexed areas from open fields to built-up subdivisions. By 1950, city limits had reached Fennell Avenue on the Mountain, Rifle Range Lane to the west, and Red Hill Creek valley on the east, in the latter case absorbing the Bartonville area south of Main Street and east of Kenilworth Avenue. By 1955, the city's southern thrust had reached Mohawk Road, with a western Mountain movement carrying city limits to the township line between Barton and Ancaster by 1958.

"On the Mountain," says Waldo W. Wheten, B.Sc., appointed as successor to Mr. McFaul in 1959, "water is the problem. It requires extra power to pump water up. There is no problem with sewage. Sewage flows by gravity."

Beginning with the great tunnel sewer in 1951, running east on Fennell Avenue from James Street, with lateral sanitary sewers constructed from this trunk, the city spent thirty million dollars in little over a decade extending sewers into new areas. At Red Hill Ravine the Fennell Street sewer drops into a ninety-foot shaft, emerging at Greenhill Avenue, the continuation of Fennell below the Mountain. Here the dry weather flow enters city sewers, while overflow and storm water is carried off by Red Hill Creek, to the detriment of that once lovely watercourse.

Leading to the rapid development of the western Mountain a heavy sewer program was completed in 1958 in that area, with drainage into the Fennell Street trunk.

Below the mountain, old sewer systems also demanded attention. To the west of Burlington Heights so heavy was pollution of West Hamilton Creek, emptying into Cootes' Paradise, from raw sewage discharged in time of storm, that the Ontario Water Resources Commission registered increasing concern. The culprit was the obsolescent pumping station at Royal Avenue and Stroud Road, with an assist from the Valley Street pumping station at the rear of the Basilica of Christ the King, which lifted its sanitary flow of western sewers up the ridge, beneath Victoria Park to King Street and along King to James and the city's old brick sewer system.

In the east end a main trunk sanitary sewer ran north on Gage Avenue to a pumping station below bay level, which connected with the city's first sewage treatment plant at the corner of Hillyard and Munroe. In 1928 a large interceptor sewer, connected to the Wentworth Street plant, was built westward along Burlington Street from Gage to Ferguson Avenue, picking up sewers along the way. When a second sewage disposal plant was built at Depew Street in 1931 on later Stelco property, sewage was pumped to this plant through a force main.

The city's first incinerator was also erected on the Depew site, it being determined at this time to concentrate the city's garbage and sewage facilities in one area. When sale of the property for Stelco expansion made this impossible, the ten-million-dollar Woodward Avenue sewage treatment plant was built and opened in 1962.

The Woodward plant is primary treatment type, reducing pollution from sewage by about fifty per cent. Ultimately, to satisfy tightening anti-pollution legislation, it will be expanded to give full treatment (85-95 per cent) at additional expenditure of over ten million dollars.

The plant is the key to the city's growth, for where sewers go, settlement and industry follow. Today over five hundred miles of city-owned sewers honeycomb Hamilton's sub-basement, with countless additional miles of private sewers connecting homes and businesses to the public system. First to connect with the new plant, the western (west of the plant) interceptor trunk sewer ran east along Burlington Street from Gage Avenue to Parkdale and by Glow Avenue to its destination—a two-mile giant tunnel, eight feet across, dug out of th depths of the earth sixty feet below the homes it services.

258

To open desperately needed Saltfleet industrial sites, the eastern (east of the plant) interceptor trunk followed—from the Woodward plant east along Brampton Street and a right-of-way along the southern side of the Queen Elizabeth Way to the city limits on the east side of Gray's Road, county line between Barton and Saltfleet. For this excavation two huge boring machines were used to corkscrew the giant tube through the earth at such a depth, because of seepage and soil conditions beneath Augustus Jones' Stoney Creek pond, that engineers adopted the compression chamber system, with an air lock separating the shaft from the tunnel, and workmen entering a decompression chamber before surfacing, to avoid the deep sea diver's dreaded hazard of "the bends."

Today beneath the city, westerly from Gage Avenue, an extension to the western interceptor trunk is boring its way along Burlington Street to the distant Valley Street pumping station. "When completed," said R. C. Monaghan, deputy city engineer, "this sewer will provide an outlet for all sewage reaching the Valley Street pumping station which will then be closed, and will also provide an outlet for almost all sanitary sewage flow west of Gage Avenue."

As several districts in this area discharge raw sewage directly into Hamilton Harbour, the importance of the sewer program becomes evident. Already the West Hamilton Creek trunk sanitary sewer, constructed for the city by the provincial department of highways in conjunction with the Chedoke Expressway, has resulted in closing the pollution-breeding Royal Avenue pumping station.

In Hamilton's immediate future lies a new sewerage system for central Hamilton where the city's old brick sewers are becoming increasingly inadequate under the high rise apartment boom in the city's core and on its perimeter, and in view of north end redevelopment under urban renewal; and sewers to service Lake Avenue, Saltfleet and even more remote areas. Eventually a second east-west trunk just north of Highway 53 will allow for Mountain expansion southward.

In North America the well-being of the twenty-first century will depend considerably on the beginning battle of the twentieth against pollution of air and water, the latter by sewage, detergents, fallout and industrial waste, and by foreign shipping.

Today local plants at considerable expense are seeking programs designed to lessen pollution, both of air and water. Pollution from shipping is a factor about which less can be done, however, under present legislation.

Polluted or not, the bay is big business. During the 1950's alone the Hamilton Harbour Commission and Hamilton industry spent more than thirty million dollars expanding handling wharves and freight terminals in preparation for the increased cargo tonnage expected with the opening of the St. Lawrence Seaway in 1959.

As a result, annual reports of the St. Lawrence Seaway show that for the first three years of operation the port of Hamilton surpassed the tonnage of any other port in volume of Seaway cargo. In 1961 the port of Hamilton totalled 7,787,895 tons of cargo handled,[1] as compared with 5,079,433 tons for the port of Toronto.

At the foot of James Street, from its enclosed rooftop observation deck the five-storey Harbour Commission administration building commands the bay. Below, movement of vessels within the port is clearly visible, including the white-waked course of the powerful patrol boats of the marine police whose operation under Harbour Police Chief Howard Sager has saved many lives. Visible too the activity of the Catharine and Wellington Street docks and their marine freight terminals, their cavernous interiors filled with cargoes of foreign ports—French wine and Italian cheese, rubber from Singapore, plasterboard from London, Egyptian cotton, crockery and soya beans.

Package freight, this, valuable and romantic, hailing from ports such as Jaffa, Lisbon, Naples, Yokahoma or Bombay, but comparatively small in tonnage in proportion to the bulk cargo—coal, ore, oil and grain—handled by the port.

On the city's waterfront the future is measured not up but down, in multi-million-dollar dredging and filling operations to convert water lots to land, to advance the harbour headline, and provide more mooring space, more wharfage, more warehousing, more roads and rails and straddling cranes—more of everything, in fact, needed to move tonnage in and out of a deep sea port.

Two developments enhancing the efficiency and speed of operations at Hamilton have been the building of the Burlington Skyway bridge, completed in 1958, which clears the harbour entrance at standard Seaway height of 120 feet, and the federal vertical lift bridge, which carries rail and local vehicular traffic, replacing the old bascule and swing bridges.

Port navigation is controlled by both signal lights and radio telephone, the former adding their metronomic flash to the jewelled circle that nightly rings the harbour from the Skyway's lovely arc to glowing Burlington, backdropped by the lighted city and the Mountain trailed with gold.

The Seaway has brought changes to the fourth largest port of Canada. E. D. Hickey, chairman, Hamilton Harbour Commissioners, enlarged on this: "During most of the first half century, from 1912 on, development of the port of Hamilton was oriented to providing harbour facilities for movement of raw materials by water to meet the ever-increasing demands of the vast industrial complex rising along its harbour front.

"With the advent of the St. Lawrence Seaway, however, it became necessary to broaden the function and services of the port to take advantage of the new waterway as a giant conveyor belt, not only bringing bulk materials to its industries but also distributing products of southern Ontario to world markets, in return for a variety of imports."

The pleasant balding man behind the desk paused thoughtfully. "How Canada's world trade will affect future development of the port depends upon many economic factors, including mode of travel and transportation of tomorrow's world. Present trends suggest that the port will become an increasingly important seaport gateway through which an ever-growing volume of exports and imports will be shipped.

"Although the port of Hamilton," said Mr. Hickey, "is adaptable to major changes within the foreseeable future, these are not presently anticipated. Currently the Centennial Docks terminals constitute the final project in the port's 'Seaway Mile', a complex of general cargo and bulk storage wharves, stretching from James Street to Hillyard Street. East from Hillyard to Strathearne Avenue extends the port area of greatest industrial activity, surrounding the steelmaking companies.

"Expansion of this industrial complex will undoubtedly occur along the east, the Burlington Beach side of the harbour and its southern approach, where water lots have been already reclaimed and filled in by the Harbour Commission and industry.

"North of the harbour entrance, where shore lands now lie in the town of Burlington, the first of a series of wharves has been constructed which will accommodate the growing industrial needs of Burlington, Oakville and other communities to the north."

The commissioner walked to the wide window and looked down at the port. "For industry and commerce requiring rail development," he said, "the west end of the harbour, between Simcoe Street and the old Desjardins canal entrance, is in line for early development. A major program of wharf construction will ultimately develop in this area."

His eyes circled the bay, dotted with white sails. "Within the harbour boundaries the potential for further development is still far from fulfilment. Let us say that the total future development of the port is as expansive as the demands of our economy and the future of the vast southern Ontario community the port serves."

Mr. Hickey's forecast will have an ominous ring for conservationists who view the port of Hamilton's encroachment on the bay as a disaster; for owners of choice north shore residential properties; and for Director Leslie Laking, and other R.B.G. officials, hard pressed by McMaster expansion into Gardens property, and by appropriation of T. B. McQuesten holdings for provincial expressways.

Much more directly affected is Mr. Wheten's engineering department, whose city water supply comes from Lake Ontario immediately east of the developing beach strip, and who must service a vigorous port with sewers, waterworks and roads.

When Hamilton began its second hundred years as a city in 1947, its waterworks system was capable of pumping an average daily 30 million gallons, with a maximum of 35 million. With the postwar boom already in evidence, and the high lift pumping equipment showing signs of age, council approved a new high lift pumping station capable of producing ninety million gallons a day as extension to the low lift pumping station at the Beach plant; additional feeder water mains; a new 33-

million gallon reinforced concrete, covered reservoir[2] immediately east of the Barton reservoir; and new pumps and switching gear at the Ferguson Avenue pumping station.

To service the Bartonville area east of Kenilworth a booster pumping station and towering elevated tank, with 100,000-gallon capacity, had been erected earlier. Now an elevated water tank of 1,250,000 gallons, together with connecting mains, was installed on Fennell Avenue beside the 750,000-gallon tank in use since 1945.

To permit coordination with the Ontario Hydro frequency standardization program in southern Ontario, City Engineer McFaul delayed installations at the Ferguson Avenue pumping station until 1955 when a 33 million gallon per day pump was placed in the Beach low-lift pumping station. The program was then completed, obsolete pumps removed and others converted. In 1959, to keep pace, the filtration plant increased daily capacity from forty to eighty million gallons.

Possibly the city's available water supply will never meet the demands placed upon it. In 1960 annexations in Barton, Ancaster, Saltfleet and Glanford townships added eighty-three hundred acres to Hamilton and pushed the city's southern boundary from Mohawk Road to well south of Highway 53. By 1963 Mountain water shortages, varying according to locality from restrictions on lawn watering and car washing to compulsory use of boiled well water, and water purchased by the so-called "bucket brigade" from circulating trucks, raised a storm of complaints. Simultaneously heavy industrial expansion began to push the Burlington Street main beyond its capacity.

Nor was Mountain shortage to be overcome simply by building water mains, difficult as that might be. To lay water mains in areas not serviced by sanitary sewers was courting danger of infection, warned M.H.O. L. A. Clark, M.D.,[3] while the "watchdog of the treasury", Controller S. Leslie Parker, speaking from twenty years' experience as city alderman and controller, termed such action "playing with dynamite."

When a new waterworks program was undertaken, its three phases were planned to accommodate Hamilton's expansion for the next twenty years and serve a community of 600,000 people, providing a minimum of 200 gallons per person per day.

"We have already in operation," said Hamilton's dark haired, square-set and affable chief engineer, "a new low lift pumping station at Lakeland Beach capable of pumping 175 million gallons a day. Under construction is a 25-million-gallon underground reservoir on the Mountain plus a feeder main. By new techniques, using new chemicals and micro strainers, we hope to increase production of the filtration plant without extending buildings. And we are designing a new steel and concrete intake, eight feet in diameter, to extend 3,100 feet into Lake Ontario, with 5,000 feet extension possible. In twenty years we expect to have a pumping station good for 350 million gallons a day.

"To service industry along Burlington Street a new main will be laid, probably in conjunction with the widening of the street, which is one of our top priorities. Today half the water pumped in the city goes to industry."

Throughout the city new buildings as avant-garde as the future water intake were replacing the old. The original Y.M.C.A. built in 1889 — the first Y.M.C.A. building in Canada — whose indoor swimming pool was criticized as being too secular for a Christian institution, was torn down in 1958 and replaced by a modern building which emphasizes in its facilities the importance of health of body for health of mind, and stresses the value of leadership training of youth. At this time the Mount Hamilton joint Y.M.C.A.-Y.W.C.A. was opened, under a new post-war policy which permits women and girls to participate in certain Y.M.C.A. programs.

Taking a similar step, the Y.W.C.A. raised funds under campaign chairman Hon. Ellen Fairclough to replace its antiquated structure with a new up-to-date building on the southeast corner of Jackson Street and MacNab. In line with the growing policy of joint use of facilities, the city contributed $250,000 for a swimming pool providing some public use of the pool be allowed. Since 1940 Miss Margaret Heilig has served as executive director.

In 1959 the Canadian National Institute for the Blind transferred from its outgrown Gyro-sponsored Eastwood home on Main Street East to new Edgewood Hall on Main West.

Erected in 1949, the Jewish Community Centre on Delaware Avenue has developed a full non-sectarian program of youth activities for all ages and makes its attractive rooms available to philanthropic and civic groups without charge. In the decade following opening of the Centre, three handsome houses of worship were erected by the congregations of Anshe Sholom, Beth Jacob and Anshe Sfard.

On the other hand Dale Community Centre, first of its kind in the city, occupying James Jolley's square stone house on the Mountain, ceased to function as a centre in 1951, and in 1964 was sold to make way for building. Dale Centre dated from 1936 and was a joint project of the Family Service Bureau and the unemployed, designed to provide non-sectarian social, educational and craft opportunities during the depression. Stemming from the same period and also inspired by Miss Jean McTaggart, executive-secretary, and members of the Family Service Bureau, were the twelve Amity (friendship) Clubs operating in city churches for men, forerunner of today's Amity Rehabilitation Centre of Hamilton.

Retired also, with some ceremony, on June 10th, 1960, was Old Flo, last milk wagon horse on city streets, gone with the dripping ice truck tailed by eager children scrambling for frosty splinters.

Required instead by the motor car age is a new four-storey million-dollar market parking ramp for city motorist and farmer producer. Occupying the northern section of the market the ramp, opened on November 5th, 1960, is geared to efficiency with elevators, waiting room, automatic ticket dispensers and an electronic instrument panel that does everything but park the car. An increasingly important city body is the three-member parking authority composed of R. K. Fraser, H. H. Leather, and James Stowe.

Equally modern is the fourth Wentworth County Court House on Prince's Square. Excellently designed, the dignified structure is a happy combination of cut stone, walled glass and frescoes. At the opening ceremonies, on June 18th, 1958, guest of honour was the late Mrs. John G. Farmer,[4] daughter of Canon George A. Bull, who as a child of seven had attended the opening of the third Court House with her uncle, Senator Harcourt Bull.

Four years after the new Court House opened, William K. Warrender resigned from the provincial cabinet to accept the newly-created post of roving judge for the County and District courts of Ontario, with chambers in the Court House. Following eight years on city council and board of control, interrupted by three years' war service with the R.C.A.F., Mr. Warrender was elected member for Hamilton Centre in 1951. Appointed minister of planning and development, he later held other cabinet posts.

In 1953 the Canadian Bank of Commerce (now Imperial) modernized its main branch at King and James. At one time Sir Allan MacNab property, the land featured in 1921 in one of the biggest realty transactions in Hamilton to that date when the Bank of Hamilton increased its corner holding by purchasing the remaining MacNab property from the estate of the late Dowager Countess of Albemarle (Sir Allan's daughter, Sophia) for $175,000.

There were other new buildings. At the end of May, 1956, residents of Macassa Lodge were moved to a new up-to-date functional home on Upper Sherman Avenue, and the old Lodge razed. After years of controversy the site was sold to a developer in 1966 for urban renewal's first large private project, a luxury high-rise apartment complex. Nearby, to be completed in 1967, the city's first "new idea" pensioners' apartment complex will feature twin high towers containing 146 government-subsidized apartments for low-income pensioners.

As the city increased in size and population, following World War II, the incidence of crime steadily mounted. As vehicle traffic increased, traffic violations multiplied. In 1950 and 1951, to meet changing conditions, 146 new police officers were recruited, bringing the force under Chief Leonard Lawrence to 356 by 1952.

To provide the enlarged force with badly needed accommodation and to serve the eastern portion of the city, a composite building was erected on Kenilworth Avenue, housing police station and fire and health departments. Three years later, in 1955, the Mountain Police station, a one-floor completely modern structure, was built on Wellington Street South.

Updating methods also, a stepped-up program of instruction and training was instituted, and an identification laboratory under specially trained personnel was installed, its equipment including cameras, darkrooms,

264

fingerprinting apparatus, firearm identification devices, and moulding and etching tools. In 1957 breathalyzer equipment was added.

When three women police officers were enrolled in 1958, a longtime crusade of the Local Council of Women — which wished female police officers to attend women and children — proved successful. Later the number was increased to seven.

In the kindred civic field of fire protection, the post-World War II period of accelerated changes in industrial, commercial and domestic buildings resulted in new fire-fighting problems. To these problems the fire department of the 1950's was able to apply modern scientific approaches learned from the lessons of war.

The steam fire engine was still in use when Chief Alexander W. Aitchison, 1879-1905, introduced the first swinging harness and sliding pole in Canada; replaced the cumbersome hose reel with the combination chemical engine and hose wagon; reduced the force to paid members; and taught the importance of early arrival at a fire. When he died on duty the "Big Chief" was mourned by the fire department and city at large.

Chief Arthur B. TenEyck, 1905-22, introduced the city's first motor combination hose and chemical car in July, 1911, and relieved his force of 24-hour duty, except meal hours, by instituting 10-hour day and 14-hour night shifts, another first in Canada. The last fire horse retired to the farm in 1926, and the bright red motor trucks took over. Down through the years, new office buildings, new fire alarm headquarters, new fire alarm systems, new street alarm boxes were instituted, particularly under Chief Wallace T. James (1923-33).

A two-way radio transmitter was installed in Chief William Murdoch's car in 1942, operating on police radio frequency, and by 1958 all mobile firefighting apparatus was equipped with three-way radios, operated by the department's own transmitter.

Post-war developments instituted under Chief Edward Nixon, 1949-55, and Chief Reginald F. Swanborough, a youthful 48 when appointed in 1955, include a three-platoon shift system; an electronic speaker system linking all fire stations to relay fire alarms; a modern efficient training program; water fog application in firefighting; home fire inspection; and formation of an arson squad.

In 1950 the Hamilton Fire Prevention Bureau was established, six years after the disastrous Moose Hall inferno which ended a gay Royal Oak Dairy dance with 10 dead and 47 injured. In later years Chief Swanborough has introduced decentralization of fire stations by relocation, removal of street fire alarms, and amalgamation of firefighting services throughout Wentworth County.

Today Hamilton's 400-man force is one of the best in Canada. Its chief, a former president of the Canadian Association of Fire Chiefs, was elected president of the International Association in 1964.

In other civic departments besides fire and police, Mayor Jackson made his support felt. His mayoralty was noted for appreciation of the work of volunteers engaged on the city's seventeen community councils.

"The willingness of citizens," he said, "to serve on independent boards such as hospital, parks, library, housing, welfare and beautification, is the single most extraordinary phenomenon of community life on this continent. It is basic and the very fabric of our civic life."

From his travels, Mayor Jackson conceived the idea of the tea house in the Rock Garden, opened in July, 1962, during chairmanship of the late Judge William F. Schwenger. Designed by Alex German to fit the contour of the converted quarry, the two-storey balconied tea house is built of random limestone and wood, and gay with window boxes. Its upstairs glass-walled air-conditioned tea room derives character from slate floors, a fireplace and Pecky Cypress panelling.

In cutting the ribbon of the new building, in its setting of flower tapestries, foliage, and flowing water, the mayor used the same scissors with which C. V. Langs had cut the ribbon opening the High Level bridge in 1932, when the city's western entrance was still a dream.

From his travels the mayor also brought back ideas which led to the successful beautification of waste spaces and homeowners' properties. *Trillium* awards and plaques are presented annually for individual, group or street achievement.

"Every city," said the tall, strong featured, forceful man who represented Hamilton for thirteen years and travelled widely in the city's interest, "every city has a character and atmosphere distinctly its own. Wherever I go, and I *mean* wherever, from Victoria, B.C., to London, England, and beyond, I am always greeted with four questions.

"People come up beaming and shake hands and the first thing they say is, 'How's the old Hamilton Mountain? How's the market? That wonderful market!' And then, 'How about the rock garden? Still as lovely as ever?' And finally, 'The Tiger-Cats? What are they doing now?' "

The mayor settled his large frame more comfortably into the armchair behind his big uncluttered desk in the mayoralty suite of Hamilton's new City Hall, which he would grace for two years.

"Hamilton is frequently termed the 'Pittsburgh of Canada'," he observed, "and there is more to it than the mere extent of our industry."

He gazed past the tubbed philodendron, through the northern glass wall of the building, to crowded Main Street, stripped of the towering shade trees of a more casual era, and restricted to eastbound traffic under the city's progressive traffic program.

"Hamilton is changing from early days, becoming more cosmopolitan. The ethnic groups in the city are expanding rapidly. One finds different nationalities from the oldtime Irish, Scotch and English once so notable in Hamilton industry. The large percentage of Europeans that are, say, of Slavic origin is apparent today from the rolling mills of Stelco to McMaster's graduating class. Like Pittsburgh, we too are becoming a

266

melting pot. Races have intermarried here, resulting in a mixing of strains. Workers have a different appearance. It is obvious to any eye.

"These ethnic groups," concluded the mayor, "are an asset to the city. Their music, dancing, costumes and folklore add liveliness, colour and Old World charm to our more conservative culture."

No one who has attended the Germania Society's gay carnival of jesters and fools, where mirth and nonsense dull for a time the edge of life's daily fears; or inspected the tempting merchandise of the Netherlands Exhibition and Trade Fair at the Forum; thrilled to the excitement of Jaroslaw Klun's dancing and the choreography of his Ukrainian Chaika troupe with their untamed gipsy music, difficult 'squat-fling' or *prisjadka,* and powerful soaring leaps and bounds; or totalled the number of professional men and outstanding athletes given the city by the Italian colony, could doubt the value of all these to the community.

His Worship the Mayor, an indefatigable attendant at city functions, was probably recalling these events when he added thoughtfully, "The flavour of life in Hamilton is different from that of other cities, and this is because of our type of heavy industry and the workers that industry employs."

In 1959 the selling value of Hamilton's factory shipments totalled $1,114,137,000,[5] a production exceeded in Canada only by Montreal and Toronto.

In 1960, following opening of the St. Lawrence Seaway, capital investment in new plant, equipment and repair broke all previous records for the city and surpassed all previous marks established by any Canadian city for a similar twelve months.

"Hamilton's total capital and repair investment," said the Ontario Department of Economics, "in 1960 reached $179,200,000, a figure twenty-three per cent higher than in 1959, and more than seventy-five per cent above the level of 1958. This represents a postwar record.[6] Over the past fourteen years new capital investment and repair expenditures have increased more, both in absolute terms and proportionately, than in any of the other four Ontario metropolitan areas.

"Last year's increase," concludes the department, "is owing wholly to increased new investment, about forty-three per cent greater than 1959 and more than double 1958."

"As much wealth is generated in this city each year," said Milford L. Smith, business editor of *The Hamilton Spectator,* "as is produced by the four Atlantic provinces together."

Stelco's molten metal pouring in a fiery stream from a giant's cauldron to form an ingot fifteen tons in weight . . . copper strands like bright cobwebs at Greening Industries, spinning into screening on a flying shuttle . . . Canadian Liquid Air's pure oxygen . . . a looming waterwheel generator of 185,000 KVA dwarfing the Westinghouse workmen that fashion it . . . modern textiles from Hamilton Cottons . . . Lifesavers speeding in bright millions along an aseptic conveyor belt . . . giant 750-pound tires at Firestone, destined for the Canadian far north, curing in reeking vulcanizer . . . Bright's native *Mazeltov* and champagne: these are merely an indication of the wealth and variety of products that roll from Hamilton assembly lines.

In July, 1965, North America's top thirty-six steel companies sent their ace steelmakers to Hamilton to study methods developed by the Steel Company of Canada and Dofasco.

An acknowledged pacemaker in open hearth methods, Stelco has won and held the world record for output of a single furnace, its Big Inferno. Designed to produce five hundred tons of steel every eight hours, Big Inferno has consistently poured in excess of this and halved the time through use of oxygen.

"In 1963," said President V. W. Scully, "Stelco's ingot production reached 3,110,000 tons — the first time annual production of any Canadian steel producer had passed the 3,000,000 ingot ton mark — and sales came to nearly $371,000,000. In 1964 ingot production reached 3,500,000 tons. Stelco makes approximately forty per cent of all iron and steel produced in Canada and is among the largest Canadian producers of low alloy steels. The diversity of its overall operation enables it to contribute to practically every branch of Canadian industry."

At Hilton Works, Stelco's basic steel plant, visiting steelmakers studied the application of oxygen to open hearth methods and inspected the multi-million-dollar electrostatic precipitator equipment which reduces air pollution by trapping dust and gases from the fast-cooking furnaces.

At Dofasco, which pioneered in North America in 1954 in the use of the oxygen steelmaking furnace, replacing its open hearths and electric furnaces with the European process, the steelmen visited Dofasco's bay front plant, one of the heaviest industrial users of oxygen in Canada. To supplement its own production Dofasco has piped large quantities of oxygen from the plant of the Canadian Liquid Air Company Limited, on Burlington Street, and recently contracted with the company to build a 400-ton Oxyton near the Dofasco melt shop.

A fiery pot of steel nearly three storeys high, lined with brick, shaped like an old-fashioned bean pot and pivoted for loading and discharge, the basic oxygen furnace has transformed the future of steel and sounded the knell of the open hearth furnace — used as recently as 1961 for eighty-five per cent of United States' industrial output — just as the open hearth largely displaced the earlier convertor. A single two-furnace oxygen shop can replace twelve to sixteen open hearths.

Used in conjunction with another cost-reducing new step in steelmaking known as continuous casting, together with associated industrial technology, the oxygen furnace, according to some experts, can within five years reduce the cost of steel production twenty to twenty-five per cent, or $30 to $40 a ton.

In his term of office possibly no achievement gave His Worship Mayor

Jackson more satisfaction than erection of Hamilton's new City Hall, first proposed in 1940.

Of the four sites advanced — Central Collegiate grounds, the existing City Hall location, the old Macassa Lodge grounds, and a property bounded by Main Street and Hunter, Park and Bay — the Main Street site ultimately chosen was consistently favoured by Mayor Jackson. It provided a western anchor for the downtown business section, forming a nucleus of administrative buildings with the new federal building, erected on the northeast corner of Main Street and Caroline in 1954, and the Public Library. Only today is the wisdom of that choice fully apparent.

On December 12th, 1959, Mayor Jackson laid the cornerstone for the estimated $10,000,000 building with a silver trowel presented by the late Joseph M. Pigott, its contractor, whose father, Michael A. Pigott, founder of the Pigott Construction Company, had built the old City Hall. Architect of the new building was Stanley M. Roscoe.

Westward in the city the restoration and refurnishing of Dundurn Castle to the period of MacNab's occupancy was taking its initial step. Under the guidance of general consultant Prof. Anthony Adamson, historical architect Arthur Wallace, Mrs. Jeanne Minhinnick, consultant of furnishings, Mrs. Gwen Metcalfe, since 1955 Dundurn's capable and devoted curator known widely as "Lady MacNab," and William J. McCulloch, Hamilton's centennial chairman, the big Regency mansion with its Italianate towers and colonnaded Classical portico by 1967 would achieve the grace of Sir Allan's era.

"Today," said Bill Lyttle in *The Hamilon Spectator* of April 16, 1966, "plumbers, carpenters, electricians and masons saw, hammer, chisel, splash and drill with space age machinery in century-old cellars and halls.

"But out of the unearthly chaos they create, Dundurn will emerge with its former glory restored and its charm intact."

Responsibility for the $500,000 city project lies with a 16 member executive board which includes centennial chairman McCulloch, vice-chairman, T. W. D. Farmer, T. J. Newlands, Controller A. H. R. McCoy, Alderman Anne H. Jones and Dr. Freda Waldon.

As part of the restoration *The Hamilton Spectator* will sponsor conversion of Dundurn's former cockpit into a children's open-air theatre.

26

Victor Kennedy Copps

BUILT of white Cherokee marble, glass-walled to north and south, the eight-storey City Hall fronts on Main Street with semi-circular steps mounting to a marble-columned entrance which supports the projecting second floor council chamber.

On November 21st, 1960, to a fanfare of trumpets from the balcony of the council chamber, Governor-General Georges P. Vanier snipped the red ribbon that bound the glass wall of doors, and Hamilton's new civic administrative building became a reality.

The doors opened. Crossing the airy glass-walled lobby, the party ascended the central open staircase to the second floor, nerve centre of the building, admiring the rich gold carpet that would raise such a city up-roar that no one would accept responsibility for it, and yet which would still be in use five years later, standing up to the brunt of thousands of feet.

Low-slung blue leather furniture, glass dividing walls, tall tubbed philodendron . . . murals, one a sunbright nostalgic memory of the central market and old City Hall by Frank Panabaker, A.R.C.A. . . . and in the mayor's office a painting of Westlawn, stately home of Colin C. Ferrie, Hamilton's first city mayor, built in 1836.

In the council chamber, seat of municipal government, symbolically situated in the eye of the building, functionalism and luxury unite: gold carpet, wood-panelled walls and a virtual ceiling of light . . . steeply tiered Chinese red leather seats overlooking the open horseshoe of desks and bright blue chairs of the elected representatives of the people and the table of dignified City Clerk James F. Berry, in office since 1933[1] . . . on the raised podium the tall dark leather chair of the mayor, a far cry from the red velvet upholstered, carved Victorian throne of the old City Hall.

Observing in his inaugural address that certain older citizens winced at the modernity of the new City Hall and found it hard to accept, Mayor Jackson concluded with unconscious prophecy, "This is a building of youth . . . of looking forward!"

For many departments it was a building of convenience. For the first time in years city administration, including the fire department, was consolidated under one roof, either located in the two lower stories of the new building or in the office tower which rose to a crowning penthouse cafeteria, operated with cheerful efficiency by the C.N.I.B.

Here through the panoramic sweep of glass commanding on the south the Mountain with its green-clad summit broken by the excavation of Sam Lawrence Park, and on the north the city and busy harbour, with the Burlington Skyway arced against the blue lake, one could see across a welter of roofs the old City Hall in its death throes.

It came down stone by stone, some blocks in the 155-foot tower[2] weighing three tons apiece. Its four-foot-thick walls were lined with brick, and they must be toppled inwards because of busy streets below. The demolition as seen from the cafeteria was frequently attended by the sorrow felt in loss of a close friend. Forgotten were cramped quarters, rickety stairs, heat, dust and mice.

"It goes awfully slowly," observed charming and diplomatic Marjorie Marshall, whose 39 years of cheerful, friendly and efficient service, twenty as mayor's "girl Friday," gave her a unique knowledge of the city and its citizens. "I'll be glad when it gets down where I can't see it!"

The move from the old City Hall to the new, ably organized by Mr. Berry and his staff, was more than a move of a few blocks across a city. When it went, the old James Street building took a generation with it.

In the 1960's Septimus S. (Seppi) DuMoulin died, at eighty-four; and Billy Sherring; Captain J. R. Cornelius, who launched the golden era of amateur sport in Hamilton; Benjamin L. Simpson, aged eighty-six; at eighty-five, Michael J. (Mike) McGarvin, former principal of Delta Collegiate, frail, wiry, kindly and noted for his outstanding sense of humour; and Charles W. Houghton of Central Secondary school, who organized and conducted the Houghton Educational tours for students to New York City for seventeen years.

In 1962 the city lost two faithful and able servants with the death of popular Walter E. Griffin, deputy city clerk, 1942-59, and Bernard J. Mathews, veteran fire department official who served under five fire chiefs.[3] Music lost heavily in the sudden death of Cyril Hampshire, outstanding musician, teacher, arranger and composer; of Edward Lester, founder of the Harvester Male chorus, Hamilton Philharmonic Society choir, Excelsior Male and Orpheus Ladies' choirs, and the Lester Choraliers; of D'Iril Coons, music and drama critic with the old *Hamilton Times* until it closed in 1920, and popular orchestra leader; and of Harry J. Allan, for 47 years organist-director of First United Church.

Representative of Hamilton women: Mrs. Manley B. Morden, graduate of Wesleyan Ladies' College and alumnae officer, lifelong adherent and worker in city organizations; Mrs. Grace Puma Miceli, widow, whose grocery store on James Street North which she operated for nearly fifty years was a Hamilton landmark; and Miss Ellen Ewart, R.N., director of nursing for the H.H.A., whose sudden death on duty shocked the city. A sister of Dr. Hugo Ewart, medical superintendent of the H.H.A., Miss Ewart had spent twenty-three years with the Mountain institution, joining after overseas service in the Second World War during which she was mentioned in despatches.

One by one, each leaving his mark upon the city, a long-lived generation made way for the next: Ross Gerald Harstone, former Harbour Commission chairman, ardent Thistle Club curler and sportsman; Rev. Norman Rawson, D.D., formerly of Centenary Church, dynamic nonconformist and one of the city's notable ministers and Lt.-Col. William J. Deadman, B.A., M.D., V.D., internationally known soldier, doctor, author, and speaker, Hamilton's Man of the Year in 1949, for forty-two years city pathologist and director of the laboratory of Hamilton General Hospital, and later chief provincial medical examiner with the attorney general's department.[4]

Well known to courts as an expert medical witness, Dr. Deadman performed and supervised more than 10,000 autopsies. Of these one thousand were medico-legal and included examinations relative to murders, one of the most interesting from a pathological viewpoint being identification of Hamilton's famous armless, legless, headless "torso murder" victim in the sensational Dick case of 1946.

Contemporary with Dr. Deadman's service was the movement of city hospitals into the present era — at the H.G.H., the modernizing and expanding of operating theatres; replacement of west and east wings; building of a new nurses' residence; and in 1951 construction of the Cooper wing, named for W. H. Cooper, board chairman. In the 1930's the first laboratory technician's school in Canada was instituted at the H.G.H., with Dr. F. B. Bowman first pathologist, and Frank J. Elliott, for many years chief laboratory technician, also a pioneer. In the H.G.H. Dr. Albert E. Walkey was the first full-time radiologist.

In 1938 the first cancer clinic in Hamilton was established at the H.G.H., and operated with government support until 1949 when it was taken over by the Ontario Cancer Treatment and Research Foundation. Hamilton clinic director, O.C.T.F., is R. L. Green, M.D., D.M.R.T. In 1965 the clinic was transferred to the Henderson Hospital.

Working in conjunction with the cancer clinic, since its formation in 1948, the Hamilton unit of the Canadian Cancer Society has devoted itself to raising funds for research, to public education, and to assisting patients undergoing treatment. Today the Hamilton unit, housed at the Little Red Door, the former Charles G. Kelly home, on Victoria Avenue North, has become part of the Metropolitan Hamilton District Council which covers Wentworth County. Executive secretary, 1948-66, was Mrs. Frank S. Dewey, succeeded by field secretary Roy W. Delaney.

Contemporary, too, to the Deadman era were Drs. J. K. McGregor,[5] thyroid surgery; F. B. Mowbray, newly developed surgery of the chest; Victor Lapp, otolaryngology; Myles G. Brown, medical superintendent,

H.G.H., 1940-47; John A. Bauer, father of internal medicine in Hamilton; and Gerald Glassco, pioneer in psychiatry, all deceased; Dr. E. C. Janes, with new techniques in orthopaedics and thoracic surgery; Dr. Ambrose G. McGhie, goitre; and Basil Bowman, skin specialist; and the late Drs. G. S. Rennie, Daniel P. Kappelle, L. L. Playfair, and John R. and Robert Y. Parry. Pioneers in a biasedly male field were Drs. Alice McGillivray, Mabel Henderson, and Florence Smith, now deceased, and of a later period, Dr. Marian Templin, presently M.H.O. of Windsor, Ontario.

"In the old days," said Coroner R. H. McAlister, "doctors became specialists because they were naturally adroit in certain lines. Now they become specialists by examination and their membership in the Royal College of Physicians and Surgeons. Dr. R. T. Weaver was the first city doctor to limit his practice to obstetrics and gynecology. Dr. D. G. McIlwraith specialized in obstetrics, Drs. Donald A. Warren and W. M. Cody in anaesthesia."

In 1957 Dr. John B. Neilson resigned his ten-year position as general superintendent, Hamilton General Hospitals, to accept a post as chairman of the Ontario Hospital Services Commission and director of hospital services. At the H.G.H. he was replaced by Dr. H. E. Appleyard, who in turn resigned in 1965 to accept a position with the O.H.S.C. He was succeeded by Dr. William E. Noonan. In 1962 the Hamilton General Hospitals — comprised of the Hamilton General, the Mountain and the Henderson — were legislated an individual instead of a municipal corporation and their name changed to Hamilton Civic Hospitals.

At the Mountain Hospital, a maternity wing had been opened in 1938; the nurses' residence enlarged, the 1915 wing converted to a chronic care unit. In 1954 the Nora-Frances Henderson Hospital for convalescent patients was opened, to be converted in part two years later to active medical patients.

By 1958, realizing that direction of maximum growth of the city was south and east, full general hospital status, including surgery and emergency care, was planned for the Nora-Frances Henderson, thus achieving the dream Dr. J. Heurner Mullin had envisaged three decades earlier of a full scale Mountain hospital.

In January, 1965, the separate Mountain units were integrated into the Henderson General Hospital complex of 868 adult beds and 150 bassinets, constructed, equipped and outfitted to the most modern hospital standards.

With the Cooper wing, formerly housing the cancer unit, converted to a neuro-surgical unit and special surgical theatres established, H.G.H. will specialize in future in lengthy, complicated heart, brain and genito-urinary surgery.

Nursing director at Henderson General is Miss Elizabeth Ferguson; at the Hamilton General, Miss Merle Smith, who succeeded Miss Ada Squires. Preceding Miss Squires were Miss Marie E. Hudson and Miss Constance E. Brewster. Following retirement from the H.G.H. Miss

Squires was appointed the city's first regular inspector of nursing homes in a program designed to raise the standard of these institutions.

At the Mountain Sanatorium marked changes have occurred. In 1950 the San housed 753 tubercular patients in hospital buildings largely named after donors: the Southam building, erected with funds from sale of the Southam Home for Incurables on City Hospital (H.G.H.) grounds; the Bruce building; the Wilcox; the Evel; the Brow Infirmary; the Patterson Nurses' residence and the Holbrook Pavilion, named in honour of Medical Superintendent John Howard Holbrook, M.D. Generous gifts and bequests made other expansion and construction possible.

As success in treatment, due in part to use of new drugs, emptied beds — by 1964 to a needed 35 to 40 — Eskimos were accepted at government request, some thirteen hundred in all being treated, and the H.H.A. began expansion into the general hospital field. With government and city grants the H.H.A. established in San buildings a chronic and convalescent hospital, the Chedoke General and Children's Hospital, the Hamilton and District Rehabilitation Hospital. A new Children's Psychiatric Centre for emotionally disturbed young patients was part of an area pilot project in community care of the retarded. This leaves Lynwood Hall and Mount St. Joseph for moderately disturbed children only.

In 1964 also the independent Hamilton and District School of Nursing opened on H.H.A. grounds, with hospitals in Burlington and Oakville offering clinical facilities to student nurses.

Medical superintendent of the present Chedoke General Hospital complex is Hugo T. Ewart, B.A., M.D., appointed in 1947; assistant medical superintendent, H. E. Peart; Miss Roslyn Martin, secretary since 1929. With long service to the San: Drs. Paul Robinowitz, 1928-64, and D. B. Aitchison, 1931-64; and to the H.H.A., the late W. H. Lovering, Q.C., O.B.E.; Harold F. Lazier, Q.C., and Mrs. Victor Vallance.

In its specialized field St. Peter's Infirmary has also progressed. On November 25th, 1931, the infirmary changed its status and was approved as a hospital for incurables, a step made possible by the efficient administration of Miss Annie I. Browne, A.R.R.C., First World War hospital matron. Also innovated under Miss Browne was the admitting of female patients in 1929. Three years later the George C. Coppley wing was built and named in honour of the president of the board.

In 1938 Miss Merle O. Watson, R.N., succeeded Miss Browne as lady superintendent, Dr. K. E. Cooke (later Lt.-Col. K. E. Cooke, M.C., V.D.) became medical superintendent, and George F. Webb president of the board.

Two years later the ground floor of the two-storey, 100-bed west wing was opened, with the second floor completed for occupation in 1950, and a third storey built and opened the following year when a more liberal government policy eased funds.

By 1957 a new heating plant and laundry were installed as first phase in a program aimed at replacing the main wing and developing St.

Peter's into a modern 300-bed hospital. The second phase will proceed upon approval of the O.H.S.C., which controls hospital construction in Ontario and relates bed capacity and future requirements to terms of regional needs. Today's president and chairman of the board is John Kenyon; medical superintendent, Dr. E. L. Page; and director of nursing services, Mrs. E. M. Rowles, R.N.

At the head of John Street, St. Joseph's gleaming new hospital and medical centre, opened on October 18th, 1962, towers above a block of older buildings which have now become a wing of the new. Expanded in 1941 by Our Lady of Victory wing, St. Joseph's increased its capacity in 1947 to over 400 beds with erection of a new hospital, to which three years later a maternity wing was added. By the 1950's, however, mounting population and the advent of government hospitalization insurance had again created a critical shortage of city hospital beds.

Obliged for the first time in its history to appeal for public support, the $9,000,000 hospital was built by funds raised by the Sisters, by federal, provincial and municipal grants, and by generous public contributions. Its opening gave St. Joseph's 765 beds and 125 bassinets.

Constructed of concrete and steel, with a sand-lime brick exterior effectively contrasted with blue glazed brick panelling, with stainless steel flashing and aluminum doors, the hospital rivals City Hall in dignified simplicity. It offers the ultimate in service to patients with its tinted, chintz-hung rooms, glazed tile, chrome and glass; the gleaming sterilizers of its decontamination and reprocessing areas; its automatic conveyors, discharging onto each ward untouched trays from spotless kitchens; its despatch centre forwarding fresh supplies and collecting soiled articles in continuous rotation; and saving steps and speeding operation, a two-way voice communication system.

Could Osler but return, one might imagine his delight with the explosion-proof, shockproof multibeam lights of today's operating suites — as in other Hamilton hospitals; the well stocked instrument room; the intensive care unit; and supplementing these, the powerful, delicate instruments employed in modern pathological and surgical procedures.

In 1960 St. Joseph's Hospital became the first North American institution to establish officially the nuclear-age partnership of scientist and doctor, with appointment of three McMaster University nuclear scientists to the hospital's medical staff with equal status with doctors of medicine. Appointees were Dr. H. G. Thode, nuclear scientist, Dr. R. H. Tomlinson, nuclear chemist, and Dr. Paul Nace, biologist.

Today the hospital functions under Sister Mary Grace, administrator, with Dr. (Col.) J. D. Galloway, O.B.E., medical director, Sister Celestine, director of nursing and Sister Cleophas, public relations.

As revolutionary in their field as the hospitals were the new schools in architecture and education. No longer adequate was the general education of the past, specialized only in professions such as law, medicine and engineering. To afford greater variety of approach to both academic and

275

technical, or occupational, education, the so-called Robarts plan was formulated offering a curriculum organization for secondary schools that would provide students of varying scholastic abilities with courses designed to meet individual differences.

The plan was greeted with scepticism. In view of the longtime tradition of prestige of arts and science it was thought parents would reject business and technological courses offered, as being blue collar. The sceptics were wrong. Possibly today's most significant development in education is the swing to vocational training, with half or more of the student body choosing specialized courses which lead to graduation in business and commerce or technology and trades.

Today's educational system therefore seeks to provide a solid general education at the elementary and secondary school levels, gradually permitting students to specialize in fields in which they display interest or competence. The system has proved successful in combatting the problem of dropouts, but has aggravated the problem of overcrowded schools.

In 1965, eight secondary, three junior vocational and seventy-six elementary schools enrolled some 36,000 public and 17,000 secondary and vocational students. To cope with this increased number, two high schools, Central and Delta Collegiates, operated on shift system and twenty-six portable classrooms were used. On the separate school front three high schools, twenty-eight elementary and five portable schoolrooms, supervised by F. P. Cunningham, William M. McRae and T. A. Hennelly, separate school inspectors, handled an enrolment of 16,326 public and 2,400 high school students.

Among the impressive new schools in the above systems, Briarwood Junior vocational girls' school, Parkview boys' school in lower Hamilton, Crestwood junior vocational boys' school and Southmont secondary composite school on the Mountain were built under the federal-provincial technical and vocational training agreement of 1961, whereby $12,000,000 of new schools, additions and renovations were constructed at a total cost to Hamilton of only $1,900,000.

The schools are a direct government attack on drop-outs and unemployment and an indirect attack on poverty. If a healthy percentage of young people refuse to attend school to grade twelve level, then the two governments must see them launched in today's "increasingly sophisticatd labour market" with job equipment of training commensurate with individual capacity.

While Canada badly needs professional technicians, craftsmen and qualified office personnel, the country also needs shop assistants, garage attendants, cashiers, telephone operators and receptionists. All these and many more semi-skills are taught. On the other hand, in the 56-room, 1,500-pupil Southmont secondary school, near Sherman Avenue and Highway 53, students may take drafting, auto and power mechanics, toolmaking, testing and metallurgy, building and construction, electrical installation and industrial electronics.[6]

In its own revolution, the elementary school has met the problem of retardation and acceleration — slow child and bright — by a unit system whereby the student advances at his own ability level. In Hamilton the system was started experimentally in 1939 and by 1945 was generally adopted. For students with an I.Q. below 80, "Opportunity" classes are provided, with promotion to junior vocational schools after the age of thirteen. For handicapped children special classes are provided, with itinerant teachers for children confined for over three months to home or hospital. In the children's ward, H.G.H., Mrs. Eileen Carey taught for twenty years (1942-62).

In another specialized field the seriously retarded are taught in three schools operated by the Hamilton and District Association for Retarded Children, under president A. E. Ferguson and director K. M. Leslie: Centre Haven, Mount Haven, and the new functional Easthaven. Emotionally disturbed children, on the other hand, housed in Hamilton's attractive new Lynwood Hall, are placed individually in elementary school classrooms.

In work with the handicapped, the Amity Rehabilitation Centre, executive director, Gordon Mann, has achieved results which have brought international recognition. Born of the depression, Amity became one of Canada's top salvage collectors during the war, working for some time with the local branch of the Red Cross, and donating its profits of sixty thousand dollars to the Red Cross and war services. Following the war, Amity turned to rehabilitation and training of the physically and mentally handicapped. Today it operates a workshop and three outlets where donated used furniture, clothing and appliances are reconditioned and sold. A non-profit organization, its payroll to handicapped employees, many of whom graduate to work elsewhere, totals $100,000 annually. Assistant executive directors are Miss Berta Sullivan and Ivan Roper.

Under the Board of Education,[7] (chairman, R. J. Stewart who succeeded John E. Trimble), the "big business" of the Hamilton school system is administered by the director of education, Gordon E. Price, M.A., LL.D., a former city student, teacher, principal of city schools, and superintendent of Hamilton secondary schools; D. A. Cooper, B.A., M.Sc., superintendent of secondary schools; L. A. Freeman, B.A., B.Paed., superintendent of public schools; and business administrator, R. S. Cartmell, B.A.

Chairman of the separate school board is David A. Warme, 1937-66, while other long term members are Edward I. Duffy, 1942-66, and Gordon F. McInnes, 1939-66.

Seek a common denominator in school buildings today and you will find it in individualism. Gone with the past is the regimented uniformity of the traditional school. Rubble stone from the Credit River to project solidity . . . pyramid and vaulted roof to catch the eye from Mountain roads above . . . windows to offset the shadows of the Mountain . . . the city's first circular, or near-circular, school, with five-sided classrooms . . .

a school glass-walled about a landscaped courtyard, 128 by 96 feet . . .
classrooms resembling a de luxe huddle of six-sided African native huts,
with conical roofs above wall murals: these are the new schools.

"Light!" pronounces architect J. D. Kyles, selecting the most salient
characteristic of today's glass-bright schools. "Without windows!" decide
Prack and Prack, architects of Hamilton's latest and most radical secondary school, built on Scott Park, site of the old Gage home. Previously
selected to house the Football Hall of Fame, the property was reluctantly
surrendered by the parks board. Combining recreational with educational
facilities, the five-storey building features public areas on the lower floors,
boiler room and cafeteria on the third floor, and classrooms on fourth
and fifth. It is windowless because of its restricted site and proximity to a
main traffic artery.

In life the only constant is change. The year 1960 will always be
remembered in civic circles as the year of upsets in the civic election. In
1960 realigned wards ran from the Mountain to the bay and representatives who had held office for years with a strong north end or south end
following, now with a north-south ward found themselves dispossessed of
their seats. In 1960 eight new aldermen were elected to council.

The election was also noted for the meteoric sweep of an unknown
star into the civic firmament. Using what some termed "American elec-
tioneering tactics," Board of Control candidate Victor Kennedy Copps,
who prefers to be known as Vic Copps, flaunted a campaign balloon from
his headquarters under the nose of City Hall, a gimmick he supplemented
in his subsequent mayoralty election campaign with free-ride, sight-seeing
trains about the city, and hand-out candy bars inviting, "Vote Copps."
Also offered electors was a cordial handshake and an election program
promising industrial development and redevelopment of downtown
Hamilton.

Medium in size, dark haired with a retreating hairline, dark eyed,
possessing a ready smile — sincere, hardworking, aggressive — the new
aspirant to board of control was born in Haileybury, in northern Ontario,
one of seven sons, had been sports reporter for the Timmins' *Daily Press,*
had served with the R.C.A.F. during World War II, and for fifteen years
had been Station CHML's highest paid radio time salesman. He had a
wife and four children and was noted as a family man, was a dedicated
member of the Knights of Columbus, a staunch liberal, and—important
today—was bilingual.

In his landslide into office, Vic Copps pre-empted top place on the
Board of Control from Controller Jack MacDonald and dispossessed Controller Leslie Parker of a seat. Completing the board were Controllers Ada
Pritchard and Archie McCoy, the latter solidly enough ensconced in public
esteem to ride out charges of conflict of interest involving city contracts
and the McCoy Foundry Company Limited, and McCoy Machinery and
Supply Company. The charges were brought by Copps, who proved a
board member who attracted press coverage as champion of the peoples'
interests.

Only Mayor Jackson was not affected in 1960. In appreciation of his long service to the city, and to assure him a term in the new City Hall, he was returned by acclamation. In 1962, however, when he determined to try his luck in a three-cornered mayoralty race with Vic Copps and Jack MacDonald, Copps repeated his earlier victory and became mayor by a margin of 14,722 votes. When the successful candidate swept into City Hall on election night, surrounded by a youthful jubilant throng of supporters, it was obvious that the city had embarked on a new era. Equally jubilant were Controller Leslie Parker, who had staged a comeback, and Brian Morison, elected first Mountain controller after nine years as alderman.

In summing up Mayor Jackson's administration, "Lloyd Jackson," said *The Hamilton Spectator*, "steps aside with a record few public men in Canada could rival. He built the postwar city we know now in a way that will be more impressive to us as the years roll on. Even above his great material achievements was a sort of camaraderie with Hamiltonians everywhere that made Mr. Jackson a public servant in the truest sense . . . He was never too tired nor too busy to do the little things that are the big things.

"In this he was assisted in a touching and inspiring way by his wife. The two may be bowing out of politics. They are still with and of this city and its people and always will be."

In January, 1963, the Jacksons were jointly presented with the annual Distinguished Citizenship award at the 26th Civic Night of the Ad and Sales Club of Hamilton. On the following October 22nd they celebrated their golden wedding anniversary.

Mrs. Jackson was the fourth woman to receive the award, the first having been Mabel Burkholder, district historian, honoured in 1938 for writing the history of the city. In 1951 Mrs. J. D. Taylor was the recipient, for her educational contributions as president of the Ontario Federation of Home and School Associations, president of the National Home and School and Parent-Teacher Federation, editor of *Canadian Home and School,* and president of the Ontario Educational Association. Seven years later Mrs. John Humphreys was awarded the distinction for her twenty-six years of civic service with the Y.W.C.A. and various other groups; for counselling young married couples, and for work with senior citizens in formation of community "Over 60" clubs.

In 1964, Hamilton had a fifth woman recipient, Mrs. Herbert A. Ricker (now Mrs. Stewart A. Reeves), the vice-chairman of the Hamilton Housing Authority and director of the central division of the Ontario Association of Housing Authorities, and a member of numerous other organizations including the Urban Renewal committee, Hamilton Juvenile Court committee, and the Salvation Army Red Shield campaign committee.

Mayor Jackson left behind one issue of top priority. "We had three projects," he said, "urban renewal, Confederation Park, and the Chedoke Expressway. We took Confederation Park first. Conditions were bad at

Van Wagner's and Crescent beaches, the land washing away, waves pounding the cottages. We gave Confederation Park priority. Next we took the Chedoke Expressway. The city badly needed a west end north-south access. If we gave the land, the province would build the road. So we tackled the expressway. That left us with urban renewal."

On June 25th, 1964, Confederation Park was officially opened. With assistance from senior levels of government 173 acres of lakeshore, classified as a physical blemish area, was converted to large-scale recreational use with landscaping, parking lots, and a $90,000 combined bath house and snack bar. Chairman of the Beach committee was Alderman Reginald Wheeler. Opened on July 1st, 1966, the Confederation Park seven-acre model domestic animal farm, for which Controller Archie McCoy worked indefatigably, contains rustic fences, corrals, and a barn for livestock.

Approaching the twenty-first century with its promise of the good life of constantly decreasing hours of labour and constantly lengthening hours that must be filled with some alternative pursuit, parks are enjoying a resurgence of popularity. "Take Me Out to the Ball Park," with ball park loosely interpreted, may well become the theme song of the gay carefree 1990's.

In sixty odd years since Hamiltonians in 1900 established a board of park management of six citizens and the mayor, and selected Henry G. Wright as first chairman,[8] the parks system has expanded to forty-three properties covering some two thousand acres. Besides the sedentary recreation of park visiting and flower and bird watching, the parks provide opportunities for swimming, skating and hockey, golf, lawn bowling and tennis; for track and field, football and soccer, soft ball and hard ball; for hiking in the 816-acre King's Forest occupying William Davis' Mount Albion valley and mountain top, and in the Hamilton section of the Bruce Trail, which in part follows the abandoned mountain-side right-of-way of the old Brantford and Hamilton radial line.

In Royal Botanical Garden properties, too — developed under supervision of Director Norman W. Radforth, M.A., Ph.D., F.R.S.C., expert on Canada's northern muskeg, and his gardens-minded successor, Leslie Laking, B.S.A. — which now encompass 1,900 acres, trails in abundance wind through the lovely wooded glades behind McMaster University which border the south shore of Cootes' Paradise (today a wild life sanctuary), along the northern shore of the marsh where a 350-acre arc of Gardens land swings to the outskirts of Dundas, and in the marshes of Hendrie Creek, near Aldershot.

In making sports facilities available to the public in the most efficient and economical manner, parks staff and recreation department work closely together. In addition to operating its own facilities, the recreation department also regulates the programs governing pools, playgrounds, and ball fields in city parks. Only in those parks from which revenue is derived — Civic Stadium with its football and soccer fields and its quarter-mile track, the H.A.A.A. grounds,[9] and Victoria and Woodland parks with their fastball diamonds — does the parks board regulate the program. Similarly the Chedoke Civic Golf Club, the Victoria, Hamilton, and Rosedale Tennis Clubs, and the Churchill Fields and Roselawn Bowling Clubs operate under the parks board. To these a golf course in King's Forest will be added.

On the Mountain, parks and pools strive to keep ahead of the population explosion. "To meet future Mountain requirements alone," said E. R. Seager, secretary to the board of parks management, "we will need three to four hundred acres of park land of different types." Park land on the Mountain is still available. "What is in short supply," said Mr. Seager, "is funds."

Says J. T. C. Waram, city planning commissioner, "By 1990 Hamilton will need 910 more acres of park land and the city may expect to pay $100,000 an acre for some of the sites it needs."

In view of these factors and the mounting cost of construction, parks, recreation and education departments are being called on to develop new channels of thinking and new approaches to problems.

"Parks are no longer hallowed ground," declares Controller A. H. R. McCoy, a potent force at City hall, with thirteen years in municipal government, ten as controller, and with a realistic, successful business man's approach to city problems. "Petunias are fine but I am sure we can combat juvenile delinquency better by providing adequate recreational facilities than by planting flowers."

"Parks," retorts parks board chairman, T. J. Newlands, with equal vigour, "must provide for the population as a whole. Thousands of citizens and tourists visit the annual tulip display in Gage Park, the 4,000 rose shrubs in bloom in June, and the November chrysanthemum show with its 50,000 flowers. Sunday evening instrumental and vocal concerts held in the Gage Park bandshell have drawn 8,000 listeners a night.

"This year the city has added in Dundurn Park a brand new form of entertainment, unique in Canada, the dramatized Sound and Light presentation of the life of Sir Allan MacNab, laird of Dundurn Castle. Fifty per cent of our parks," said Chairman Newlands, "are fifty per cent or more recreational. Twelve per cent are all active recreation. It takes all kinds of people to make a city. City parks belong to them all and must serve them all."

To accomplish this to the best advantage old fetishes are being discarded. "Facilities of parks, recreation department, and schools should be available one to the other," declares Mr. Newlands.

"Community centres as planned today," agrees George Force, chairman of the Hamilton Recreation committee, "will be dual-purpose recreation-educational facilities built as school additions. Under the system inaugurated last year, recreation department swimming pools can be used by students in school hours. During weekends, evenings, and holidays the pools, school gymnasiums, other rooms and playgrounds will be available to the public in recreation programs."

Agreement is also voiced by Miss Florence Meiler, the efficient director of recreation appointed in 1957 to a department which had grown in the previous ten years by nineteen new playgrounds, a day camp in Cootes' Paradise, Central Memorial[10] and Wesley Community centres, Strathcona Community centre, and the Jessie Patterson Memorial pool.

Florence Meiler greets the new departure enthusiastically. "The most exciting development in recreation," she says, "is the present plan of combining schools and district centres. Three additions to schools are now in use, at Westmount Secondary, Dalewood public, and Bennetto public in the urban renewal area. Each contains a 25-metre pool, craft room, kitchen and office. The addition is built adjacent to the school gymnasium which completes facilities for the centre. Schools in the neighbourhood will use pool and gymnasium during school hours. At other times these will be open to the general public."

Mayor Jackson left the incoming administration two legacies. Thanks to the efforts of a committee chaired by the late Dr. George P. Gilmour, a new city coat of arms duly registered in July, 1963, with the College of Heralds, London, England; and on the south wall of the second floor of the new City Hall, a symbolic mural presented by the Steel Company of Canada, painted by the Canadian artist, Franklin Arbuckle.

Superimposed on an abstract drab background broken by the thin sunshine yellow of a clouded day, Mr. Arbuckle has depicted in a fabric of tenuous lines symbols to represent the crude might of the mills; factory processes; electrical devices; the multiple vocations and professions of city workers; McMaster University's nuclear reactor, landmark in the school's research program of nuclear fission and isotope chemistry; the Hamilton Art Gallery; the natural wealth of the city's famous marketplace; the vivid accent of the Royal Botanical Gardens; ships and the port; the Tiger-Cat football team; and the Mountain.

But Mayor Copps also inherited less pleasant legacies: the perennial headache of Hamilton's Mountain access roads, aggravated now by the need of east-west freeways; shortage of industrial land; deterioration of the city's heart, the twentieth-century plague sweeping the cities and towns of North America; additional down-at-heels areas bound to become slums unless redeveloped; new remote sections requiring integration; and pollution.

"There are problems," Mayor-elect Copps had said on election night, "but with teamwork and energy and a good council we shall solve them. The people wanted a change," he added. "Younger candidates have more vigour, and the people realize more vigour is needed."

No one can deny that vigour has characterized the Copps administration. Devoted to downtown redevelopment, the mayor strongly supported erection of Terminal Towers and location in the building of the magistrates' courts; opposed the licensing of outlying plazas with their diversion of trade from the city core; and supported an early closing by-law for stores, thus lessening plaza competition.

282

In December, 1964, following Mayor Copps' flight to Ottawa to oppose a federal bill giving the government complete jurisdiction over development of the port of Hamilton, the Senate transport committee responsible for the legislation killed it by adjournment. In raising the last difficult $50,000 necessary to secure the Canadian Football Hall of Fame for Hamilton, Vic Copps displayed the same strategy that had won two elections — a direct and bold frontal assault. At $100 a plate, the black-tie dinner he offered Hamiltonians netted $45,000, all costs, including food, being met privately. As a memorable assembly of consequential citizens helping push a civic project over the top, it may well have established a precedent.

In his bid for leadership of Ontario Liberals, Vic Copps was less successful. Entering the race late as seventh aspirant, he posed little threat to leaders at the convention in Toronto in September, 1964. If this was a wound and not mere political jockeying for future recognition, then its pain was partly alleviated by his election the following May as president of the Canadian Federation of Mayors and Municipalities, an office held first in Hamilton's history by ex-Mayor Jackson in 1958.

In the master traffic plan prepared by consulting engineers C. C. Parker, and Parsons, Brinckerhoff, the widening of Burlington Street to six lanes was offered as the first phase of a $200,000,000 program to correct the city's traffic problems.

As early as 1943 Thomas J. Mahony, M.P.P., Wentworth South, 1923-34, deputy speaker of the Ontario legislature, president and director of the Hamilton Automobile Club, known as Canada's "Mr. Good Roads," urged Hamilton's need of an improved eastern access. Fifteen years later Controller A. H. R. McCoy turned the first sod at Kenilworth Avenue and Beach Road to start construction of the Beach Road expressway connecting Burlington Street with the Queen Elizabeth Way. With its few thousand feet of paving, the expressway overcame one of the city's worst bottlenecks leading into Burlington Street, the city's main artery through the heavy industrial district.

In the master traffic program, the conversion of Burlington Street from Kenilworth Avenue to the beginning of the north-end urban renewal area at Wellington Street is complementary to the proposed future construction of a $54,000,000 east-west freeway, possibly elevated to reduce roadway demands on built-up property, which will cross the city between Burlington and Barton Streets carrying through traffic between Highway 403 on the west and Highway 20 on the east.

Later a second east-west freeway is scheduled for the Mountain, probably located between Lime Ridge and Stone Church Roads. Gridding these from north to south, the traffic program calls for four new Mountain accesses within the next twenty years, with Gage Avenue a north-south artery carrying crosstown traffic.

"Hamilton," said City Engineer Wheten, "will eventually be rimmed with expressways. On the west we have Highway 403 which will climb the escarpment to join Highway 2 near Duff's Corners. On the east is Highway 20, broadened to four lanes. When a trunk sewer is laid up the Red Hill Creek valley, the Red Hill expressway will accompany it. The Victoria Avenue-Claremont Hill access, planned to sweep over the Jolley Cut and link Victoria Avenue and Upper James Street, has been on the drawing boards for a decade. Then there will be a freeway in the neighbourhood of York Street and Dundurn."

He blackpencilled lines on a city map covering his desk. "In the P.P. and B. plan, however," he added, "overall priority goes to a north-south freeway winding up the Mountain between Wentworth and Ottawa Streets."

By 1985 experts estimate that twenty-four Mountain access lanes will be required to carry traffic between the lower and upper city whose population then may well exceed a quarter of a million.

Of the pioneers' Mountain roads only the central Jolley Cut, rebuilt in 1953 to become the city's first major Mountain access, and the eastern Flock Road incorporated five years later into the even more ambitious Kenilworth east end access, have grown in importance. When completed, both were proclaimed permanent structures, built on "a safe shelf of rock." Within months the Mountain had closed both routes, setting their shoulders to slipping and sliding, and bombarding them from above with shale and boulders in its century-old fashion.

Recalling the steeper, loftier, and more pretentious slopes common to Italy and other Mediterranean countries and the Middle East, with orderly drained and terraced vineyards, olive groves and dizzy roller coaster roadways, one wonders if Hamilton's Mountain roads have been correctly engineered.

Says Mr. Wheten, "It will be a costly procedure, but some day the shale will have to be removed from the Mountain face, the rock pared back, and the whole Mountain side drained, terraced, graded, and returned to its original state of turf and trees. It will make a wonderful backdrop for the city and provide space for walks, trails and picnic areas."

With the terraced Mountain belong the Mountain access tunnels of the future, advanced as the only permanent solution to Streets Commissioner William Muirhead's perennial headache of snowbound and rain-slicked Mountain roads. Among tunnel advocates is former Controller Ada Pritchard, today first woman chairman of a standing committee of the Ontario legislature, that of Education, Health and Welfare.

Elected in 1951 in Ward 3, Mrs. Pritchard succeeded Ellen L. Fairclough who had represented the same ward, 1947-49, before advancing to head the board of control in 1950 and become federal member of Hamilton West in a by-election the same year.

Dynamic, smart in appearance, smiling and imperturbable in stress, Hon. Ellen Fairclough, P.C., C.A.,[11] carved out for herself a notable career in top-level Canadian politics. In 1957 as Secretary of State she became Canada's first woman cabinet minister. In 1960 she was appointed Minister of Citizenship and Immigration, and in 1962 Post-

284

master General. An astute business woman, with pre-political experience in the printing business owned and operated by her husband, Gordon Fairclough, she followed her defeat at the polls by Alderman Joseph Macaluso in 1963 by accepting the position of Secretary of the newly formed Hamilton Trust and Savings Corporation.

Remaining longer in the municipal field, English-born Ada Pritchard served for three years as alderman and ten as controller before moving into provincial politics. Because of her interest in the problems of youth and age, low rental housing, and recreation, the Ada Pritchard Court apartments for senior citizens were named in her honour. Supported strongly by the Local Council of Women and the Hamilton Civic Club, Mrs. Pritchard has always been assured of a powerful women's vote. Her husband, Charles H. Pritchard, recently retired after twenty-five years as organist of the Church of the Ascension.

In the city, five other women have held seats in council: Mrs. A. Sharpe; Helen M. Anderson, avowed communist; Mrs. Bessie Hughton; Mrs. Margaret Standen; and currently Mrs. Anne Jones, widow of Rev. Aubrey Jones, who possesses a political presence that should carry her far. In her husband's honour the low rental Aubrey R. Jones Memorial Apartments for senior citizens were constructed and opened in June, 1965, by Downtown Kiwanis.

In recent years it would seem that the Hamilton municipal field has proved a convenient stepping stone to government office. In 1964 Joseph Lanza, first of the city's large Italian colony to win a seat on council, resigned to accept an Ottawa appointment as a member of the Hamilton Harbour Commission. Mr. Lanza had served as campaign manager for Thomas H. Ross, M.P., Hamilton East, 1940-56. In 1962, the seat, after having been taken by Quinto Martini following the death of Mr. Ross, was recaptured by Liberal Alderman John Munro.

Hamilton's north end renewal program, first broached in 1958 and again in 1961, differs from the usual urban renewal project in that the latter involves simple slum clearance and rehousing of the bulldozed area and is recommended for districts without strong neighbourhood feeling. Hamilton's urban redevelopment, however, calls for a maximum of rehabilitation and minimum of bulldozing and involves an area noted for its community pride and sense of tradition—the jealously proud north end.

Unique in Canada, Hamilton's scheme comprises a complete change of design of the 257-acre section of the city bounded on the south by the C.N.R. tracks, on the east by Wellington Street, and on the north and west by the bay—a section containing 2,500 houses with 8,400 people occupying them. Besides involving millions of dollars in real estate and commercial and industrial ventures, it affects the lives of people who have lived for generations in the same locality—some even in the same house.

As approved by the Ontario Municipal Board, urban renewal plans call for a massive face lifting, with removal of blighted buildings and others needed to provide space for facilities; renovation and improvement of run-down buildings, preferably by private enterprise; new schools, parks, and recreational areas; a shopping centre; public housing for residents who wish to remain in the area but whose homes have been demolished, and geared to income, for families from other city areas; construction of a sub-trunk sanitary sewer to hook into the western interceptor sewer; realignment of streets, and—key to the whole area development— its isolation by closing Burlington as a dead-end at Wellington and carrying it as a limited access perimeter road south to the C.N.R. tracks, then following them west to link up with the Chedoke expressway.

Within the redeveloped area traffic movement will be further reduced by closing certain streets, by removing two bridges over the C.N.R. tracks on north-south thoroughfares, and by converting many streets into courts and dead ends. As finally developed, only vehicles bound for a definite area will travel into it.

Naturally such plans aroused public outcry, doubts and fears. "A ghetto!" protested one fiercely of the closed streets. "We'll pay dearly," said many. "We'll improve our places and they'll raise our taxes!" Many wished merely to be left in peace to live out their remaining days. Few wished to move away. Some feared financial disaster. By 1965 however, much of the opposition had ceased. This resulted largely from the urban renewal committee policy of explaining each move, exercising patience, and reducing inconvenience to a minimum.

Chairman of the urban renewal committee, responsible for the development from its beginning, is Kenneth D. Soble, president of the Maple Leaf Broadcasting Company Limited, and owner of station CHML, purchased from Senator Arthur C. Hardy in 1942; CHML-FM opened in 1964; president, Niagara Television Limited, operating the pioneering independent Station CHCH-TV — Channel 11, Hamilton — opened in 1954 and featuring the Ken Soble Amateur Show of radio fame; owner of the Hamilton Forum and Hamilton Red Wings, an OHA Junior "A" hockey team; governor, Tiger-Cat football team; president, Tiger-Cubs Hockey Club; first president, Hamilton Jewish Community Centre; director, H.H.A. (Chedoke General Hospital); chairman of the Ontario Housing Corporation and of the newly formed Ontario Student Housing Corporation.

Mr. Soble's right hand man, who has borne much of the brunt of the project, is D. Graham Emslie, originally executive secretary, now urban renewal commissioner. Formerly Mr. Emslie was with Station CKOC, Hamilton, as director of news and public relations.

Today the first stage of the north end program is a visible entity. Bennetto senior public school and the community centre erected as a joint recreational-educational project with shared gym and swimming pool facilities is already in use. A modern progressive junior public school and a separate school are under construction. Also planned is a new secondary school at York and Bay, and a replacement for the old Hess Street School. Homes have been purchased and renovated for occupation.

Encouraged by the success of this pilot plot, Hamilton authorized the urban renewal committee to undertake similar studies of the York Street and downtown areas, the former a narrow, congested, shabby street linking the city's landscaped western approach to its prosaic business core.

"This is a building of youth—of looking forward," Mayor Jackson had said of the new City Hall. On July 29th, 1964, James F. Berry, who had brought dignity, distinction and efficiency to the office of city clerk for thirty-one years, resigned and was succeeded by thirty-nine-year-old Edward A. Simpson, an R.H.L.I. veteran of World War II, with youthful Keith Avery as deputy clerk. Of comparable age is John R. Jones, secretary to the board of control. During the half century since he had joined the municipal staff in 1912 as a junior clerk of fifteen, James Berry had served under fourteen mayors.

In 1964 Francis G. (Frank) Dillon, senior alderman on city council, died suddenly. When his death was followed in 1965 by that of ex-Alderman Hugh F. Brown, Q.C., Hamilton's "dean of city council," defeated in the 1964 election, the cult of youth — today's great North American mystique — became predominant in city administration. Top ranking controller was James E. Campbell who had replaced Mrs. Pritchard when she left the board. In the aldermanic field four newcomers, in age twenty-seven to thirty-seven years, ousted older incumbents, while young Alderman Anne Jones, the only woman elected, topped the polls for the city.

On February 15th, 1965, the city raised a new flag. . . . In March the planning committee of the Hamilton Police Department, consisting of Chief Leonard Lawrence, Deputy Chief Gerald Reed, Assistant Chiefs Howard Moreau and John Arno, and Inspector Gordon Torrance, began a major overhaul of the department. Objective was to streamline administration and operations; reclassify the city's patrol areas; institute a new rank system; and reorganize department divisions. By simplifying and tightening organization and command it was planned to change an unwieldy outdated police operation into a rejuvenated efficient force. When completed, Magistrate Walter Tuchtie, Police Commission Chairman, expressed approval of the revised organization.

Following removal of magistrates' courts to Terminal Towers, the interior of Central Police station was completely renovated in 1966, turning grim, depressing and cramped rooms into spacious, cheerful quarters.

27

Today

ON APRIL 8th, 1965, Murray Jones, whose firm had been engaged to design a plan for development of York Street and the downtown core, disclosed its details at a public meeting at City Hall. Board of education members were present in force, including chairman John Trimble and the six women members, Mrs. Dorothy Cooke, Mrs. Katherine McAuley, Mrs. Doris E. Gasse, Mrs. Olive Ritchie, Mrs. June Robertson and Mrs. Kathleen Nolan, the last three newly elected. With Ada Pritchard up from Toronto they brightened the council chamber with their spring pastels and hats like spun confections of candy floss.

Present too were Dr. Gordon Price and members of the Theatre-Auditorium Foundation, established the previous year with Colin S. Glassco as president to undertake promotion of a theatre-auditorium to serve Hamilton and the surrounding area.

Interest of the board of education lay in Murray Jones' proposed site for the new $3,000,000 education and administration building that would replace the present building on Hunter Street West. In the interests of downtown redevelopment, council, sparked by Mayor Copps, had fought long and valiantly to secure location of the new building on a downtown site.

For months controversy had raged. School trustees had determined on the former site of Hillfield College in Westdale and plans had been drawn to suit the location. When an urban renewal plan was announced by Kenneth Soble for York Street, council renewed its pressure, offering land concessions if the education centre were built within the boundaries of the York Street development. Finally, in 1964, the board of trustees agreed reluctantly to accept the York Street site. At this same time Mr. Soble announced preparation of the urban renewal scheme for the downtown core which was to be presented tonight.

What everyone expected was a presentation similar to the north end renewal plan. What Murray Jones unfolded was vastly different and more exciting. "A bold new plan," said *The Hamilton Spectator*, "designed to leapfrog Hamilton into the twenty-first century."

Dealing with the city west of James only, Mr. Jones presented two plans. One dealt with the square north of City Hall, bounded by MacNab Street, Bay, Main and Merrick Streets—a hodge-podge of unassorted, time-stained buildings, shabby streets, and drab parking lots. The other plan converted congested grimy York Street into a sweeping boulevard uniting the western entrance of the city with the new Civic Square.

Completely eliminating parking lots and ancient buildings, replacing Park and Charles Streets with new one-way thoroughfares, and wiping out York Street between Bay and James, Murray Jones created a spacious square with a complex of architecturally coordinated buildings set in green spaces.

Across Main Street to the west of City Hall, stood the new education headquarters; to the east, the expanded Public Library so badly needed; north of the library, a new art gallery necessitated by McMaster University expansion; far to the north, centred with City Hall, at the end of a green vista, the theatre-auditorium. A new tower office building, an arcaded hotel, shopping areas, and a parking garage—Murray Jones' plan was a coordinated downtown revitalization.

Suddenly, unbelievably, the doubts, dissensions, and uncertainty were past. The plan was revolutionary, yet at the same time so simple, so logical, so fitting that once having seen it, there seemed no other future for this heart-of-the-city area. Before the meeting ended, city council voted unanimously to expropriate the thirty-five acres required for the estimated $50,000,000 development.

Without too much effort the school board changed its thinking once again, accepting the location north of Main Street for its new building instead of one north of York. After some grumbling, York Street merchants reconciled themselves to loss of the education building, in return for other promised considerations.

There can be no doubt of Mayor Copps' elation with the Civic Square complex. "It is the most exciting thing that has ever happened to Hamilton!" he declares.

Westward, however, on the campus of McMaster University, a development fully as exciting and more controversial was taking form.

"McMaster today," says President H. G. Thode, appointed October 27th, 1961, when ill health forced Dr. Gilmour's retirement, "is riding towards the crest of a sudden explosive growth in student population. By 1970, when it is expected that more than 8,000 students will be studying there, the university will have come through one of the great watershed periods in its history.

"In the 1959-60 academic year 1,408 students were enrolled at McMaster. By 1964-65 the number had risen to 3,312. The university had added a faculty of engineering and had redoubled its efforts in graduate teaching and research. Producing this upsurge in enrolment was the arrival of postwar babies at university age; increasing prosperity, permitting parents to send more children to university; and increasing government aid to students."

To accomodate the upsurge came additional university buildings, playing fields and parking troubles. Westdale residents began to grumble. In 1960 McMaster indicated to the Ontario government its interest in establishing a school of medicine. To house it, the university purchased with government funds 230 acres of land belonging to the Royal Botanical Gardens. In 1963 the university was quietly given powers of expropriation. The same year it advised the city that its plans for complete integration of medical school and teaching hospital with departments of arts and science would require the closing at Forsyth Avenue, east of the campus, of King Street, then routed through university grounds to meet Highway 102 (now Coote's Drive).

McMaster then visualized a $24,000,000 completely-integrated medical school complex with a 360-bed teaching hospital fronting on Main Street West. By 1966 the medical complex had expanded to $50,000,000 and was now designated as a regional centre to serve communities throughout the Niagara Peninsula and west to Brantford. It would also contain a school of dentistry, and a family practice unit, an innovation in Canada. In June, 1965, John R. Evans, M.D., was appointed first dean of medicine of the new school.

The new plans, however, would call for closing of King Street at Dalewood, a block east of Forsyth, and its rerouting south to Main, and expropriation of some ninety high class residential homes in the area. Only twenty-six houses, however, would be immediately required. Although Westdale residents rallied under leadership of the Westdale Community Council to combat the plan, a divided city council approved the McMaster medical centre plan in full on June 14, 1966.

City Engineer W. A. Wheten and W. E. Ewens, former city traffic director, opposed the diversion of King Street.

"If a major sewer or water main collapsed on Main Street, as one did recently," said Mr. Wheten, "the west end would be virtually isolated."

J. D. Campbell, president of Canadian Westinghouse, and chairman of the McMaster Growth Fund, possibly expresses the view of the majority of Hamiltonians towards the university, whatever their attitude in the present controversy. "McMaster University has adapted itself vigorously to the educational needs of a rapidly growing industrial city and area. Its graduates are found everywhere in business and the professions. Its faculty members are active in civic, cultural, educational, and church organizations. More than 5,000 people attend evening classes, about one-third of them taking courses leading to academic degrees, the others seeking to expand their knowledge.

"McMaster," said Mr. Campbell, "has vastly enriched the community in many ways."

In the opinion of John Trimble, former chairman of the Hamilton board of education, the part played by schools and cultural forces in the life of the average adult will increase materially in the near future.

"Education for employment," says John Trimble, "will be a continuing factor during each person's productive years. Going to school will become as commonplace as going to church or the drive-in. Most adults will spend some time in school upgrading skills, perfecting hobbies, appreciating the arts, discovering great literature. Curricula will achieve dramatic changes. Ethics, morality, comparative religion, the arts, and philosophy will assume a larger share of teaching time. The objective will be the steady expansion of man's understanding of both the why and how of living.

"But the primary function of education will be to teach people how to find facts for themselves, to research and evaluate, to answer their own questions, to think."

Labour supported McMaster University in its expansion program, so possibly Labour will agree with Mr. Trimble when he declares, "It will be common for collective bargaining agreements to provide for a shorter work week, conditional upon a certain amount of leisure time being spent in school."

In this he is echoed by the city's new chief librarian, Charles E. Brisbin, Ph.D., who succeeded Freda F. Waldon, M.A., LL.D., chief librarian from 1940 to 1963, a dedicated public servant under whose guidance the Hamilton library system attained a standard unsurpassed by libraries functioning on a much higher per-capita grant. Tall, personable Mr. Brisbin is outspoken. "The library," he declares, "must prepare for the day of automation, of increased leisure, of intensified and prolonged formal education, as well as more adult self education."

The winds of change are blowing in the lunch-pail town. Almost throughout Hamilton's industry the plant cafeteria has replaced the lunch pail. The new class of worker today, accustomed to the cultural advantages of Europe, is protesting the city's sterility. The impact of McMaster is taking effect.

Yet prior to World War II the Hamilton library had added only four branches—the Barton, Locke, Mountain and Kenilworth—and since the war, the functionally designed, attractive Western branch; a new replacement for the outmoded Barton Street branch opened in 1908; and the modern Sherwood on the Mountain.

By careful management of the Library Board—present chairman, Marvin R. Farewell—and knowledgeable planning by Chief Librarian Mrs. Norman Lyle and her successor, Dr. Waldon, and by Mrs. Isabelle Skelly, assistant librarian, and the staff, the popular boys' and girls' department of the main library was supplemented by three school branches, by boxes of books circulated to classrooms, and finally by a bookmobile.

In 1924 the library under E. W. Browning pioneered in Canada with an arts and science department, offering both reference and circulating books and magazines in science, technology and the arts. To meet coming demands, however, much more is required. As a minimum, library expansion on the Mountain and a main library several times the size of the present Carnegie building are urged by Charles Brisbin.

Today the Hamilton Art Gallery[1] has a membership exceeding twenty-five hundred. "In the last fifteen years," says director T. R. MacDonald, RCA, appointed in 1947, "from a static collection we have gathered an ever growing permanent and quite outstanding collection of paintings, sculpture, drawings and prints by Canadian artists and those of other countries, which serves as a nucleus for important gallery activities.

"Lecture programs," said the gallery director, "bring fresh viewpoints and insight. Classes for children and adults provide opportunities for personal participation and creation. Visits from children and the films and slides program are a very important part of gallery work."

In Little Theatre the upswing of interest has resulted in a drama group, it would seem, in every church and parish hall and in every school from McMaster University down. Among the leading groups in the city the Players' Guild, founded by Miss Caroline Crerar in 1930 and now owning its own headquarters building on Queen Street South, was joined in the 1950's by the Hamilton Theatre Company (later, Hamilton Theatre Incorporated), a lively, ambitious musical theatre organization which hires professional directors and choreographers and has attained "sold out" status for its productions; the Temple Players and the Hamilton Opera Company, both young and promising groups; and St. Thomas More Players founded by the late David W. Farr in 1956, which with the Players' Guild has won awards in both the Western Ontario Drama League and the Dominion Drama Festival.

Changing both name and status, the Royal Hamilton College of Music, formerly the Hamilton Conservatory, opened in 1965 with a faculty of sixty-four teachers, five district branches, and an expanded program. From Bach to barbershop to bop, old and new musical groups are flourishing, the Hamilton Police Male Chorus and The Fire Department Drum and Bugle Corps winning special renown.

The Head-of-the-Lake Historical Society—president Miss Mary H. Farmer—with the help of a city council grant brought out its sixth issue of Wentworth Bygones, edited by Rev. T. M. Bailey, T. R. Woodhouse and William M. McCulloch. In 1944 the society was founded by Col. C. R. McCollough, with Dr. A. H. Wingfield president. Several writers in the city and at McMaster University are being published. And in the Bohemian Coffee House at 26 Gore Street, a group of university students, under the direction of James Cox, for three nights presented a reading of Dylan Thomas' play for voices, Under Milk Wood.

Only from Hamilton's lone angry young man, chief librarian Charles Brisbin, comes a monitory word. "If Hamilton is to be revitalized as is planned, it will need to be more than an ambitious city. It will have to be a daring city, an imaginative city, a city with an identity beyond the Botanical Gardens, steel mills, and even, possibly, a football club!"

The daring city and the imaginative city are on the drawing boards thanks to Kenneth Soble and the man he engaged, Murray Jones. When he speaks of the future, however, Mr. Soble discusses the city in prosaic, everyday terms.

"Changes in Hamilton over the next quarter-century," he says, "will be prodigious. Citizens are beginning to appreciate that our developing environment can be made to conform, through proper planning and, where necessary, urban renewal, to all of our hopes for this community. Because of this it is not likely that Hamilton will be a city with an archaic and dying centre, ringed by mushrooming, poorly integrated suburbs. Rather it will be a city of nearly half a million people, which shows the results of intelligent restoration and positive, well directed growth.

"In many areas of the city we shall see little radical change, but decay will no longer be evident. Really bad structures will be removed. Reasonably good ones will be restored so that citizens who wish to do so may live in homes that incorporate the best in spaciousness and elegance of the past.

"Throughout the city, public and private buildings will offer oases of greenery; and malls and walkways with trees and attractive landscaping will invite strollers to shop at their pleasure."

All these are brave new things. To remind the city of its past, Murray Jones included in his Civic Square, on the southwest corner of Jackson and MacNab Streets, the dignified square stone town house, Whitehern, given the city by the family of the late Isaac McQuesten, to be maintained as a memorial to Calvin McQuesten, iron founder, and his grandson, the Hon. T. B. McQuesten. Built about 1843 by Richard Duggan, the twenty-four-room house behind its high stone wall was purchased in 1852 by Dr. McQuesten. A manufacturer of stoves, Dr. McQuesten heated Willow Bank, as the house was first named, with one of the earliest furnaces in the community.

Today its original furnishings, lovingly preserved, remain practically intact. In the drawing room the high-ceilinged walls are covered with paper hung over a century ago—a formal pattern of grape clusters in hand-applied gold leaf on a white background.

"Everything came from Boston," says the Rev. Calvin McQuesten, who occupies the house with his sister, Miss Hilda Belle, under a lifetime tenancy, "wallpaper, carpets, curtains, lambrequins, furniture." He added, with satisfaction, "There was nothing good enough in New York City!"

About the house on its double terrace the garden of the Hon. Thomas B. McQuesten, park lover, still flourishes. Above the carpeting myrtle and lily of the valley, laburnums hang their tasselled gold. Against the south wall, giant sunflowers and lilies, forged in the family foundry, glow timelessly.

Says Eric R. Arthur, professor of architectural design, school of architecture, University of Toronto, ". . . Whitehern [is] a unique example in perfect state of preservation of a gentleman's estate of the first half of

the nineteenth century. House and buildings and gardens are all there.
. . . In its peace and quiet, so close to the hurly burly of Main Street,
future citizens, and particularly the children of the future, may have a
vision of a vanished world of highly civilized, well mannered people—a
small world perhaps in the 1840's but nevertheless one that laid the
foundation of the city of Hamilton today."

When Willow Bank was young and the great willows that gave it its
name stood at the four corners of the house, the Mountain had looked
down on meadow land and wood lots between its lower slopes and the
gray house walls. Now on the pasture where the McQuesten children
had driven the family cow to graze, the gleaming glass and concrete
layers of today's "vertical expansion" thrust upwards.

So much had been accomplished in such a little time—only a fraction
of the Mountain's life span. Yet the city forgot how far it had come in its
concern over how far it had to go. The Mountain tunnels would arrive;
the inevitable system of rapid transit; and the linking crosstown arteries.
The north end, rejuvenated, would bloom again. York Street would
emerge like Cinderella from the drab chimney corner and triumphantly
don the glass slipper; and the Civic Square would some day stand, a
centre of culture, much as it had been planned.

Above, the Mountain's city-within-a-city at a future time would out-
grow its parent below. Only one constant would remain, separating each
from the other, yet at the same time binding them with a common bond—
the enduring Mountain.

Each generation the Mountain had looked down upon had considered
its problems unique—more formidable and more urgent than any before.
Impatiently the people harried and drove themselves to overcome the
difficulties that confronted them. Yet after their generation had vanished,
the problems they solved so triumphantly would generate even greater
perplexities for those who followed them.

Unmoved, the Mountain had withstood the quarrying of his strength
for their short-lived homes and troublesome streets, their inept blasting
and boggling of mountainside roadways. They had used his slopes for rape,
for canned heat orgies, for brawls, for violence. Under the shield of night
they had tossed incriminating bodies upon him—the young and beautiful
and the beheaded, armless and legless—both to be found on a happy
day's hike by the inevitable enquiring child.

Yet they had also sent him lovers, in all generations, and children to
make trails across his face, to explore and climb, and sometimes to fall,
discovering here a whole wonderful world of make believe. For a time
the busy people of the city had turned from him. Now with this generation
and the next they were returning again to his slopes.

Generation by generation they had come and gone: John Depue,
Robert Land, and Richard Beasley, Sir Allan MacNab, Isabella Hyde, the
five Johns, Ethel Kinrade, Tom Longboat, Dr. Ingersoll Olmstead,
William Southam, the blue-eyed Nora Frances Henderson, Dr. P. W.

294

Philpott, Rabbi Arthur Feldman, Sam Lawrence, Captain Cornelius and the Rev. Aubrey Jones, Judge William Schwenger and several million more. Each had come and gone leaving his mark, to grow fainter and fainter as the years passed.

The people came and went and were forgotten. Only the city would survive and only the mark each put upon the city would remain.

It had outgrown its puny infancy and gangling youth. The city now is indestructible.

And the city is the sum total of all its people of all time.

Acknowledgements

WITHOUT THE assistance of a great many people this book would never have been written.

Initially, of course, it was His Worship Mayor Lloyd D. Jackson and the City Council of 1961-62 who approved and made the project of a city history possible, and Mayor "Vic" Copps and City Council of 1965-66 who encouraged and supported its completion.

While the various departments of City Hall were universally helpful, my special gratitude must go to former City Clerk James F. Berry for accommodating me in his department for a much longer time than he had anticipated, for making city records available, and on occasion for interpreting these from his wide knowledge of corporation legislation; to his successor, Mr. E. A. Simpson, for similar courtesy, and to the department itself for making my stay in City Hall a most pleasant one. To Miss Marjorie Marshall, mayor's secretary during three administrations, to Keith E. Avery, deputy city clerk, and to Jack R. Jones, secretary to the Board of Control, my warmest thanks for their many acts of helpfulness.

Especially am I indebted to City Engineer Waldo A. Wheten and his department for information, for maps and reproductions, and for making available Mr. William Cust and his knowledge of early city developments; and to R. C. Monaghan, deputy city engineer, for reading the manuscript; to the legal department and Solicitors J. B. Chambers and W. M. McCulloch for their many patient interpretations of legal mysteries, and to Solicitor K. A. Rouff; to William Muirhead, Commissioner of Streets and Sanitation, and his department; to Miss Florence Meiler, Director of Recreation; and B. Harrison, of the Service Department, for copies and reproductions; and to City Treasurer J. C. Jaggard and N. A. Wilkes, assessment commissioner, and their staffs for data and figures.

To Chief of Police L. G. Lawrence and Chief of the Fire Department R. F. Swanborough, my appreciation for their cooperation and for the assistance given by Inspector Gordon V. Torrance and Douglas A. Jehan of their respective departments.

As representative of Hamilton industry, it is a pleasure to acknowledge the contribution of information and illustrations supplied by The Steel Company of Canada Limited, Dominion Foundries and Steel Company Limited, and Canadian Westinghouse Company Limited. Special thanks to Mr. W. A. Campbell, president and general manager of Wallace Barnes Company Limited, who as chairman of the Hamilton Industrial Commission provided material relative to Hamilton industry in general. In this field also my thanks to Milford L. Smith, financial editor of *The Hamilton Spectator.*

To *The Hamilton Spectator* itself my appreciation for the wealth of information obtained from its daily files and anniversary and special publications, including the historical features of Mabel Burkholder, Ella J. Reynolds, former managing editor, James G. O'Neil, Erroll Boyd, Frank L. Jones, and Fred Howe. To other city publications of the past— *The Hamilton Times, The Hamilton Herald* and *The Hamilton Review* —my appreciation also.

My warmest gratitude to the Hamilton Public Library: to Mr. Charles E. Brisbin, Chief Librarian, who added to my indebtedness by reading manuscript, and to Dr. Freda Waldon, former Chief Librarian; to Miss Dorothy Simpson, Miss Mary Farmer, Miss Katharine Greenfield, and other staff members of the Reference Room, and Miss A. Elizabeth Mullin, department of Arts and Science, who helped immeasurably with the research required for this book. To McMaster University library and *The Hamilton Spectator* library, to the Department of Public Records and Archives, Toronto; and the Public Archives of Canada, Ottawa, my appreciation also.

In the educational field, assistance is gratefully acknowledged from the Board of Education of the City of Hamilton, and the Inspector of Separate Schools, Hamilton Division; from McMaster University; from Hillfield-Strathallan Colleges; from Loretto Academy; and from Cathedral High School (Boys) and Cathedral High School (Girls). Thanks also to Katherine (Mrs. Frank) Panabaker for recalling schools of the past, and to John Trimble for forecasting the school of the future. In allied fields, acknowledgement also to the Royal Hamilton College of Music, and the Hamilton Art Gallery.

To the Hamilton Civic Hospitals, St. Joseph's Hospital, Chedoke General and Children's Hospitals (Hamilton Health Association), the Ontario Hospital, and St. Peter's Infirmary my thanks.

As it is impossible to name individually even a fraction of the Hamilton institutions which have generously contributed material to this history may I offer, as representative, the Hamilton Harbour Commission, the Board of Park Management, with special thanks to Chairman T. J. Newlands and E. R. Seager, secretary; the Royal Botanical Gardens; the Hamilton Street Railway Company, by virtue of W. J. McCulloch; and Radio Stations CKOC, CHML, CHML-FM, CHIQ, and Station CHCH-TV.

For the city of the future, encompassing North End Urban Renewal,

Civic Square, and York Street, thanks are due Mr. Kenneth D. Soble, chairman of the Renewal Committee, and Urban Renewal Commissioner Graham Emslie.

Of the many individuals who have given family histories, recollections of old times, or stories of bygone Hamiltonians, space again permits mention of only a few. To the Hon. Lester B. Pearson, Prime Minister of Canada, who found time to write a personal reminiscence of the city, my most sincere appreciation.

To the Hon. Ellen L. Fairclough my thanks, and to Mrs. William Hendrie and the late Miss Caroline Crerar; to Donald O. Cannon, registrar, County of Wentworth, for immeasurable help; to A. F. Stewart, clerk-treasurer of the County of Wentworth; W. L. McFaul, former city engineer; Mr. F. I. Ker, former vice-president and publisher of *The Hamilton Spectator*; Mr. C. Hunter MacBain; Dr. H. R. McAlister; Mrs. Gwen Metcalfe, curator of Dundurn Castle; James Stowe, president of the Hamilton and District Labour Council; Robert R. Gage; and T. Roy Woodhouse, historian.

To the descendants of the founding Stewart, Depew, Land, and Beasley families and of other pioneers who feature in these pages, my hope that I have not failed them.

Lastly, and above all, to my long-suffering family who for four years have lived with the City of Hamilton almost as a living entity, my profound appreciation.

M. F. C.

Notes

NOTES TO CHAPTER ONE

1. Earlier called Marcassah Bay, Big Washquarter, Lake Geneva, and Burlington Bay.

2. Also called Little Washquarter, Coote's Paradise gained its name from Captain Thomas Coote, 8th King's Own Regiment, a keen sportsman who devoted all his spare time to shooting the ducks, geese and wild pigeons that fed by the thousands on the wild rice beds of the marsh.

3. C. Hunter MacBain, B.A., "Hamilton—One Hundred Years Ago," Hamilton: The Hamilton Association for the Advancement of Literature, Science and Art, 100th Anniversary, 1957, p. 12.

4. Escarpment height varies from under 300 feet to over 1,000 feet in the Blue Mountain section near Collingwood . . . L. J. Chapman & D. F. Putnam, *The Physiography of Southern Ontario*, Toronto: University of Toronto Press, 1951, p. 135.

NOTES TO CHAPTER TWO

1. All food consumed in Fort Niagara and other western forts was transported by slow sailing ship from Britain to Quebec or Montreal and thence by canoe, batteau, and schooner up the portage-impeded St. Lawrence River to Lake Ontario. So many Indians starved near the fort in the winter of 1779-80 that in the spring 1,500 were moved upstream and settled about Buffalo Creek. Log cabins (not longhouses) were erected and corn fields cultivated.

2. Francis Goring, *Reminiscences*, quoted from Land Board Records, P.A.C., N.H.S., No. 28, p. 26.

3. P.A.C., quoted by E. A. Cruikshank, N.H.S., No. 39, p. 30.

4. To all who had remained loyal to Great Britain during the American Revolution and who had lost their property through abandonment or confiscation, Britain promised land: 200 acres to each loyalist, man or woman, and 200 acres to each child of a loyalist as he or she came of age; and a graduated scale for soldiers and officers who had seen active service varying from 50 to 5,000 acres.

5. In 1782 and '83 John Depew, George Stewart and their families are listed as settlers drawing rations at Niagara. On the 1784 list John Depew, George

Stewart and Hamilton Loyalist Robert Land all appear. No list is available for 1785. In 1786 Charles De Pugh (!), Robert Land and George Stewart are listed. Charles De Pugh (Depew) appears for the first time as head of a family, with a wife and female infant. George Stewart, previously with three sons, now has an infant daughter. John Depew and his family are missing from the 1786 list. The 1787 list contains none of the above names. One can only deduce therefore that John Depew left for the Lakehead prior to the 1786 listing, and the other three followed him sometime before the ration list of 1787 was compiled . . . Loyalist Victualling List for the district of Niagara, 14 Nov., 1786, (R.G. 19, C 35, vol. 1, file 1), P.A.C.

6. Lots 3, 4 and 5, B.F., and Cons. 1, 2, and 3.

7. Remains from both cemeteries reinterred in Sunken Gardens, Hamilton Cemetery.

8. Direct descendants of Charles Depew, Jr., their great-grandfather: Miss Mary E. Bates, retired Hamilton primary school teacher, Miss Beatrice G. Bates, Mrs. Ernest Shirlaw, Mrs. J. R. West and James M. Bates, all of Burlington, Ontario, the latter Burlington's Citizen of the Year for 1962 and principal for 35 years of Burlington Central High School. Also the late John F. Bates, Stoney Creek, Miss Mary Depew, Simcoe, and Miss Lydia Depew, Paris, Ontario.

9. New Jersey Archives, Second Series, Vol. III, 1779, p. 226.

10. Prof. John M. Coleman, O.H.S., Vol. XLVIII, No. 2, 1956, pp. 47-62.

11. Pennsylvania Archives, Harrisburg, Series 1, Vol. VIII, p. 597.

12. Petition, Robert Land to Sir Henry Clinton, July 10, 1780, The University of Michigan, Ann Arbor.

13. Register of baptisms, Parish of Trinity Church, New York City, Jan. 21, 1781.

14. Haldiman Papers, B-102, p. 150.

15. E. A. Cruikshank, N.H.S., No. 39, p. 42.

16. Bourinot, *Memoirs of Dundurn and Burlington Heights*, Toronto: The Copp-Clark Company, 1900, p. 6.

17. Loyalist Victualling List for the district of Niagara, 14, Nov., 1786, (R.G. 19, C 35, vol. 1, file 1), P.A.C.

18. Lot 11, B.F., and Cons. 1, 2 and 3, Barton Twp., May 17, 1802.

19. Before razing in 1928 "Landholme" served during World War I as the Victoria Convalescent Home; was transferred to the Military Hospital Commission; later became the Children's Home. Today's direct descendants of Robert Land are Mrs. John F. Alton and Mrs. C. M. Clinton, both of Burlington.

NOTES TO CHAPTER THREE

1. Until 1791 Canada, from the St. Lawrence to the prairies, was the province of Quebec. The Constitutional Act of 1791 divided Quebec into Upper and Lower Canada.

2. E. A. Cruikshank, Extract from the Quebec Land Book, N.H.S., No. 40, pp. 55, 56.

3 E. A. Cruikshank, N.H.S., No. 38, 1927, p. 69.

4. This would seem the source of the story first related by Mrs. Mary E. Rose Holden ("Burlington Bay, Beach and Heights in History," W.H.S., 1899, Vol. 2, p. 27), that Simcoe in 1792 intended to locate the "little town then springing up" on Burlington Bay, on Burlington Heights, but was forced to withdraw his offer of purchase because of the exorbitant price demanded for his land by

Beasley. The story is obviously erroneous. In 1792 there was no town at the head of the Lake. Beasley did not own the land. By 1799, when it was finally patented to him, Simcoe had been gone from Canada three years. Furthermore, if Simcoe had wanted the site he would have expropriated it, as the government reserved Burlington Heights. Simcoe was undoubtedly referring to the King's Head Inn built the following year at the southern end of Burlington Beach.

5. The J.P. tried petty offences and heard minor civil actions in his neighborhood. As a member of the Court of General Sessions he sat on criminal cases, enacted local legislation for his district, levied and disbursed taxes, granted licenses, and superintended the erection of court houses and gaols and the building of bridges.

6. O.A.T.: Twp. Papers, Barton Twp., Con. 2, Lots 14 and 15.

NOTES TO CHAPTER FOUR

1. George E. Mason, *The Barton Lodge*, Hamilton, 1895, pp. 37, 127.

2. This was the home of the Widow Morden, first settler of Dundas, whose husband, Ralph, was hanged for guiding Robert Land. The latter is said to have suggested their location at the Lakehead.

3. Letter, Jan. 24, 1895, Peter Spohn Van Wagner, to F. H. Lynch-Staunton, P.L.S. (Provincial Land Surveyor), Hamilton. Family Papers owned by Miss Myra M. Hamilton, Toronto.

4. Under French feudal tenure land could not be owned outright, sold, or traded, willed, or even fully controlled as to use, being held and worked by the tenant under a scheme of quit rents of the produce raised.

5. Mabel Dunham, *Grand River*, Toronto: McClelland and Stewart Limited, 1945, p. 97.

6. Rousseau Collection, 1774-1871, 27 Feb. 1797, O.A.T., p. 14.

7. W.H.S., 1902, p. 47.

8. Throughout North America the end of the 18th and beginning of the 19th centuries was a time of gigantic land swindles: millions of acres of land were exploited for settlement purposes and raped of forests and natural resources.

9. Charles M. Johnston, "An Outline of Early Settlement in the Grand River Valley," O.H.S., Vol. LIV, No. 1, March, 1962, pp. 54-55.

10. Mabel Dunham, op. cit., pp. 85-96.

11. Of the total Indian crown grant of 768,000 acres along the Grand River, some 352,707 acres was acquired by white speculators, mostly leading citizens of the province, who bought the land with the smallest possible down payment, terms spread over 999 years, and annual interest on which they defaulted. Government interference to protect Indian rights created such strong Indian displeasure and distrust that the government reluctantly approved the action taken by the Council of the Six Nations in endorsing Brant.

NOTES TO CHAPTER FIVE

1. E. A. Cruikshank, *Documentary History of the War of 1812*, Pt. III, pp. 84, 85, 87, 88.

2. William Wood, *The War with the United States*, Chronicles of Canada, 14, Toronto: Glasgow, Brook and Company, 1915, p. 74.

3. In 1789 it was decreed that all loyalists "who had adhered to the Unity of the Empire and joined the royal standard before the Treaty of Separation in the year 1783, and all their children and their descendants, by either sex," should

be registered and distinguished by having the capitals, U.E., affixed to their names.

4. George E. Mason, *The Barton Lodge*, Hamilton, 1895, p. 127.

5. Since Captain Hamilton served under Major P. L. Chambers at Detroit, he may have been with the detachment of the 41st Regiment and militia under Chambers' command already waiting for Brock at Point aux Pins, Lake Erie.

6. E. B. Biggar, *The Hamilton Spectator*, Hamilton, June, 1873.

7. E. B. Biggar, Reprint, J. H. Smith, W.H.S., Vol. 10, 1922, p. 120.

8. P.A.C., C. 679, p. 30.

9. P.A.C., C. 679, p. 28.

NOTES TO CHAPTER SIX

1. E. A. Cruikshank, N.H.S., No. 44, 1939, p. 78.

2. *The Daily Spectator*, Oct. 4, 1875, Copy from Gen. Mewburn's Papers, courtesy Frank L. Jones, H.P.L., Ref. Rm.

3. Hon. Wm. R. Riddell, "The Ancaster Bloody Assize," O.H.S., No. XX, 1923, pp. 109-113. Also, P.A.C.,Sundries, 1814; E. A. Cruikshank, O.H.S., No. XXV, 1929, pp. 212-213.

4. H. H. Robertson, "Gore District Militia," W.H.S., Vol. 4, 1905, p. 31.

5. Widow of Private James Gage, 2nd Regiment, Ulster County, New York Militia, killed defending Forts Clinton and Montgomery against the British, Oct. 6, 1777. Proof of Service: Archives of State of New York, Vol. 1, p. 549; Year Book of the Sons of the Revolution in the State of New York, 1909, p. 439. From formal declaration of James Gage Beemer, Jr., great-great-grandson of James Gage and Mary Jones Gage, in membership application, Sons of the Revolution. Verified and accepted, March 22, 1915. All data courtesy Hamilton Alderman William McCulloch, authority on the James Gage family, and Mr. Clyde V. Gage, Worchester, New York, genealogist, Gage family.

6. Letter, A. Hamilton to Mrs. Henderson, No. 1 Park Street, Edinburgh, 1813, P.A.C., N. AM. War of 1812, R.G. 8, "C" Series, Vol. 679, 1.

7 Patented to Daniel Springer, May 17, 1802. Sold April 2, 1803, for £50 to John Springer. On Nov. 10, 1803, John Springer sold 27 acres to Thomas Dexter, innkeeper, for £120, and on Dec. 28 eight acres to James Durand for £40.5.0. Later Durand purchased the remainder of John Springer's holding but because of the loss of this deed and destruction of the Lincoln County Registry office during the War of 1812, date of this final purchase can only be inferred as 1806.

Two arguments support this date. In April, 1806, Durand bought Thomas Dexter's 27 acres for £312.10.0; and in the *Reminiscences of Charles Durand*, Charles, the son of James, dates in 1806 his father's transfer from Norfolk County to the Barton farm and his stepmother's death by being thrown from the carriage descending Hamilton Mountain to her new home.

Certainly Durand possessed the farm in 1809, for in that year, on May 24, he bought from Nathaniel Hughson the block of land to the north lying between Main and King Streets, in order to extend his farm to the travelled road, King Street, Main being then only a concession line not yet opened. Abstract of Titles, George Hamilton Survey, The Registry Office, County of Wentworth, Hamilton: Courtesy Mr. Donald O. Cannon, Registrar.

8. Charles Durand, *Reminiscences of Charles Durand*, Toronto: The Hunter-Rose Co., Ltd. 1897, pp. 15, 19, 21.

9. *Ibid.*, p. 17.
10. See note 6, above.
11. Agnes H. Lemon, W.H.S., Vol. 2, Hamilton, 1899, p. 136.
12. *Acts of Great Britain Applying to Upper Canada.* Printed by R. C. Horne, York, 1818, Chap. XIX.
13. "Report of Committee on the Gore," H.C.C., Mar. 3, 1847.
14. *Ibid.*, Mar. 19, 1847.
15. *Ibid.*, Feb. 8, 1847.
16. *Historical Atlas, County of Wentworth,* Toronto: Page & Smith, 1875.

NOTES TO CHAPTER SEVEN

1. Charles Durand, *Reminiscences of Charles Durand,* Toronto: The Hunter-Rose Co., Ltd., 1897, p. 151. Direct descendants of Charles Durand are his great-grandson, James V. Bacon, Hamilton, and his children, Susan, Elizabeth, and Mrs. Ann-Marie Edwards; and great-grandsons Charles E. and Paul H. Durand.

2. Captain William Johnson Kerr, by blood one-quarter Mohawk, was the son of Dr. Robert Kerr, prominent surgeon of Niagara, and his wife Elizabeth, daughter of Sir William Johnson, British agent of Indian Affairs for North America, and the famous and beautiful Molly Brant, sister of Chief Joseph Brant. W. J. Kerr married his cousin, Elizabeth Brant, daughter of Joseph Brant.

3. *The Hamilton Spectator,* 100th Anniversary, "Early District Journal Key to Past," July 15, 1946.

4. W.H.S., Vol. 2, 1899, pp. 88-89.

5. For 55 years, 1833-1888, the old minutes of the Board of Police and the subsequent city council are written in longhand. After 1888 council minutes are printed and indexed, simplifying research but losing in the process their personal touch and sense of immediacy.

6. In 1840 elections of three of the four members were protested. In addition the protest against the election of one member was itself protested. Furthermore, the four, after being declared elected, were unable to elect a fifth member and a general election became necessary. Minutes, Hamilton Board of Police, 1833-1847.

7. H. H. Robertson, "Desjardin's Canal," W.H.S., Vol. 5, Hamilton, 1908, pp. 19-30. Peter Desjardin was James Durand's clerk in Simcoe. He accompanied Durand to the Lakehead and settled in Dundas, and was riding with the party on horseback when Mrs. Durand was killed.

8. George E. Mason, *The Barton Lodge,* Hamilton, 1895, pp. 157-158.

9. Mr. B. Charlton, *Journal and Proceedings of the Hamilton Association,* Session 1890-'91. The tombstone of Capt. McKeen bears the following inscription: "Sacred to the memory of Captain John McKeen who was a partner of James G. Strowbridge for the construction of Burlington Bay Canal, who died September, 1824 . . . This monument Was Erected by J. G. S., 1831." Two years later Mr. Strowbridge was interred nearby.

10. In 1825 the first Hamilton Post Office, operated by William B. Sheldon, stood on Main Street near James; in 1827 was moved to James North, near Gore, the postmaster being A. R. Smith; the following year to James, north of Rebecca, with the postmaster, J. M. Cameron. In 1831 Edmund Ritchie was appointed. In early years a flag was hoisted to show arrival of the mail.

NOTES TO CHAPTER EIGHT

1. This and all future Board of Police records will be found in the Minute Books, City Hall, Hamilton, under the individual dates quoted.

2. In future the simpler King Street and John Street, gradually adopted, will be used.

3. Prior to incorporation "Hamilton's Plot" had undoubtedly served as a rudimentary market site, with markets held on certain days. One visitor described a Saturday market with one wagon, three or four wheelbarrows and several baskets of produce for sale.

4. William J. Gilbert, William Daley and Alexander Carpenter, all and each to be only liable for his proportion of the amount of said note, or of the deficiency if any there shall be in payment of the same out of the taxes and monies of the Corporation.

5. Part of Lot 14, Cons. 2, Barton, granted by the crown to Ralph Clinch and transferred in 1801 to John Askin, who sold it in 1805 to Nathaniel Hughson, Sr., for £100. On May 24, 1809, Hughson sold the southernmost 14 acres, lying between King and Main, James Street and the line of Mary, to James Durand for £10, Durand in turn disposing of it in 1815 to George Hamilton. The remaining 86 acres of Lot 14, lying north of King Street, Nathaniel Hughson, Sr., sold to three purchasers: the front part to Ebenezer and John Stinson for £1,000; the west half to James Hughson, his son, for 1,000 guineas; and the east half to Nathaniel, Jr., for 1,000 guineas.

6. In 1846 the corporation bought an additional 20 feet, fronting on King William Street east of the fire engine lot, making the latter 50 feet in width.

7. Descended from Lieut. William Milne, R.N., who served at the Nile and the battle of Trafalgar, Thomas W. D. Farmer, Editor-in-Chief of *The Hamilton Spectator*, his brother, G. R. D. Farmer, and sisters, Mrs. P. M. McCormack and Miss Eleanor, are connected by marriage with George Hamilton and also with John Law.

8. In 1834 Stephen Randall resigned as headmaster of the Gore District School, then located at the corner of King and Wellington Streets, to become publisher of the Hamilton *Free Press*, established in 1831 by William Smith. His place was taken by his assistant, James Cahill. When Mr. Cahill left in turn to study law, Dr. Rae and Mr. Tassie were appointed.

9. Opened in 1820 by Edward Leslie and William Lyon Mackenzie, later purchased by Mackenzie, and sold about 1823 to John Leslie who operated it successfully for forty years.

NOTES TO CHAPTER NINE

1. Of eight children born to the founder and his wife, three had died as infants, leaving to survive their father, besides the heir, three daughters, Maria, Catharine and Augusta Caroline, and a second son, George, Jr., who would die in 1840, aged nineteen. Today William Harvey Hamilton and his descendants, of Redonda Beach, California, are direct descendants of John, son of Robert Jarvis, and his wife, Ann Elizabeth Farmer. Hamilton descendants of Peter Hunter Hamilton are Miss Lydia, Miss Kathleen E. and George Wilfred Hamilton.

2. Registry Office, County Halton, Milton, April 7, 1870, D. Henderson, Deputy Registrar.

3. Records, City Hall, Hamilton, Beasley File.

4. *Ibid.*

5. P.A.C., Beasley File.

6. Local descendants today of Thomas Beasley include James and Alec Z. Beasley, Hamilton, brothers of David; Bruce C. Beasley, Burlington, and his sons David B. and Gary D. Beasley. Great-granddaughter of Richard is Miss M. L. Beasley.

7. George W. Spragge, Editor, *The John Strachan Letter Book*, 1812-1834, O.H.S., 1946, p. 171.

8. *Western Mercury*, July 4, 1833, No. 125, H.P.L.

9. F. Kidner, W.H.S., Vol. 3, 1902, pp. 73-74.

NOTES TO CHAPTER TEN

1. As with the fire engine house, first award, £7.10.0, went to William Hardy, with Messrs. Tassie and Samuel Shenstone receiving 25 shillings each for their submissions. In addition to drawing the plans, Mr. Hardy also built the market house, receiving from the board a total of £800, divided into twenty instalments spread over six years.

2. First located to Ralph Clinch (Clench), Lot 15, Cons. 2, extending from James Street to Bay Street and from Barton to Main, became in 1801 a Crown grant to John Askin. In 1805 the latter sold the whole to Nathaniel Hughson. After passing through several hands a plot of seven acres, lying north of York Street and west of James, was purchased by Andrew Miller. Of this plot, now a bearing apple orchard, 2 roods, 10 perches (slightly over one-half acre) was presented on April 14, 1837, by Mr. Miller to the corporation in perpetuity, providing the land was used as a market site and for a market house.

3. Deeds, James Street Market File. Minutes, Hamilton Board of Police, Oct. 1, 1849.

4. Victor Ross, *History of the Canadian Bank of Commerce*, Vol. 1, p. 174.

5. Although the bank directors supported MacNab in a public statement, Colin Ferrie was returned as president. Later MacNab resigned as solicitor, his place, however, being taken by his partner, Mr. Hatt of Dundas.

6. On the mountain the Stone Church in Barton was the stronger part of the charge.

7. June 6, 1846: Act of Incorporation of the City of Hamilton, Provincial Statutes, 9 Victoria, 1846, p. 981.

8. Council: *St. George's Ward*, Samuel B. Freeman, Samuel Mills; *St. Patrick's*, Daniel Kelly, H. R. O'Reilly; *St. Lawrence*, Nehemiah Ford, Charles O. Counsell; *St. Andrew's*, Daniel C. Gunn, Hugh B. Willson; *St. Mary's*, Mr. Ferrie, Andrew Miller.

9. W. H. Smith, *Canadian Gazetteer*, pp. 49-50, 75-77.

10. Dr. Beverley Ketchen, "Centennial Year, 1854-1954," MacNab Presbyterian Church, Hamilton, 1954.

NOTES TO CHAPTER ELEVEN

1. Municipal Corporations, U.C., Act 12 Victoria, Chap. 81: Baldwin's Act, May 30, 1849.

2. Election of inspector discontinued in 1858.

3. See note 1, above.

4. H.C.C., Dec. 31, 1850: Annual Report of the Finance Committee.

5. Drs. W. L. Billings, John W. Hunter, William G. Dickinson, William

Craigie, Gerald O'Reilly, Kellogg, John Mackelcan, William Case III, Macartney and Thomas Duggan.

6. Previously orphans and indigents were supported by the city in foster homes. On March 15, 1852, the newly formed Roman Catholic St. Mary's Relief Society applied for and received a city grant.

7. Edward Glackmeyer, first manager. Lamps lighted at the rate of £6 each per annum, with the company responsible for lighting, extinguishing, and cleaning, and the corporation for keeping them in repair. Gas sold metered or flat rate. Minutes, Bd. of Pol., Jan. 29, 1851.

8. In July, 1837, direction of Hamilton pathmasters was transferred from the provincial Board of Road Commissioners to the Hamilton Board of Police.

9. Directory, City of Hamilton, 1858, p. 10.

10. Niagara to Windsor, 226 miles. Built at a cost of £15,000 per mile. Celebrations also held at Niagara Falls and London, Ontario, in January, 1854.

11. H.C.C., Aug. 8, 1850. Also By-Law No. 51, Aug. 29, 1850. Amended to £50,000 subscription by By-Law 74, Aug 20, 1852; debentures, already issued, as above.

12. H.C.C., July 10, 1848: Resolved to purchase from Miles O'Reilly and Hugh C. Baker, church wardens of Christ's Church, 18½ acres of 23½ purchased by said wardens from Sir Allan MacNab, church retaining 5 acres as an Anglican burial ground. Purchase price of £1,804.5.7 to include Sir Allan's conveyance to city of his license of occupation to 45 acres of military reserve to the north. Fenced by Thomas P. Kinreade, summer, 1849, and grounds laid out.

13. In consideration of this, council allowed Terence Branigan, market clerk, a reduction in his lease fee (£470.15.0) for 1849. Originally auctioned annually, the market lease was now tendered for, the successful candidate receiving in return the rent of market stalls.

14. *Spectator,* daily, semi-weekly and weekly. Published also at this time: *Hamilton Banner,* daily and weekly; *Journal & Express,* semi-weekly; *Canada Christian Advocate,* weekly; *Canada Evangelist,* monthly; and *Globe,* daily, semi-weekly and weekly, in Toronto, Hamilton agency corner King and James Streets.

NOTES TO CHAPTER TWELVE

1. Increased to meet additional construction costs developing from rock encountered on Barton Street and quicksand underlying John Street and Catharine, conditions of which council felt the city engineer and sewer contractors should have been aware.

2. City Engineer, 1856-1862; Manager, Hamilton Waterworks, 1861-1896.

3. *The Hamilton Spectator,* Sept. 12, 1908, Ref. Rm., H.P.L.

4. Records, City Hall: By-laws 103, 108, 119, 122, 124, 133, 134, 138, 145, 147, 152, *et seg.*

5. Twelve acres first acquired, ten added later, extending grounds to Dundurn Street. Crystal Palace committee, appointed at a public meeting held in the Mechanics' Hall, October 30, 1858: George H. Mills, Mayor, chairman. Architect, A. H. Hills; contractor, Robert Gordon. Total cost of Palace: $29,233. Donations: $9,874. Cost to city: $19,359.

6. In honour of Sir Allan MacNab, T. C. Keefer, waterworks engineer, and Adam Brown, water commission chairman. Mr. Brown's elm alone survived, standing to the present.

7. William John Simcoe Kerr, Hamilton barrister, married Catherine M., daughter of John W. Hunter, M.D., Hamilton. They had no issue.

NOTES TO CHAPTER THIRTEEN

1. Nathaniel Burwash, *Egerton Ryerson,* The Makers of Canada, Vol. VIII, Toronto: Morang & Co. Limited, 1910, p. 180.

2. Building on York Street about four doors west of Walton's Blacksmith shop. Benches for the school, 13/S 1½ d.; teaming benches, 2/S 6d.

3. New names show the lively turn-over in the Hamilton teaching staff of that day. The sixth name resulted from a recent ruling of the board that the 5 school sections be retained in everything except disbursement of the school fund but that the town be nominally divided into 6 coequal portions for this matter.

4. J. H. Smith, *The Central School,* Hamilton: Hamilton Spectator Printing Co., Ltd., 1905, p. 71.

5. The system included competent teachers trained in teachers' training schools, proper inspection, uniform textbooks, and a sufficient government grant and municipal school tax to finance the program.

6. Smith, *op. cit.,* pp. 67, 70.

7. Of school trustees outstanding in service in the 1850's and 60's, Dr. Sangster lists Messrs. James Cummings, Colin C. Ferrie, William L. Distin, Oliver T. Springer, John Winer, Joseph Lister, W. G. Kerr, Tristram Bickle, Edward Magill, J. M. Williams, Hutchison Clark and Dr. W. L. Billings. "They did a noble work and the city owes them a generous debt of gratitude," he declared. "Their names should be written in letters of gold on tablets of bronze and deposited in a place of honour." Smith, *op. cit., The Central School,* pp. 78-79.

8. On original Richard Beasley land, track lay north of Cons. 4, Barton, and between Garth (Dundurn) Street and the line of Locke. Bounded on the north by a stream south of William Street.

9. Logan Stewart, *This Is Where I Live,* Hamilton: Davic-Lisson, Ltd., 1946, p. 59.

10. H.C.C., Sept. 16, 1861. On Lot 174, Bond Street.

11. Mrs. Pratt, a noted hostess, entertained largely at *Rose Arden.* In 1915 Mr. Pratt built the present Hampton Court apartments, remodelling and incorporating the old mansion into them. In 1929 the apartments were sold to Marshall M. Lounsbury, Sr., realtor. Although again remodelled and a wing added, the Smiley home was retained and still stands.

12. H.C.C., March 19, 1851. Inmates of the House of Industry now 30-odd.

13. Refused to the Ladies' Benevolent Society as an Orphan Asylum and to A. Bryson for dairy purposes in 1853, the building was restored, refurnished and returned to use as a Female House of Refuge in 1857. Male indigents were accommodated at the City Hospital. With opening of the City Hospital on Barton Street, the John Street Hospital became a House of Refuge for both sexes.

14. In 1849, the Customs House still occupied Hughson's hotel. It was then moved to a building at the foot of MacNab Street. In 1860 a new cut stone Customs House was erected on Stuart Street, west of MacNab. Today the stately building houses the Naples Macaroni Co.

NOTES TO CHAPTER FOURTEEN

1. $1,000 annually for city chamberlain (treasurer) and city clerk and $500 for the city engineer.

2. H.C.C., Oct. 15, 1860; Aug. 19, 1861.

3. *Ibid.*, Nov. 25, 1861; Dec. 6, 1861.

4. *Ibid.*, Finance Committee Report, Oct. 13, 1862.

5. In 1842 Bishop John Strachan and Sir John Beverley Robinson having withdrawn from politics, MacNab became leader of the Conservative opposition in the legislature of United Canada. From 1844-1848 he was Speaker of the House of Assembly, from 1848-1854 again Leader of the Opposition.

6. *A History of the Grand Lodge, A.F. & A.M. of Canada, in the Province of Ontario*, McCallum Press, Ltd., 1955, pp. 23, 24.

7. Mary Stuart MacNab died of tuberculosis on May 8, 1846. Her second daughter, Mary Stuart, married George Daly, second son of Sir Dominick Daly, in 1861. Sir Allan's daughter by his first wife, Anne Jane, Protestant, married John Salisbury Davenport in 1849. Her brother, Sir Allan's only son, was killed in a hunting accident in Hamilton in 1834, aged eleven.

8. Mrs. David Archibald MacNab, née Sophia Mary Stuart, sister of Sir Allan's second wife, a devout Roman Catholic. Allan and his brother married sisters. After her sister's death the widowed Mrs. D. A. MacNab remained at Dundurn as chatelaine. She had great influence with Sir Allan.

9. From the letter file of Dr. Freda Waldon and Mrs. Woodburn, daughter of the late F. W. MacBeth. Charles Burrows, 1837-1931, was a newspaper reporter, travelling correspondent, and editor (as above). At the time of MacNab's death, young Burrows was a clerk in the office of Best, the bailiff. H.P.L.

10. To John J. Anderson, New York City, Colonel William McGiverin, Hamilton, and Robert Bloomer, New Orleans. Vague stories of a "southern lady at Dundurn" may refer either to Eliza N. Bloomer or Theresa Antoinette Anderson, wives of the above. The above three owners in turn sold the property to Donald McInnes for $27,000 . . . Hamilton City Records: Abstract of Titles, Messrs. Burton and Bruce, March 2, 1868.

11. Prior to his death Sir Allan had sold 5 acres of Dundurn property to the government as site for a Deaf and Dumb Institute for $20,000. So clouded was the land with mortgages, however, that the deed was never surrendered to the government. Until 1869 the matter dropped from sight, when it became a subject of parliamentary enquiry and investigation . . . Suit in Chancery, Nov. 24, 1873, Donald McInnes, Plaintiff, and the Attorney General for the Dominion of Canada, Clause 7. Records, City Hall.

12. W. A. Child, M.A., "Iron Trade Built by Determined Men," *Hamilton Spectator*, July 15, 1926.

13. One of the twelve children of the Hon. Adam Ferrie, of Glasgow, Scotland, descendant of Admiral Ferrier, a Grandee of Spain who commanded a ship of the Spanish Armada, wrecked off Scotland in 1588. Salvaging plate and treasure Admiral Ferrier settled ashore. In 1808 Adam Ferrie emigrated to Montreal (moving to Hamilton in 1833) and founded the firm of Adam Ferrie and Company, wholesale merchants, branches of which were located in Hamilton and neighbouring communities by Colin and his brothers, John and Adam Jr., the Hamilton firm being C. and J. Ferrie and Company. Hamilton descendants of the family today include Miss Jean E. Haslett, Mrs. J. C. van Nostrand and her children, Miss Elsie McPherson, W. George Ballard, and members of the Ferrie, Young, Burbidge and Parker families.

14. Toronto: Longmans Canada Ltd., 1961.

15. McKenzie Porter tells of two sons. Lytton Strachey, David Duff, Dormer

Creston, Joan E. Morgan, Edgar A. Collard, Hector Bolitho and others carry references too numerous to mention. Lewis Melville in *Farmer George*, London: Isaac Pitman and Sons, 1907, estimates the number of children of the Duke of Kent and Madame de St. Laurent as twelve. In 1957 Archbishop Carrington of Quebec told Tom Jarvis, then church editor of *The Hamilton Spectator*, that Robert Wood, 1792-1847, commemorated by a stained glass window in the north gallery of the Cathedral of the Holy Trinity, Quebec, was the son of the Duke of Kent and Madame Julie and therefore elder half-brother of Queen Victoria... Tom Jarvis, *The Hamilton Spectator*, Aug. 3, 1957.

16. Today, descendants of Isabella Hyde include her great-granddaughters: Mrs. W. Grayson Brown (Marjorie Colquhoun), Toronto; Mrs. C. A. McClenahan (Rosomund Colquhoun), Burlington; Mrs. Westropp Armstrong (Winnifred Colquhoun), Philadelphia; and her great-great-granddaughter, Valerie L. G. Armstrong, Philadelphia.

NOTES TO CHAPTER FIFTEEN

1. In addition the Great Western Fire Brigade, organized in 1862, comprised 4 companies with a membership of about 300 men. Chief Engineer was W. H. Robinson. The Great Western also contributed land on which a fire station was opened, Jan. 1, 1857, at the corner of James and Stuart Streets.

2. The second Engine house, completed March 20, 1850, was an outsize two-storey stone building on East Market Street (King William, east of John), between Mary and Catharine site of the present Central Police station. The third was a frame and roughcast Engine house on the Market Square.

3. H.C.C., June 7, June 24, 1865.

4. Agreement with county, May 1, 1875, to Jan. 1, 1880. Mins. of the Mun. Coun. of the Corp. of the Cnty. of Wentworth, 1847-77, Dec., 1875, p. 97.

5. A branch of the United Empire Loyalist Association has existed in Hamilton since February 10, 1902, when the founding meeting was held at the home of Dr. and Mrs. G. E. Husband, with J. E. O'Reilly elected president. Current president is Dr. J. G. Dillane. Lifetime members include Brigadier Armand Smith, C.B.E., M.C., E.D., Howard Williams, R. Colin Mills, Mrs. N. M. Spack, Capt. Langsford Robinson, Miss Grace Smith, Miss Mabel Kelly, the late centenarian Miss Gertrude Smith, Stanley Mills, Miss Doris Schutz and Mrs. J. Bryce Mundie. Further descendants of James Mills today are Edwin W. Mills, S. A. Mills, W. H. Mills and Mrs. C. H. Greenway.

NOTES TO CHAPTER SIXTEEN

1. Largely built by members of the Shaver family descended from loyalist William Shaver and his wife, Catherine Book, and their 13 children. A Shaver reunion is held annually at Bethesda Church. In 1937 when 1,000 Shaver relatives gathered, a family tree was presented showing 3,600 descendants. Hamilton descendants include Miss Mabel Kelly, Dr. Gordon Kelly, Mrs. Charles H. Hubble, A. M. Shaver, Jay Shaver, Mrs. John Devitt, Miss Clara and Miss Cora Hewitt, Mrs. Edgar C. Brown, and the late Mrs. Ira Shaver, George V. P. Shaver and Warner Howell.

2. Founded in 1854 as the daily and weekly reform *Hamilton Banner* by Editor William Nicholson, Thomas McIntosh and William Bowen. Office on Hughson Street on present site of the Right House. In Jan., 1857, the *Daily*

Banner became the *Hamilton Evening Times,* a morning paper. In Feb., 1860, under Editor George Sheppard it was changed to an evening paper; in 1861 was acquired by Messrs. Jones and Holbrook; and in Jan., 1862, was purchased by Messrs. C. E. Stewart & Company, under whose management its circulation shortly increased to a healthy 40,000 weekly.

3. T. Roy Woodhouse, "Hamilton—The First Telephone Exchange in the British Empire," Wentworth Bygones, No. 3, Walsh Printing Service, Hamilton, 1962, pp. 24-29. Also, Lillian M. Shaw, "The Baker Family of Hamilton," ibid., pp. 30-34.

4. Presently by Arthur R. Peacock, the founder's grandson. Among direct descendants of Mr. and Mrs. Peacock are Mrs. William Milne, daughter; E. Manson and Frank E. Milne, grandsons, all of Burlington; and Dr. H. A. Peacock, Hamilton.

5. H.C.C., Feb. 12, 1849.

6. Of Stoney Creek. Not to be confused with Alexander Carpenter, foundry-man, son of Alexander Carpenter and Elizabeth Smith, Saltfleet, and grandson of Ashman Carpenter.

7. Under *The Toll Roads Municipal Expropriation Act,* H.C.C., Apr. 12, 1893, p. 137.

8. An early undated map also shows a road running on the Heights, past today's Rock Garden, to the old outlet where it connected by ferry with a mainland road marked, "To York."

9. As owner, John Brown, wholesale grocer, preceded Mr. McInnes, while Thomas Robertson, M.P. (later Judge) succeeded him. The latter renamed the house Rannoch Lodge. In 1911 it was purchased by Frank A. Merrick, then general manager of the Canadian Westinghouse Company, later vice-president and director. In 1950, following his death, the estate was sold by his son, Lester F. Merrick, and converted into apartments.

10. At the turn of the quarries, stormiest and coldest spot in the township in winter, muddiest in spring, dustiest and hottest in summer, and windy always.

NOTES TO CHAPTER SEVENTEEN

1. The Bank of Hamilton was chartered and opened in August, 1872, on King Street East, with a capital of $1,000,000. First officials: Donald McInnes, president; John Stuart, merchant, vice-president; H. C. Hammond, cashier and general manager.

2. Mr. Hensen and his son, Russell, under the name Sam Hensen Apartments, have converted some 25 of Hamilton's most distinguished homes to apartment use, preserving their outward appearance and, to a great degree, their original interior features.

3. Dr. William Henry Hewlett, a prominent, popular and well loved figure in Hamilton musical circles. From 1918-39, principal of the Hamilton Conservatory of Music, founded in 1897 by Dr. C. L. M. Harris with a faculty of 23 and some 75-100 pupils. Today faculty numbers 64, pupils 1,500.

4. It was enfranchised on March 29, 1873, as the Hamilton and Lake Erie railway; it amalgamated the following year with the Hamilton and Northwestern railway, and in 1880 with the Northern to become the Northern and North-western railway with terminals at Port Dover on Lake Erie, Collingwood on Lake Huron, and a junction with the Canadian Pacific near North Bay. In 1882 the Grand Trunk took over the Great Western, and in 1888 the Northern and

Northwestern. Trains previously using the Ferguson Avenue depot were routed from Stuart Street. In 1890 the roundhouse and shops were closed, and the freight sheds became the Canadian National freight office.

5. Cornerstone laid July 18, 1888. Municipal offices during construction moved to the old post office building on the east side of James Street North, later the Sun Life building, and then the Home Bank. The clock supplied by Howard Clock Company, New York, at a cost of $2,318, was serviced throughout its lifetime by the pioneer firm of Thomas Lees, watchmakers and jewellers.

6. Opened on November 29, 1880, on the east side of James Street with exit and stage doors on Gore Street, the big unadorned red-brick Grand Opera house possessed one of the largest stages in Canada, although its seating capacity was only 1,200. The Grand had two galleries. Renovated in 1892 and 1905, it was sold on Dec. 1, 1919, along with his other theatre interests for $1,700,000 by Ambrose Small who disappeared the following day and was never heard of again. As the Granada it became a vaudeville house; in 1954 was converted to cinema and renamed the Downtown; in 1961 was demolished.

NOTES TO CHAPTER EIGHTEEN

1. At the end of the century, in addition to physicians already named were, among others, Drs. John Duff Macdonald, John Mackelcan, L.R.C.S., and George Mackelcan, E. A. Gaviller, George E. Husband, James Lafferty, William Philp and M.H.O. Isaac Ryall, Jr.

2. For over one hundred years there has been a White in city medical practice, beginning in the 1860's with Thomas White, M.D., brother of Dr. James, the latter being succeeded by Dr. R. W. K. White, son of Thomas.

3. The company was founded in 1880, and in 1900 was sold to Col. James R. Moodie, brother of the founder. The company operated three mills in Hamilton until February, 1958, when they closed. Mills specialized in men's, women's, and children's underwear.

4. In 1889 the Wentworth Historical Society was formed with George H. Mills as president. In 1899, following disagreement over the site for a monument commemorating the battle of Stoney Creek, the Ladies' Auxiliary of the W.H.S. defected and formed the Women's Wentworth Historical Society under president, Mrs. John Calder, granddaughter of James Gage. Having raised funds the W.W.H.S. purchased the Gage homestead and land, and the property was opened as a public park. On June 6, 1913, Queen Mary unveiled the tower monument which had been erected with government aid. Dauntless workers for the project were Mesdames John Crerar, John S. Hendrie, T. C. Watkins, and M. O. Sealey. In 1961 homestead and park, maintained until then by the W.W.H.S., was turned over as a gift — with adjacent property purchased by the federal and provincial governments — to the Niagara Parks Commission for development as an historic site.

5. A devout Roman Catholic, on visits to Hamilton, Sophia paid her respects to the Sisters of St. Joseph to whom she had presented the castle bell which hung, says one account, "in the wooden tower next to the west turret." The bell was placed in the belfry of the Park Street chapel, to remain until 1951 when it was removed to St. Joseph's convent. In the entrance hall of the convent stand two tall graceful urns of marble, also a gift of Sophia MacNab.

6. The Canadian Club was organized on Feb. 1, 1893, to foster Canadian pride in Canada through greater knowledge of the country's history, literature

and resources. From a local beginning the Canadian Club became national in scope and came to include women's clubs. The Hamilton Women's Canadian Club was organized in 1911 by Mrs. H. D. Petrie and inaugurated in 1912.

7. The park was located south of Barton between Wentworth Street and Sanford Avenue, with entrance where the present Forum stands. Owned by Andrew Ross, carriage builder, and William Yates, contractor, the park contained a quarter-mile track for bicycle and foot racing. Later Bristol Street was opened through park and city lots laid out. In the 1930's the house was moved to Sanford Avenue when the School of Commerce was built.

NOTES TO CHAPTER NINETEEN

1. William Southam was president and managing director of the Spectator Printing Company. In 1877 Southam with William Carey purchased the *Spectator* from Alexander Lawson and David McCulloch, successors to the White brothers, and formed the company. On Jan. 23, 1884, *Spectator* premises, on present site of Parke and Parke, Limited, were gutted by fire. As temporary quarters the company purchased and absorbed the rival Hamilton Tribune Printing and Publishing Company, later moving to James Street South, where the G. W. Robinson Company store now stands. In 1898 another move carried the paper a few doors south to the present St. James building, and from there it was transferred on June 4, 1921, to its present location on King Street East.

2. Brown was married twice, Elizabeth (Mrs. Hendrie) being the youngest of his twelve children. In 1887 he was elected to the federal house, representing the city. In 1890 he served with outstanding success as honorary commissioner for Canada at the Jamaica Exhibition, where he established new markets for Canadian wheat in both the West Indies and South America. He had earlier created an overseas export market for Canadian cheese, founding today's lucrative cheese export trade. A big man, Mr. Brown's fine leonine features, his kindly good nature and erect bearing inevitably attracted attention. He was an outstanding orator.

3. Following Peter Horning's death his 5,600 acres of land was divided among his children, each inheriting 600 acres. With her marriage to Andrew Gage, Deborah Horning's dowry became the Gage farm at the Delta. Other daughters married into the Land, Filman, Hesse, Depew, and House families. Sons were Abraham, Isaac and Lewis.

4. The Local Council of Women was organized in 1893, following establishment of the National Council of Canada, by Lady Aberdeen to work for the betterment of laws and conditions affecting women and children. In Hamilton the first president, Mrs. J. Rose Holden, after one year in office, was succeeded by Mrs. Lyle who served for 33 years.

5. Marjorie Freeman Campbell, *Holbrook of the San*, Toronto: The Ryerson Press, 1953.

6. The will reserved sufficient means from the estate to provide perpetual care of the plot.

7. Gladstone Woolley and his brother Joseph are great-great grandsons of William Rymal. Children of Gladstone and Elsie Woolley are Stanley, Joseph and Bernice (Mrs. Floyd Fair). Their children make the seventh generation of William Rymal's family on the Mountain, youngest being Christine Anne, daughter of Stanley and Marilyn (née Buttenham).

NOTES TO CHAPTER TWENTY

1. A Liberal, John Gibson narrowly defeated Hugh Murray in 1879. He represented Hamilton in the Provincial House in various appointments until 1908, when he was made Lieutenant-Governor of Ontario. He filled this post until 1914. In 1912 he was knighted by King George V.

2. Lt. Hubert Howells Washington and Lt. Francis Gibson were killed at Armentières.

3. In 1886 the wooden drill shed had been destroyed by fire with heavy loss of military records and music, uniforms, and equipment. In 1888 it was replaced by a two-storey brick building with shingle roof, 200 feet by 80 feet. In 1908 the present capacious brick Armouries was erected to the south. The architect was Lt.-Col. Walter W. Stewart who raised the 86th Machine Gun Battalion and fell at Vimy Ridge. In 1965 the 1888 building was torn down.

4. *Hamilton, Canada, Its History, Commerce, Industries and Resources.* Issued under the auspices of the city council in the Centennial year of 1913, Hamilton Spectator Printing Company, Limited, 1913.

5. The Commission consisted of three members, two appointed by the government and one by city council.

NOTES TO CHAPTER TWENTY-ONE

1. In 1904 wages at the International Harvester Company of Canada were 15 cents an hour; $9 for a 60-hour week. At Canadian Westinghouse a carter commanded 43 cents an hour for man and team.

2. In a widespread merger the Dominion Power and Transmission Company now assumed the Hamilton and Dundas street railway, the Dundas Electrical Company, Limited, the Hamilton, Grimsby and Beamsville Electrical Railway, the Brantford and Hamilton Electrical Railway, the Hamilton Terminal Company, Limited, and several non-local companies. In 1903 and 1911 the capacity of the De Cew plant was increased. Two years later, however, power demands forced the company to commence construction of a steam plant on Burlington Bay. Interrupted by the outbreak of World War I, this was not completed until 1916.

3. In 1864, per capita debt was $146.67; in 1964 gross per capita debt, $379, net per capita, $295; 1964 per capita expenditure, $177.

4. In 1952 King Street was extended westward through the grounds of McMaster University, to enter Highway 102 and sweep into Dundas by the lower entrance. In 1966, to permit McMaster University expansion, entrance to Highway 102 was closed off and King Street diverted around the McMaster campus.

5. H.C.C., 1924: Report of Judge Gauld, p. 474, and Report of C. S. Scott and Company, Auditors, p. 480.

6. Not until 1929 did the city annex the area south of Main Street to the mountain brow, and west from Paradise Road to Lot 56, Ancaster Township (today West Hamilton).

7. First officers of the Hamilton branch, V.O.N. were elected May 22, 1899: Hon. W. E. Sanford, president; W. H. Ballard, secretary, and B. E. Charlton, treasurer; assisted by a ladies' board. Miss Emily Dakin was first V.O.N. nurse in the city. Fees were set at 5 to 50 cents a call. Following the president's death in July, 1899, Thomas W. Watkins replaced him.

8. Also in Hamilton in 1915, besides the Benevolent societies were: Boys'

Home, 5-14 years, organized in 1869, and in 1876 established permanently on Stinson Street. Boys were trained and placed for adoption or indentured to an employer. By 1915 over 2,000 boys had been admitted; Girls' Home, George Street, founded in 1865, with girls taught home duties, deportment and personal cleanliness. Otherwise the same as Boys' Home; Aged Women's Home, Wellington Street South, conducted by Ladies' Benevolent Society; St. Mary's Orphan Asylum, Park Street, under the Sisters of St. Joseph, with some 56 boys and 40 girls in residence; Women's Christian Temperance day nursery, John Street North, organized in 1895 to care for children of working mothers, at a charge of 5 cents a day. During 1914 the nursery cared for 5,175 children. Home of the Friendless and Infants' Home, Caroline Street South, established about 1875; National Children's Home, end of Main Street East; Children's Aid, founded in 1894; and the Salvation Army Rescue Home, forerunner of the present Grace Haven, opened in 1882 on Wentworth Street South and transferred in 1905 to 27 Mountain Avenue, a home and hospital for social service redemptive work, especially caring for unwed mothers.

9. This was furnished largely by the combined effort of the Ladies' Aid Societies of St. Paul's and MacNab Street Presbyterian Churches and Gore Methodist (later Centenary) and the Women's Christian Association, formed in 1873, which called the organizational meeting. Mrs. F. G. Malloch paid the first year's rent of $400. In 1892 the W.C.A. determined to join the Young Women's Christian Association movement and added 'Young' to their name.

10. The new Queen Victoria, opened in September, 1964, cost $645,000.

11. In 1930 King George V granted permission for use of the word "Royal."

NOTES TO CHAPTER TWENTY-TWO

1. City government: *1867*: 5 wards, each electing 3 aldermen (no councillors); school trustees no longer elected but appointed by council. Mayor elected by council. *1869*: 3 aldermen for each ward, elected for terms of 1, 2 and 3 years, one retiring and one elected annually. Statutes of Ontario, 31 Victoria, 1867-68, p. 175. *1871*: 3 aldermen as before but reversion to 1-year term. Assessment & Municipal Act, 1870. *1874*: election of mayor returned to voters at polls. *1875*: city divided into 7 wards, now numbered; 3 aldermen for each ward for 1-year term. *1902*: city's 21 aldermen now elected by a general vote of electors. Mayor elected at polls. *1909*: 7 wards, each represented by 3 aldermen, elected by wards. Mayor elected at polls for 2-year term.

2. In 1964 tax arrears were $7.92 per capita.

3. In 1940 Lt.-Col. Gibson was elected to the federal government for Hamilton West. After holding four portfolios in the Mackenzie King cabinet he was appointed to the Ontario Court of Appeals.

4. Another brother was A. Bruce Peene, and a sister Miss Vida Peene, of Toronto, the past president of the Dominion Drama Festival and chairman of the Dominion Drama Festival centennial committee.

5. Other sons: William F., Daniel, George, Alexander, and Hamilton W., all musical. In 1904-05, W. F. Robinson toured the world with the Canadian Kilties' band, playing two royal command performances in England and receiving a medal and baton from King Edward VII. He succeeded his father as bandmaster of the 13th.

6. In 1915 Russell T. Kelley founded the advertising firm bearing his name.

In 1945 he was elected M.P.P. for Hamilton-Wentworth and the following year was appointed provincial Minister of Health. His death occurred Feb. 20, 1952.

NOTES TO CHAPTER TWENTY-THREE

1. Son of Mr. and Mrs. Adam Inch after whom Inch Park is named. Five sons, Alexander, William C., and Adam Murray, all deceased, Robert F. and George all saw active war service. In 1927 George Inch was appointed local registrar of the supreme surrogate courts and clerk of the Wentworth county court, succeeding the late A. C. Garden. In 1965 he retired, and was succeeded by Miss Joan Beat and presently by H. M. Guild.

2. Postmaster, 1921-1948, succeeding Adam Brown, M.P., appointed in 1891. During their two terms of office rural mail delivery was instituted in 1910; parcel post, 1914; in 1921, insurance of parcels; and the following year, C.O.D. service. These services stimulated the exchange of merchandise throughout Canada. During Postmaster Webber's term of office the present handsome six-storey gray stone building was erected and opened in 1936. Succeeding Frank Curtis, 1948-52, popular Charles Depew Stipe, great-great-grandson of Capt. Charles Depew, Sr., the city's founder, served until 1962. Present postmaster is P. M. Arnold.

3. *National Geographic*, June, 1918, p. 578.

4. Charles II and William IV, of England, are both credited with authorizing the drinking of the Loyal Toast while seated, after the king, rising to reply to a toast to himself aboard ship, had struck his head on a low beam. He is reputed to have added, "Gentlemen, your loyalty is not questioned." Authority: J. A. Jamieson, Lt. Cmdr., R.C.N.R.

5. H. H. Leather was the father of Sir Edwin Hartley (Ted) Leather, former British M.P. for Somerset North, knighted in 1962 and recipient of the British Legion's meritorious service medal. After serving in World War II on Gen. Crerar's staff, Capt. Leather settled in England. His wife (Sheila Greenlees) is daughter of the late Alexander Greenlees, city surveyor.

6. Robert Land . . . son, Ephraim . . . son, John Scott Land, merchant, Hamilton, later moved to U.S. . . . son, Dr. C. H. Land, dentist, Detroit . . . daughter, Evangeline L. Land, married Charles A. Lindbergh . . . son, Charles A. Lindbergh.

NOTES TO CHAPTER TWENTY-FOUR

1. An area of 72 acres, Gage Park consists of the Gage farm purchased in 1917 for $320,000 from R. R. Gage (the vendor retaining use of the homestead and 13 acres during Eugenie's lifetime), plus later purchases from the Charles Schwenger estate to the west, the owners of the National Children's (Barnardo) home on the east, and Swann and Mason. The Gage home, The Retreat, is now administration building of the parks board.

2. In 1941 by act of the provincial legislature the Gardens were established as an independent organization with an independent board as its governing body. First president was T. B. McQuesten. Prior to this the R.B.G. was a development of the Board of Parks Management. Of the one mill annually apportioned to the parks board by the city, the board after 1941 allowed the R.B.G. one-quarter mill. The western entrance on Burlington Heights and the city's famous Rock Garden, converted from an old gravel pit, were developed by the Parks Board.

3. In 1962 a new clubhouse was opened at the foot of Bay Street, with accommodation for dancing, banquets, and all club rowing equipment.

4. In 1919 Cornelius had been appointed director of physical education at Central Collegiate. By 1930 the school had won 142 trophies in track and field against topflight competition. Cap was twice coach of Canada's Olympic team. In 1934 Central Collegiate's sharpshooters won five Dominion and two provincial championships. In 1961 Cap retired. He died Dec. 15, 1964.

5. "Canada's Basic Steel Strike," The *Sample Case*, Columbus, Ohio, May and June, 1947, H.P.L., Ref. Rm.

6. Elected alderman, Ward 1, 1932, '33 and '34. Headed polls as controller, 1935, 1944, 1945, 1946 and 1947. Interested in social problems, especially of women and children, in unemployment, relief, and low rental housing, Nora Frances was strongly supported by women's groups such as the Local Council of Women and the Hamilton Women's Civic Club which she founded in 1932 to interest women in assuming public office. In her memory the Nora Frances Henderson Hospital on the mountain, now the Henderson General Hospital, was named.

NOTES TO CHAPTER TWENTY-FIVE

1. *Economic Survey, Niagara Region*, Ontario Department of Economics and Development, 1963, p. 174.

2. Capacity was reduced to 33 million gallons when mountainside slippages during construction endangered the C.N.R. right-of-way to the south and required that the reservoir be moved north.

3. Dr. Clark, appointed assistant M.H.O., 1941, and M.H.O. in 1947, died suddenly in office, April 19, 1964, and was succeeded by Dr. J. S. Kitching. The Dr. L. A. Clark mountain health centre building at Mohawk Road and Upper Wentworth Street, which he had planned and which was named in his honour, opened on Nov. 4, 1964.

4. Mrs. Farmer was the mother of Lt.-Col. John A. Farmer, D.S.O., of Galt; Mrs. W. B. Duncan; Mrs. W. F. Wallace, wife of Archdeacon Wallace, rector of the Church of the Ascension, 1932-62; Mrs. J. G. Milligan, Montreal; and Miss Mary H. Farmer. H. E. G. Bull, Hamilton, is a son of Senator Bull.

5. Economic Survey, Niagara Region, Ontario Department of Economics and Development, 1963, p. 165.

6. Planned expenditure, 1965, $239,800,000, amounting to $700 per capita. Department of Trade and Commerce, Ottawa, Mar., 1965.

NOTES TO CHAPTER TWENTY-SIX

1. When the Act of Incorporation was passed, in the summer of 1846, Leggatt Downing was clerk to the Board of Police. On Jan. 6th, 1847, immediately prior to election, Mr. Downing died and Robert J. Yeott was appointed clerk *pro tem*, serving until Jan. 21st, 1847, when Charles H. Stokoe was appointed by the newly elected first city council. On Sept. 1st, 1852, health forced Mr. Stokoe's resignation and John Kirby became city clerk. When he resigned Sept. 4th, 1854, Thomas Beasley took office, remaining until 1907. He was followed by Samuel H. Kent, noted for his knowledge of municipal law, his dignity and good grooming. His successor, Mr. Berry, remained in office until Aug. 31st, 1964, being succeeded by Edward A. Simpson.

2. Bell and four-faced clock were removed for future use, possibly in Sam

Lawrence Park atop the Jolley Cut, then building with a mountainside waterfall, later discontinued. Since its installation the clock was serviced by Thomas Lees, jeweller, with Walter Voelker, since 1937, doing the actual cranking of gears which constituted winding.

3. Following Chief A. B. TenEyck: Wallace T. James, 1923-33; Robert Aitchison, 1933-38; Kenneth Cassel, 1938-42; William Murdoch, 1942-49; Edward Nixon, 1949-55; and Chief Swanborough.

4. In World War 1 Dr. Deadman saw service in Egypt and Salonica. Following the war he served among many appointments as president of the Hamilton Academy of Medicine, chairman of the laboratory section of the Canadian Public Health Association, member of the Royal Commission to investigate cancer research remedies, member of the New York Academy of the Sciences, and member of the Royal Society of Health in Great Britain. His writings in scientific and medical fields found wide publication.

5. With D. U. McGregor, M.D. sons of J. O. McGregor, M.D., of Waterdown, whose family also includes Mrs. Orrin H. Baker, Mrs. Frank A. O'Brien, Mrs. O. D. Peat and Mrs. H. P. Frid, all of Hamilton.

6. Similar courses are taught in the city's other secondary schools, including Barton, Glendale, Hill Park and Westmount not previously listed. In 1950 F. R. Close Technical Institute and Central High School of Commerce were amalgamated with Central Collegiate.

7. In 1949 the union board which had operated for over 75 years was abolished and a board of education for the city of Hamilton was established, consisting of 2 representatives elected from each ward and 2 appointees from the separate school board. The same year Mrs. Katherine McAuley, first woman board member, and Henry Eydt were elected (both are still serving), while Lloyd D. Jackson, 1944-49, resigned to run as mayor. In 1965 Mrs. Edward P. Nolan became the first woman elected to the separate school board.

8. Other chairmen with especially long years of service as members were George Wild, 15 years; George Hope, 12; A. Pain, 14; T. M. Wright, 22; Samuel R. Manson, 19, serving until his death in August, 1954; Judge W. F. Schwenger, 12 years, 6 as chairman; Dr. W. S. T. Connell (presently Hamilton's chief coroner), 18 years; and A. G. Bain, 19 years as a member.

9. These were purchased in 1945 for arrears of taxes ($7,000). By legislative act the corporate existence of the H.A.A.A. was terminated. Priority and reasonable terms in use of the field were assured Tiger Cats and Hamilton Tennis Club.

10. In June, 1946, Hamilton Central Collegiate Institute was totally destroyed by fire, only the gymnasium escaping. In 1954 renovated and converted, this became the Central Memorial centre.

11. A fifth-generation Canadian, Mrs. Fairclough is great-granddaughter of Jacob Cook (son of Andrew, farmer settler from Pennsylvania to Ancaster, 1803) after whom Cooksville is named. Jacob operated the first stage coach and carried the mail between York and Wellington Square. In 1904 her family moved to Hamilton. She has a son, Howard G. Fairclough.

NOTES TO CHAPTER TWENTY-SEVEN

1. In 1914 the Art Gallery was founded to receive 32 paintings donated by the family of William Blair Bruce, Hamilton artist, a board of directors being established and the first charter in Ontario obtained. The gallery was housed in

the old public library, 22 Main Street West. With appointment of Mr. MacDonald a campaign for a new building was waged, spearheaded by Dr. C. H. Stearn and James Garrow. The active women's committee was formed in 1950, and in 1953 the new gallery was opened on Main Street West, on Royal Botanical Gardens land.

ABBREVIATIONS USED IN THE NOTES

B.F.: Broken Front
Cons.: Concessions
H.C.C.: Hamilton City Council (Minutes)
H.P.L.: Hamilton Public Library
N.H.S.: Niagara Historical Society
O.A.T.: Public Archives of Ontario, Toronto
O.H.S.: Ontario Historical Society, Toronto
P.A.C.: Public Archives of Canada, Ottawa
Twp.: Township
W.H.S.: Wentworth Historical Society, Hamilton

Bibliography

Manuscript Sources

Minute Books, State Papers and Land Records of the Executive Council to Upper Canada, P.A.C., Ottawa, and on microfilm, P.A.O., Toronto.

Reports of the Department of Public Records and Archives of Ontario, 17th-20th, P.A.O., Toronto, 1928-31.

Land Books, A, B, C and D, with grants of Crown Lands in Upper Canada, 1787-1798.

Records, Registry Office, County of Wentworth, Hamilton.

Deeds, Abstracts and original papers, City Hall Files, Hamilton.

Board of Police and City Council Minutes, Folios in longhand, 1833-1888, City Hall, Hamilton.

City Council Minutes, 1888-1965, printed, Library, City Hall, Hamilton.

Papers, Van Wagner Estate, courtesy Miss Myra M. Hamilton, Toronto.

Diaries, Canon George A. Bull, courtesy Miss Mary H. Farmer.

Records, Allan Napier MacNab and Dundurn property, City Hall File, Hamilton.

Records, First Battalion of Incorporated Militia of Upper Canada, 1839-1843, courtesy Mrs. C. A. McClenahan, Burlington.

Minutes, Babies' Dispensary Guild, 1911-34, courtesy Hamilton Academy of Medicine, Hamilton.

Beasley Papers, P.A.C.

Cartwright Papers and Cartwright Letter-Book, P.A.C.

Haldimand Papers, P.A.C.

Land Papers, P.A.C.

W. L. Mackenzie Papers, P.A.C.

W. H. Merritt Papers, P.A.C.

Simcoe Papers, P.A.C.

Newspapers
(Incomplete Files)

Gore Gazette, 1827-29.
Western Mercury, 1830-35.
Hamilton Free Press, 1831-37.
Colonial Advocate, 1824-37.
Hamilton Express, 1836-39.
Hamilton Gazette, 1835-56.
Canadian Illustrated News, 1863.

Publications

O.H.S.—Ontario Historical Society Papers and Records.
N.H.S.—Niagara Historical Society Papers and Records.
W.H.S.—Wentworth Historical Society Papers and Records.
Wentworth Bygones—Head-of-the-Lake Historical Society Papers and Records.

Sources, Primary and Secondary

Acts of Great Britain applying to Upper Canada. Printed by R. C. Horne, York, 1818, Chap. XIX, p. 367.
Adamson, Anthony, "Dundurn Castle, an Undeveloped Asset," Toronto, 1961.
Alden, John Richard, *The American Revolution, 1775-1783,* Harper, New York, 1954.
Austin, P. R., "Two Mayors of Early Hamilton," Family Papers, Mrs. J. C. van Nostrand, Hamilton.

Bailey, T. Melville, *Traces, Places and Faces,* Hamilton, 1957.
——, *The History of Dundurn Castle and Sir Allan MacNab,* Hughes and Wilkins Limited, Hamilton, 1943.
Barton Township, County of Wentworth, Abstract Index, Apr. 1, 1926, Registry Office, Hamilton.
——, Township Papers, P.A.O., Toronto.
Beasley File, Records, City Hall, Hamilton.
Beasley, Richard, "Dwelling House to Let," *Western Mercury,* July 4, 1833, No. 125, H.P.L.
Beattie, Jessie L., *John Christie Holland,* The Ryerson Press, Toronto.
Bidwell, Norma, "Birth Control Society Survives Despite Opposition, Indifference," 2 parts, *The Hamilton Spectator,* Mar. 8, 9, 1962.
Biggar, E. B., *The Hamilton Spectator,* Hamilton, June, 1873.
——, "Account of the Battle of Stoney Creek," Reprint, J. H. Smith, W.H.S., Vol. X, 1922.
Bourinot, Sir John George, *Memories of Dundurn and Burlington Heights,* The Copp Clark Company Limited, Toronto, 1900.
Boyd, Erroll, "When the School Bells Rang," *The Hamilton Spectator,* Sept. 16, 1961.
——, "Olympic: Ship Magnificent of World War I," *The Hamilton Spectator,* Apr. 25, 1964.
Breithaupt, W. H. *The Railways of Ontario,* Reprint, O.H.S., Vol. XXV, 1929.
Brock, A. Maude (Cawthra), *The Mills, Holton and Smith Families,* James and Williams, Toronto, 1927.
Brown, G. W., "The Durham Report and the Upper Canadian Scene," *Canadian Historical Review,* Vol. XX, No. 2, 1939.
Bull, W. Perkins, *From Brock to Currie,* The Perkins Bull Foundation, George J. McLeod, Toronto.
Burkholder, Mabel, *The Story of Hamilton,* Davis-Lisson Company Limited, Hamilton, 1938.
——, *Barton on the Mountain,* Hamilton, 1956.
——, "Out of the Storied Past," Weekly Column, *The Hamilton Spectator.*
Burwash, Nathaniel, *Egerton Ryerson,* The Makers of Canada, Vol. VIII, Morang, Toronto, 1910.

Caley, J. F., *Palaeozoic Geology of the Toronto-Hamilton Area,* Ontario, King's Printer, Ottawa, 1940.
Campbell, Marjorie Freeman, *Holbrook of the San,* The Ryerson Press, Toronto, 1953.

————, *The Hamilton General School of Nursing*, The Ryerson Press, Toronto, 1956.

————, "Life in a Strike City Is Ugly," *Saturday Night*, Toronto, Sept. 14, 1946, H.P.L.

————, "Canada's Basic Steel Strike," *The Sample Case*, Columbus, Ohio, May and June, 1947, H.P.L.

Campbell, Patrick, *Travels in North America*, The Champlain Society, Toronto, 1937.

Canada, Province of, *Statutes*, Act of Incorporation of the City of Hamilton, 9 Victoria, 1846, p. 981; Municipal Corporations, Upper Canada, 12 Victoria, Chap. 81 (Baldwin's Act), 1849.

Canadian Illustrated News, May 16, 1863, H.P.L.

Canniff, William, *History of the Settlement of Upper Canada*, Dudley and Burns, Toronto, 1869.

————, *History of the Province of Ontario*, A. H. Hovey, Toronto, 1872.

Chapman, L. J., and D. F. Putnam, *The Physiography of Southern Ontario*, University of Toronto Press, 1951.

Charlton, B., Journal and Proceedings of the Hamilton Association, Session 1890-91, Hamilton, H.P.L.

Charlton, R. S., "Administrative Beginnings," *Wentworth Bygones*, No. 2, 1960.

Coleman, John M., "Robert Land and Some Frontier Skirmishes," O.H.S., Vol. XLVIII, No. 2, Toronto, 1956.

Cowan, John M., "The Great Western Railway," *Wentworth Bygones*, No. 5, Hamilton, 1964.

Cox, Isaac, *The Journeys of René Robert Cavelier, Sieur de La Salle*, A. S. Barnes and Company, New York, 1905.

Coyne, J. H., *Exploration of the Great Lakes, 1669-70, Galinee's Narrative*, O.H.S., Vol. XVII, No. 4, Pt. 1, Toronto, 1903.

Child, W. A., "Iron Trade Built by Determined Men," *The Hamilton Spectator*, July 15, 1926.

Craig, Gerald M., *Upper Canada, The Formative Years, 1784-1841*, McClelland and Stewart Limited, Toronto, 1963.

Creston, Dormer, *The Youthful Queen Victoria*, Macmillan and Company Limited, London, 1952.

Cruikshank, E. A., *Documentary History of the Campaigns on the Niagara Frontier, 1812-14*, Vols. I-IX, Lundy's Lane Historical Society, Welland, 1896-1908.

————, "John Beverley Robinson and the Trials for Treason in 1814," O.H.S., Vol. XXV, Toronto, 1929.

————, *The Simcoe Papers*, O.H.S., Toronto, 1923-31.

————, "Notes on the History of the District of Niagara," N.H.S., No. 26, Welland.

————, "Extract from the Quebec Land Book," N.H.S., No. 40.

Curtin, Joe, Series on Land, *The Hamilton Spectator*, Feb. 17, 24, March 7, Hamilton, 1958.

Davis, Calvin, *Centennial Souvenir of First Methodist Church, Hamilton, Ontario*, 1924.

Davis, Phyllis, *Adventure in Faith*, 125th Anniversary of First Church Congregation, Hamilton, 1949.

Dent, J. C., *The Story of the Upper Canada Rebellion*, 2 Vols., C. B. Robinson, Toronto, 1885.

————, Canadian Portrait Gallery, Vol. IV, p. 73, J. B. Magurn, Toronto, 1880-81.

Directories, City of Hamilton, 1853, '56, '58, '62, '63, 1865-1965, H.P.L.

Directory of Community Services of Hamilton and District, 1964-65, The Social Planning Council of Hamilton and District, 1964.

"Dominion Power and Transmission Company: Historical Sketch," Appendix "A",
Hydro Electric Power Commission of Ontario, courtesy Hydro Electric System
of Hamilton.

"Dominion Power and Transmission Company: Central Electric Stations in Canada," Department of Northern Affairs and National Resources, Water Resources, Paper No. 27, 1918, p. 107, Hydro Electric Power Commission of
Ontario and Hamilton Hydro.

Duff, David, *The Shy Princess*, Evans Bros. Limited, London, 1958.

Dunham, Mabel, *Grand River*, McClelland and Stewart Limited, Toronto, 1945.

Durand, Charles, *Reminiscences of Charles Durand*, The Hunter-Rose Company
Limited, Toronto, 1897.

Durham, John G. L., The Report and Despatches of the Earl of Durham, Ridgways, London, 1839.

Fenwick, G. Roy, "Some Musical Memories," *Wentworth Bygones*, No. 6, 1965.

Farmer, Mary, "The Preston and Berlin Railway," O.H.S., Vol. LII, No. 3, Sept.,
1960.

Gardiner, H. F., "The Hamiltons of Queenston, Kingston and Hamilton," O.H.S.,
Vol. VIII, 1907.

Goodale, Edward, "Origin of Some Street Names of Hamilton," *Wentworth
Bygones*, No. 2, 1960.

Gourlay, Robert F., *Statistical Account of Upper Canada*, Vols. I and II, Simpkin
and Marshall, London, 1822 and 1826.

Great Railway Catastrophe on the Desjardins Canal Bridge, The, Pamphlet, Hamilton, 1857. Family papers, courtesy Misses Clara M. and Ada Kilvington.

Greenfield, Katharine, "The Rev. John Gamble Geddes and Early Days at Christ's
Church, Hamilton," *Wentworth Bygones*, No. 4, 1963.

Guillet, Edwin C., *Pioneer Life*, The Ontario Publishing Company Limited,
Toronto, 1938.

———, *Pioneer Settlements*, The Ontario Publishing Company Limited, Toronto,
1947.

———, *Pioneer Social Life*, The Ontario Publishing Company Limited, Toronto,
1938.

———, *Pioneer Travel*, The Ontario Publishing Company Limited, Toronto, 1939.

Haldimand Papers, B-102, p. 150.

Hamilton, Alexander, "Letter Addressed to Mrs. Henderson, No. 1, Park Street,
Edinburgh," P.A.C., North American War of 1812, R. G. 8, "C" Series, Vol.
679.

Hamilton Association for the Advancement of Literature, Science and Art, The,
100th Anniversary, 1857-1957, Davis-Lisson Limited, Hamilton, 1958, H.P.L.

———, *Journal and Proceedings, Season 1890-91*, H.P.L.

Hamilton, The Birmingham of Canada, The Times Printing Company, Hamilton,
1893.

Hamilton, Canada: Its History, Commerce, Industries and Resources, Spectator
Printing Company Limited, Hamilton, 1913.

Hamilton Centennial, 1846-1946, ed. Alexander H. Wingfield, Hamilton, 1946.

Hamilton City Council Minutes, "Report of the Committee on the Gore," Feb. 8,
March 3, March 19, 1847, City Hall, Hamilton.

———, Toll Roads Municipal Expropriation Act, Apt. 12, 1893, p. 137.

Hamilton, George, Abstract of Titles, George Hamilton Survey, The Registry
Office, County of Wentworth, Hamilton.

Hamilton, Myra M., Van Wagner Family Papers, Toronto.

Hamilton Spectator, The, 100th Anniversary, "Early District Journal Key to Past,"
July 15, 1946.

Hanley, Robert J., "The Little Irish Ladies Tell of Early Corktown Days," *The Hamilton Spectator*, Jan. 22, 1953.

Historical Atlas, County of Wentworth, Page and Smith, Toronto, 1875.

History of The Grand Lodge, A.F. & A.M., in the Province of Ontario, A., Mc-Callum Press, 1955.

Holbrook, J. H., M.D., "A Century of Medical Achievement," *The Hamilton Centennial*, 1946.

Holden, Mary E. Rose, "Burlington Bay, Beach and Heights in History," W.H.S., 1899.

Howe, Fred, "Early Car Era Was Lively," *The Hamilton Spectator*, Nov. 5, 1961.

——, "Matt Hayes," *The Hamilton Spectator*, Feb. 24, 1962.

James Street Market File, Deeds, City Hall, Hamilton.

Jameson, Anna, *Winter Studies and Summer Rambles in Canada*, London, 1838.

Jefferys, C. W., *The Picture Gallery of Canadian History*, 2 vols., The Ryerson Press, 1942.

Jenness, Diamond, *The Indians of Canada*, The King's Printer, Ottawa, 1932.

Johnson, Melville B., "The Year We Mounted Guard on the Mountain," *The Hamilton Spectator*, Jan. 25, 1964.

Johnson, Wm. F., "The Historical Evolution of Hamilton Beach," *Wentworth Bygones*, No. 2, 1960.

Johnston, Charles M., *The Head of the Lake*, Robert Duncan and Company Limited, Hamilton, 1958.

——, "An Outline of Early Settlements in the Grand River Valley," O.H.S., Vol. LIV, No. 1, March, 1962.

——, *A Battle for the Heartland*, in collaboration with Richard Diubaldo and John Hammill, Pennell Printing, Stoney Creek, 1913.

Jones, Augustus, Survey Map, Twp. No. 8, now Barton, District of Gore, showing original Crown grants, P.A.O., H.P.L.

——, Surveyor's Letters, J. 1787, Dept. of Lands and Forests, Toronto, p. 448.

Jones, Frank L., "The Militia of Upper Canada: The Formative Years, 1793-1864," *Wentworth Bygones*, No. 6, 1965.

Keenleyside, Hugh L., and Gerald S. Brown, *Canada and the United States*, Knopf, New York, 1952.

Ketchen, Beverley, *Centennial Year, 1854-1954, MacNab Presbyterian Church*, Hamilton, 1954.

Kidner, F., W.H.S., Vol. 3, 1902, pp. 73-74.

Kilbourn, William, *The Firebrand*, Clarke, Irwin and Company Limited, Toronto, 1956.

Kingsford, William, *The History of Canada*, Roswell and Hutchison, Toronto, 1887-98.

Laidler, George, "The Story of the Land Family," *Wentworth Bygones*, No. 1, 1958.

Lamoureux, W. J., "Cootes Paradise Sanctuary," *The Gardens Bulletin*, R.B.G., Hamilton, Feb., 1960.

Land Board Records, P.A.C., Ottawa; P.A.O., Toronto.

Land, John H., "Record of Robert Land, U.E.L.," W.H.S., Vol. 7, 1916.

Lautens, Trevor, "Mountain's Oldest 'Own' Citizen, Miss Alice McConnell," *The Hamilton Spectator*, July 29, 1957.

Laver, James, *Taste and Fashion*, George G. Harrop and Company Limited, London, 1937.

Lemieux, L. J., M.D., *The Governors-General of Canada*, 1608-1931, Lake and Bell Limited, London, 1931.

Lemon, Agnes H., "Biographical Sketch of a Noted Pioneer," W.H.S., Vol. 2, Hamilton, 1899.

Lower, A. R. M., *Colony to Nation*, Longmans, Green, Toronto, 1946.
Loyalist Victualling List for the District of Niagara, 14 Nov., 1786, (R.G. 19, C 35, Vol. I, File I), P.A.C., Ottawa.
Lucas, C. P., *Lord Durham's Report on the Affairs of British North America*, 3 vols., Clarendon Press, Oxford, 1912.
Lynes, Russell, *The Taste Makers*, Harper and Brothers, U.S.A., 1949.

MacBain, C. Hunter, "Hamilton—One Hundred Years Ago," The Hamilton Association, 100th Anniversary, 1857-1957, Hamilton, 1958, pp. 7-29.
McCulloch, W. J., "City Now Owns Canada Coach," *The Hamilton Spectator*, Nov. 12, 1960.
————, "City Sixth Owner of Street Railway," *The Hamilton Spectator*, Nov. 12, 1960.
McCullough, Charles R., "The House of Hamilton," Series, *The Hamilton Spectator*, Apr., 1931.
McInnes, Donald, Suit in Chancery, Nov. 24, 1873, Donald McInnes, Plaintiff, and the Attorney General for the Dominion of Canada, Clause 7, Records, City Hall, Hamilton.
Mackenzie, W. L., "The Seventh Report from the Select Committee of the House of Assembly of U.C. on Grievances," Toronto, 1835, P.A.O.
Macrae, Marion, and Anthony Adamson, *The Ancestral Roof*, Clarke, Irwin and Company, Toronto, 1963.
McRae, William, "Our North American Background: A Brief History of the Hamilton Elementary School System from 1856 to 1940," Hamilton, 1961.
Makers of Canada, various authors, Morang and Company Limited, Toronto, 1910-11.
Marshall, Fred, "Short Lived but Busy Radials," *The Hamilton Spectator*, Nov. 12, 1960.
Mason, George E., *The Barton Lodge*, Hamilton, 1895.
Melville, Lewis, *Farmer George*, Isaac Pitman & Sons, London, 1907.
Merrilees, Andrew, "A History of the Railways of the Dominion Power and Transmission Company," Andrew Merrilees Limited, Toronto, courtesy Robert R. Gage.
Merritt, J. P., *Biography of the Hon. W. H. Merritt, M.P.*, St. Catharines, 1875.
Millar, Joseph, "St. Mary's Roman Catholic Church," *Wentworth Bygones*, No. 3, 1962.
Miller, Ivan, "Champions of Sport," *The Hamilton Centennial*, Hamilton, 1946.
Mills, Stanley, *The Mills and Gage Families*, The Reid Press Limited, Hamilton, 1926.
————, *Lake Medad and Waterdown*, The Reid Press Limited, Hamilton, 1937.
————, *The U. E. Loyalists*, Hamilton.
Mills, Tom F., "City Hall," Column, *The Hamilton Spectator*.
Minute Books, Records of the Hamilton Board of Police and City Council, City Hall, Hamilton.
Moodie, Susanna, *Roughing It in the Bush*, Bell and Cockburn, Toronto, 1913.
Morgan, Joan E., *Castle of Quebec*, J. M. Dent and Sons Limited (Canada), Don Mills.
Municipal Council of the Corporation of Wentworth County, Minutes, 1847-77, Dec., 1875.

National Geographic, June, 1918, Washington, D.C., p. 578 (Major Robert Dodds).
Nelligan, David M., "North End Produced Lively Crop of Characters," *The Hamilton Spectator*, Dec. 31, 1958.
New Jersey Archives, Second Series, Vol. III, 1779, p. 226.
Niagara Historical Society Papers and Records, especially Nos. 26, 28, 38-44, Niagara Historical Museum, Niagara-on-the-Lake.

Notman, William, and Fennings Taylor, *Portraits of British Americans*, Vol. II, W. Notman, Montreal, 1867, pp. 297-324 (A. N. MacNab).

Oates, T. W., "From the Little Red School," *The Hamilton Centennial*, Hamilton, 1946.

O'Neil, J. G., "Chronicles of Corktown," *Wentworth Bygones*, No. 5, 1964.

Ontario, Department of Economics, Economic and Social Aspects, Ontario Survey, 1961.

——, Department of Economics and Development, Economic Survey, Niagara Region, 1963.

——, Department of Lands and Forests, Conservation Authorities Branch, *Spencer Creek Conservation Report, History*, Toronto, 1962.

——, Provincial Economist and Bureau of Statistics and Research, Economic Survey of Ontario, 1955.

——, Public Archives, Dept. of Public Records, Seventeenth Report, King's Printer, Toronto, 1929; Eighteenth Report, 1930; Nineteenth Report, 1931; and Twentieth Report, 1932.

Pantazzi, Ethel, "Youthful Days in Hamilton: A Record of the Eighties," *The Hamilton Spectator*, 10 instalments, Sept. 22-Oct. 8, 1960.

Parkman, Francis, *La Salle and the Discovery of the Great West*, G. N. Morang, Toronto, 1898.

Paterson, G. C., "Land Settlement in Upper Canada," Report of the Ontario Dept. of Records and Archives for 1920, Toronto, 1921.

Pearson, Norman, "Hamilton: Setting for Disaster," *Community Planning Review*, Vol. VIII, No. 3, Ottawa, Sept., 1958.

——, "Hell Is a Suburb," *Community Planning Review*, Vol. VII, No. 3, Sept., 1957.

Pennsylvania Archives, Harrisburg, Series I, Vol. VIII, p. 597.

Plewman, W. R., *Adam Beck and the Ontario Hydro*, The Ryerson Press, Toronto, 1947.

Porter, McKenzie, *Overture to Victoria*, Longmans, Green and Company, Toronto 1961.

Powell, William Dummer, "Summary of the Rise, Progress and Actual Settlement of U.C.," Powell to Portland, July 21, 1796, "Q" Series, Vol. 282-2, pp. 60-61, P.A.C.

Petition, Robert Land to Sir Henry Clinton, July 10, 1780, The University of Michigan, Ann Arbor, Michigan.

Read, D. B., *Life and Times of Governor Simcoe*, G. Virtue, Toronto, 1890.

Reaman, G. E., *The Trail of the Black Walnut*, McClelland and Stewart Limited, Toronto, 1957.

Regehr, Theodore D., "Land Ownership in Upper Canada, 1783-1796," O.H.S., Vol. LV, No. 1, Toronto, 1963.

Register of Baptisms, Parish of Trinity Church, New York City, Jan. 21, 1781.

Reynolds, Ella J., "Days Before Yesterday—the Arts," *The Hamilton Centennial*, 1946.

Riddell, The Hon. Wm. R., "The Bloody Ancaster Assize of 1814," O.H.S., XX, Toronto, 1923.

Ridout, Thomas, "Report for Sir Peregrine Maitland on U.C. Land Policy, 1783-1818," Aug. 22, 1818, U.C. Sundries, R. G. 5, A I, P.A.C.

Robertson, H. H, "Desjardins Canal," W.H.S., Vol. 5, Hamilton, 1908.

——, "Gore District Militia and Militia of West Lincoln and West York," W.H.S., Vol. IV, Hamilton, 1905.

Robertson, John Ross, *The Diary of Mrs. John Graves Simcoe*, The Ontario Publishing Company Limited, Toronto, 1934.

Robinson, John Forbes, *Oh Christopher!*, 100th Anniversary, The T. B. Greening

Wire Company Limited (Now Greening Industries Limited), 1859-1959, Hamilton, 1959.

Ross, Victor, A History of the Canadian Bank of Commerce, Vol. 1, Oxford University Press, Toronto, 1920, pp. 205 ff.

Rousseau Collection, 1774-1871, P.A.O.

Scadding, Dr. Henry, Toronto of Old, Willing and Williamson, Toronto, 1878.

Shaver, Richard L., Incidents in the History of the Shaver Family, 1786-1937, Hamilton, 1937, Reprinted, 1962.

Shortt, Adam, "History of Canadian Currency, Banking and Exchange," Journal of the Canadian Bankers Association, VIII, p. 317, H.P.L. (MacNab and the Gore Bank).

Sissons, C. B., Egerton Ryerson: His Life and Letters, Vol. I, Clarke, Irwin and Company, Toronto, 1937.

Smith, Milford, "This Changing Hamilton," Series, The Hamilton Spectator, May 9, 10, 11, 1962.

Smith, J. H., The Central School, Hamilton, 1853-1903, Spectator Printing Company Limited, Hamilton, 1905.

———, Historical Sketch of the County of Wentworth, W.H.S., Vol. 10, Hamilton, 1922.

Smith, Wm. H., Smith's Canadian Gazetteer, H. and W. Rowsell, Toronto, 1846.

Sons of the Revolution in the State of New York, Year Book, 1909, Archives of the State of New York, Vol. I.

Spack, Vivian M., "The Story of a Pioneer Doctor—Harmanus Smith," Wentworth Bygones, No. 5, 1964.

Spalding, L. T., The History and Romance of Education (Hamilton), 1816-1950, Hamilton.

Spragge, G. W., ed., The John Strachan Letter Book: 1812-34, O.H.S., Toronto, 1946.

Springer, H. Isabel, "A History of the Hamilton Street Railway," Wentworth Bygones, No. 2, 1960.

Steubing, A. Douglas, "Our Churches," The Hamilton Centennial, Hamilton, 1946.

Stewart, Logan, This Is Where I Live, Davis-Lisson Limited, Hamilton, 1946.

Strachey, Lytton, Queen Victoria, Harcourt, Brace and Company, New York, 1921.

Talman, J. J., "Travel in Ontario before the Coming of the Railway," O.H.S., XXIX, 1933.

Turnbull, Margaret Leslie: Family Papers, James Wesley Ross and Andrew Miller, Hamilton.

Turner, J. E., "Albion Mills," Wentworth Bygones, No. 3, 1962.

Traill, Catherine Parr, The Backwoods of Canada, C. Knight, London, 1836.

United Empire Loyalist Association of Ontario, The, Head of the Lake Branch, Hamilton, Minute Book.

Waldon, Freda F., "Hamilton Learns to Read," The Hamilton Centennial, 1946.

———, "Early Provision for Libraries in Hamilton," Wentworth Bygones, No. 4, 1963.

———, Letter File, Freda F. Waldon and Mrs. Francis MacBeth Woodburn: item MacNab and the bailiff, H.P.L.

Wallace, W. S., The Family Compact, Glasgow, Brook and Company, Toronto, 1915.

———, The Knight of Dundurn, Toronto, 1960 (private printing).

———, The United Empire Loyalists, Glasgow, Brook and Company, Toronto, 1914.

Waller, Dulce, "Dundurn Curator, Gwen Metcalfe, to Study on Canada Council Grant," The Hamilton Spectator, Sept. 25, 1961.

———, "Gallery Show Features Local Artist—Ida G. Hamilton," *The Hamilton Spectator*, Oct. 31, 1962.
Water, J. E., *Annual Reports of the Board of Park Management*, Hamilton, 1960-65.
Watson, J. W., "Industrial and Commercial Development," *The Hamilton Centennial*, 1946.
———, "The Changing Industrial Pattern of the Niagara Peninsula," O.H.S., XXXVII, 1945.
———, "Hamilton and Its Environs," *Canadian Geographical Journal*, Ottawa, May, 1945.
Wentworth Historical Society, *Papers and Records*, Hamilton, H.P.L.
Wentworth Landmarks, The Hamilton Spectator, Hamilton, 1897, H.P.L.
Western Mercury, July 4, 1833, No. 125, H.P.L.
Wood, William, *The War with the United States*, Glasgow, Brook and Company, Toronto, 1915.
Woodhouse, T. Roy, *The History of the Town of Dundas*, Pt. I, Dundas Historical Society, Dundas, Ontario, 1965.
———, "Hamilton, the First Telephone Exchange in the British Empire," *Wentworth Bygones*, No. 3, 1962.
Woodruff, Norris Counsell, *Twelve Generations, 1636-1959*, Hamilton, 1959.
Wrong, George M., *The United States and Canada*, The Abingdon Press, New York, 1921.
Whyte, E. E. E., Diary of Emily Esther Elizabeth Whyte, 1843, Gourlay Family Papers, Hamilton.

Young, A. H., *The Rev. John Stuart, D.D., U.E.L. of Kingston, U.C., and His Family*, Whig Press, Kingston.
Young, Scott, "The History of a Hot Potato," *The Globe and Mail*, Toronto, Apr. 15, 1966. See also: "Mac Medical School Plans—and Issues," *The Hamilton Spectator*, May 9, 1966.

Index

A

Abcowser, Christopher, 46
Aberdeen, Lady, 193, 225
Aberdeen, Lord, 193, 225
Acres, William H., 239
Act of Incorporation, 95-96
Act of Union, 99
Adam, A. E., 211
Adams, Cmdr. Kenneth F., 242
Adams, Mary Electra, 161
Adee, Lt. Harry, 207
Adolescent School Attendance Act, 220
Ahrens, Hermon F., 152
Aiken, W. M. (Max), 185
Aikman, Hannah, 55
Aikman, John, 28, 55, 63
Aitchison, Alexander W., 151, 176, 230, 265
Aitchison, Dr. D. B., 274
Aitchison, Robert, 173
Albermarle, Dowager Countess of, 264
Aldous, John Edmond Paul, 229, 230
Alexandra Dance Hall, 232-33
Alger, Major, 46
Allan, Mrs. George, 229
Allan Studholme Memorial Labour Temple, 245
Ambrose, Miss, 229
American Can Company of Canada Limited, 211
American Federation of Labour, 244
American Revolutionary War, 3, 6
Amity Rehabilitation Centre of Hamilton, 263, 277
Amor, James, 151
Ancaster Bloody Assize, 47-48
Anderson, Helen M., 285

Anderson, Dr. James, 198
Applegarth, William, 18, 63
Appleyard, Dr. H. E., 273
Arabian, launching of, 175-76
Arbuckle, Franklin, 282
Archibald, David, 93
Argyll and Sutherland Highlanders of Canada, 235
Armstrong, Det., 152
Armstrong, Chief Magistrate G. H., 102, 153
Arno, John, 287
Arrell, Dr. William, 182
Arthur, Eric R. on Whitehern, 293-94
Arthur, Julia, 173
Askew, George, 175
Associated Musicians of Ontario, 228
Astor, John Jacob, 33
Asylum for Inebriates, 194
Asylum for the Insane, 194
Atomic Energy of Canada, 222
Attwood, W. Matthias, 148
Aussem, J. H., 141
Automobile, age of, 183-84
early laws regarding speed, 183
Avery, Keith, 287
Aviation, 238-41

B

Babies' Dispensary Guild, 216-17, 218
Bagshaw, Dr. Elizabeth, 225;
on the automobile of 1911, 184;
on early transportation of doctors, 182
Bailey, Rev. T. M.,

Baker, Hugh Cossart, 97;
founder of the Canada Life Assurance Company, 98
Baker, Hugh C. II, 162;
and first telephone exchange in British Empire, 161-62
Balfe, Dr., 196
Ball, Margaret W., 182
Bank of Upper Canada, 80;
and the Gore Bank, 93
Barker, Samuel, 193
Barnes, George, and Company, 164
Barnes, Thomas, 164
Barren, Walter, 196
Barron, Constable James, murder of, 196
Barrow, E. G., 214
Barter system, prevalence of, 74
Bartmann, William, 230
Barton and Stoney Creek Road Company, 165
Bastien, H. L., 175, 178
Bates, Mrs., 37
Bates, M. Banker, 243
Bates, William, 36
Batstone, Harry, 250
Bauer, Dr. John A., 196, 273
Baugh, Dr., 196
Baum, James, 198
Beasley, Catherine, 99
Beasley, David C., 69, 86;
on the character of Richard Beasley, 82;
on the sale of Richard Beasley's lands, 81
Beasley, Henry, 12, 99
Beasley, John, 12
Beasley, Johanna (Cartwright), 12
Beasley, Keziah (Ford), 99
Beasley, Richard, 38, 46, 47, 48, 54, 55, 57, 294;
appointed justice of the peace, 15;
on Clergy Reserves, 81;
credit from Richard Cartwright, 28;
death of, 99;
elected to Legislative Assembly, 24;
expansion of holdings, 12-15;
first arrival at lakehead controversy, 12-13;
forced to sell land, 29;
friendship with Chief Joseph Brant and Augustus Jones, 24;
lineage, 12;
marriage to Henrietta Springer, 16;
overextending land holdings, 24;
petition for crown lands, 12;

postwar economic hardships, 45-46;
sale of lands, 80-82;
sale of lands to Mennonites, 29-30;
trading business, difficulties, 28-29
Beasley, Thomas C., 99;
disappearance of assessment rolls, 135-36
Beasley, Thomas W., 156
Beddoe, Mrs. Harold S., 229
Bedford, Reginald, 231
Bedford Music Studio, 231
Beeby, A. E., 289
Bell, Alexander Graham, 161
Bell Telephone Company of Canada, 162
Bennett's Vaudeville House, 213
Benthuysen, Lydia van (Beasley), 12
Berrie, Robert, 66, 71
Berry, James F., 270, 271, 287
BeSaw, E. W., 237
Best, Thomas N., 139
Betts, Lorne, 231
Biggar, E. B., on the Battle of Stoney Creek, 40
Biggar, Robert, 71, 72
Biggar, S. D., 207, 210
Biggar, Lt. Warren, 207
Billiken Club, 246
Billings, John, 141, 191
Billings, Dr. William, 113
Bengham, Dr., 182
Birge, C. A., 141
Birge, Cyrus, 185
Birge, M. B., 141
Birth Control Society of Hamilton, 225
Bisby, George H., 192, 193
Black, George, 148, 162
Blackford, John, 141
Blackstock, George Tate, 198
Blackwood, Thomas, 80, 81
Blakely, Olive Berlow, 229
Blatz, Dr. William E., 173
Bleakley, John W., 188, 199
Blennerhassett, Miss, 88
Blennerhassett, Mr., 88
Board of Health, establishment of, 102-3
Boer War, 184
Booker, Lieutenant Colonel Alfred, 111, 131, 143
Booker, Rev. Alfred, 114
Booker, Charles Goodenough, 247-48
Booker, Mayor, 203, 208
Booker, Lt. Stewart C., 248
Boulton, Capt. A. G., 242
Boulton, D'Arcy, 85
Boulton, Henry, 80, 85

Bowan, Miss Carrie M., 181
Bowen, Major, 126
Bowers, Lawrence, 150
Bowlby, Reid, 155
Bowman, Basil, 273
Bowman, Dr. F. B., 216, 272
Boyd, Miss Annie B., 217
Boyd, Erroll, 203
Boyd, Hugh, 151
Boys' Home School, 218
Brad, John, 38
Bradley, John, 72
Brant, Lt. Cameron D., 207
Brant, Isaac, 30
Brant, Chief John, 31, 67
Brant, Chief Joseph:
    arrival at lakehead, 23;
    death, 30-31, 48;
    friendship with Augustus Jones and
        Richard Beasley, 24;
    trips to England, 23
Brant, Molly (Mary), 23
Brewster, Constance E., 273
Brickers, Sam, 30
Brigger, Major W. J., 236
Brisbin, Charles E., 291;
    on future of Hamilton, 292
Bristol Bill, 153
Brock, General Isaac, 33, 36;
    appreciated inevitability of war, 32;
    on numbers of settlers loyal to U.S.A.,
        34;
    on state of the militia, 35
Brooke, Lieutenant Daniel, 85
Brooke, Elizabeth (McNab), 85
Brouse, Mrs. A. M., 228
Browe, Miss Annie I., 274
Brown, Adam, 118, 119, 122, 192, 251
Brown, D. P., 219
Brown, George, 138, 147
Brown, Sir George McLaren, 251
Brown, Hugh F., 257, 287
Brown, James, 128
Brown, John, 225
Brown, Myles G., 272
Brown, Richard, 140
Brown, William Arthur, 251
Brown, William Evatt, 251
Browne, Edward, 170
Browning, E. W., 291
Bruce, Alexander, 155
Bruce, Mrs. R. S., 226
Brulé, Etienne, 20
Brydges, C. J., 114
Buchan, John M., 160
Buchanan, Elsie, 122

Buchanan, Isaac, 95, 97, 100, 120, 122,
    123, 136, 142, 178, 194
Buchanan, Isaac, and Company, 135
Buchanan, Joshua G., 162, 178
Buchanan, Mrs., 142
Buchanan and Company, 136
Bucke, Dr. Richard M., 194
Buckland, Charles, 92
Bull, Mrs. Charles E., 229
Bull, Eleanor, 114
Bull, Canon George A., 114, 264;
    on Dr. Roe's Grammar School, 77-78
Bull, George Perkins Boothesby, 77
Bull, Senator Harcourt, 264
Bullock, William, 73
Burgess, James, 168
Burgess, Sophia, 168
Burkholder, Jacob, 26, 28, 99
Burkholder, Mabel, 297;
    on the arrival of the Burkholder fam-
        ily, 26;
    on churches, 159;
    on life of the pioneer Burkholder fam-
        ily, 27;
    on Methodism, 159
Burlington and Hamilton Glass Works,
    177
Burlington Bay Canal:
    construction of, 62, 63-64;
    economic importance, 66, 97;
    opening, 65;
    tolls, 65
Burlington Heights, importance of dur-
    ing War of 1812, 33
Burn, W. Scott H., 84
Burnfield, Alexander, 114
Burrill, W. S., 211
Burton, Alice, 227
Burton, Jack, 238
Burton, Mayor William, 239
Burwell, Lewis, 62
Bury, Viscount, 137-38
Byng, Governor-General, Lord, 249

C

Caffery, Jack, 173
Cahill, E. D., 170
Cahill, James, 60
Cahill, Magistrate James, 153, 208
Cameron, J. M. A., 129
Cameron, John H., 180
Campbell, Donald, 188
Campbell, J. D., 290
Campbell, James E., 287
Campbell, Mrs. Laura, 125

Campbell, Capt. Patrick, 14;
  on the soil between the mountain and
    lake, 27
Campbell, Judge William, 47
Canada Land Company, 63
Canada Life Assurance Company,
  founding of, 98
Canada Screw Company, 185
Canada Steamship Lines, 247
Canadian Automobile Association, 184
Canadian Bank of Commerce, 142
Canadian Congress of Labour, 245
Canadian Coloured Cotton Mills, 211
Canadian Drawn Steel Company Limit-
  ed, 205
Canadian Field Artillery, 11th Battery,
  236
Canadian Football Hall of Fame, 282
Canadian Industries Limited, 8, 205
Canadian Liquid Air Company Limited,
  268
Canadian National Institute for the
  Blind, 263
Canadian Press Association, 131
Canadian Rowing Association, 178
Canadian Wesleyan, 70
Canadian Westinghouse Company Lim-
  ited, 186, 236
Canadian Women's Press Club, 208
Cannon, Donald O., 52
Carey, Dr. Bruce A., 208, 230-31
Carey, Mrs. Eileen, 277
Carey, Mrs. Vernon T., 229
Carey, Lt. William V., 207
Caroline affair, 89
Carpenter, Albert Edward, 165
Carpenter, Alexander, 72, 76, 96
Carpenter, Eliza Jane, 50
Carpenter, Joseph J., 76
Carr, Col. Leeming A., 242
Carroll, Peter, 167
Carroll, William, 206
Carruthers, John, 134, 152
Carruthers, Miss, 126
Carscallen, Col. Henry G., 200
Carscallen, Wing Cmdr. Henry M., 240
Cartwright, John Solomon, 81
Cartwright, Richard, 12
Cartwright, Richard, Jr., 12, 13, 81;
  and Beasley's notes of credit, 28-29;
  influence on Beasley, 14;
  lineage, 12
Case, Dr. William, 41, 88, 100
Case, Dr. William II, 106, 113, 187
Casey, Thomas, 125
Casson, Francis Dollier de, 20

Cataract Power Company of Hamilton,
  210, 211, 212
Cauman, Kalman, 160
Celestine, Sister, 275
Chambers, Stewart C., 203
Champ, H. H., 140, 217
Champ, W. B., 205
Chandler, Gen. John, 38, 40
Charlton, B. E., 38
Charlton, Benjamin, 127
Charlton, Mayor Benjamin E., 148
Chauncey, Commodore Isaac, 36, 37,
  41, 42, 43
Chedoke General Hospital, 274
Cheevers, George, 94
Child, W. A., 140
Chipman, Holden Company Limited,
  205-6
Chisholm, John, 65
Chisholm, William, 63
Chisholm, Col. William, 89, 99
Cholera:
  control of, 70-71;
  epidemic of 1832, 66-68;
  epidemic of 1854, 112-13;
  hospital built, 71
Chowne, Miss Lucie, 192
Christian Brothers of Toronto, 220
Church:
  activities, 1798, 55
  site of first, 18
Church of England: monopoly on mar-
  riage, 15
Churches, 159-60
City Council: appointment of school
  board trustees, 126;
  first meeting, 96;
  members increased, 101;
  stock in Great Western Railway Com-
    pany, 110
City Ditch, construction of 168-69
City Hall (new):
  description, 270-71;
  erection of, 269
City Hospital, 180;
  deaths from cholera infantum, 216;
  expansion of, 191;
  first Nurses' Training School, 181
  first operating suite, 181-82;
  the new, 180-81
City limits, extension of, 96, 101
Clark, H., 76
Clark, Hutchinson, 101
Clark, L. A., 262
Clemens, R. Eugene, 218
Cleophas, Sister, 275

Clergy, Reserves, 81
Cline, George, 250
Clinton, Sir Henry, 10
Cockburn, Dr., 196
Cockburn, G. F., 116-17
Coffin, Lt.-Col. A. F., 242
Colborne, Sir John, 85
Cole, Joseph, 57
Coleman, Kathleen Blake, 208
Coleman, Dr. Theobold, 208
Coles, Eric M., 243
Collinson, John H., 225
Commercial interests, growth of, 97
Commonwealth Air Training Plan, 237-38
Communications:
    development of, 70, 91-92;
    Jolley Cut, 167-68;
    solving the problem, 165-68
Community activities, 96
Confederation, 147-48
Confederation Park, 279-80
Constitutional Act, 1791, 81
Cooch, Harold A., 207
Cooke, Mrs. Dorothy, 288
Cooke, Dr. K. E., 274
Coombes, Major S. H., 235
Cooper, D. A., 277
Cooper, W. H., 247, 272
Copps, Victory Kennedy: biographical sketch, 278;
    as controller, 278;
    elected mayor, 279;
    vitality of his administration, 282-83
Corktown, 172-73
Corktown House, 173
Cornelius, Capt., 295
Corman, Ellis, 241
Corman, Isaac, 33, 39
Cornelius, Capt. John Richard, 250, 271
Correspondent and Patriot, on McNab's unsatisfied debts, 93
Cory, Charles D., 162
Coulter, David, 188, 196
Counsell, Charles Ozen, 125, 126
Courthouse, erection of new, 154-55
Courthouse and Gaol, first, 56-57
Court sessions, first recorded, 57
Cowman, Jean, 239-40
Cox, Ernie, 250
Cox, James, 292
Craigie, George, 119
Craigie, Dr. William, 100, 119, 126, 138, 144

Crerar, Caroline, 292;
    on her home, 171;
    on the social life of her time, 171-72
Crerar, Capt. Harry D. G., 200
Crerar, John, 155, 157, 171
Crerar, Mrs. P. D., 193
Cresswell, R. H., 187
Crime, rash of murders (1899-1909), 195-99
Crimean War: cannon incident, 131-32
Crinnon, Right Rev. Peter F., 160, 178-79
Crocker, Joseph R., 253
Crompton, Thomas, on the upswing in real estate, 206
Crooks, James, 57, 60
Crooks, Matthew, 60
Cross, Tom, 177
Crystal Palace, 121-23, 132, 179
Cummings, Alice, 229
Cummings, James, 101, 102, 111, 135
Cummings, Dr. Samuel, 181, 182
Cunningham, F. P., 276
Cust, William C., on early surveying methods, 21
Cutaia, Angelo, 232
Cutaia, Anthony, 232
Cutaia, Nicholas, 232
Cutaia, Richard, 232

D

Daily Spectator, on pension inadequacies of War of 1812, 46
Dale Community Centre, 168, 263
Dalton, Thomas, 175
Dalley, F. F., 225
Daly, Mrs. Mary Stuart, 188
Daniel C. Gunn Shop, manufacture of locomotives, 139-40
Davey, Dr. J. Edgar, 207, 217, 218
Davidson, Thomas, 111
Davis, Elizabeth, 26
Davis, Joseph, 71
Davis, Mary Long, on the aftermath of the Battle of Stoney Creek, 41
Davis, Ralph, 152
Davis, William, 26, 34, 77
Davis, William, Jr., 39, 56
Daw, Canon Samuel, 160
Deadman, Dr. William J., 216, 272
Deadman, Mrs. William J., 229
Deborah Ladies' Aid Society, 160
Deering Company, 185
Delaware and Cayuga Indians and the Fenian raids, 143-44

Delaware Land Company, 9
Denman, R. O., 238
Depew, Capt. Charles, Sr. (Depue), 7, 8, 55
Depew, Capt. Charles, Jr., 8
Depew, John, 7, 8, 13, 55, 294;
  land grant to, 8
Depew, Mary, 7
Depew Family, contribution to Hamilton, 8-9
Depot, Canadian Mounted Rifles, 202, 203
De Pugh, Charles, 10
Derby, William, 244
Desjardin, Peter, 62
Desjardins Canal, 80, 97, 167;
  construction of, 62
Desjardins Canal Company, 62
Davey, Dr. J. Edgar, 190
Devely, D. R. and Son, 176
Dewey, Daniel, 141
Dewey, Mrs. Frank S., 272
Dexter, C. O., 211
Deyman, Emma J., 216
Dickenson, John, 165, 210
Dickinson, Dr., 104
Dillon, Frank G., 257, 287;
  on the north end, 175
Distinguished Citizen Award, women honoured, 279
Dixon, Ewart (Red), 190
Dixon, W. H., 121
Dodds, Major Robert, 238, 239, 240
Dominion Foundries and Steel Limited (Dofasco), 8, 186, 268
Dominion Power and Transmission Company Limited, 211, 212-13
Dominion Steel Castings Limited, 186
Dominion Telegraph Company, 161
Donohue, Denny, 178
Donohue, Jerry, 178
Doolittle, C. E., 140
Dorchester, Lord, 15, 21
Douglas, Fenner, 240
Douglass, John, 98
Dowling, Bishop T. J., 192, 218
Downs, Timothy, 46
Drennan, William, 117
Drew, Commander Andrew, 89
Duet Club, 229
Duff, Sir Lyman Poore, 155
Duff, William, 92
Duffy, Edward I., 277
Duggan, Dr. Thomas, 113
Duke of Devonshire, 192
Dumbrille, Douglas, 185

Du Moulin, Septimus S., 250, 271
Duncan, Robert, and Company, 164
Duncombe, Charles, 89
Dundurn Castle, 86, 132;
  sale of, 139
Dundurn Park, opening of, 188-89
Dunham, Mabel, 24, 29, 30
Dunn, Dr. John G., 113
Dunstan, R. W., 141
Durand, Alonzo, 51
Durand, Charles, 36, 51, 58, 60, 71, 74, 75;
  on the assault of George Rolph, 57-58
Durand, Ferdinand, 51
Durand, Harriet, 75
Durand, James, 34, 50, 51, 52, 54, 58, 75, 79;
  death, 77;
  sale of land to George Hamilton, 51
Dymal, William, 54
Dynes, John, 87

E

Eastman, Miss Eliza, 88
Eastwood, John M., 246
Eaton, Col. W. F., 250
Eaton, T., Knitting Mill, 206
Edgar, Dr. James W., 182
Education, 124-28, 224-29;
  act establishing public school in Canada, 60;
  board of examiners, 125;
  the Central School System, 126-28;
  changes, 275-77;
  Common School Act, 125;
  financing, 126;
  first board of trustees, 126;
  first efforts, 59-60;
  first school premises, 125;
  growth, 160-61;
  integration, 125;
  medical practice of public schools, 216;
  pay scales of teachers, 124, 125-26;
  the Separate School Act, 160;
  separate school system, expansion of, 220-21;
  technical training, 219;
  in the twentieth century, 218-22
Edward, Duke of Kent, and Julie de St. Laurent, 144-46
Edward, Prince of Wales, 118, 146, 247-48
Eleanor Callaghan Lees Scholarship, 229

334

Electricity, first experiment in lighting by, 148
Eleventh Field Regiment, 236
Elliott-Fairchild Air Service, 238
Elliott, Frank J., 272
Elliott, Jack V., 238-39
Elliott, Miss, 124
Ellis, Norman, 207
Elmslie, George, 78
Emergency Measures Organization, 243
Emslie, D. Graham, 286
English, James, 73
English, Dr. Walter M., 194
Eustis, William, 34
Evans, John R., 290
Evans, Mrs. Robert, 193
Evatt, Maria Z., 122
Ewart, Miss Ellen, 271-72
Ewart, Dr. Hugo T., 272, 274

F

Fairclough, Gordon, 285
Fairclough, Ellen L., 263, 284-85;
  on period of peak immigration, 191
Fairgrieve, Capt. Hugh, 247
Fairgrieve, Capt. J. B., 176
Family Compact, 48, 98;
  vs the Reformers, political influence on Hamilton, 58
Family Service Bureau, 263
Farewell, Marvin R., 291
Farmer, Col. G. D., 207, 235
Farmer, Lt.-Col. G. R. D., 235
Farmer, Mrs. John G., 264
Farmer, Mary H., 292
Farr, David W., 292
Farrell, Right Rev. John, 100, 150, 156, 227-28
Fay, Anna Eva, 198
Fearman, F. W., 59, 75-76, 87, 88
Fearman, Lt.-Col. H. D., 202, 235
Feldman, Rabbi Arthur, 295
Fenian Raids:
  and the Delaware and Cayuga Indians, 143-44;
  Hamilton's contribution, 142-43
Fenwick, Dr. G. Roy:
  on music, 228;
  on Hamilton musical families, 230
Ferguson, Archibald, 27, 75
Ferguson, A. E., 277
Ferguson, Bessie Gowan, 208
Ferguson, Elizabeth, 273
Ferguson, Florence, 55
Ferguson, G. Howard, 239

Ferguson, Messrs, and Company, 68
Ferguson, Peter, 55, 117
Ferrie, Adam, 99
Ferrie, Adam, Jr., 114
Ferrie, A. E., 178
Ferrie, Colin Campbell, 69, 71, 93, 99, 114, 144;
  first mayor, 96, 270
Ferrie, R. B., 178
Ferris, Frederick H., 257
Fessenden, Clementina, 188-89
Fessenden, Rev. E. J., 189
Fidler, Dr. E., 216
Findlay, Strathmore, 246
Finney, James, 76
Fire of 1833, 68
Fire Department Drum and Bugle Corps, 292
Fire protection: by-laws for (1833), 70;
  cost of, 73;
  erection of fire engine house, 72;
  fire engine, purchase of, 71-72;
  first engine company, 72-73;
  modernizing of department, 265
Firestone Tire and Rubber Company of Canada Limited, 237
Fisher, John, 77, 101
Fitzgerald, Eileen, 226
Fitzgibbon, Lieut. James, 40
Fitzpatrick, Johnny, 250
Fitzpatrick, Maurice, 125
Flint, Joseph, 141
Foley, Flt.-Lt. Roden, 240
Foley, Samuel S., 239
Fonger, David, 46
Football Hall of Fame, 277, 283
Foote, Major John, 236
Force, George, on planning community centres, 281
Ford, Nehemiah, 99
Forneret, Ven. George, 160, 217
Forsyth, Caleb, 55
Fourth Field Battery, 200
Fortieth Field Battery, 236
Frame, Andrew, 236
Frank, William, 71
Fraser, R. K., 264
Freeman, L. A., 277
Freeman, W. A., Coal Company, 11
French, Caroline Sophia, 188
Frey, Philip, 16
Friar, Miss, 126
Friar, W. M., 124
Frost, Harry L., 205, 232
Frost, Russell W., 250

Frost Wire Fence Company Limited, 205
Fuller, Right Rev. T. B., 174
Funston, William H., 237
Furlong, Charlie, 178
Furnivall, T. G., 129

G

Gage, Andrew, 157, 165
Gage, Cynthia Elizabeth, 189
Gage, Eugenie Helen, 248
Gage, Hannah Jane, 248
Gage, James, 39, 41, 49, 202
Gage, J. Walter, 206
Gage, Mary, 49
Gage, Robert R., 164
Gage, William, 41, 49
Gale, Alexander, 99, 100
Gale, Rev., 125
Galinée, René de Brabant de, 20
Galloway, Dr. J. D., 275
Galt, John, 63
Gaol, erection of new (1875), 153-54
Garah, John, 73
Gardiner, H. F., 178
Garland, The, 70
Gartshore, John, Company, 119
Gartshore, Mrs. John, 208
Gas illumination, 105-6
Gasse, Doris E., 288
Gatchell, Nathan B., 141
Gates, Frederick W., 130, 152, 167
Gauld, Judge John Gordon, 215
Geddes, Very Rev. John Gamble, 76, 125, 126, 138, 174
Geohegan, Rev. Thomas, 160, 192
German, Alex, 266
Germania Club, 230
Germania Society, 267
Ghent, Thomas, 26
"Ghost of the Canal Story", 64-65
Gibb, Bert, 250
Gibson, Major Colin W. G., 155, 202, 226, 241
Gibson, Sir John M., 119, 155, 174, 189, 201, 205, 210, 225
Gilbert, Charles, 76
Gilbert, William J., 72, 76
Gilkison, Jasper T., 95, 112
Gillan, Gladys, 243
Gillesby, Thomas, 71
Gillespy, William, 131
Gillrie, M. E., 196

Gilmour, Dr. George Peel, 282;
    on the first ten years of McMaster's life, 221
Girls' Home School, 218
Gisborn, Reginald, 245
Glassco, Dr. Gerald S., 218, 232
Godden, Reginald, 231
Gompers, Samuel, 244
Gompf Brewery, 150-51
Gordon, Howard, 243
Gordon, John S., 219
Gordon, Rev. Mr., 126
Gore, Lieutenant-Governor Sir Francis, 52;
    on beauties of the area, 19
Gore Bank, 73, 80, 94;
    and Bank of Upper Canada, 93;
    bankruptcy of, 141;
    Board of Directors, 93;
    and Hamilton bankruptcy, 134-35;
    refusing to honour city's cheques, 122
Gore Gazette, 59;
    on Burlington Bay canal, 65
Goring, Francis, 6
Gourlay, Robert, 58
Gourlay, Col. William, 100, 145
Gourlay, Mrs. William, 194
Grafton, J. B., 194
Grafton, Col. J. J., 194
Grafton Infirmary, 194
Grand Trunk Railway, 139;
    and Great Western Railway Company, 120, 209
Grant, Peter, 164
Grantham, Mrs. Charles D., 232
Grasselli Chemical Company of Cleveland, 205
Gray, E. R., 215
Gray, Thomas, 119
Gray, William A., on first public transportation, 163
Great Western Railway Company, 95, 167;
    absorption by the Grand Trunk, 209;
    city council stock in, 110;
    construction of first rolling mill, 140;
    destruction of bridge over Desjardins canal, 186;
    disaster at Burlington Heights, 113-15;
    and Grand Trunk Railway Corporation, 120;
    loan from Hamilton, 120;
    opening of line, 108-111;
    rolling stock shops, 111, 139
Green, Mrs. Caswell R., 229

Green, Dr. R. L., 272
Green, Levi, 39
Green, William, 39, 46
Greenfield, Lt.-Col. T. W., 235
Greening, Benjamin, 186
Greening, Harry B., 186
Greening, Samuel Owen, 183, 184, 186
Greening, Timothy, 186
Greening, B., Wire Company Limited, 186
Grey, Governor-General Earl, 193
Griffin, Dr. H. S., 181
Griffin, Walter E., 271
Griffith, J. B., 162
Griffith, T. B., 162, 247
Griffith, Mrs. W. Eric
Grosman, A., 95
Guillet, Edwin C., on Beasley-Land controversy, 13;
on the Stump Act, 107
Gunn, Kate, 227
Gurney, Charles, 140
Gurney, E. & C., Company, 141
Gurney, Edward, 140
Gurrie's Hotel, 173

H

Hagerman, Judge, 58
Halcrow, George G., 245
Hale, Cmdr. Edward B., 243
Hale, William, 73
Halford, Harry J., 245
Hamill, Thomas, on the community at the lakehead (1797), 18
Hamilton:
    act of incorporation, 1833, 60-61;
    bankruptcy, 134-36;
    capital expenditure, 1919, 24, 214
    centennial celebrations, 189-90;
    a conservative stronghold, 98-99;
    and death of Queen Victoria, 184-85;
    development, 1830-36, 62;
    and disappearance of the assessment rolls, 135-36;
    early financial problems, 72;
    first municipal election (1833), 69;
    first settlement (Head of the Lake), 3-11 passim;
    heading for bankruptcy, 119-20;
    Homes, 84, 170-71;
    industry (1816), 54;
    municipal debt, 102, 149;
    municipal government, changes (1909), 223;

municipal government set up (1833), 61-62;
municipal officials, appointment of (1833), 69-70;
municipal services, attention to (1866), 149;
municipal tax, first assessed, 71;
and the Navy, 241-43;
north end characters, 177-78;
roads (1816), 54;
and the Roaring Twenties, 224;
return to solvency, 136;
selected as county town, 51-52;
social life (1816), 54-55;
tax exemption for new industries, 140-41;
territorial expansion, 75-76, 96, 101;
topography, 1-5;
underwriting loan to Great Western, 120;
and the visit of H.R.H. Prince of Wales, 122-23
Hamilton, Right Rev. Charles, 192
Hamilton, Fred, 204
Hamilton, George, 14, 36, 54, 57, 67, 75, 126;
    death of, 77, 79;
    exploits during War of 1812, 50;
    postwar economic hardships, 46;
    purchase of Durand's lakehead land, 51
Hamilton, Ida G., 219
Hamilton, Myra M., on naming the village of Waterdown, 49
Hamilton, Peter Hunter, 58, 69, 71, 75, 126, 128, 130, 131, 204
Hamilton, Robert, 14, 15, 50
Hamilton, Robert Jarvis, 91, 104, 107
Hamilton Aero Club, 239, 240
Hamilton Amateur Athletic Association, 129
Hamilton and District Association for Retarded Children, 276
Hamilton and District Trades and Labour Council, 245
Hamilton and Dundas Street Railway (Dundas "Dummy"), 174
Hamilton and Milton Road Company, 167
Hamilton and Saltfleet Road Company, 165-66
Hamilton Art Gallery, 292
Hamilton Art School, 219
Hamilton Automobile Club, 183, 184
Hamilton Board of Trade, 219

Hamilton Bridge and Tool Company, 175
Hamilton Bridge Work Company Limited, 205
Hamilton Business College, 218
Hamilton By-Products Coke Ovens, 8
Hamilton Cataract Power, Light and Traction Company Limited, 211
Hamilton Choral Society, 228
Hamilton Civic Hospital, 273
Hamilton Coat of Arms, 282
Hamilton Conservatory of Music, 228-29, 230
Hamilton Construction Association, 250
Hamilton Cotton Company, 202
Hamilton Council of Knights of Columbus, 246
Hamilton Cricket Club, 130
Hamilton Cycle Club, 183
Hamilton District Telegraph Company, 161, 162
Hamilton Eistedd Fod, 230
Hamilton Electric Light and Cataract Power Company Limited, 211
Hamilton Electric Light and Power Company, 205
Hamilton Electric Radial Company, 211
Hamilton Fire Brigade: development of, 149-52;
and fire at D. McInnes & Co., 151
Hamilton Fire Prevention Bureau, 265
Hamilton Flying Club, 243
Hamilton Free Press, 70, 99
Hamilton Gas Light Company, 105, 189
Hamilton General Hospital, modernization and expansion of, 272-73
Hamilton Glass Works, 141
Hamilton Harbour Commission, 205
Hamilton Health Association, 193, 246
Hamilton Hospital Association, 274
Hamilton Iron and Steel Company, 140
Hamilton Jockey Club, 166
Hamilton Law Association, 155
Hamilton Mechanics Curling Club, 131
Hamilton Medical and Surgical Society, 181
Hamilton Medical Society, 182
Hamilton Mountain Incline Railway, 169
Hamilton Mountain Park Company, 169
Hamilton Municipal Airport, 239
Hamilton Olympic Club, 250
Hamilton Opera Company, 292
Hamilton Playground Association, 246-47
Hamilton Playgrounds Commission, 246

Hamilton Police Male Chorus, 292
Hamilton Provident and Loan Company, 141
Hamilton Public Library:
expansion of, 291-92;
opening of, 174
Hamilton Radial Electric Railway, 211
Hamilton Review: on Mayor Sam Lawrence during Stelco strike, 253;
on Nora Henderson, 253
Hamilton Riding and Driving Association, 129
Hamilton Rowing Club, 178
Hamilton School of Music, 229
Hamilton Spectator, 5, 239;
on Confederation, 147-48;
death of first editor, 131;
founding, 98;
on Mayor Jackson's administration, 279;
on the Murray Jones concept of the downtown core, 289;
on opening of the new courthouse, 155;
political ideals, 98;
on the Railway ball, 111
Hamilton Spring Steeplechases, 129
Hamilton Steamboat Company, 247
Hamilton Steel and Iron Company, 185
Hamilton Street Railway, 211;
electrification of, 210;
extension of, 210;
inauguration of service, 162-65
ownership, change of, 210;
route of, 162-64 passim;
strike, 209
Hamilton String Quartette, 229
Hamilton Symphony Orchestra, 230
Hamilton Technical School, 219
Hamilton Terminal Company, 211-212
Hamilton Theatre Company, 292
Hamilton Trades and Labour Council, formation of, 244
Hamilton Victoria Club, 131
Hampshire, Cyril, 231
Hancock, John, 154
Hand, Earl, 238
Hanley, Robert J., on Corktown people, 173
Hannon "Doc", 129
Harbour development, 112
Hardy, Charles P., 148
Hardy, William, 58
Harris, Dr. C. L. M., 228, 229, 230
Harris, Lloyd, 185
Harris Orchestral Club, 228, 230

Harrison, Gen. William Henry, 33, 39
Harstone, Ross Gerald, 272
Hart, R. S., 205
Harvey, George B., 92
Harvey, Col. John, 38, 40, 41
Haskins, William, 117, 214
Haslett, Thomas C., 155
Hassel, D. F. (Dofasco Dan), 187
Hatch, Col. Harry, 204
Hatt, John O., 93
Hatt, Richard, 52
Hatt, Major Samuel, 34, 36, 37, 48
Hawkins, Mrs. W. C., 225
Hay, Lt.-Col. A. J., 235
Hayes, Matthew, 251
Hayworth, John, 235
Hayworth, Mrs. John, 235
Hayworth, Margaret, 235
Head, Governor-General Sir Edward, 138
Head, Lady, 138
Head, Sir Francis Bond, 88
Head-of-the-Lake Historical Society, 292
Health: medical inspection of public schools established, 216
Health department: expansion of, 217; first health centre, 217
Hearst, Sir William, 207
Heaven, Rev. Cecil A., 226
Hebden, Rev. John, 168
Hebrew Benevolent Society Anshe Sholom of Hamilton, 160
Heilig, Margaret, 263
Heise, Rev. Dr., 114
Henderson, Gordon J., 217
Henderson, John C., 114
Henderson, Dr. Mabel, 273
Henderson, Nora Frances, 294; on Stelco strike, 252-53
Hendrie, John, 129
Hendrie, Sir John S., 184, 191, 200, 205, 225
Hendrie, William, Sr., 75, 128, 129
Hendrie, Mrs. William, 191, 192, 251
Hendrie, Capt. W. I. S., 200
Hendrie, William, Jr., 128, 129
Hendrie and Company, 128, 132
Henery, Governor, 157
Henery, John, 152
Hennelly, T. A., 276
Henser, Samuel, 170
Hensworth, Major L., 236
Henwood, Edwin, Sr., 113, 133, 218
Herrington, W. S., 55
Hess, Charity, 25

Hess, Michael, 25
Hess, Peter, 27, 83
Hesse, Catherine Maria, 99
Hewlett, Dr. W. H., 230, 231
Hickey, E. D., on the effect of the St. Lawrence Seaway, 260-61
Hicks, Frederick J., 232
Hill, Amos, 141
Hillfield Private School, 225-26
Hills, A. H., 154
Hilton, H. G., 253
Hincks, Francis, 93
H.M.C.S. *Patriot*, 242
H.M.C.S. *Star*, 241-42
Hitchcock, P. M., 140
Hobson, Robert, 178, 185
Hobson, Thomas, 198
Hodgins, William, 116
Holbrook, Dr. John Howard, 193
Holden, John R., 101
Holton, Aurora, 156
Holton, Brisies, 156
Holton, Janna, 156
Holton, W. A., 205
Holton, Warren, 164
Holton, William A., 164
Hoodless, Mrs. John, 218
Hooper, Lt. Bertram O., 202
Hope, Senator Adam, 162, 171
Hope, George, 217
Hopkins, Beamer W., 239
Hornibrook, Lt.-Col. J. A., 236
Horning, Abraham, 25
Horning, Elizabeth (Depew), 8
Horning, Isaac, 25
Horning, Ludwig, 25
Horning, Peter, 54
Hospitals: 180-81; development, 132-33; Hamilton's first permanent, 103-4; increased numbers of, 191-95
Houghton, Charles W., 271
House of Industry, 104, 105, 132
Howell, Walter (Spike), 203
Howitt, Canon F. E., 160
Hudson, Marie E., 273
Hughson, B. H., 169
Hughson, George, 35
Hughson, Nathaniel, 27, 51, 52, 55, 59, 133
Hull, General William, 35, 36
Humphreys, Mrs. John, 279
Hunter, Dr. J. W., 103, 133
Hunter, George, 79
Hunter, Peter, 79
Hunter, Robert, 250

Huron and Erie Trust Company, 141
Hyde, Isabella, 145, 294
Hydro Electric Power Commission of
    Hamilton, 212
Hydro Electric Power Commission of
    Ontario, 212, 213
Hyslop, 67, 71

I

Immigration, 104-5, 191
Imperial Cotton Company Limited, 211
Imperial Order Daughters of the Em-
    pire, 193
Inch, Adam, 169
Inch, Lt.-Col. George T., 236
Inch, Lt.-Col. Robert F., 243
Industrial Growth, 139-41, 185-86, 205
Inglis, Rev. David, 100
Inksetter, Dr. D. G., 246
Inkson, William, 151
Inns; as barometer of community econ-
    omy, 59;
    rash of (1820-30's), 59
International Airways Limited, 238, 239
International Harvester Company of
    Canada, 185
Ireland, Samuel John, 219
Irvine, James, 187
Irvine, Rev. Dr., 114
Irving, Aemelius, E., 155

J

Jackson, Edward, 28, 76, 161
Jackson, Lloyd Douglas, 255-69, 282,
    286;
    on Confederation Park, 279-80;
    defeat, 279;
    on Hamilton and Hamiltonians, 266-
    67;
    municipal changes during term, 255-
    69 passim;
    on the new City Hall, 270, 287
Jackson, Mrs. Lloyd, 279
Jaimet, Charles H., 222
James, John W., 156
James, Wallace T., 265
Jardine, J., 169
Jarvis, Robert, 75, 79, 104
Jarvis, William Munson, 60, 92
Jeffrey, John, 178
Jelfs, Magistrate George F., 208
Jerome, Harold, 231
Jewish Community Centre, 263
John By (First Hamilton Steamer), 63

John Street North Hospital, 93
Johnson, James, 99
Johnson, James, 207-8
Johnson, Sir William, 23
Johnson, W. F., 65
Johnston, Mrs. James, 196
Johnston, Mimi, 229
Johnston, William, 87
Jolley, James, 167-68
Jolley Cut, 167-68
Jones, Anne, 285
Jones, Rev. Aubrey, 295
Jones, Augustus, 16, 21, 31, 36, 50;
    friendship with Joseph Brant and
    Richard Beasley, 24;
    as land surveyer, 21-22;
    move to Brant County, 48-49
Jones, Dr. E. C., 273
Jones, Frank L., on Richardson's navi-
    gating ability, 44
Jones, John R., 287
Jones "Mickey", 173
Jones, Murray, 288, 293;
    and downtown development, 288-89
Jones, Rev. Peter, 22, 31
Jones, Philip, 49
Jones, Robert, 55
Jones, Seneca, 38
Jones Ruthven and Company, 95
Jubal Club, 229
Judiciary, development of, 154-56
Juson, Richard, 122, 168, 170
Juson, Mrs. Richard, 174
Jutten, Thomas W., 175, 248

K

Kappelle, Dr. Daniel P., 273
Keen, Major Frank J., 236
Keith, David, 148
Keith, George E., 148
Kelley, Russell T., 231, 250
Kelly, "Collar Button", 177
Kelly, Robert, 125
Kennedy, John, 69
Kennedy, Reginald, 170
Kennedy, Reginald Aemilius, 170
Keogh, Major David, 236
Kerr, Archibald, 153, 167, 170
Kerr, J. H., 186
Kerr, Kate, 123
Kerr, Robert, 185
Kerr, Robert, W., 156
Kerr, Lt.-Col. William Johnson, 58, 123;
    on renovation of Burlington Bay
    Canal, 63-64

Kerr, William Simcoe, 123
Kidner, F., 87;
  on McNab and his militia departure
    from Gore, 89
Killip, Arthur F., 226
Kilvert, F. E., 175
Kilvington, Thomas, 164;
  on the Great Western disaster, 114
Kimble, C., 73
King's Head Inn, 17
Kingsthorpe Day and Boarding School,
  228
Kinrade, Ethel, 294;
  murder of, 197-99
Kinrade, Florence, 197, 198, 199
Kinrade, Thomas L., 197, 199
Kirkendall, Samuel, 23, 27
Kitchen, M. T., 228
Kittson, E. E., 178
Kittson, Dr. E. Graves, 180
Klun, Jaroslaw, 267
Knights of Labour, 244
Kough, Mary, 192
Kyles, J. D., 278

L

Labatt, Lt.-Col. R. H., 207
Labour, 244-45;
  strike at Stelco, 252-53;
  and management, first clash, 94-95
Laidler, George, 292
Lake, Rev. Samuel, 169
Laking, Leslie, 261, 280
Lamb, Harold, 178
Lamoureux, W. J., 240
Lancefield, R. T., 174
Land, Abel, 9, 11, 27, 28
Land, Ephraim, 10, 11, 38
Land, John, 9, 10-11
Land, Mary, 38
Land, Phoebe (Scott), 10
Land, Phoebe (II), 11
Land, Rebecca, 11
Land, Robert, 9, 12, 27, 33, 294;
  activities during Revolutionary War,
    9-10;
  death, 77;
  family settlement, 11;
  migration to Hamilton, 10-11
Land, Robert Jr., 10, 11, 34, 185
Land, William, 11
Langmuir, J. W., 194
Langrill, Dr. Walter F., 207
Langs, C. V., 221, 248, 249, 266
Langtree, Miss, 126

Lannin, Dr. G. E. J., 232
Lanza, Joseph, 285
Lapp, Victor, 272
La Salle, Robert René Cavelier de, 20
Laurie, Douglas, 250
Law, John, 60, 71, 77, 100, 128
Lawrence, Leonard George, 245, 264,
  287
Lawrence, Samuel, 242, 244, 245, 252,
  295;
  on William Morrison, 251
Lazier, Harold F., 274
Lazier, Stephen F., 155
Leadley, Frances R. (Pep), 250
Leander Boat Club, 178, 250
Leander Club, 178
Leather, H. H., 11, 264
LeBrocq, Mrs. Stanley E., 229
Lee, David, 229
Lees, George, 132
Lees, George H., 207, 212
Lees, Mrs. T. Jack, 229
Lees, Thomas, 141
Leland, Mrs. Frank, 159
Lemon, Agnes Hannah Hamilton, 51, 75
Lemon, Charles, 155
Lenaten, Mother Superior M. Philip,
  113, 192
Leslie, Dr. James, 181
Lester, Edward, 271
Leslie, K. M., 277
Levy, Mrs. Herman, 160
Lewis, Kitty, 177
Lewis, Thomas, 230
Lister, John, 161
Littlehales, Thomas, 229
Local Council of Women, 216, 217, 218,
  246, 265, 285
Lockwood, Heziah, 55
Logie, Lt.-Col. William Alexander, 204
Long, W. D., 170, 193
Longboat, Tom, 294
Looney, James B., 160
Loosely, Fred, A., 187
Lord Durham's Report, impact on Up-
  per Canada, 99
Loretto Academy, 227-28
Lorne, Marquis of, 146, 154
Lottridge, Capt. Robert, 13
Lottridge, William, 36
Lounsbury, Marshall J., 239
Lowell Machine Shops, 139
Lucas, R. A., 202
Lundy, William, 10
Lundy's Lane, 10
Lusitania, sinking of, 202

Lutz, Conrad, 56
Lutz, Henry; description of courthouse and gaol, 56
Lyle, Mrs. Norman, 291
Lyle, Dr. Samuel, 193
Lyle, Mrs. Samuel, 193
Lynch, Staunton George, 198
Lynch, Staunton, Mark, 233

M

McAfee, Angus, 35, 87
McAfee, David, 35
McAfee, Samuel, 35
McAllister, R. H., on specialists, 273
Macassa, 247
Macassa Lodge, 133
McAuley, Katherine, 288
McCabe, Captain, 147
McCabe, James, 151
McCallum, Andrew F., 215
McCallum, Archibald, 128
McConnell, Michael: and the murder of Nelson Mills, 156-57
McCoy, Archie H. R., 278, 280, 281
McCracken, James, 149, 152, 153, 155
McCrae, Lt.-Col. John, 208
McCullough, Col. Charles R., 188, 231, 292
McCulloch, W. S.: on electrification of the Hamilton Street Railway, 210
McCurdy, J. A. Douglas, 207, 238
Macdonald, Angus L., 241
Macdonald, Col., 36
McDonald, Jack, 279
Macdonald, J. Katherine, 229
Macdonald, Sir John A., 98, 137, 140, 145, 147, 257
Macdonald, Sheriff, 82, 87
MacDonald, T. R., 292
McDonald Institute, 219
McElroy, Robert, 118, 132, 135, 178
McFaul, W. L., 257;
on relief work during depression, 215-16;
on water works system, 216
McFetrick, Lt.-Cmdr., John, 241
McGarvin, Michael J., 271
McGhie, Dr. Ambrose G., 273
MacGill, Judge Helen Gregory, 173
McGillivray, Dr. Alice, 273
McGillivray, Dr. T. S., 232
McGiverin, Hal, 178
McGregor, Sq.-Ldr. D. U., 240
McGregor, Dr. J. K., 232, 272
McGregor, Flt.-Lt., Norman S., 240

McIlroy, Andrew, 71
McInnes, Donald, 167, 188
McInnes, Gordon F., 277
McInnes, Sanford, 141
McInnes, Senator Donald, 151
McInnes, D., and Company, 151
MacKay, Aeneas, D., 112
McKay, Alex, 173
MacKay, Lt.-Col. J. Keiller, 226
McKeand, Major David, 204
McKeen, Capt. John, 63
Mackelcan, Councillor, 136
Mackelcan, Frances, 155
McKelvey, Frank, 250
McKenna, John P., 151
Mackenzie, Alexander, 62
Mackenzie, George A., 143
McKenzie, John, 160
Mackenzie, Rev. John G. D., 143
MacKenzie, William Lyon, 25, 58, 66, 82, 88-90 *passim,* 92, 93, 98
McKid, Rev., 126
McKinnon, Hugh, 187, 188, 230
McKinstry, Henry, 121, 150
Macklem, William, 193
McLaren, Col. John I., 204, 246
McLaren, W. P., 122, 174
McLaren, Mrs. W. P., 174
McLellan, David, 230
McLelland, Dr. J. A., 160
McMahon, Inspector, 197
McMaster, R. H., 185
McMaster Divinity College, 222
McMaster University, 221-22, 224, 225;
planned expansion, 289-92 *passim*
McMenemy, J. H., 193
McMenemy, O., 187
McMullen, Walter, 190
McNab, Daniel, 96, 97
McNab, Mrs. D. A., 139
McNabb, Lieut. Allan, 84
McNab, Robert, 84
McNab, Sir Allan Napier, 67, 79-90 *passim,* 92, 98, 100, 111, 112, 120, 130, 294;
assistance to Hamilton during bankruptcy, 136-37;
biographical sketch, 84-86;
and the business community, 80;
and the *Caroline* affair, 89;
Colonel of Gore Militia, 80;
contribution to development of Hamilton, 86;
death, 138-39;
director of Gore Bank, 93;
and Dundurn Castle, 86;

first marriage, 85;
first resident lawyer, 79;
knighting, 89;
land office business, 80;
and Lord Durham's Report, 99;
as "Martyr of Toryism", 85-86;
and the Masonic Order, 137, 138;
as Prime Minister, 137;
and the proposed railroad, 95;
purchase of Beasley's location on Burlington Heights, 80-82;
and the Rebellion of 1837, 88-89;
representative in Legislature, 80;
retirement to England, 137
McNab, Sophia Mary, 137-38, 188
McNair, Gordon A., 257
McNeil, Stan, on the role of the Moun-
   tain, 5
McNichol, Dr., 199
McPherson, Col., 46
Macpherson, F. F., 251
Macpherson, James C., 157
McPowers, Mr., 117
McQuesten, C., and Company, 140
McQuesten, Dr. Calvin, 77, 140, 161,
   292
McQuesten, Rev. Calvin: on buttering
   the tracks of the Dundas
   "Dummy", 174;
on the furniture at Whitehern, 293
McQuesten, Isaac, 293
McQuesten, T. B., 221, 249, 261, 293
Macrae, John O., 152
McRae, William M., 276
McTaggart, Jean, 263
Madison, James, 32
Magee, Irish Philip, 65
Magee-Walton Ice Company, 176
Magil, Charles, 102, 129
Magor, Robert J., 205
Mahony, Thomas J., 283
Main, Mrs. Herbert A., 229
Mainwaring, George, 162
Malcolmson, Capt. John, 175
Malloch, Dr. Archibald, 181
Malloch, S. E., 184
Manasoo, 247
Mann, Gordon, 277
Manning, A. E., 188
Manufacturers' Association, 219
Manufacturing, beginnings of, 76-77
Market, 69, 71, 97
Marshall, Marjorie, 271
Marshall, Margaret, 232-33
Martin, Chief Justice Archer, 155
Martin, Edward, 155, 170

Martin, Mrs. F. R., 246
Martin, Dr. Harold: on early trans-
   portation of doctors, 183;
on medical practices of early twen-
   tieth century, 182
Martin, Kirwan, 188
Martin, Roslyn, 274
Mary Grace, Sister, 275
Mason, George E., 54, 63
Massie, James, 175
Masters, Jesse, 83
Mathews, Bernard J., 271
Matthew, Emily Esther Elizabeth, 145
Matthew, Col. James, 145
Mattice, Hortense C., 219
Mau, Frank James, 186
Mau, John, 186
Mayberry, T. M., 237
Meakins & Sons, 140
Mechanics' Institute, 95;
   forerunner of public library, 95;
   sale of, 179
Medical profession, 181-83;
   and the automobile, 184
Meiler, Florence, 282
Mennonites, land from Beasley, 29-30
Merchandise, variety of (1832), 74-75
Merrick, Dr., 128
Merrick, Frances A., 186
Merrick, Lester F., 225
Merrick, Mrs. Lester F., 225
Merritt, Thomas, 48
Mewburn, Major-General S. C., 161,
   202
Mewburn, S. G., 178
Mewburn, Thomas Chilton, 161
Miceli, Grace Puma, 271
Michigan Central Railway Company,
   109-10
Middleton, James T., 164, 210
Middlewood, Joseph, 164
Miles, O'Reilly, 116
Miles, Samuel, 167
Military Service Act, 207
Militia: 1st Battalion, disbanding of,
   100;
   passing of, 142
Militia Act, 34
Militia Act of 1855, 142
Millen, Capt. Lionel H., 204
Miller, Andrew, 59, 91, 204
Miller, John, 188
Mills, Charles, 212
Mills, George E., 168
Mills, Herbert, 249
Mills, James, 27, 131, 156

Mills, John, 28, 156
Mills, Nelson, 141, 157, 189;
  slaying of, 156-57
Mills, Robert, 249
Mills, Samuel S., 27, 69, 136, 148, 156
Mills, Stanley, 11, 155, 189
Mills, Mrs. Stanley, 155
Mills, Tom F., on Mayor Jackson, 256
Milne, John, 169, 185
Milne, William, 135, 154
Minty, James B., 117
Mitchell, Humphrey, 245, 252
Mitchell, John, 157
Modjeska, 247
Moes, Gerlacus (Gerry), 243
Mohawk Mills, 206, 237
Monaghan, Hugh B., 243
Monck, Sir Charles Stanley, Viscount,
  136
Monck, Judge, 130
Montreal Telegraph Company, 148
Moodie, Col. J. R., 183, 184, 204
Moodie, James, 184
Moodie, John, 183
Moodie, John R., 210
Moodie, Lt. R. R., 204, 217
Moore, Colonel Alex H., 178, 201
Moore, Bill, 173
Moore, Dennis, 129
Moore, Frank, 204-5
Moore, Lyman, 141, 162
Moore, John, 113
Moore, Chief Constable John, 152
Moore, John F., 114
Moore, Miss, 124
Morden, Mrs. Manley B., 271
Morden, Ralph, 10
Morden, W. J., 196
Moreau, Howard, 287
Morison, Brian, 279
Morris, A. W., 250
Morris, Joseph, 169
Morris, Thomas S., 247
Morrison, Annie, 127
Morrison, Brig.-Gen. Sir Edward, 207
Morison, Capt. Frank, 204
Morrison, Keziah, 51
Morrison, Col. Thomas, 207
Morrison, William, 207, 241, 245
Morton, David, 140, 164
Morton, Dr. John P., 217, 232
Moss, Judge, 157
Mountain Sanatorium, 193-94, 246, 274
Mountain Union Mission, 161
Mountain View Hotel, 202
Mount Hamilton Hospital, 192

Mowbray, Dr. Frederick Bruce, 232, 272
Mueller, Dr. Victoria, 173
Muir, Alexander G., 250
Muir, George, 128
Muirhead, William, 176, 257, 284
Mulcaster, Capt. Sir W. H., 43
Mulligan, C. W., 154
Mullin, Dr. John A., 180
Mullin, Dr. J. Heurner, 217, 273
Mullin, Mrs. J. Heurner, 229
Mundie, Mrs. J. Bryce, 41
Munro, John, 285
Murdoch, William, 265
Murphy, Angelina, 227
Murphy, Insole, 178
Murphy, "Long John", 177-78
Murphy, John, 178
Murphy, May, 227
Music, 228-31
Myler, Paul J., 186
Myles, James, 141
Myles, Thomas, 141

N

Nace, Dr. Paul, 275
Napoleonic War, 32
National Hosiery Mills, 206
National Steel Car Corporation, 205,
  236-37
Natural Gas, illumination with, 189
Nautilus Club, 178
Navy League Cadet Corps *Cougar*, 242-
  43
Neilson, Dr. John B., 273
Nelligan, David M., 128;
  on the "North End" of Hamilton, 66
Nelligan, Dennis, 132
Nelson, George H., 141
Newlands, T. J., 281
Newspapers, growing numbers of, 70
Niagara Peninsula, settlement, 6, 7
Nickerson, Moses C., 76
Nicolls, W. H., 152, 153
Nieghorn, William, 230
Nine Hour League, 244
Nineteenth Field Ambulance Corps, 207
Ninety-first Highlanders, 203
Nixon, Edward, 265
Nixon, Robert, 130
Noble, Maria (Beasley), 12
Nolan, Kathleen, 288
Noonan, Dr. William E., 273
Nora-Frances Henderson Hospital, 273
Normal School of Domestic Arts, 218-19
Norman, Van, 129

Norman Slater Company, 166
North End Improvement Society, 248
Norton Manufacturing Company, 211
Nowlan, Owen, 129
Nurses' Training School, 181

O

Oates, T. W., 225
O'Brien, Dennis, 87-88
O'Connor, D. D., 140
O'Connor, J. J., 221
O'Donoghue, Daniel J., 244
O'Heir, "Mush", 173
Olmstead, Dr. Ingersoll, 181-82, 294;
    introduction of first operating suite,
    181-82;
    organization of Nurses' Training
    School, 181
Omand, William, 150
O'Neil, James G., 173
O'Neill, Gen. John, 142
Ontario Agricultural College, Guelph,
    219
Ontario Department of Economics, on
    Hamilton's capital and repair in-
    vestment, 267
Ontario Motor League, founding of, 184
Ontario Normal College, 218
Ontario Pipe Line Company Limited,
    189
Ontario Rolling Mill Company, 140
Ontario Teachers' Training College, 220
O'Reilly, Dr. Charles, 181
O'Reilly, Dr. Gerald, 106, 113, 168,
O'Reilly, Dr. Gerald Jr., 232
O'Reilly, Judge, 93
O'Reilly, Michael J., 246
O'Reilly, Myles, 71, 72, 101, 125, 130,
    167, 173, 187
Ormiston, Rev. William, 100
Osborne, Dr. A. B., 181, 182
Osborne, Rev. John, first superintendent
    of common schools, 125, 126
Osler, B. B., 155, 157
Osler, Dr. William, 181
Otis Elevator Company, 205

P

Page, Dr. E. L., 275
Page, Col. John P., 226
Painter, A. J., 219
Panabaker, Frank, 270
Panabaker, Mrs. Frank S., on private
    schools, 226-27

Park, Dr. Pryse, 232
Parker, H. E., 250
Parker, Henry (Bristol Bill), 153
Parker, Joe, 152
Parker, S. Leslie, 257, 262, 279
Parker, Mrs. Luke H., 164
Parks, availability of, 279-81
Parrott, Benjamin, Sr., 195
Parrott, "Crazy Ben", 195
Parrott Matricide, 195-96
Parry, Dr. John R., 217, 232, 273
Parry, Dr. Robert Y., 207-273
Patterson, George, 162
Patterson, John, 210
Peace, Flt.-Lt. W. J., 240, 243
Peacock, Arthur, 164
Peacock, H. A., 240
Pearce, Miss H. M., 226
Peart, H. E., 274
Peebles, John, 173, 251
Peene, A. W., 229
Peene, Lilli M. W., 229
Perri, Bessie, 207;
    murder of, 254
Perri, Rocco, 207, 253-54
Perry, H. W., 129
Phin, Major J. P., 236
Philadelphia Centennial Exposition, 161
Philharmonic Society, 229
Phillips, Hannah, 26
Philpott, Pastor Peter W., 201, 294-95
Philpott Memorial Church, 201
Pickard, Victor, 250
Pierce, Bob, 250
Pigott, Joseph M., 269
Pigott, Michael A., 269
Pinfold, Lt.-Cmdr. F. H., 242
Planned Parenthood Association, 225
Platt, Wm. & Company, 72, 73
Players' Guild, 292
Playfair, Dr. L. L., 273
Police force: equipment, turn of the
    century, 196;
    expansion of, 188;
    modernizing of, 264-65;
    overhaul of department, 287
Police protection: early service, 151-
    52;
    and the Parker gang, 152;
    towards modernization, 151-53
Population: Head of the Lake (1816),
    54;
    1826-36; 62;
    1850's, 101;
    1858-1873, 148-49;
    1870-1900, 165;

1875, 159;
1880-1914, 191;
1914-32, 213;
1930-66, 251-52
Porter McKenzie, 144
Powell, Brig. Gen. H. Watson, 10
Powell, Judge William Dummer, 47
Powis, Mrs. Gordon, 246
Pratt, T. H., 131
Price, Dr. Gordon E., 277, 288
Priest, Mrs. Lloyd, 245
Princess Patricia's Canadian Light Infantry, 200
Pritchard, Ada, 278, 284-85, 287, 288
Pritchard, Charles H., 285
Procter, Major-General Henry, 33
Procter and Gamble Company of Canada Limited, 8, 207
Pugsley, Capt. George, 203
Pullar, Rev. Thomas, 160

Q

Queen's Own Rifles, 143
Queen's Plate, first running of, 129
Quimby, Alfred C., 141
Quimby and Tuckett Tobacco Manufacturers, 141

R

Radforth, Norman W., 280
Radial era, 211-12
Rae, Dr. John, 77, 78, 125
Railways: new facilities for, 251;
proposed, 95;
Ramsay, Miss I., 217
Randall, Stephen, 60, 69
Rawson, Rev. Norman, 272
Rayner, William, 87
Read, John R., 236
Real Estate, upswing in, 206
Rebellion of 1837, 88-89, 90
Reciprocity Treaty, 139
Recreational facilities, availability of, 280-81
Reed, Gerald, 287
Reeves, Mrs. Stewart A., 279
Reid, George Lowe, 167
Relief, increased numbers on, 119-20
Rennie, Dr. George S., 182, 207, 273
Rice, George L., 185
Rice, Rev. S. D., 161
Richardson, "Addie", 190
Richardson, Lieut. James, 42-44
Ridley, Dr. Henry T., 113

Riel, Louis, 57
Right House, 141
Ritchie, Edmund, 128
Ritchie, Olive, 288
Rivières, Francis des, 80, 81
Roach, Dick, 177
Roach, George, 46, 129
Road improvements, 106-7
Robert Land Home and School Association, 11
Robert Land School, 11
Roberts, Major H. L., 203-204, 207
Roberts, Dr. James, 207, 216
Robertson, Capt. Archibald, 175
Robertson, Catharine (Askin), 50
Robertson, Miss Catharine, 79
Robertson, Hon. Mr. Justice, 155
Robertson, June, 288
Robertson, Col. R. A., 202
Robertson, Thomas, 155
Robinowitz, Dr. Paul, 274
Robinson, George, 230
Robinson, Chief Justice Sir John Beverley, 36, 84
Robinson, M. M. (Bobby), 250
Robinson, Walter H., 230
Roche, Sophia de, 26
Roehm, Lorenz, 230
Rogers, Dr. James T., 217
Rollo, Walter R., 245
Rolph, George, 57, 60;
assault of, 57
Rolph, Dr. Thomas, 62
Rolston, Joseph, 69
Roper, Ivan, 277
Roscoe, Stanley M., 269
Rose, David, 141
Rosebrugh, J. W., 158
Ross, Frederick, 201
Ross, Thomas H., 285
Rothesay Castle, 148
Rottenburg, Baron de, 138
Rottenburg, Baroness de, 138
Rousseau, St. Jean Baptiste, 14, 29
Routh, Lieut. Percy Gore, 143
Rowles, Mrs. E. M., 275
Roy, George A., 243
Roy, Philippe, 243
Roy, R. M., 205
Royal Botanical Gardens, 221, 249
Royal Canadian Army Service Corps, 1st Divisional Petrol Company, 235
Royal Canadian Medical Corps:
5th Field Ambulance, 235;
12th Field Ambulance, 207;
19th Field Ambulance, 207

Royal Canadian Sea Cadet *Lion*, 242-43
Royal Connaught Hotel, 201
Royal Hamilton College of Music, 202
Royal Hamilton Light Infantry, 235-36
Royal Hamilton Yacht Club, 130, 178, 206-7
Royal Military College, 225
Rubber Workers, 245
Rumble, Harry, 257
Russell, Dr. James, 194, 226
Russell, Robert, 248
Rutherford, George, 141
Ryan, Major G. H., 242
Ryckman, Cornelius, 25, 54
Ryckman, John, description of the city, 1803, 18
Ryckman, John J., 69, 71
Ryckman, S. W., 167
Ryckman, Samuel, 25, 54
Ryerson, Dr. Egerton, 60, 124, 126; normal school methods, 127-28
Rymal, David Sykes, 161
Rymal, Jacob, 25, 54, 89, 99
Rymal, Joseph, 89, 99
Rymal, William, 25

S

Sadleir, Charles A., 101, 102, 130
Sadler, John, 187
Sager, Howard, 260
St. Elizabeth Visiting Nurses' Association, 217
St. Joseph's Hospital, 222; changes in, 275; expansion of, 191, 192
St. Lawrence Seaway, importance to Hamilton, 259-61
St. Laurent, Julie de, 144-46
St. Peter's Home for Incurables, 192-93
St. Peter's Infirmary, 192; changes, 274-75; founding, 192-93
St. Thomas More Players, 292
Samuel, Rev. Canon John, 230
Sanford, Senator William E. L., 183
Sangster, John Herbert, 127
Sassoon, Siegfried, 208
Sawyer, L. D., and Company, 140
Sawyer, Luther D., 140
Sayer, Harry, 196
Scarlet Fever epidemic, 195
Scheuer, Edmund, 160
School Act of 1871, 160

Schools: private, numbers of (1830's), 88; site of first, 18
Schwarz, Fred, 230
Schwenger, Charles, 230
Schwenger, Judge William F., 155, 266, 295
Scott, Chief Justice Thomas, 47, 48
Scott, James, 71, 72
Scott, John J., 202
Scott, Phoebe (Land), 9, 33
Scott, Lieutenant-Colonel, Winfield, 33, 41-42
Scully, V. W. on Stelco's 1963 ingot production, 268
Seager, E. R., on number of park acres needed, 281
Searls, A. S., 71
Secord, Peter, 6
Sedgwick, Hugh G., 245
Sedgwick, Rev. W. H., 217
Summers, George H., 201
Separate School Act of 1885, 160
Settlers, American, 34
Sewell, Miss, 88
Sewerage system: controversy over, 116-17; expansion of, 257-59
Sharpe, Mrs. A., 285
Slater Steel Industries Limited, 166
Sheeler, John, 83, 84
Sheldon, William, 28
Sheldon, William B., 128
Shenton, Samuel, 71
Sherbrooke, Mr., 88
Sheridan, Sister M. Philomene, 113
Sherk, Joseph, 30
Sherman, Clifton W., 186, 187
Sherman, Frank A., 187
Sherman, F. H., 187
Sherring, William J., 195, 271
Shipbuilding, 175
Showers, Magdalene (Depew), 8
Simcoe, John Graves, 17, 32; abolishing of land boards, 13; changing of Canadian names to English, 15; pattern of social development, 14; on provisioning troops from Beasley's grist mill, 14-15
Simcoe, Mrs. John Graves, —description of area, 19-20
Simcoe Canning Company, 211
Simons, Major Titus Geer, 48, 58, 66, 77
Simpson, Benjamin L., 225, 271

Simpson, Edward A., 287
Simpson, Jimmy, 250
Sinclair, Lt.-Col. I. M. R., 235
Sinclair, James Shaw, 157
Sisters of Notre Dame, 220
Sisters of St. Joseph, 160, 170, 191;
   and the cholera epidemic of 1854,
   113;
   purchase of new hospital site, 192-93
Sisters of the Institute of the Blessed
   Mary Virgin, 228
Skelly, Mrs. Isabelle, 291
Skinner, Lt.-Col., James, 201
Skinner, Lillian (Land), 11
Skinner, Major James, 143
Skinner, Nathaniel, 10
Slack, Herbert, 239
Smiley, Hugh, 98
Smiley, John, 98, 131
Smiley, Robert Reid, 98, 131
Smith, Albert Victor, 250
Smith, Alexander, 188, 208, 210
Smith, Col, Armand, 207
Smith, Dr. Florence, 273
Smith, Harold G., 237
Smith, J. H., on Beasley's time of ar-
   rival at the lakehead, 13
Smith, James:
   on cock fights, 177;
   on work in the Bay, 176-77
Smith, Lloyd H., 239
Smith, Merle, 273
Smith, Milford L.:
   on Hamilton's wealth, 267-68;
   on work gangs at Dofasco, 187
Smith, Rev., J. C., 157, 158
Smith (Smyth), Peter, 12, 13
Smith, William, 99
Smith's Tavern, first public house in
   area, 18
Snelgrove, Arthur E., 141
Snider, Judge C. G., 215
Smyth, Conn, 236
Soble, Kenneth D., 286, 288;
   on future of Hamilton, 293
Soper, Robert, 175
Southam, Major Gordon H., 207, 236
Southam, W. J., 170
Southam, William, 185, 191, 193, 207,
   294
Southam, Mrs. William, 191, 193
Spohn, Edith, 49
Spohn, Peter, 49;
Spohn, Peter:
   on Augustus Jones's Indian wives, 22;
   "The Ghost of the Canal", 64-65;

on Indians and the family mirror,
   49-50
Sports, 250;
   1830's, 87-88;
   popularity of horse racing, 128-30;
   types of, 1850's and 60's, 130-32
Sprague, Dave, 250
Spring Brewery, 164
Springer, Daniel, 16, 51
Springer, H. Isabel, 164
Springer, Henrietta (Beasley), 16
Springer, Henry, 16
Springer, John, 27, 28, 55
Springer, Dr. Lewis M., 136, 162, 164
Springer, Margaret, 16
Springer, Richard, 16, 27, 55, 76
Springer, Sarah, 55
Squires, Ada, 273
Stapley, Norman, 208
Stares, Harry, 190, 204, 208
Steamship service, inauguration of be-
   tween Hamilton, Oakville, Toronto,
   148
Steel Company of Canada, 8, 164;
   formation of, 185;
   ingot production, 268;
   nucleus, 140;
   strike, 252-53
Stern, Dr. Philip D., 289
Steven, Andrew, 93, 135
Stevenson, Mrs. P. S., 114
Steward, Lt.-Col. J. D., 235
Stewart, Alexander David, 187
Stewart, Ann, 55
Stewart, George, 10, 55
Stewart, George, Jr., 55
Stewart, Logan—on the race meeting
   of 1867, 129
Stewart, R. J., 277
Stewart, T. J., 212
Stewart, Rev. Dr. William, 159
Stewart (Stuart)-Depew cemetery, loca-
   tion of, 8
Stipes-Depew family cemetery, location
   of, 8
Stinson, Ebenezer, 69
Stinson, H. A., 178
Stinson, John, 73
Stinson, T. H., 178
Stinson, Thomas, 136, 141, 144
Stock, Thomas, 155
Stone, William L., 23
Stoney Creek, battle of, 38-41
Storms, Dr. D. G., 217
Stowe, James, 245, 264;
   on Sam Laurence, 245, 253

Strachan, Right Rev., John, 43, 60, 98; on the character of Richard Beasley, 82
Strafford, Tom (Bumble Bee), 177
Strathallan School for Girls, 226-27
Street, George C., 74
Strong, Miss I. W., 219
Strongman, William, 167
Strowbridge, James G., 63
Stuart, Donald, 114
Stuart, George, 7, 8
Stuart, John, 170
Studholme, Allan, 245
Sullivan, Berta, 277
Sullivan, Dan "Dude", 173
Sullivan, Edward, 130
Sunley, George, 124
Surveying—early method of, 20-21
Sutherland, Capt. James, 114
Sutherland, John W., 210
Sutherland, Canon R. G., 160
Swanborough, Reginald F., 265
Sweet, Judge J. A., 155
Syme, John J., 246-47
Syme, Mary Y., 229

T

Tallman, W. H., 187
Tassie, William, 77, 78
Taylor, Mrs. J. D., 279
Taxation, 122
Taylor, Cmdr. P. D., 242
Taylor, John, 154
Taylor, Judge Thomas, 57, 60, 69, 71, 76, 79; death of, 77
Taylor, Sir Thomas Wardlaw, 57
Teetzel, J. B., 155
Teetzel, J. V., 184, 188
Teetzel, Mrs. J. V., 189
Telegraph Service, early, 161
Telephone—first exchange in the British Empire, 161-62
Temperance Act (Ontario), 207
Temple Players, 292
Templin, Dr. Marian, 273
Ten Eyck, Arthur B., 190, 265
Ten Eyck, Rev. J. W., 160
Terryberry, William, 54
Textile Workers, 245
Theatre, 96-97, 213; interest in, 292
Theatre-Auditorium Foundation, 288
Thirteenth Overseas Battalion, 202
Thirteenth Royal Regiment, 200, 202

Thode, Dr. Henry George, 222, 275; on population of McMaster, 289-90
Thomas, E. Cartwright, 135
Thomas, William, 170
Thompson, James A., 175
Thompson, Dr. R. A., 160, 190
Thompson, Dr. Walter G., 251
Thomson, Robert, 171
Thornton, Patrick, 125
Tice, Capt. W. J., 240
Tiffany, George S., 68, 125
Timmis, Brian, 250
Tomlinson, Dr. R. H., 275
Toronto Automobile Club, 184
Toronto Examiner—on McNab's indebtedness to the Gore Bank, 93
Toronto, Hamilton and Buffalo Railway, 179, 205, 212
Torrance, Gordon, 287
Town bell—clash over, 94-95
Trades and Labour Congress of Canada, 244
Trades and Labour Council, 218, 219
Trade Union Act, 244
Traffic Control, future, 283-84
Transportation System, public, introduction of, 162-65
Treleaven, Jane, 249
Treleaven, Mr. Justice Russell W., 155
Treleaven, Freeman F., 248, 249
Trimble, John E., 277; on education for employment, 291
Tuchtie, Magistrate Walter, 287
Tuckett, George E., 249
Tuckett, George Thomas, 141, 156
Tuckett, John E., 141
Turbina, 247
Turnbull, James, 170
Turnbull, Jean, 228
Turnbull, Major W. R., 204
Turner, James, 131, 225
Turner, J. B., 160
Turner, Spencer, 211
Turville, Frank, 250
Tyler, Dr. W. H., 216

U

Unions—development of, 209-10
United Electrical Radio and Machine Workers, 245
United Empire Loyalists, 3, 34
United Gas and Fuel Company of Hamilton Limited, 189
United Gas Limited, 233
United Steelworkers, 245

Unsworth, Dr. A. D., 193
Upper Canada:
  1837 Rebellion, 82;
  government of, c. 1792, 15;
  pattern of social development, 14
Urban Redevelopment, 285-86;
  downtown care, 288-89

V

Vallance, Mrs. Victor, 274
Van Allen, Eli, 154
Vanier, Governor-General Georges P., 270
Van Norman, Caleb, 141
Van Wagner, Henry, 22;
  importance as millwright, 49;
  purchases Augustus Jones's property, 49
Van Wagner, Lt.-Col. Henry Picton, 200
Van Wagner, Peter Spohn, 49;
  on Augustus Jones's children, wives, 22;
  on Indians and family mirror, 49-50;
  story of the "Ghost of the Canal", 64-65
Veale, F. J., 246
Viba, Commodore Samuel, 207
Victoria Wire Mills, 186
Victoria Yacht Club, 248
Victorian Order of Nurses for Canada, 216
Villiers, Colonel, 46
Vincent, John—trial and execution of, 58
Vincent, Major-General John, 33, 38, 40, 41;
  defence of Burlington Heights, 37-38
Virtue, Miss Janet, 226

W

Waddell, R. R., 129, 130, 155, 164, 167
Wadland, Thomas H., 162
Wagner, Dr. Henrih von, 49
Waldon, Dr. Freda F., 291;
  on McNab and money matters, 94
Walker, Ken, 250
Walker, Margaret, 129
Walkey, Dr. Albert E., 272
Wallace, Dr. J. M., 194, 196
Walton, W. G., 183
Walters, Chester S., 185, 203, 236, 247
Wanzer Sewing Machine Company, 148

War of 1812, 10, 32-45;
  Burlington Heights defence, 37, 38;
  causes, 32;
  confusion of campaigns, 33;
  division of families and businesses, 33;
  formation of flank companies of volunteers, 34;
  lack of equipment for the militia, 35;
  lack of pensions, 46;
  the lakehead, initiation by fire, 36-37;
  postwar economic hardships, 45, 46-47;
  postwar treason trials, 47-48;
  victuallage, problem of, 35-36
Waram, J. T. C., 281
Wark, William, 178
Warme, David A., 277
Warnick, William J., 173
Warrender, William K., 264
Washington, S. F., 198, 201
Waterworks System, 261-63;
  addition, 214-15, 216;
  cost, 119;
  description, 119;
  development of, 117-19
Watkins, John H., 141
Watkins, Thomas C., 141
Watson, Charles, 248
Watson, Miss Merle O., 274
Watson, Mrs. W. J., 246
Weaver, Samuel, 188
Webb, George F., 168
Webb, Sam, 97
Webber, John A., 238
Webster, George, 175
Wedge, William, 27
Weir, James H., 175, 178
Welch, "Huck", 250
Welland Canal, 97
Wentworth Historical Society, 11
Wentworth House of Refuge, 193
Wentworth Motors Limited, 213
Wesleyan Ladies' College, 160-61
Westdale—educational centre of Hamilton, 224-25
Western Mercury, 68, 70, 86, 99;
  economic advantages of Burlington Bay canal, 65
Westland, Ltd. H. Lloyd G., 241
Wheeler, Reginald, 279
Whelpton, Ernie, 250
Wheten, Waldo A., 21, 257, 290;
  on future of Hamilton roads, 283-84
Whipple, H. B., 130
Whitake, Lt.-Col. W. Denis, 236
White, Glenn R., 243

White, Dr. James, 181, 182, 196
White, John, 129
White, Mrs. Lyle, 180
White, Richard, 131
White, Thomas, 131, 147
White, Dr. Thomas E., 182
Whitehern, 293
Whitton, Charlotte, 248
Whitton, Mrs. Corbett E., 229
Whyte, Col. James Matthew, 84, 93, 99
Whyte, John Lionel, 84, 145
Wigle, Wing Cmdr. Douglas H., 240-41
Wigle, Lt.-Col. Frederick E., 235
Wigle, Mrs. Gerald W., 238
Wilcox, A. E., 219
Wilcox, A. M., 140
Wilcox, Charles S., 140, 185
Wilcox, H. W., 217
Wild, George, 188
Willard, Henry, 140
Williams, Henry John, 102, 103
Williams, Dr. J. J., 194
Williams, Johnny, 173
Williamson, David, 165
Willingdon, Governor-General Viscount, 248
Wilmot, Miss, 124
Wilson, James, 14, 29
Wilson, John, 104, 132, 133
Willson, John, 52;
    on the loss of George Hamilton's writ, 53
Wilson, John W., 154
Winder, Gen. William H., 38, 40
Winer, John, 141
Wingfield, Dr. A. H., 292
Wires, Robert, 29
Wishart, W. D., 190
Witton, J. G., 219
Witton, William P., 251
Women's Christian Temperance Union, 244
Women's Wentworth Historical Society, 184, 226
Wood, A. T., 170

Wood, B. R., 170
Wood, S., 72
Wood, Andrew Trew, 170
Wood, Vallance and Company, 170
Wood, William, 150
Wood, William Augustus, 170
Woodhouse, T. Roy, 292;
    on Beasley's place of residence, 13
Woolley, Mrs. R. Gladstone, 196
Woolverton, Algernon, 246
Woolverton, Dr. F. E., 180
Woolverton, Mrs. Francis, 246
Works department, and political influence, 215
World War I:
    conscription, 207
    and Hamilton, 200-209 *passim*
World War II, 235-43
Wren, Tom, 173
Wright, Arthur G., 187
Wright, Henry G., 280
Wright, Mary, 79
Wright, Montrose, 198

Y

Yeates, Lt. R. Howard, 241
Yeo, Sir James Lucas, 42-43
Young, James, 83
Young, James M., 202
Young, Mrs. James M., 202
Young, Lt. James V., 202
Young, John, 83
Young, John, 131, 192, 202
Young, Robert, 141
Young, William, 141
Y.M.C.A.-Y.W.C.A., building, 263
Young-Sheeler case, 83-84
Young Women's Christian Association, 218

Z

Zealand, Edward, 132

351